Why has China been able to avoid the crippling hyperinflation that has bedeviled so many developing and reforming centrally planned economies? This is puzzling because the potential for inflation in the Chinese economy is enormous, the fiscal control by the central government is weak, and China's tax and monetary policies are still passive.

This book analyzes an important aspect of this issue – how the central government has been able to tame inflationary investment demand and to impose investment reduction policies that go against the economic interests of Chinese local officials. Yasheng Huang focuses on the controlling role of political institutions and argues that one of the central functions of the political institutions is to make allocative decisions about bureaucratic personnel. Drawing on institutional economics, he hypothesizes that centralized personnel allocations help reconcile some of the policy differences between the central and local governments and provide vital information to the central government about the conduct of local officials. Systematic data analysis is carried out to test the propositions developed on the basis of this hypothesis. The book also contains detailed descriptions of the roles of local governments in economic and investment management and of China's bureaucratic system.

Huang argues that China now has a de facto federalist system in which the central government specializes in political responsibilities and the local governments specialize in economic responsibilities. This, he suggests, has a number of important normative implications. Under the condition of political authoritarianism, this combination of economic and fiscal decentralizations with political centralization may be an optimal governance structure. Economically, a degree of political centralization is useful to alleviate coordination problems when economic agents lack financial self-discipline and when indirect macroeconomic policies are ineffective. Premature political decentralization in the presence of soft-budget constraints may have contributed to runaway inflation in other reforming centrally planned economies. Politically, the Chinese style of federalism can also be optimal because fiscal decentralization helps check the enormous political discretion in the hands of the central government, on which the Chinese political system itself places no formal constraints. Given China's recent history, this ought to be an important consideration in designing China's economic system.

Inflation and investment
controls in China

Inflation and investment controls in China

The political economy of central–local relations during the reform era

YASHENG HUANG
University of Michigan

CAMBRIDGE
UNIVERSITY PRESS

Published by the Press Syndicate of the University of Cambridge
The Pitt Building, Trumpington Street, Cambridge CB2 1RP
40 West 20th Street, New York, NY 10011–4211, USA
10 Stamford Road, Oakleigh, Melbourne 3166, Australia

First published 1996

Printed in the United States of America

Library of Congress Cataloging-in-Publication Data
Huang, Yasheng.
Inflation and investment controls in China : the political economy
of central–local relations during the reform era / Yasheng Huang.
p.   cm.
Partially based on the author's Ph.D. dissertation written between
1989–1991 in the Government Dept., Harvard University.
Includes bibliographical references and index.
ISBN 0-521-55483-7
1. Anti-inflationary policies – China.   2. Fiscal policy – China.
3. Intergovernmental fiscal relations – China.   4. Investments –
Government policy – China.   5. China – Economic conditions – 1976– –
Regional disparities.   I. Title.
HG1285.H83   1996   95–33092
336.3'0951 – dc20   CIP

A catalog record for this book is available from the British Library.

ISBN 0-521-55483-7 Hardback

To my mother, Tan Jiakun,
and to the memory of my father,
Huang Kang (1917–1993)

Contents

Figures and tables

Acknowledgments

I owe my foremost intellectual debt to Professor Janos Kornai of Harvard University. In 1986, I took his seminar, "The Political Economy of Socialism." His lectures and writings on the economy, politics, and ideology of socialist systems inspired a generation of students from China to undertake systematic research on economic reforms in socialist countries. Readers familiar with Professor Kornai's works will immediately recognize the influence of his ideas in this volume.

This book is based in part on my Ph.D. dissertation, which I wrote between 1989 and 1991 in the Government Department at Harvard University. I would like to thank members of my dissertation committee, Professors Roderick MacFarquhar, Jorge Dominguez, Robert Keohane, and Dwight Perkins, for their patience and guidance. Professor Dwight Perkins deserves special mention here because he shepherded my work not only during the dissertation stage but also when I was preparing this book.

I benefited tremendously from the advice and suggestions of Robert Bates and an anonymous reviewer for Cambridge University Press. I am also grateful to my colleagues at the University of Michigan, Ken Lieberthal and, briefly, Michel Oksenberg, for their detailed comments on both my dissertation and my manuscript. Jeffry Frieden, Joel Hellman, Hiroyuki Imai, Jeffrey Sachs, and Shang-jin Wei commented on ideas and research contained in chapter 8, a pivotal chapter in this book. In Beijing and then later on in Cambridge, when he was a visiting scholar at Harvard's Fairbank Center for East Asian Research, Luo Xiaopeng, formerly an official from the Rural Development Research Center under the State Council, had many conversations with me about the motives and behavior of Chinese local officials. My thanks go to Edwin Lim and Peter Harrold at the World Bank, who gave me considerable latitude so that I could accommodate my research interests when I was working as a consultant for the Resident Mission of the World Bank in Beijing in 1988 and 1989.

Over the years, I have also benefited from discussions with many scholars and friends whose contributions to this volume are important but cannot be singled out individually. These include Chris Achen, John Campbell, Cui Zhiyuan, Bob Dernberger, Fan Gang, Fu Jun, Steve Goldstein, Stephan Haggard, Hu Zuliu, John Jackson, Jing Jun, David Li, Lu Mai, Jean Oi, Qian Yingyi, Ron Rogowski, Terry Sicular, Dorothy Solinger, Ed Steinfeld, Ezra Vogel, Alan Wachman, Andrew Walder, Wang Jun, Barry Weingast, Jeff Winters, Xu Chenggang, Yan Suzher, Zhang Wei, Zhang Xin, and William Zimmerman. Numerous scholars and officials in China helped arrange for my research and fieldwork in Beijing, Jiangsu, and Guangdong during various stages. Out of respect for their anonymity, I am unable to acknowledge their help individually.

Elizabeth Neal, Janis Bolster, Lisa Lincoln, and Vicky Macintyre at Cambridge University Press guided me through the publication process. A number of students at the University of Michigan and at Harvard assiduously and tirelessly assisted me in my research and data collection and entry. They are Dandan Pan, Gloria Tsuen, and Nancy Yu at the University of Michigan and Stephanie Hui and Ying Qian at Harvard College. I owe special thanks to Nancy Hearst, the librarian at Harvard's Fairbank Center and a good friend for many years. She read this manuscript a number of times and gave excellent editorial assistance. Her vast collection of books on contemporary China facilitated my research immeasurably. Thanks also go to Jean Hung at the University Service Centre in Hong Kong.

I also wish to acknowledge the generous financial support of a number of institutions. The China Times Cultural Foundation, through its young scholar program, awarded me a fellowship in my last year of graduate school when I was struggling financially to finish my dissertation. A Faculty Development Fund, a research grant from the Center for Chinese Studies, and a Faculty Recognition Award, all at the University of Michigan, enabled me to expand my research far beyond the coverage of my dissertation. In the academic year 1993–94, I received a Chiang Ching-kuo Foundation/Joint Committee of Chinese Studies postdoctoral fellowship (administered by the American Council of Learned Societies and the Social Science Research Council), which released me from teaching at the University of Michigan and allowed me to finish writing this book. I also wish to thank the Fairbank Center for East Asian Research and its director, Professor Woody Watson, for being my host during my sabbatical. Of course, none of the persons or institutions mentioned above bears responsibility for any errors and shortcomings of this book. All the translations from Chinese are the author's unless otherwise noted.

No Chinese growing up in China in the chaotic 1970s – when schools were closed or functioning poorly – could ever hope for a measure of professional achievement later in life without the intellectual guidance of their parents. My thought first goes to my mother, Tan Jiakun, whose strong will and optimism have always been a source of inspiration. I also want to apologize to her for her many sleepless nights, worrying about my struggles in an alien land and about those plane, train, and shipwrecks in America (irrespective of their locations vis-à-vis Ann Arbor or Cambridge). My father, Huang Kang, a prominent writer and journalist in China, passed away when I was working on this book. My father and I had many differences of opinion on economic reforms in China, but as I matured, I began to appreciate his views and his sentiments. During the most adverse years for our family, it was my father who first taught me the love of books and knowledge and then taught me perseverance and thoroughness in work and honesty and fairness in life. I dedicate this book to my mother and the memory of my father.

Abbreviations

Institutions

ABC	Agricultural Bank of China
CITIC	China International Trust and Investment Corporation
CCP	Chinese Communist Party
CDIC	Central Discipline Inspection Commission
CIRES	Chinese Institute for the Reform of the Economic System
CPEs	Centrally planned economies
DOO	Department of Organization
GAA	General Auditing Administration
ICB	Industrial and Commercial Bank
LARs	Large administrative regions
MOF	Ministry of Finance
MOP	Ministry of Personnel
MOS	Ministry of Supervision
PBC	People's Bank of China
PCBC	People's Construction Bank of China
SCGE	State Commission on Government Establishment
SCRES	State Commission for the Reform of the Economic System
SEC	State Economic Commission
SEZs	Special Economic Zones
SPC	State Planning Commission
SSB	State Statistical Bureau
TIC	Trust and investment companies

Terms and variables

AP	Austerity policy
$BM_{(joint)}$	Bureaucratic model for top and secondary officials

BM$_{(top)}$	Bureaucratic model for top officials
BM$_{(sec)}$	Bureaucratic model for secondary officials
CI	Central investments
CLIR	Central/local investment ratio
DM	Development model
FI	Foreign investments
FDI	Foreign direct investment
FM	Financial model
FYP	Five-year plan
GVAO	Gross value of agricultural output
GVAIO	Gross value of agricultural and industrial output
GVIO	Gross value of industrial output
GVO	Gross value of output
LI	Local investments
LM	Lag model
NKS	Net capital stock
NMP	Net material product
NRO	Net resource outflows
PR	Personnel reforms
RC	Revenue contributions
RI	Renovation investments

Names of provinces

AH	Anhui
BJ	Beijing
FJ	Fujian
GS	Gansu
GD	Guangdong
GX	Guangxi
GZ	Guizhou
HB	Hebei
HLJ	Heilongjiang
HN	Henan
HUB	Hubei
HUN	Hunan
JS	Jiangsu
JX	Jiangxi
JL	Jilin
LN	Liaoning

NMG	Neimenggu
NX	Ningxia
QH	Qinghai
SHX	Shaanxi
SD	Shandong
SH	Shanghai
SX	Shanxi
SC	Sichuan
TJ	Tianjin
XJ	Xinjiang
XZ	Xizang
YN	Yunnan
ZJ	Zhejiang

1

Introduction

A question every Chinese leader must grapple with in crafting an appropriate governance structure is how much decision-making power should be kept at the national level of government and how much should be delegated to localities. This is indeed a perplexing question for policy makers in a centrally planned economy (CPE), where local and national objectives are often at odds with each other. On one hand, there is a desire to give operational autonomy and economic resources to local governments and enterprises so that they will have the incentive as well as the wherewithal to stimulate economic growth; on the other, there is a desire to maintain macroeconomic stability, to achieve regional equity, and to fashion an industrial structure more compatible with the long-run developmental needs of the national economy. This book is about China's attempts to resolve this question in the area of inflation control. Specifically, it is about central–local relations in China's national economic management, and about central and local controls over investments in plants and equipment for the purpose of expanding the productive capacity of the economy.[1]

At present these issues occupy a central place in China's political economy. The delegation of economic control to the localities is the cornerstone of China's economic reform program. On the positive side, the growing economic power of the localities during the reform era has infused much dynamism and innovation into the Chinese economy. This, probably more than anything else, has broken the central government's economic monopoly and in the process has facilitated the transition of the Chinese economy to a market system. There have also been unexpected benefits, mostly of a political nature. Regional decentralization has created a powerful group with a vested interest in the continuation of the economic reforms. The inability of the central

---

1. In this book, I ignore two other forms of investment that one commonly finds in market economies – investment in financial assets and in real estate – because these investments are small and of relatively recent vintage.

planners to roll back reforms completely in the wake of the Tiananmen crackdown is in part due to the resistance of regional officials, who have much to
lose from a restoration of central planning.[2]

On the negative side, economic decentralization has created major coordination problems for the management of the national economy by the central
government. Inflationary pressures have intensified, the state's fiscal burdens
have increased, and income differentials between the rich and poor provinces
may have grown. Economic decentralization has made it difficult for the central
government to mobilize resources for long-term development programs and to
manage short-term macroeconomic performance. Although some of these
problems are related to the manner and the nature of the decentralization
rather than to the decentralization per se, many policy advisers and scholars
argue that China's reforms have given excessive power to the local governments,
and that this may lead to economic and social dislocation; some even foresee
national disintegration (see Goodman 1993; Shambaugh 1993; Wang Shaoguang
and Hu Angang 1993). The latter dire scenario is now the focus of much
attention as people speculate about the health of Deng Xiaoping. A controver-
sial Pentagon study, released in February 1995, predicts that China will have
a "50-to-50 chance to experience a Soviet-style breakup" after Deng dies.[3]

Often a contentious issue in central–local relations is the apportionment of
investment controls between the Center and the localities. Investment is probably the most powerful tool localities can use to pursue their economic and
political interests. Investment also affects the macroeconomy. Unlike market
economies, where inflation is usually caused by private and public consumption, CPEs are more prone to investment-driven inflation. Between 1978 and
1993 China experienced five bouts of inflation; each time the main catalyst was
investment surges, and each time the central government attempted to control
inflation through reductions in investment and recentralization of investment
authority.

Political or policy conflicts arise when these inflation control policies – or
austerity programs – pit the interests of the central government directly against
those of the local authorities. Local officials gain prestige, power, and tangible
economic and fiscal benefits from investment expansion; any effort to reduce
investment growth or to direct investment resources away from sectors favored

---

2. For this line of analysis portraying local officials as a vested interest group, see Huang (1990)
and Shirk (1993).

3. Some participants of the study contend that the conclusion distorts their views. See Newcomb
(1995). My own study shows that the economic and political control by the central government
is still quite authoritative (Huang 1995c).

by local officials often meets with both passive and active resistance at the local level. Thus a study of investment conflicts is at heart a study of the distribution of power in the Chinese political system and of the manner in which one group of actors is able to achieve its preferences at the expense of the interests of the other groups. What are the economic and political interests of Chinese local officials? How do those interests arise? Are they different from or even conflicting with those of the central government? Are local officials defenders of the regions over which they preside, or are they the agents of the central government faithfully implementing its mandate? With considerable fiscal and economic power at their disposal, are local officials able to challenge the authority of the central government by excessively pursuing their own investment interests? If not, what is the power base of the central government that enables it to impose its policy preferences on local officials from a position of general economic weakness? I try to answer some of these questions in this book.

To understand how local investment behavior is affected by the distribution of economic and political resources between the central government and the localities, it is necessary to examine the subject in two broad contexts. The first is China's vast geographic expanse. One of the great challenges in fashioning an integrated, national planning effort in China is its poor transportation and communication infrastructure, weak administrative skills, and the uneven levels of social and economic development in its various regions. For Chinese leaders, regional economic decentralization is often a matter of administrative necessity. During the Maoist era, China had a relatively decentralized economic system. As I explain in later chapters, the reforms in the 1980s brought decentralization into more decision-making arenas and deepened and, to some extent, institutionalized decentralization already present in others. Thus economic decentralization has been a constant theme in China's national economic management; centralization, except during the First Five-Year Plan (FYP), is often a policy response to the problems associated with decentralization.

The other broad context is the political one. In sharp contrast to the decentralized economic control, political power in China has always resided firmly with the central government, and with the Chinese Communist Party. This feature of the Chinese political system has remained fundamentally unaffected by the economic reforms. It is obviously still a one-party system, and it can be extremely repressive and brutal when the political authority of the Chinese Communist Party is challenged. The system manages central–local *political* relations in a highly centralized fashion. The central government directly appoints all the top provincial officials and uses an elaborate system to supervise and regulate personnel and administrative affairs at the local levels. As I will show in greater detail in chapter 4, the political or administrative control exercised by the Center over the localities has in fact been tightened during the reform era. The central monopoly over personnel allocations plays a pivotal role in my explanation of investment and inflation controls in China.

Any account of the behavior of local officials – be it economic or otherwise – must incorporate explicitly these two forces that seem to work at cross purposes. Measured in economic terms, the Center is rather weak; measured in political and bureaucratic terms, the Center is fairly strong. How does this fundamental reality impinge on local investment behavior? In the general balance of things, that behavior is strongly influenced by both the economic power and the political dependency of local officials. Unfortunately, conventional wisdom focuses only on the economic side of the equation. Those who fail to see the political side erroneously conclude that economic decentralization in China has greatly weakened the central state. The analytical task of this book is to provide theoretical and empirical support for this statement. The discussion opens in this chapter with the groundwork, namely, an explanation of my analytical purpose and method of investigation.

Research aims and strategy

The foremost objective of this study is to give as complete as possible an account of the substantial economic and investment activities in which local Chinese officials are engaged. Important subtopics are the role of local officials in the political and bureaucratic hierarchy, the phenomenon of "investment hunger" and the institutional causes for its existence, and the macroeconomic and industrial policy issues during the reform era.

Another objective is to explore the central question posed by this book, "How should one explain the behavioral characteristics of local officials as both powerful economic actors *and* as political and bureaucratic subordinates? Specifically, how are these behavioral characteristics exhibited in their investment conduct?" The concepts and analytical approaches presented here are borrowed from institutional economics. Using a principal–agent model, I hypothesize that local officials behave strategically and opportunistically to maximize their investment preferences, subject to the constraints imposed by the central government. Thus, all else being equal, investment behavior – across time or across regions – can be expected to vary in some systematic relationship with the force of the centrally imposed constraints. This hypothesis and its implications are examined by comparing local investment behavior across two macroeconomic policy regimes, contractionary and reflationary, and by studying investment behavior under the same policy regime but across different regions.

Centrally imposed constraints can vary in a number of ways. For one thing, austerity rounds can be different in their severity. This variation can be intentional; by all accounts, the three-year austerity program between 1989 and 1991 was more far-reaching than, say, the investment reduction in 1986. Or the variation in the severity of austerity programs can be a result of political conflicts at the top. For the first two years of the three-year adjustment (1979–81), the central leadership was locked in a divisive debate about some of the fundamental political issues of the day (such as a political appraisal of Mao Zedong and of the Cultural Revolution) and about economic development strategies. These conflicts were not resolved until the end of 1980, and the resolution ushered in the biting investment reduction of 1981. When there are sharp policy conflicts at the top, it appears that local officials might doubt the credibility of the central austerity programs and choose to ignore central strictures against investment expansions.

Central constraints vary in other ways as well. For example, provincial officials differ markedly in their relationships with the central government. Some serve, concurrently, as national Party and government officials; for example, the Party secretaries of Beijing, Shanghai, and Tianjin have traditionally been members of the Politburo. Others worked extensively in the central ministries before assuming their current provincial posts. Still others have climbed to the top provincial posts via a strictly local career trajectory. Do those officials with closer institutional ties with the central government behave differently from those with looser ties? Other variations are more subtle. Central constraints would only have an impinging effect if the action in question is measurable, that is, if there is a clear criterion to separate successes from failures. Thus the degree of measurability of the tasks is closely related to the stringency of the constraints: the more measurable the tasks, the more stringent the constraints, all else being equal.

Some may question my premise that political and bureaucratic constraints can meaningfully condition local investment conduct; surely, they might argue, there are some very powerful local leaders who, for whatever reasons, can challenge the central government without punishment. This scenario, ipso facto, sounds plausible, but it does not refute my approach, because my approach per se does not exclude this possibility. It would be more appropriate to formulate an alternative hypothesis based on a different understanding of the way the Chinese system works and to see if the empirical evidence on local investment behavior is consistent with the alternative hypothesis.

Although this discussion is limited to China, the findings have implications for general political economy research. To begin with, this is an explicit attempt to incorporate politics into economic analysis. Because the object of this inquiry is an economic activity intermediated through direct governmental actions, it is necessary to include both economic and political variables.[4] The political economy approach separates this book from many of the existing studies on this topic. Second, my research sheds light on the successes and failures of the economic reforms in some of the CPEs. Although policy makers and economists differ over prescriptions to cure inflation, the consensus is that economic reforms can only be implemented when inflation is not serious. To the extent that certain political features can serve to limit demand for inflation, an understanding of this dynamic makes it easier to assess the political requirements for successful economic reforms. Other normative implications concern designing an appropriate governance structure for China, taking into account the political power of the Center vis-à-vis the economic power of the localities. These issues are examined in greater detail in the conclusion of this book.

Political scientists tend to study subnational politics in communist countries by using the "interest group" approach. In this approach, which began in the 1960s as an intellectual rebellion against the traditional image of communist polities as highly rigidified political hierarchies with uniform societal interests (see Brzezinski and Huntington 1964), policy outcomes are considered an aggregation of pluralist interests.[5]

My approach differs from the interest group approach in a few important respects. First, I do not view the formation of interests as a function of the "structural characteristics" of the actors involved – in this case, top decision makers and local officials.[6] The differences between central and local officials with regard to their investment interests are a function of the way the Chinese

---

4. As Alt and Chrystal (1983: 37) put it, "The formulation and adoption of economic policies involves the selection of priorities among economic targets or goals, often through political conflict."

5. A statement from H. Gordon Skilling's article (1966: 443), "Interest Groups and Communist Politics," best epitomizes this approach: "There can be no doubt that Communist society, in spite of its monolithic appearance and the claims of homogeneity made by its supporters, is in fact as complex and stratified as any other, and is divided into social classes and into other categories distinguished by factors such as nationality or religion. Each group has its own values and interests, and each its sharp internal differences, and all are inescapably involved in conflict with other groups."

6. The interest group approach usually deduces commonality of interests among members of a group, usually along professional, functional, or regional lines, by identifying certain structural characteristics of the group. Skilling (1971: 24), for example, makes the following observation: "We shall consider as a political interest group an aggregate of persons who possess certain common characteristics and share certain attitudes on public issues, and who adopt distinct positions on these issues and make definite claims on those in authority." Following this approach, Domes (1984) identifies "structural groups" in Chinese politics. Structural groups consist of members who share common origins in education, experiences, or regions.

economic system operates. The intrinsic characteristics of the actors them-selves, such as their perspectives on particular issues and educational back-grounds or their professional roles, are assumed to matter little in the formation of their interests.[7]

Second, my treatment of group activities in the Chinese political process is a disaggregated one. Even though I assume that local officials share an interest in maximizing investment shares, this assumption in itself does not lead to the prediction that they are equally successful in obtaining the outcome they desire or, indeed, that they uniformly act on their interests in a collective manner. The plan here is to focus on the variations – on the differences among Chinese local officials – and to explore the reasons for such variations, rather than to treat them as an aggregate category.[8] Such an approach may help explain why some groups are more effective than others in pursuing their preferences.[9]

This approach proceeds along two main paths. First, the approach em-ployed in this study is explicitly comparative: local investment behavior is compared either between different points in time or among provinces. Al-though most comparative studies are concerned with the relationships be-tween characteristics of the so-called macro-social units, the nation-states, and some outcomes of interest, comparing subnational units may have a few ad-vantages.[10] It excludes the confounding influences of factors that are difficult to define and measure, such as the political system or the political culture. Furthermore, it isolates the outcome under investigation from factors whose effects are fairly well understood. Thus it helps us concentrate on those factors that are less well known. For example, the notion that administrative efficiency and compliance are a function of bureaucratic professionalism, which, in turn, may be attributable to a high level of socioeconomic development is a plau-sible one but is not of concern here because the subject matter in this study is placed in *roughly* similar socioeconomic settings.[11] In short, choosing a

7. Of course, this is by assumption only and it may or may not fare better than the original assumption empirically. The strength of this assumption lies in the fact that it can facilitate the construction of accounts that are testable. Ultimately, it should be the quality of the accounts that helps us make decisions about retaining or rejecting a particular assumption (Friedman 1953).

8. This approach is also adopted by Goodman (1986), who compares the roles of Sichuan and Guizhou in the national policy debates between the mid-1950s and mid-1960s.

9. For Soviet politics, see Skilling and Griffiths (1971: 19–45); for Chinese politics, see Falkenheim (1987: 1–15).

10. The classic examples include Moore (1967) and Skocpol (1979). An exception to this tra-dition is Shorter and Tilly, *Strikes in France, 1930–1968* (1974), which tests competing theories on strike activities taking place across different French departments.

11. Bureaucracy, viewed in the Weberian tradition, is characterized by a "hierarchy of author-ity" (Weber 1958: 77–128). Authority is exercised to the extent that a subordinate accepts a decision by a superior without independently questioning its merits and haggling over the reward accorded to performance, at least not on a quid pro quo basis (Simon 1976: 11).

subnational comparison over a cross-national one yields some of the same dividends as a careful experimental design.[12]

Second, I employ what Frieden (1991) calls a "modern political economy" approach. I assume that actors maximize utility and take into account the benefits and costs of the measures to achieve their ends. Although this approach is often challenged for its empirical inaccuracy, its utility lies in the fact that it permits one to construct a priori expectations about behavior by specifying a set of constraints impinging on the actors in question (see Tversky and Kahneman 1990). These expectations, in turn, can be falsified only when one assumes that the force of constraints works on the actors in similar ways. Arguably, the rationality assumption is the only means whereby we can carry out systematic research on comparative behavior.

That actors may have different definitions of utility in no way invalidates the modern political economy approach itself. Utility itself is not given, even though utility-maximizing behavior is. Thus different actors may pursue quite different goals, depending on their positions in the economy or society. In the case of China, the central government pursues macroeconomic stability, whereas the local governments pursue income and employment objectives in ways often detrimental to macroeconomic stability. The analytical framework also does not require that definitions of utility always be consistent; the central government has alternated between macroeconomic stability and income objectives. What the analytical framework does require is that the central government, on balance, should care about macroeconomic stability more than local governments, a condition easily satisfied in the Chinese situation.

Local officials in the Chinese political system

In Western studies of central–local relations in China, local officials are usually put into one of two categories. On one hand, they are classified as economic agents and their economic conduct is said to be driven principally by the economic resources they possess. According to this view, in the current reform era decentralization has shifted economic resources into the hands of localities and has weakened central economic control. Local investment and production behavior often contravenes central policy objectives (Naughton 1987; Wong 1985, 1987). Relatedly, the declining revenue share claimed by the central government has often been blamed for the lax macroeconomic management and inflation (Wang Shaoguang and Hu Angang 1993; World Bank 1990a).

---

12. For further discussions along this line, see Lijphart (1971).

On the other hand, local officials are considered active, if not powerful, political players able to bargain effectively with the central government over the terms of their interactions and over national policies (Chang 1978). Local officials also form political alliances to demand economic reforms and to have some say in the pace and the fashion of these reforms (Shirk 1990). They are, in addition, "political brokers" who intermediate the interests between their localities and the central government (Goodman 1984), or they are skillful opportunists who exploit the weaknesses of the system to maximize their own interests (Huang 1990).[13]

This book departs from such perspectives. In this book, intergovernmental relations are not just about divisions of economic resources but are bureaucratic and hierarchical in nature. Chinese local officials are treated in much the same way that they would be treated in the Chinese official bureaucratic literature – as subordinate members of the Chinese bureaucratic and administrative system. This is not to suggest that traditional perspectives are wrong, but that this bureaucratic perspective does lead to a substantive shift from the traditional perspectives. Local investment behavior cannot be characterized simply as "defiance" of or compliance with central investment directives. Instead, local officials comply selectively and strategically. If this administrative characteristic of Chinese local officials is overlooked, one is likely to exaggerate the effect of economic and fiscal delegations. There is also an analytical shift. The focus here is on hierarchy and on the effect of hierarchy on behavior, in addition to the economic and political resources that localities may possess. Thus this study focuses on a number of bureaucratic characteristics of the Chinese system, such as administrative divisions of labor, appointment and promotion practices, and the effects of duration of service and tenure security.

As explained later in this chapter, the data on which this study is based encompass both provincial and subprovincial investment activities, but the bulk of the analysis applies to the provincial-level bureaucracies. One might well ask to what extent provincial-level officials can be treated as an appropriate unit of analysis. There are three principal justifications for singling out provincial governments as a unit of analysis. First, the aim here is to explore interactions between the central government and local authorities, rather than the behavior of local officials per se. In this regard, provincial officials occupy a rather unique position in the Chinese political system in that they are a cross between policy makers and policy implementors.

Although China specialists disagree over the extent, impact, and regularity

---

13. See also Li and Bachman (1989), Walder (1992), and Zang (1991).

of provincial participation in national policy deliberations, the consensus is that provincial officials play a formal role in the policy-making process.[14] Since 1977, for example, all the provincial Party secretaries have routinely been full members of the Central Committee, and in 1987 the first Party secretaries of Sichuan, Beijing, Tianjin, and Shanghai were promoted to the ranks of the Politburo; in 1992, the Party secretaries from Guangdong and Shandong were also given the same status. Other provincial officials are drawn into the policy deliberation process by their participation in economic work conferences (*jingji gongzuo huiyi*) or conferences on industry and transportation (*gongjiao huiyi*), held regularly at the beginning of the year, as well as by their attendance at provincial governors' and mayors' conferences (*shengzhang shizhang huiyi*).

The second reason to treat provincial governments as a unit is their important economic role. According to a study done by the Chinese Institute for the Reform of the Economic System (CIRES) in the mid-1980s, provincial officials were responsible for setting 37.8 percent of the mandatory production targets, compared with 51.9 percent set by the central government and 10.3 percent set by the city-level authorities (Zhang Shaojie, Cui Heming, Xu Gang, and Ji Xiaoming 1986: 162). In essence, economic decision-making power roughly corresponds to the Chinese political hierarchy; provincial officials, after the central government, are the most important economic players.

The third reason is that the salience of provincial officials typically increases during a retrenchment phase. In 1983, 1986, and 1989, the central government explicitly stated that it would hold provincial officials personally responsible for investment excesses within their jurisdictions. This measure puts provincial officials in a rather awkward position as political brokers (Goodman 1984). In effect, provincial officials are asked to choose between the two constituencies whom they normally strive to placate simultaneously: they are asked to adhere to central policies and to advance local interests at the same time. A study of provincial officials during retrenchment sheds light not only on this dilemma and how this dilemma is resolved but also on the dynamics of Chinese political processes.

Investment policy conflicts in China

Investments to build new plants and facilities – the focus of this study – cause policy conflicts in China because excessive investment growth increases inflationary pressures and because the central government and localities disagree

---

14. For two opposing views, see Chang (1978) and Barnett (1967).

about how to apportion the costs of containing these pressures.[15] Investment policy conflicts are not incidental, and they do not occur between specific national and local leaders as individuals. Instead, these conflicts have deep institutional roots in the way the Chinese economic system works. That is to say, they are a product of budget constraints and the way in which the economic and political benefits (and costs) of investment expansions are allocated. Investment policy conflicts are a specific example of the kind of coordination problems created by economic decentralization during the reform era.

Investment and inflation

Development economists have long argued that a country's long-term economic growth depends critically on how willing people are to save and what proportion of the national income is spent on investment in relation to consumption activities. Although as of late this view has lost some of its traditional luster, principally because of the neoclassical emphasis on the efficient utilization of resources, many policy makers and economists still maintain that capital formation holds the key to economic growth and development.[16]

In socialist economies, policy makers believe even more fervently in the link between capital formation and economic growth. In part, this belief is a by-product of the emphasis on heavy industry; heavy industry is more capital intensive than light industry and agriculture, and therefore a keen policy interest in heavy industry inevitably drives up investments. Indeed, socialist governments have traditionally resorted to forced savings – such as agricultural price scissors and consumption rationing – to finance capital construction. As a share of the national income, socialist countries put more resources in capital construction than do market economies.

Reforming socialist economies face a different investment problem. Typically, the governments have long given up on "investment fetishism" or the blind emphasis on heavy industry; yet the investment growth rate is still quite high or higher than when the economy was more tightly controlled. Indeed, one of the most vexing economic policy challenges to current policy makers is how to rein in the explosive growth of investment volume once economic reforms are under way. Their task is made all the more difficult by the urge to invest and to launch new projects, which runs deep and is pervasive in

---

15. Investments in existing capacities are less relevant to central–local relations mainly because those operational investment decisions are made overwhelmingly by enterprises themselves. However, I also examine the behavior of renovation investments, the investments that ostensibly modify the existing capacities but are in fact intended to create new capacities.

16. See Wade (1990) for a representative view.

bureaucratic offices and enterprise headquarters. This is the phenomenon the Hungarian economist Janos Kornai describes as "investment hunger."

In studies of comparative economic systems, the conventional wisdom is that CPEs are "supply constrained." An economy is supply constrained to the extent that an endemic pressure exists to gear the economic system toward full capacity utilization. Given that prices do not adjust to changes in demand, shortages typically occur, first in investment goods and factors and then in consumer goods via derived demand for wage goods. This situation of shortage contrasts with that of market economies, which are typically "demand constrained" and exhibit a constant tendency to slip into recession on account of sluggish demand. This contrast is demonstrated by the nature of the inventories held in the two types of economies. Whereas inventories in market economies are final goods kept as a buffer against demand shocks, in CPEs they tend to be inputs to production which are to insure against taut planning (Levine 1969).

A systematic and cogent illustration of this view is found in Janos Kornai's work, *The Economics of Shortage* (1980). His argument rests on the critical distinction between the two actors in CPEs, households and firms. These two actors, according to Kornai, are governed by fundamentally different decision rules in their economic behavior: households operate under "hard-budget constraints," as a result of which household spending cannot exceed the levels of their income; in contrast, state-owned firms face "soft-budget constraints," in the form of fiscal grants and deferred or unserviced bank credits to subsidize enterprise losses.[17] The readiness to prevent bankruptcy can be viewed in part as an act of "a paternalistic state" (Kornai 1986b) and in part as a shrewd effort to preserve political and social stability by keeping workers employed.[18] In either case the incentive effect is the same: soft-budget constraints imply zero risks to firms' investment behavior and zero risks feed investment expansions.

This distinction in the decision rules of households and firms explains the centrality of capital investment in affecting macroeconomic stability in a CPE. The household demand for goods and services is bound by hard-budget constraints and thus, to some extent, is self-restrained. Firms, in contrast, face soft-budget constraints and their demands tend to be "insatiable." These demands translate into investment hunger and are present at all levels of the

17. Indeed, households in socialist economies face harder budget constraints than their counterparts in market economies because they cannot borrow to finance their consumption.

18. One can argue that this political motive is stronger in China because the state-owned firms not only provide jobs but also housing, education, social insurance, and other such amenities to their employees. See Walder (1986).

economic system: planners, economic bureaucrats, and managers alike seek to increase their shares of investment funds until shortages, or repressed inflation, become too severe. In reaction, the top leadership imposes strict controls on investment activities by tightening numerical targets and (re)centralizing many economic decision-making rights (Bauer 1978; Kornai 1980).

Investment hunger is linked with open or repressed inflationary pressures in several ways. Although in principle investment increases the supply capacity of the economy and therefore should moderate demand/supply imbalances in the medium to long run, in the short run, there is usually a significant time lag before the supply-side effect is realized. An investment surge with a time lag is inflationary for two reasons. First, investment expansion leads to an increase in the total wage payments, that is, in household incomes, which leads to a higher demand for consumer goods. The higher demand for consumer goods translates into inflationary pressures.[19]

Second, and closely related to the first reason, an investment surge typically lengthens the investment completion cycle.[20] CPE firms are often said to maximize or to compete to initiate as many investment projects as possible; finishing a project and making it productive are a secondary concern. The reason for this type of behavior is that a project, once officially approved and initiated, will guarantee resource commitments to it at some point in the future; thus in order to claim additional resource commitments a rational strategy is to concentrate on initiating projects rather than on completing them.[21] No matter what the reason for the time lag, investment time lag produces inflationary pressures because all the investment activities have to be financed either by the budget or by bank credits. Both methods can lead to an increase in money supply, which is the most direct reason for inflation.

Two other factors accentuate the inflationary character of investments as well. First, an overwhelming proportion of investment activities in the Chinese economy are carried out by state-owned enterprises, which have access to bank credits. Such access easily leads to increases in the money supply because nonstate firms typically finance their investment demand by savings or retained earnings, which crowd out consumption and therefore are not necessarily inflationary.[22] Second, in recent years more and more investment

19. For this line of analysis, see Imai (1994).

20. Investment completion cycle refers to the period from the inception of a project to the time when the project becomes productive.

21. Various strategies are used to maximize project initiation rates. One deliberately attempts to underestimate anticipated costs so that approvals will be more forthcoming. This strategy is known in both East European countries and in China as "hooking in the plan." See Grosfeld (1989: 364).

22. I thank Professor Dwight Perkins for this point.

resources have been devoted to nonproduction-related purposes, such as the construction of luxurious office buildings or recreational facilities. Because these investment activities do not add directly to the productive capacity of the economy, they can fuel inflation by raising the total wage bills and the demand for investment goods.

The consensus within policy and academic circles is that enhanced macro-economic instability in China since the early 1980s has been due primarily to the investment component – as opposed to consumption and external shocks – of aggregate demand.[23] Even though policy makers have disagreed quite widely over the deep and systemic causes for investment expansion and over prescriptions for long-term solutions to tame aggregate demand, the short-term reaction has never been in doubt. Since 1979, the Chinese government has launched five rounds of economic austerity to combat inflation: in 1981, 1983, 1986–87, 1989–91, and in 1993. Although these five episodes have differed in their severity and in their approaches, they clearly have one characteristic in common: they have all been aimed at reining in the expansion of aggregate demand by cutting the rates of investment growth and, especially, the growth rates of local investment.

Inflation control and adjustment costs

In general, the policy responses to inflation have been swift. Inflation has always been a politically sensitive issue in China, in part because the Chinese Communist Party (CCP) traces its rise to power to the hyperinflationary days of the Nationalists in the late 1940s. The political impact of inflation was underscored by the prodemocracy movement in the spring of 1989, when inflation, along with corruption, featured prominently in the protests by intellectuals, students, and workers.[24]

No less significant, in political terms, are the processes and policies to control inflation. The political significance of inflation control arises not only from the fact that political institutions shape and constrain the mix of policy choices

---

23. A less orthodox view among a small group of Chinese economists is that Chinese inflation is consumption driven. They base their position on the observation that much of the investment is not made to enhance productive capacity but to augment artificially depressed income and thus acts as a form of welfare. In their view, investment in housing, athletic, educational, and cultural facilities for employees should be counted as consumption expenditures (see Cao Erjie 1988).

24. According to a survey conducted by the People's University in early 1989, in terms of the importance of their concerns, inflation ranked number three among respondents, many of whom were high-ranking government officials at or above the bureau level (see *Shijie jingji daobao* [World Economic Herald] April 3, 1989: 1). For an analysis of how inflation fed workers' political demands, see Walder (1989: 33–35).

with which a government is faced (Alt and Chrystal 1983: 36), but also from the fact that the representation of economic interests becomes an intrinsically political issue to the extent that government retrenchment policies affect the distribution of economic interests in the society. "The central political dilemma," Haggard and Kaufman write about developing countries' efforts to cope with debt crisis, "is that stabilization and adjustment policies, no matter how beneficial they may be for the country as a whole, entail the imposition of short-term costs and have distributional implications" (1989a: 210). In China, as elsewhere, political battles are waged over the distribution of the burdens and costs of efforts to combat inflation.

Different actors bear the adjustment costs – the costs of containing inflation – in different economic systems. In market economies, economic adjustment often requires that fiscal deficits be reduced via cuts in entitlement programs, government expenditures, and urban subsidies. The allocation of the burdens of these cuts among social, economic, and political actors is a major test of a government's political authority (Haggard and Kaufman 1989a; Nelson 1988). Typically, well-organized economic and social groups aspiring to maximize or defend their shares of the social product are in an advantageous position to shirk adjustment costs. This argument – known as the structuralist thesis – views the incidence of inflation or the failure to restrain inflation as a product of pressures emanating from effectively organized "inflation coalitions," as in the case of a number of Latin American countries in the 1970s (Hirschman 1985).[25]

The situation in China differs from this in two marked respects. First, as in other centrally planned economies, austerity often takes the form of a reduction in the resources available for investment purposes, rather than in the factors that principally affect consumption, such as income policies and welfare expenditures. Second, opposition to austerity programs does not come so much from social or economic groups, which lack an organized representation of their interests. The conflicts over the direction of economic policies cut across powerful bureaucratic actors and between these actors and the central policy authorities.

Because austerity programs invariably seek to curb investment growth and

---

25. Robert J. Gordon (1975), in his important contribution to the field of political economy, "The Demand for and Supply of Inflation," argues that "accelerations in money and prices are not thrust upon society by a capricious or self-serving government, but rather represent the vote-maximizing response of government to the political pressure exerted by potential beneficiaries of inflation." Charles Maier (1985) offers a critique of this approach. The stakes in inflation, he argues, are often too ambiguous to the actors involved, and under such conditions it is generally difficult to induce cohesive group actions purely on the basis of a concern for inflation.

local investment growth in particular, who should bear the adjustment costs often becomes a question of who reduces investment growth more. Investment conflicts between the central government and local governments occur because their investment preferences systematically diverge. At the risk of oversimplification, I argue that the central government wants investment resources to flow to "strategic" sectors such as energy and raw materials, whereas local governments want investment resources to go to more profitable processing sectors. Furthermore, the central government desires a more or less stable investment growth rate, whereas the local governments want a faster investment growth rate. These differences in investment preferences are stable, and they in turn give rise to stable preferences over policy alternatives.

Central and local investment preferences differ with regard to how investment resources should be allocated. Whereas central investment strategy stresses the development of what it designates as "priority sectors" – infrastructure and energy – local governments tend to steer resources toward investment activities that generate revenue, many of which produce consumer durables. Sometimes, this divergence in investment preferences can lead to a situation of bluff: the central government purposely underfunds priority sectors to "shift costs" to the localities; local governments, on the other hand, refuse to comply in the expectation that the central government will ultimately balance the books (World Bank 1990a: 98–99). Typically, this tug-of-war grows more intense in a stringent fiscal and monetary environment, as the central government musters its political weight to exert extra pressures and thereby ensure that its investment preferences will prevail.

The differential preferences in the area of investment structure between the central government and local officials are an endogenous outcome of the working of the system, as well as of the economic nature of the projects in question. First of all, many of the priority investment projects possess "positive externalities" – their benefits accrue to those other than the bearers of the costs of the projects. For example, transportation and power plant construction projects typically do not benefit just a single province and often are interregional in character. Thus provinces often have a disincentive to put up the financing and consider it fair game for the Center to pick up the tab.

The price structure further enhances this disincentive. In China, the prices of finished goods are set very high in relation to the prices of the raw materials that are used to produce them. For example, heavy fuel oil is priced at one-third of the international level and the price of coal is only 60 percent of its long-run marginal costs (World Bank 1985: 71). Low prices for raw materials create high profits in the processing sectors that use these raw materials. According to Wong (1985: 270), profit rates in watch-making, rubber processing, and bicycle production are 30 or 40 times those of coal and iron-ore mining, cement, and other such sectors. This price divergence – after the normal costs of creating the final products have been taken into account – leads to strong incentives for regions with comparative advantage in raw materials to invest in expanding their processing capacity to produce finished goods locally. Producing finished goods locally is a way to keep accounting profits at home. Thus, acting rationally, localities presiding over resource-rich regions want to allocate more of their resources to the processing sectors, leaving the others to finance the construction of priority projects.

The second difference has to do with inflation preferences, more specifically, preferences for investment growth rates. In a sense, Chinese policy makers face classic Phillips curve trade-offs between the rate of inflation and levels of unemployment: higher rates of inflation are associated with lower levels of unemployment and vice versa. Although driven by fundamentally different dynamics than their counterparts in market economies, Chinese politicians also have different but stable preferences for different choices along the Phillips curve.[26] National policy makers are more concerned with high rates of inflation and thus less concerned about high levels of unemployment; local officials have the opposite preferences.

To say that top decision makers are more concerned about inflation (and therefore about investment expansions) than subnational officials, by no means suggests that top leaders are motivated by a higher notion of public good in their conduct. Nor are they necessarily more "rational" in assessing the objective consequences of their policy choices.[27] A principal factor is that central leaders absorb a disproportionate share of costs of inflation, whereas to the local governments inflation control is a public good in that the benefits of its provision are small as compared with the costs. For that reason, the central policy makers are "balancers of the last resort": if they do not balance the macroeconomic situation, no one else in the system will. They cannot "pass the buck," so to speak. Since the costs of investment expansion do not reflect their true scarcity values, one gains by claiming as many resources as possible. But this behavior – however rational it is to the individuals engaging

---

26. In developed market economies, left-wing governments tend to pursue economic policies that maximize employment at the cost of a higher rate of inflation; these policies may encompass, for example, more government spendings. Right-wing governments pursue an opposite mix of economic policies that tend to curb inflation but create a higher level of unemployment in the process. These different policy preferences are commonly attributed to the different constituent bases to which these governments appeal. See Hibbs (1977).

27. This is what is known as "the rationality model." For a fuller explication of this model, see Allison (1971: 10–38). For an illustration of its application and limitations in analyses of Chinese politics, see Lieberthal and Oksenberg (1988: 11–14).

in it – produces economywide consequences. Investment expansions cause shortages in energy and raw materials or, when prices are adjustable, cause their prices to rise. They also cause budgetary deficits. If investment expansions lead to a rise in local budgetary deficits, the central government is left holding the bag and ultimately has to finance these deficits. Central planners, not their local counterparts, have to deal with these economywide consequences. The obverse side of the "planners' sovereignty" is that they are the ultimate bearers of responsibility.[28]

There are also political costs. Inflation reduces the living standards of those people on fixed incomes, most of whom are civil servants, intellectuals, students, and urban workers with a strong political voice. Because national leaders are more closely identified with the political system, they, more than subnational officials, shoulder a disproportionate share of the political blame for inflation. (As a Beijing bus passenger once commented on inflation and Deng Xiaoping, who is barely 5 feet tall, "These days, everything rises, except the height of Deng Xiaoping.") This is so despite the fact that on objective grounds inflationary pressures should be attributed to local economic behavior. The Chinese reformist leaders are highly aware of the political sensitivity of inflation. Zhao Ziyang (1982b), the former Party secretary and premier, explicitly linked inflation with politics in a speech on the economic austerity program in December 1980: "That [failure to control inflation] will not be an economic issue only; political stability will be affected."[29]

Central policy makers in China sometimes express concern that local officials may not obey the central government in reducing investment growth. In 1983, a report on the progress of investment control drafted by the State Planning Commission (SPC) singled out a number of provinces for their

28. Contrast this situation with a market economy, where losers and gainers from inflation are more evenly spread in the system. John Woolley (1985), in an article entitled, "Central Banks and Inflation," argues that it is not so much the legalistic status of the Federal Reserve that gives it its ability to balance the executive branch's fiscal policy with a cautious monetary policy. Rather, it is the ability of the Federal Reserve to enlist support from the constituency of stable money, namely, the financial community, that gives it a degree of political independence.

29. He repeated the same comment again in 1982 (Zhao Ziyang 1982a). It should be pointed out, however, that central concerns over investment expansion are not necessarily temporally consistent. When the economy is, or is perceived to be, in equilibrium, top leaders often share a desire to achieve fast economic growth and they often set high investment targets. This was the case in 1958 and again in 1978 when unrealistically high investment targets were set by the top decision makers; in the first case the aim was to achieve Mao's grandiose ideological ambitions, and in the second case it arose out of the desire to recover from the disruptions of the Cultural Revolution (Zhao Dexing 1989a: 480–83, 1989b: 176–85). The second reason that these concerns may not be consistent over time is that top leaders may feel that at times it is politically expedient to tolerate an inflationary bout. This was very much Zhao Ziyang's calculation in 1986–87.

ineffective implementation of central investment policies (SPC 1987: 584–85). Zhao Ziyang revealed the difficulties of getting Chinese provinces to bear the adjustment costs by subordinating their "partial interests" to the "interests of the whole." In his report to the Third Plenum of the Thirteenth Party Congress, convened in October 1988 to launch another round of austerity measures, he made the following remarks:

All the regions and departments should be responsible for the safeguarding of the interests of the whole nation and for subordinating their own interests to the interests of the whole nation. This relation between the part and the whole should not be ignored, much less turned upside down. This problem deserves special attention in the process of improving the economic environment. . . . Putting the economic environment in order will never be an easy job. We have to suffer and make sacrifices. Faced with such difficulties, we should pull together, and each one of us should never act simply as he pleases. We should never do anything that benefits a locality at the expense of the whole, such as would happen if the practice of "countering a central measure with a local one" were condoned. (Zhao Ziyang 1988b: vi)

The apportionment of adjustment costs aside, local officials are positively motivated to expand investments to generate employment. There is a simple reason for this: local officials run enterprises that employ about 85 percent of China's work force and that are concentrated in labor-intensive sectors. In contrast, enterprises run by the central ministries not only employ fewer workers per industrial output value, but they are in centrally designated strategic sectors that are usually protected from austerity programs. Thus austerity programs have more severe employment implications for the localities than for the central ministries. Writing in November 1988, one month after the start of a three-year austerity program, Zhong Zhangrun (1988), the deputy director of the Economic Research Center for the Nanjing municipal government, estimated that at least 10 percent of economic growth was required to fulfill central tax obligations and to keep people on the enterprise payroll. Otherwise, he warned, perhaps with greater foresight than he realized at the time, "there will be social chaos."

There is direct documentary evidence showing this systematic difference in central and local policy preferences. In 1991 the State Commission for the Reform of the Economic System (SCRES) conducted a survey asking ministerial and provincial officials to assess the economic situation over that year. The survey supports the central/local divisions in policy preferences for Phillips curve trade-offs between inflation and unemployment. For example, 61.6 percent of the central officials rated the economic situation in 1991 – a contractionary year – as favorable, whereas only 41.2 percent of the local officials did so. Local officials also showed less concern about inflationary pressures in the economy: only 32.4 percent of them were alarmed about

Table 1.1. *Survey results of central and local officials on their opinions of the 1991 economic situation: percentage of those in agreement with various statements.*

By central–local division	Central officials	Local officials
1. Demand and supply is in equilibrium in 1991.	61.6	41.2
2. Aggregate demand is insufficient.	30.6	44.1
3. Industrial growth is too fast.	83.3	76.5
4. Credit growth is too fast.	52.8	32.4
5. Unemployment is a problem.	8.3	29.4
By bureaucratic ranks	Ministerial-level officials	Bureau-level officials
1. Industrial growth is too fast.	36.4	16.9
2. Unemployment is a problem.	0.0	22.0

Source: Huang Yunchen, Lu Jian, and Fan Yu (1992).

credit expansions, compared with 52.8 percent of the central officials. In addition, 8.3 percent of central officials viewed unemployment as a problem, compared with 29.4 percent of local officials.

The same Phillips trade-off divisions apply to bureaucratic ranks. Xue Muqiao (1987: 5), a prominent Chinese economist, remarked on the overambitious development objectives set by local officials at the seven regional development conferences he attended in 1986, adding: "These are only provincial and city-level officials; the township officials are even more ambitious." In general, concerns about inflation increase at the higher end of bureaucratic ranks and concerns about unemployment increase at the lower end: 36.4 percent of the ministerial-level officials thought that industrial growth was too fast in 1991, whereas only 16.9 percent of the bureau-level officials concurred with this view. At the same time, none of the ministerial-level officials believed that unemployment was a problem whereas 22 percent of the bureau-level officials thought so.[30] These results are summarized in table 1.1.

Some definitions

Throughout this book, the term "local government" corresponds exactly to *difang zhengfu* in Chinese official literature. That is, it denotes any level of the government below the central government. Whenever necessary, I use

30. As explained in chapter 4, top ministerial and provincial officials have the same rank, ministerial-level officials here include top officials working in the provinces. Thus the survey here shows that provincial-level officials are more concerned about inflation than county-level officials.

"province," "prefecture," or "county" to refer to specific levels of local government.[31] I also use "province" (*sheng*) to denote the three cities of provincial rank – Beijing, Tianjin, and Shanghai – without referring to them separately as directly administered municipalities.

The analysis focuses on the investment activities undertaken by state enterprises. Although investments in the nonstate sector are considerable and are growing rapidly, the bulk of investment activities are still concentrated in the state sectors. In 1990, for example, state investments accounted for 65.6 percent of the total fixed-asset investments, which was only a slight decrease from the 1985 level of 66.1 percent. Moreover, investments in the state sector contribute far more to inflation than investments in nonstate sectors, mainly because state-owned enterprises are less constrained by financial discipline and economic caution and therefore they have a more serious investment hunger problem.[32]

The quality of data also limits my focus. Nonstate sectoral investment data are not as consistently available as the state-sector data; for some years, especially the earlier years, data are particularly sketchy. The quality of nonstate sectoral data is also poorer; one problem is that some village enterprises report investment and production data evaluated in current prices as constant, thus inflating the numbers by the margins equivalent to the inflation rates.

State investment activities can be broken down in a number of analytically useful ways. In this book, they are most frequently broken down along the lines of administrative supervision, that is, between central (*zhongyang*) and local (*difang*) investments. A narrower definition would focus on the output of investment activities – namely, those investment projects under construction. If the project is supervised by a central government agency, then the project in question is classified as a "central project" (*zhongyang xiangmu*); otherwise it is classified as a "local project" (*difang xiangmu*). Here, "supervision" means that the appropriate authority formulates the project proposal, seeks or issues its approval, and is responsible for (*fuze anpai*) the project financing and for securing the necessary inputs. In the case of projects jointly financed by central and local authorities, the sources are separated, with the local part classified as local projects and the central part as central projects. The investment data disclosed in the official Chinese sources and the ones used in this study do not cover military investments.[33] This narrower definition is the prevailing

---

31. For an introduction to the Chinese *nomenklatura* system, see Burns (1987a). For details on the operation of the system, see Manion (1985).

32. For an analysis of different investment motives, see Development Center of the State Council (1986).

33. Interview with Zhang Sai, director of the State Statistical Bureau (SSB), Ann Arbor, March 8, 1993.

convention used by the Chinese statistical authorities to collect investment data (see Zhou Hanrong 1991: 685–86; SSB 1993b: 331).

A wider definition would focus on the input side of the government's investment activities. In this case, local investment activities would include not only the arrangement of inputs and project financing but also economic policies and administrative practices that expand or constrain investments. Thus administrative decrees issued to local banks or the effort to woo outside investors on the part of local governments should all be considered part of local investment behavior.[34]

Obviously, there should be some correlations between the wider and narrower definitions; the more active a local government agency is on the input side, the higher the volume should be expected on the output side. In this book, I attempt to describe local investment behavior both from the input and the output sides, but because of the more systematic availability of information on the latter, this study relies more heavily on data on the output side.

Investment activities can also be broken down according to their purposes. The total fixed-asset investments (*guding zichan touzi*) consist of capital construction (*jiben jianshe touzi*), technical renovation investments (*gengxin gaizao*), and other investments (mainly for oil development and road maintenance). Capital construction investments stress the creation of new enterprises or a major expansion of existing enterprises, and technical renovation investments aim to modify existing enterprises. Traditionally, the distinction was maintained only because of the difference in their financing sources: capital construction was financed through the budget, whereas technical renovation was financed through the retention of capital depreciation funds. This distinction has been blurred because of the diversification in funding sources for capital construction projects and because technical renovation investments are increasingly used for capital construction purposes. However, the Chinese planning and statistical authorities still maintain the distinction and use different reporting procedures for each. This has implications for investment control purposes, because the central authorities monitor and measure local investment activities mainly through capital construction (see chapter 7).

Organization of the book

This book is organized into three parts. The first part focuses on the economic and political roles of Chinese local officials from the point of view of central–local relationships in the era of reforms; the second part deals with a set of

---

34. For a more detailed discussion, see Zhong Chengxun (1993).

macroeconomic policy issues in China during the reform era; and the third presents the analysis. By and large, the first and second parts are a straightforward discussion of the characteristics of China's economic and bureaucratic systems; the third part, especially chapter 8, is more technical and relies heavily on data analysis.

The first part, beginning with chapter 2, portrays in detail the various economic roles Chinese local officials play in the Chinese system in the areas of administrative control of enterprises, output planning, regional trade policies, banking, and taxation. Chapter 3 examines the role of local governments in initiating, financing, approving, and implementing investment projects. Chapter 4 describes the position that local officials occupy in the Chinese political system and explains the mechanisms by which the central government controls and supervises the administrative behavior of local officials.

Chapter 5 turns to the phenomenon of excess investment demand in China and traces the systemic reasons that have given rise to its persistence. The purpose is to illustrate the root causes of overheated investment expansions, a problem common in reforming CPEs, and the institutional reasons why investment expansion – as opposed to consumer spendings – is a main contributor to inflation. Chapter 5 also details the policy responses by which the central government has proposed to deal with the inflationary pressures in the economy.

Chapter 6 lays down a theoretical framework and a model of local investment behavior. This framework makes inferences about behavior on the basis of two variables – information distribution and divergent policy preferences. On the basis of these general inferences, I propose a number of specific hypotheses about how information distribution and preference divergence can affect local investment behavior. These hypotheses are then tested in chapters 7 and 8 in two ways: by examining investment patterns across different time periods, and by examining these patterns and their relationships with the posited causal variables across different provinces. The hypotheses are then evaluated on the basis of the consistency in the empirical findings. In chapter 9, I briefly consider a number of larger issues, such as the relevance of the findings to evaluating the strength of Chinese political institutions, the effectiveness of inflation control in transition economies, and the optimal sequence between economic and political reforms.[35]

---

35. See also the various appendixes in this volume for details on the sources of Chinese data and supplementary empirical factors used in the analysis.

Part I

The economic and political roles of local government officials

2

Local government officials as economic agents

Studies of the Chinese economic system usually present two contrasting images. One portrays a "cellular" system in which the regions of China are encouraged to be self-reliant and self-sufficient (Donnithorne 1981). The other depicts a high degree of regional interdependence, with the central government mobilizing and distributing economic and fiscal resources quite effectively (Lardy 1978). Empirical evidence seems to support both these images. On the one hand, Chinese economic development strategy during most of the Maoist period was largely egalitarian in character, which led to a concentration of centrally financed investment in the interior and western regions during the Second, Third, and Fourth Five-Year Plan periods (1958–65, 1966–70, and 1971–75).[1] On the other hand, despite the egalitarian character of China's development strategy, regional economic disparities persisted well into the 1980s. According to a comprehensive study conducted by economists at the State Council and the SPC in the mid-1980s, the industrial structure mirrored the regional divisions in the 1950s and the 1960s. Even today the coastal provinces still have higher labor and capital productivity and much more developed processing industries; the interior and western regions are rich in energy and natural resources but are underdeveloped in manufacturing industries (State Council and SPC 1990: 410–16).

These regional disparities have served as one of the important rationales for limiting the economic power of the central government and for preserving the autonomy of local governments. This argument was most forcefully put

---

1. For more details, see Yang (1990: 233–37). It should also be noted that the decision to build up the industries in the interior regions involved national security considerations as well. In the wake of deteriorating Sino-Soviet relations and with the United States fighting a war in Vietnam, Chinese leaders became increasingly concerned about the vulnerability of industrial plants and transport facilities, most of which were located on flat coastal terrain. Thus a decision was made sometime in the mid-1960s to build up the so-called third-front industries in China's mountainous interior. For more details, see Naughton (1991a).

forward by Mao Zedong in his famous speech of 1956, "On the Ten Great Relationships." Mao argued that a highly centralized planning system based on the Soviet model was inappropriate for China because of the great differences in stages of economic development among the Chinese provinces.[2] With the abandonment of an egalitarian development strategy during the reform era, there has been more emphasis on the developmental role of local governments; the economic reforms, as a deliberate policy measure, have shifted much economic decision-making power away from the central government.

Local investment is being conducted in a context of increasing economic power in the hands of local officials. This power is manifested in both local policy autonomy and local control over economic resources. This chapter is about the central–local institutional arrangements that endow local governments considerable operational autonomy and the areas in which local governments have direct economic control at their disposal: supervision of enterprises, product allocation, regional trade policies, bank lending, and taxation. The most important economic control in the hands of local governments – the ability to sponsor, undertake, and finance investment activities – is discussed in chapter 3.

Central–local economic institutional arrangements

The Chinese political system is a unitary system in the sense that local governments derive their authority and decision-making rights solely from the central government and their duties at the local level are performed on behalf of the central government. Each sectoral ministry in Beijing has corresponding bureaus in the provinces.[3] However, the relationship between the two can be extremely confusing at times. Although one should expect some variation across the provinces (for example, Shanghai, Guizhou, and Xinjiang have a Bureau of Chemical Industry and Liaoning and Henan have a Bureau of Geology and Mineral Resources, whereas most of the other provinces do not), the unitary system is such that the institutional design at the local level is meant to mirror that at the central level rather than to accommodate local conditions. The majority of central economic ministries have provincial equivalents.[4]

Although the relationship between the State Council and the top officials in

---

2. At the time, this view clashed with that of China's central planners, represented by Li Fuchun, who argued for a greater central allocative role and who viewed the concentration of 70 percent of industrial value in the coastal regions as irrational (MacFarquhar 1974: 63–66).

3. *Ju* is also translated as "department." In this book, I use "bureau" to refer to government units and "department" to refer to the Party units, such as the Department of Organization.

4. For details of these ministries, see the appendix to this chapter.

Table 2.1. *Rank equivalents among government organizations*

Center	Province	County
Ministry (*Bu*)	Province (*Sheng*) Centrally administered cities (Beijing; Tianjin; Shanghai)	
General Bureau (*Zongju*)	Commission	
Bureau (*Ju* or *Si*)	Provincial bureau (*Ting* or *Ju*) Prefecture	
Division (*Chu*)		County (*Xian*)
Section (*Ke*)		County Department

Source: Lieberthal and Oksenberg (1988: 143).

the provincial governments is one of direct subordination, the authority relationship between the central ministries and their provincial bureaus is more complex. Three factors affect this relationship. The most straightforward of these, but also the least illuminating, is bureaucratic rank (see Lieberthal and Oksenberg 1988: 142–43). In the Chinese system, central ministries and provincial governments have the same bureaucratic rank and, although on the surface the provincial bureaus are clearly lower in bureaucratic rank than their ministerial counterparts in Beijing, as shown in table 2.1, provincial bureaus do not necessarily take orders from their ministries. This is because each sectoral provincial bureau answers to two superior units: the central ministry and the provincial government. For any system to operate smoothly in such a situation, the primary lines of authority must be specified.

The way responsibilities are divided up between these two chains of command is the second factor affecting the relationship between central ministries in Beijing and the provincial governments.[5] Formally, the Chinese bureaucratic system distinguishes between so-called administrative leadership relations (*xingzheng lingdao guanxi*) and professional leadership relations (*yewu lingdao guanxi*). Administrative leadership relations exist in such areas as the appointment, removal, and transfer of cadres at a lower level and payroll expenditures for personnel. If a superior unit has a primary say over these areas, then it is said to have an administrative leadership relationship with the

---

5. Administrative chains of command are not the only area in which there is a division of labor between the central government and their territorial authorities; in economic management, other divisions of labor are also in effect. In foreign trade, for example, local governments are encouraged to export their own products once the central foreign exchange quota is fulfilled. Also central trade organizations have a monopoly over certain products while local governments are free to trade in other products (Lou Jiwei 1992: 26–27).

local units. Professional leadership relations exist when a superior unit can issue binding operational directives and when it enjoys some degree of prerogative over personnel decisions affecting the top officials of a provincial unit.[6] What is extremely confusing at times is the fact that these two relations often do not coincide with each other and that professional leadership relations can sometimes exist across different government agencies if the issues concerned are highly interrelated or classified as approximately belonging to the same economic sector.[7]

Third, how administrative and professional leadership relations are structured affects the "verticality" (*chuizhi*) of the authority relationship between a central ministry and a provincial bureau in the same sector. One of the following two conditions is sufficient to establish a *chuizhi* authority relationship. Either the central ministry exercises both administrative and professional authority over a given provincial bureau, or the central ministry, while not controlling administrative functions, exercises the *primary (yi zhongyang weizhu)* professional authority. The specific implication of central control over administrative and professional relations is that the central ministry, not the provincial government, makes operational decisions in the following areas: (1) the central ministry formulates investment plans and secures the funds and inputs for investment projects on behalf of the provincial bureaus, and (2) the central ministry has control over the bureau's *nomenklatura* and over its payroll. In the case of primary central control over professional relations, the central ministry possesses the former prerogative but not the latter.[8] As of 1990, there are about fourteen central units exercising vertical authority over their provincial bureaus along administrative lines.[9]

Most provincial bureaus do not have a *chuizhi* relationship with their central ministries and most receive commands directly from the provincial authorities. The fact that administrative leadership is lodged with the provincial governments implies that the power to manage bureau-level personnel lies with the provincial Party committees. Also, professional leadership relations are *primarily* local. From this, it appears that provincial authorities exercise primary control over personnel decisions, payroll, and other operational issues. This does not necessarily suggest that these units are not faithful to the preferences of their ministries in Beijing; what it does imply is that operational

---

6. As explained in the next section, personnel control also depends on the bureaucratic ranks of the cadres in question.

7. For more details, see Lieberthal and Oksenberg (1988: 148–51).

8. The above discussion is based on the State Commission on Government Establishment (1990: 579–81).

9. For a list, see the appendix to this chapter.

autonomy vested in these units is considerable and that ministerial instructions are less binding or detailed than they would be under a more centralized arrangement.

The way responsibilities are divided up affects the transmittal of interagency documents. The issuing of interagency documents itself is governed by "professional jurisdictions" (*yewu quanxian*), although how binding the instruction is depends on the leadership relations. Ministries can issue documents to other ministries within the same professional jurisdiction; ministries can also issue documents to provincial bureaus in the same professional jurisdiction, but they are not allowed to issue documents directly to provincial governments unless specifically authorized by the State Council (State Council 1991). As an illustration of this rule, the Ministry of Personnel can issue documents to the personnel bureaus of the provinces and to the personnel bureaus of other ministries as well as to other ministries themselves; yet it cannot issue documents to provincial governments, except in areas of local *nomenklatura* and wage policy where it is specifically authorized to do so by the State Council (Ministry of Personnel 1991b).

As these restrictions show, rank considerations cannot be all-important since ministries can issue documents to one another but not to provinces, even though ministries and provinces have the same rank. Thus there seems to be a fairly explicit concern that the sectoral chain of command should not usurp the territorial chain of command, except in those sectors that are vertically controlled. Complaints about excessive ministerial interference are viewed as quite legitimate and are taken seriously by the State Council. In 1990 the State Council criticized some ministries for inappropriately using their funds, goods, and investment approval power to entice local governments to set up an administrative structure similar to their own (State Council 1991). Luo Gan (1991), the director of the State Council Secretariat, asked ministries not to issue documents to local governments without proper authorization. Complaints about excessive ministerial interference arise even when the instructions are issued within the appropriate professional jurisdictions. In 1982 the State Council Secretariat issued a circular to various central ministries criticizing them for having issued documents requiring their subordinate bureaus not to abolish certain posts that the provincial governments had intended to eliminate (State Council 1985 [1982]: 132).

Detailed administrative rules govern not only the issuance process but also the kinds of documents that government units can issue to one another. Documents have a hierarchical order; at the top of the hierarchy are *mingling* (commands), used to issue the most important administrative regulations, to remove personnel, and to overrule lower-level decisions. Next are *jueding*, or decisions, which announce important events or important policies, followed by *zhishi* (instructions), and *tongzhi* (circulars). Both *zhishi* and *tongzhi* refer to documents issued from a superior unit to a lower-level unit; the difference between the two is that *zhishi* are more binding and are issued between units with leadership relations. In addition, *zhishi* set out detailed work instructions for the lower-level unit (*buzhi gongzuo*). *Tongzhi*, on the other hand, are used to transmit (*chuanfa*) documents from a superior unit, a unit of equal bureaucratic rank, or a unit with different leadership relations. When used as an instruction to a lower-level unit, the document is more of a request or of a requirement (*yaoqiu*), and therefore is less binding.[10]

Two inferences can be drawn from the above discussion. First, unless specifically authorized, ministries cannot issue documents to provincial bureaus; rank equality seems not to be the deterrent since ministries can issue documents to other ministries. The intention is to preserve the operational autonomy of the territorial governments. Second, where leadership relations are not of a vertical type, documents and instructions are more likely to be of a *tongzhi* nature than of a *mingling, jueding*, or *zhishi* nature. To put it another way, in most situations the central ministries can only govern the operations of their provincial bureaus via the force of nonbinding instructions and guidelines. This is not to say that these instructions and guidelines are not obeyed, but the consequences of not obeying them are obviously less severe than they are under a more vertical arrangement.

Control over economic resources

Developmental imperatives cannot be implemented without economic resources. In China, the flow of those resources is controlled in part through the administrative supervision of enterprises, product allocation, regional trade policies, bank lendings, and taxation. These instruments of economic control all have an impact on central–local relations.

Under a traditional CPE, administrative supervision and product allocation are of great importance in determining the balance of economic control between the Center and the local governments. Since the market plays little or no allocative role, bureaucratic coordination relies greatly on administrative means. Thus the assignment of administrative control over enterprises in essence determines the chains of command and sources of instructions that

---

10. The above discussion is based on State Council (1991: 207–10).

enterprises receive for their operations.[11] Product allocation is in fact a corollary of the way in which enterprise controls are assigned, inasmuch as the responsibility for product allocations arises from the way administrative control is divided. In principle, local governments are in charge of making product allocations for the enterprises over which they have administrative supervision; likewise, the central ministries allocate products for their own enterprises.

Prior to the reforms, the Chinese economic system, unlike the Soviet economic system, placed a significant share of enterprise control, and therefore of product allocation responsibility, in the hands of the local governments. China thus had a type of "decentralized planned economy." The economic reforms of the 1980s gradually rendered enterprise control and product allocation less important. Instead, attention turned to organizing and financing investment activities, control over money, and interregional trade policies.

Administrative control over enterprises

The most direct form of economic control is the supervisory authority that local governments exercise over a significant percentage of state-owned enterprises. The Chinese system classifies enterprises according to the level at which administrative supervision takes place; a "central enterprise" (*zhongyang qiye*) is one in which the responsibilities for personnel, finance, product allocation, and other administrative affairs rest with a central ministry. A local enterprise (*difang qiye*), as the name suggests, is one in which the same responsibilities belong to a local government. Local enterprises can be further divided into provincial enterprises (*shengshu qiye*) or city or county enterprises (*shishu or xianshu qiye*). In reality, however, there is a considerable degree of overlapping of administrative control among central, provincial, and subprovincial authorities. Sichuan province is a case in point. In 1970 the Center placed sixty-five of its enterprises under provincial management, yet their wage and financial management, product allocation, and production planning were in fact distributed among central ministries, the provincial government, and the city authorities. The precise breakdown of management control is presented in table 2.2.

It should be pointed out, however, that the central government continued to exert dominant control – particularly in areas such as product supply,

---

11. Very often, as I will show later, chains of command among different levels of economic authorities often overlap, depending on the issue areas; these overlapping chains of command often make it difficult for analysts, as well as for enterprise managers themselves, to determine who the real bosses are.

Table 2.2. *Managerial responsibilities of sixty-five enterprises in Sichuan,*
1970

Responsibility	Center	Provincial governments	City governments
Administrative supervision	9	49	7
Wage control	0	59	6
Financial operations	14	44	7
Product supply	60	5	0
Production planning	51	14	0
Investment planning	56	9	0

Source: Tang Gongzhao (1983: 62–63).

production, and investment planning – because these enterprises were so large
that it was beyond the capacity of the Sichuan provincial government to supply
the necessary products for production and investment activities. Furthermore,
there could be multiple and overlapping chains of command: that is, different
aspects of an enterprise's operations could be managed by different levels of
government. Wage and financial operations appear to be more decentralized,
but production and investment are more centrally coordinated. These
overlapping control patterns have given rise to much confusion and chaos in
enterprise management; indeed, Chinese managers often complain about interference from too many "mothers-in-law" (Tang Gongzhao 1983; Tidrick
and Chen 1987).

This system is rather unique among the CPEs in two respects. First, tax or
profit collections are closely tied to how an enterprise is administered. By and
large, the central profit or tax base consists mainly of revenue streams from
central enterprises; the provincial base consists of revenue streams from provincial enterprises. Although Chinese enterprises are nominally owned by the
"whole people," the immediate supervisory agencies exercise many of the ownership rights, including the right to income and control over personnel in the
enterprises under their charge. Investment, according to the doctrine "whoever builds and manages the enterprise has the use of its output" (quoted in
Wong 1985: 260), has become in effect a purchase price and a principal means
of acquiring de facto ownership rights. David Granick (1990) has found strong
empirical support for the notion that ownership of Chinese state enterprises
is a function of past investment patterns.

Second, the size of the local sector in China is quite large. In comparison
with their counterparts in the former Soviet Union, Chinese local governments have significant economic control, and this control long predates the

reform era. Before *perestroika*, there were two main episodes of economic decentralization in the Soviet Union. The first took place between 1921 and 1928 under the New Economic Policy (NEP), which sought to integrate the market with central planning (see Gregory and Stuart 1981: 46–60; Billon 1973: 215–16). The second – Khrushchev's *Sovnarkhozy* experiment in 1957 – was in many ways similar to the administrative decentralization efforts attempted in China. It abolished most of the central ministries and assigned enterprise supervisory responsibility to about 105 regional economic councils. As a result, the share of industrial output under the supervision of the national republics increased from 31 percent in 1953 to 55 percent in 1957 (Billon 1973: 221–28).

However, the dominant tendency in Soviet economic organization and industrial management was centralization. Lenin's experiment with the NEP was reversed by Stalin, who "viewed the role of a plant director not as that of a decision maker but as that of a state employee who would carry out faithfully the decision made for him at a higher level" (Billon 1973: 217). The Khrushchev experiment ended with his ouster in 1964, whereupon a "ministerial system of management" was reinstated. Economic centralization deepened during the Brezhnev era; enterprises in important economic sectors reverted back to central control and, as was the case in China in 1954, many intermediate chains of command were removed. This enabled the Center to exert more direct control.[12] As a result, quite a large part of the Soviet industrial sector was under central control. The all-union enterprises – those managed by the central government – accounted for about 62 percent of the industrial output; union–republican enterprises, which were jointly managed, accounted for about 31 percent; the purely local enterprises only accounted for 7 percent of the output.[13]

Despite the many similarities in their economic systems during what Kornai (1992) calls "the classical stage of socialism," there were also sharp differences

12. For example, all the machine-building enterprises reverted back to a dozen or so central ministries in 1965, as did the gas, oil, chemical, and other large enterprises in the following years. The coal industry, with the exception of that in Ukraine, encountered a similar fate. Furthermore, even among those under dual control – such as electricity, metallurgy, timber, paper and woodworking, construction materials, light industry, and food processing – many enterprises and planning and research institutes were transferred to sole union control. A bureaucratic streamlining attempt in 1973 with the creation of the "three links" system eliminated the republican rung in the economic hierarchy and gave the Center a more direct managerial role. For example, the coal industry's six links – consisting of the union ministry, republican ministry, combine, trust, mine administration, and mine – were converted to a union ministry–combine–mine system (Kushnirsky 1982: 49–72; Nove 1986: 54–55).

13. In reality, the central ministries had effective control as they were responsible for plan formulation and investment fund allocation. See International Monetary Fund et al. (1991: 200).

between the Soviet and Chinese systems.[14] In general, the Soviet system organized its economic activities on a sectoral basis, with one government agency, usually a ministry, governing most activities in one sector across different geographic boundaries. This is known as the *tiaotiao* (vertical) management principle in Chinese economic literature (or the "branch management" principle in Soviet economic literature). The Chinese system was, and to a large extent still is, based on territorial or regional planning. That is, one government agency – the local government – governs most economic activities in one geographic region across different economic sectors.[15] This is known as the *kuaikuai* (horizontal) management principle.

After taking power in 1949, the Chinese communists sought to establish an economic system based on the *tiaotiao* principle. The First Five-Year Plan (1952–57) is credited with creating a centrally planned economic system closely modeled on that of the Soviet Union. An important administrative step in this direction occurred in 1952 when the central government converted the six large administrative regions (LARs) into regional branches; this consolidated central control over the economy because the LARs had been largely responsible for running the economy. In 1954 the Center abolished the LARs; enterprises previously administered by the LARs then reverted back to ministerial control.[16] In 1953 there were about 2,800 central enterprises; in 1957 this number increased to 9,300. The central government accounted for 49 percent of industrial output, but in certain sectors it had a dominant position. In 1956, for example, it accounted for 57 percent of the output in chemical industry, 72.2 percent in coal production, 83.3 percent in electricity, and 94 percent in steel (Zhao Dexing 1989a: 387). Central economic control reached its apogee during this period.

Before the economic reforms of the 1980s, China experienced two episodes of large-scale decentralization. The first, which occurred in 1958 during the

---

14. Similarities include, for example, the dominance of the state sector, bureaucratic coordination of the economy, and the drive toward industrialization, etc.

15. This distinction is similar to what Qian and Xu (1993) refer to as the M- and U-form of corporate governance. The choice of one organizing principle over another is beyond the scope of this discussion. Suffice it to say that the choice was in part accidental and in part due to the structural conditions faced by the leaders of each country. One such structural difference was the role of ethnic nationalities in each of the countries, which had implications for the political feasibility of one strategy over the other. In the former Soviet Union, Khrushchev's *Sovnarkhozy* movement – regional decentralization – was opposed and was quite politically contentious when the measure was deliberated in 1957. Later on it was reversed by his successors, explicitly on the grounds that economic decentralization would lead to "centrifugal forces and bourgeois nationalism" (Billon 1973: 224). In China, the concern over the linkage between economic decentralization and ethnic nationalism was virtually nonexistent.

16. See Schurmann (1968) for an account of the administrative evolution during the 1950s.

Great Leap Forward, saw the transfer of management rights over some 8,000 enterprises from central ministries to the provinces; the central ministries retained control over about 1,200 enterprises, mostly large enterprises in strategic sectors such as metallurgy, chemical industry, energy, precision machine-building, and defense. Also the provinces were given the authority to plan and allocate for provincial production; the central government set targets for the interprovincial transfer of key producer goods. In 1961, in the wake of the failure of the Great Leap Forward, the central government began to re-cover some decision-making rights, restoring the 1957 level of centralization in a number of areas. From the mid-1960s until 1970, a more protracted round of decentralization took place. In 1966, for example, steel, cement, fertilizer, coal, and farm machinery produced by small enterprises were under local allocation, and in 1970 about 2,400 key enterprises were turned over to the provinces for management.[17]

The cumulative impact of these episodes was that industrial organization became highly decentralized. In the early 1980s, for example, the central government directly owned only 3 percent of the 83,000 enterprises (Wong 1986: 585) and, in terms of industrial output, state-owned enterprises subordinate to the central ministries only accounted for 9 percent of total industrial output for the state sector (He Jianzhang and Wang Jiye 1984: 67). The first effort to reverse this administrative decentralization was in 1977, when the central government reclaimed control over most of the large enterprises in the strategic sectors (energy and steel, for example).

During the reform era, the main thrust of the industrial reforms has shifted away from adjusting central–local supervisory responsibilities to making Chinese enterprises truly economic institutions. These enterprise reform measures include profit-retention schemes, tax reforms, an enterprise responsibility system, and recently the corporatization of the enterprise governance structure. As far as central–local enterprise controls are concerned, in the 1980s there have been both centralizing and decentralizing shifts. Between 1982 and 1987, for example, the Center established three nationwide corporations – for the petrochemical industry, the automobile industry, and the nonferrous metals industry – and in the process recentralized enterprises in these three sectors. On the other hand, enterprises in machine-building, electronics, textiles, and metallurgy were given over to local governments ("Difang zhengfu . . ." 1991). The net impact was a moderate increase in the share of central industrial output; in 1985, the central government accounted for some 25 percent of industrial output (State Council and SPC 1990: 489).

---

17. The above discussion is based on He Jianzhang and Wang Jiye (1984) and Wong (1985).

Table 2.3. *Number of products under central allocation in the former Soviet Union and China, 1950–85*

Year	Other than producing ministries		Producing ministries		Central bodies combined	
	China	FSU[a]	China	FSU	China	FSU
1950	8	—	0	—	8	—
1952	55	—	0	—	55	—
1953	112	—	115	—	227	—
1957	231	—	301	—	532	—
1959	67	—	218	—	285	—
1965	370	20,438	222	—	592	—
1966	326	21,655	253	0	579	21,655
1968	—	14,498	—	1,814	—	16,312
1972	49	—	168	—	217	—
1973	50	8,426	567	40,000	617	48,426
1978	53	—	636	—	689	—
1979	210	—	581	—	791	—
1982	256	—	581	—	791	—
1983	—	9,200	—	—	—	—
1985	23	—	—	—	—	—

[a] FSU = former Soviet Union.
Source: Granick (1990: 73).

Product allocation

The different organizing principles behind the Chinese and Soviet economies and their different histories of centralizing and decentralizing shifts have given rise to very different patterns of product allocation. Under a standard CPE, the allocation of products is conceptually equivalent to production coordination (Granick 1990: 72), and thus the level at which goods are allocated is indicative of the level at which the bureaucracy coordinates production activities. Everything else being equal, the higher the bureaucratic level of the allocation, the more centralized the economic coordination. Table 2.3 presents one analyst's estimates of the number of products under central coordination in China and in the former Soviet Union. It shows that the Soviet central bureaucracies were responsible for allocating a significantly larger number of goods than were their counterparts in China.

The degree of local control over product allocation in China is striking and it predates the industrial reforms of the early 1980s. Eckstein (1981) attributes the discrepancy in Soviet and Chinese planning to the fact that the Soviet economy was much more advanced. A more advanced economy, so the argument goes, is able to generate information more quickly and to produce a greater array and variety of goods; in the process, different industrial branches become more interdependent. There is some truth to this line of reasoning, but this is obviously not the whole story. The figures across the rows in table 2.3 show considerable fluctuations over time, and these are not correlated with the direction of economic development. In the Soviet case between 1966 and 1968, the number of products under central allocation fell by about 20 percent, and in the Chinese case between 1957 and 1959, the number fell by almost half. Both the direction of this reduction and its magnitude suggest that the scope of the central allocation of products is subject to considerable discretion by central planners and is a result of policy choices, as opposed to underlying economic factors such as the level of economic development.[18]

During the reform era, the shares of control over product allocation for the Center and the local governments have not drastically changed; both the central and local governments have lost some ground because of the increasing importance of direct marketing by firms themselves. As early as the late 1970s, goods-ordering conferences of a cross-regional nature were already taking place for a wide range of products; the prices at which these products were transacted were negotiated among the buying or selling parties, subject to some central pricing guidelines (Eckstein 1981). As a result of the reforms, much of the material allocation process is now not only outside the administrative control of the central government, but also outside that of the local governments. To take but two examples, 17.5 percent of steel output and 32.7 percent of coal were directly marketed in 1987 (SPC and SSB 1992: 42). This is consistent with the industrial reforms: the emphasis has not been solely on balancing central–local economic controls; equally important has been the move to marketize an ever-increasing share of economic activities. Thus the production role of the central government and of the local governments has to some extent given way to their financing and regulatory roles, as discussed in the following sections.

Regional trade policies

As production inputs or construction materials are increasingly available on the open market and as the material allocation process becomes progressively more decentralized, indirect policy instruments have become more important in regulating economic activities. One such instrument is used to regulate

18. The clearest indication of this is the drastic reduction in the number of products under central allocation in China between 1982 and 1985, from 256 to 23.

interregional trade flows. There is some evidence that during the reform period interprovincial trade has declined somewhat, at least as far as trade conducted through state channels is concerned. For example, the percentage of total consumer imports originating from other provinces declined from 38 percent in 1979 to 29 percent in 1986. In some provinces, this reduction has been quite drastic. Inner Mongolia imported 100 percent of its consumer goods in 1979, but only 22 percent in 1986 (World Bank 1990b: 109–11).

The most immediate reason for this reduction is the increasing dispersion of industries among provinces. That is, the industrial structures of the provinces have come to resemble each other and there is a great policy emphasis on developing manufacturing. As already explained, this keen interest in the manufacturing sector is a function of fiscal incentives and of price distortions that favor manufactured goods.[19] Industrial convergence is a structural barrier to interregional trade because the comparative advantages of trade are reduced among provinces similar in economic structure. The evidence for increasing industrial convergence is an increase in the importance of the manufacturing sector in provinces producing raw materials: between 1979 and 1984, Yunnan and Hunan, two tobacco-producing provinces, increased their share of national cigarette production by 3 percentage points, whereas two traditional cigarette-producing provinces, Shanghai and Shandong, saw their share decline by 3 and 2.4 percentage points, respectively (World Bank 1990b: 209).

The second reason for the decline in interregional trade is the active antitrade policy stance of provincial governments. Provincial governments can reduce interregional trade flows in a number of ways. First, they can simply order their marketing departments not to import from or export to other provinces. Imports hurt local industries and indirectly undermine the revenue base of the local governments. Exports are also considered harmful because the first priority for local governments is to supply goods to local users. With more trade activities taking place outside the state marketing channels, however, local governments are using less direct methods to regulate interregional trade. For one thing, they have made interregional trade very costly by imposing tariffs on traded commodities; local governments have established "checkpoints" on the trade routes for this purpose.

Interregional trade protectionism has passed through three stages. The first

19. In general, economists consider the regional convergence of industrial structures to be wasteful in that regions do not develop along the lines of comparative advantage because the industries that are promoted lack economy of scale. However, more innovative economic thinking has begun to view industrial convergence in a more advantageous light; specifically, industrial convergence promotes interregional competition. For the former view, see Shen Liren and Dai Yuanchen (1990); for a sample of the latter view, see Qian and Xu (1993).

stage, roughly from 1979 to 1984, was the buildup stage: the local governments invested heavily in expanding the manufacturing capacities of their regions, aided greatly by the decentralization of economic decision making and economic resources. During the second stage, from 1985 to 1988, the local acquisition of manufacturing capacity boosted demand for upstream goods, such as raw materials, and induced provinces producing raw materials to erect export barriers against flows of these goods to other provinces. Trade wars became heated during this period because general macroeconomic policies were quite lax; credit expansions and large government and enterprise spendings further upset the demand-and-supply balance, giving rise to stronger incentives for setting up trade barriers.

The third stage has coincided with the latest round of economic retrenchment (since 1989), which drastically reduced demand not only for raw materials and intermediate goods but also for final goods. Although this situation considerably alleviated the demand for upstream goods and reduced incentives for trade protectionism in these areas, it has had a mixed effect on local protectionism. On the one hand, the existence of a buyers' market for certain consumer goods increased the incentives for local governments to establish trade barriers against final goods from other regions. During this stage, local protectionism changed from focusing on stopping the exports of raw materials to stopping imports of consumer goods; the calculation was to preserve market demand for goods produced by local enterprises. On the other hand, during the latest period of austerity the central government also liberalized a considerable number of prices of raw materials and energy. The profit equalization between manufacturing and upstream sectors has dampened the impetus for developing manufacturing locally. This has boosted interregional trade.[20]

Bank lending

During the reform era, financial resources have become the primary policy instruments used to regulate economic performance and behavior. Indeed, as Byrd (1983) argues, even before the reforms, Chinese banks had a more important role to play in allocating resources than did their counterparts in other CPEs because of the relative weakness of China's material product planning and because of its decentralized economic administration.

In typical CPEs, bank lending strictly complements production plans and banks act as a "cashier" for the government's development programs. In the case of the People's Construction Bank of China (PCBC), the branches are

---

20. The above discussion is based on Guo Wanqing (1992) and Watson, Findlay, and Du (1989).

responsible for channeling budgetary investment resources. Since they have access to data on almost all economic activities, banks also monitor enterprise spending on wages and investment.[21] The financial reforms have aimed at transforming a "mono-banking" system into a system that gives banks some degree of independence, lending institutions some flexibility, and banks more operational autonomy.[22] Between 1979 and 1984 regulatory and lending activities were made into separate operations: the People's Bank of China (PBC) removed itself from lending operations, and commercial lending was turned over to a group of specialized banks, such as the Agricultural Bank of China (ABC), the Industrial and Commercial Bank (ICB), the PCBC, and the Bank of China. Since this major organizational change, a number of nonbanking financial institutions have emerged as important actors in financial mobilization. The most prominent among these is the China International Trust and Investment Corporation (CITIC). Local governments also set up their own trust and investment companies (TICs), and these have played some role in project financing (see chapter 3). The development of the TICs has been particularly rapid since 1988. In the first six months of 1988 alone, the total number of TICs increased from 563 to 745.

To ensure that banks would operate as profit-maximizing enterprises, lending rates were raised in 1979 so as to better reflect the true costs of capital, and an interest charge was levied on capital construction and working capital loans. In addition, limited autonomy was given to banks in the area of credit allocation and bank branches were authorized to charge rates within 20 percent of the published rates given by the PBC. Banks were also encouraged to explore new ways of mobilizing savings and to determine the level of lending on the basis of the level of their savings mobilization. Thus the PBC credited the accounts of the specialized banks with less than sufficient funds to cover their planned expenditures; banks were thus forced to raise funds on their own. This was known as the policy of "more deposits, more loans" (*duocun duodai*). Corporatization has also been experimented with; instead of remitting all profits, the banks are allowed to retain 35 percent of their profits as additions to their capital stock and to distribute 10 percent of their profits for employee bonuses and welfare.[23]

21. For a summary discussion of the characteristics of the Chinese banking system before the reforms, see Bowles and White (1993); for more details, see Byrd (1983) and De Wulf and Goldsbrough (1986).

22. Chinese publications sometimes use "finance" to describe tax operations. Here I use "finance" to refer to monetary operations (*jinrong*) and fiscal operations to describe tax collections and expenditures.

23. The above discussion is based on Bowles and White (1993), World Bank (1990c), and Zhou and Zhu (1988).

In formal terms, the localities seem to have gained relatively little financial control from these reforms; indeed, Shanghai planning officials have voiced frustration over their lack of control over bank credits.[24] The effect of these financial reforms on central and local relations is somewhat subtle and may occur indirectly. Because of the lack of firm data, I offer a number of conjectures about ways the financial reforms may have altered central–local relations, mainly to the advantage of the localities.

To the extent that financial reforms have succeeded in converting banks from passive to active financing institutions, the local governments, as well as the central ministries, have developed a new financing facility under their wing. The importance of this new financing facility must be understood in the context of the fiscal decentralization during the reform era (see the next section). The tax reforms of the 1980s aimed to achieve balanced budgets at the local level by instituting what amounted to a lump-sum tax system. The banking reforms have, however, considerably eroded the original purpose of the tax reforms – hardening local budget constraints – by separating control rights from financing rights over local banks. The control rights belong largely to the local governments; the financing rights ultimately belong to the central government. In addition to separating control from financing rights, China separates fiscal and monetary responsibilities. Maintaining fiscal balance is a local responsibility, whereas maintaining monetary balance is a central responsibility. These two kinds of separations have led to the predictable moral hazard behavior – rapid credit growth and a huge problem of nonperforming loans.[25] Viewed this way, the excessive liquidity growth has in part been able to monetize the debt that local governments would have incurred under a different tax system.

Local governments have control rights over banks in that they can powerfully influence credit decisions because they have a say in the appointment of the regional directors of the PBC, some of whom also serve concurrent posts in the local governments and all of whom have ties with the local Party committees (*dangde guanxi*). Apart from these formal controls, local governments have an indirect influence that banks cannot ignore except at their own peril. For example, the supply of water and electricity, housing, recruitment of bank employees, and schooling for their children are all potentially under the influence of the local governments (Fu Caixiang and Xu Meizheng 1988; Zhou Mubin 1988). Local governments intervene in lending decisions in two ways:

24. In reality, the PBC branches of Shanghai, as well as those of Shenzhen, were granted greater autonomy vis-à-vis the PBC headquarters to plan and regulate credit flows in their areas. See Bowles and White (1993: 88).

25. According to one staggering estimate, as of 1993 the nonperforming loans amounted to 17 to 25 percent of the GDP. See Qian Yingyi (1995).

they issue instructions directly to banks; and they express general support for certain projects and at times even link loan decisions with career promotions. By way of example, local governments effectively used bank lending to support the rapid expansion of township and village enterprises (TVEs) in the 1980s (Dittus 1989a). Encouraging banks to act more like enterprises has enhanced the profit motives of lending operations. As a result, the economic interests of banks and local governments have converged somewhat: both want to develop industries with high accounting profits, which are often concentrated in the manufacturing sectors in downstream products. Banks thus have developmental urges similar to those of the local industrial bureaus. This convergence of incentives means that it is harder for the central government to use the banks to achieve its industrial policy goals. The local branches of the specialized banks and the local governments are natural allies in macroeconomic and industrial policy debates.

Although the formal power over money issues and credit creation rests with the headquarters of the PBC (and ultimately with the State Council), the operational autonomy granted to the local branches of the specialized banks to some extent attenuates this central power. This may occur in two ways. First, the *duocun duodai* policy motivates some bank branches to create credit on their own, by converting the loans they make into deposits. In 1986, for example, the actual loans made by the ICB exceeded the planned quotas by some 30 percent (Bowles and White 1993: 89). TICs are particularly hard to control, and they make loans far in excess of their allotted quotas. Between January and August 1988, the loans outstanding at the TICs were 2.4 times their quotas (Tang Lingyun 1992: 74). Second, the greater leeway specialized banks have in determining the sectoral composition of their loan portfolio also increases the pressure on credit creation. The specialized banks undertake two kinds of lending: profit-oriented commercial lending and "policy lending" (*zhengce daikuan*). Policy lending supports low-profit activities or those activities given high priority in the central government's industrial policies; agricultural procurement and the construction of key investment projects in energy and raw materials are examples. The returns banks receive for supporting such activities are usually lower than the returns from commercial lendings because lower interest rates are charged.

The differential returns between commercial and policy lending motivate specialized banks to allocate their own funds for commercial lending, while leaving the PBC to pick up the tab for policy lending. Thus, credit plans for state priority items are often underachieved whereas credit plans for nonpriority items are overachieved. In 1988 the PCBC exceeded its credit plan for working capital by 81 percent, but, arguing that it was short of funds, it failed to fulfill its credit plan for transport vehicle procurement, as mandated by the state plan (Tang Lingyun 1992). Another tactic is to underfund those activities that have a "rigid" demand for funding; agricultural procurement has this kind of demand: produce will rot if not purchased and stored promptly. Between January and August 1988, the ABC made loans about 48 percent in excess of its quota and then demanded additional credits from the PBC during the fall procurement of agricultural produce (Tang Lingyun 1992). Typically, the phenomenon of IOUs (*dabaitiao*) to farmers is serious when the PBC does not create enough credit to cover the difference.

The increasing number of financial institutions has also undermined the credit control exercised by the PBC and therefore has indirectly strengthened the ability of local governments to affect credit creation. One of the main sources of funds at the TICs consists of various government deposits in the specialized banks; in 1988, for example, the Beijing branch of the ICB lost 1 billion yuan in deposits to the TICs run by the central ministries. Thus an increase in the TICs' funds amounts to a decrease in government deposits and in the funding ability of the specialized banks. And because the specialized banks are responsible for implementing industrial policies, the PBC often creates special facilities to help solve liquidity problems, thus putting additional credits into circulation.[26]

The tax system

The central–local tax relationship is at the core of the Chinese tax reforms. Some Chinese policy makers and analysts have become concerned about the evolving fiscal relationship between the Center and the localities during the reform era, which has been increasingly in the latter's favor. The evidence they most often cite is the decline in the share of central revenue collection and in the share of central tax revenue in relation to gross national product (GNP). The central share of consolidated revenue dropped from 66 percent in 1980 to about 45 percent in 1989. Central revenue, as a share of GNP, hovered at about 7 percent in 1990, which is rather low in comparison with revenue in a number of developed and developing countries. This trend greatly alarmed Chinese central planners. Chen Yun (1984b: 195), in a letter to Zhao

---

26. For this line of analysis, see Tang Lingyun (1992). In recent years, many TICs have used their funds to engage in speculative activities on the stock and real estate markets and often cannot fully recoup the value once they are required to recall these investments. In part this is because austerity policies tend to depress the value of speculative investments. This was the problem with Zhu Rongji's brief austerity program between July 1993 and December 1993. Reportedly less than one-third of the speculative investments were recalled.

Ziyang in 1983, suggested that the central share of government revenue should be increased to 70 percent, approximately the norm during China's First Five-Year Plan. Others have concluded that the central macroeconomic capability, and even the central political capacity, has fallen to a dangerous level (Wang Shaoguang and Hu Angang 1993; Wang Shaoguang 1994).

These concerns arise from two closely related but conceptually distinct issues. One is the degree of revenue losses from the formal tax system as a whole; the other is the degree of revenue losses from the central government to the local governments. The implications of the latter revenue losses are clear enough: the fewer resources available to the central government, the more difficult it is to achieve central economic objectives and to affect the economic behavior of the local governments. The implications of the former revenue losses are less apparent and require some explication.

Although revenue losses from the formal tax system weaken the economic ability of the government as a whole, the central government may be affected more than proportionately. First, the central government is the "balancer of last resort." That is, in a case where there is a general budgetary deficit, the central government may eventually assume financing responsibility because, unlike the provincial governments, it cannot "pass the buck," so to speak. Thus the central fiscal burdens increase even when all the revenue losses occur at the local level. Second, to the extent that the central government has firmer control of an *administrative nature* (through, for example, personnel appointments – to be discussed in chapter 4 – and ad hoc policy interventions) over local tax and industrial departments than over local enterprises, these administrative instruments have less effect on enterprise behavior when local tax departments possess less revenue. General revenue losses, in a sense, devalue the administrative resources available to the central government.

One way to assess the degree of revenue losses is to examine tax revenues as a share of GNP. This will measure the effectiveness of the tax system in capturing the fruits of economic growth. If the shares continue to decline, then there is prima facie evidence that the formal tax system is becoming weaker because the increments of economic growth that the tax system is able to capture become smaller. Two steps must be taken, however, to reconfigure Chinese budgetary data. First, it is necessary to make the Chinese budget conform to international definitions. The Chinese budget counts government debts as a revenue item and debt payments as an expenditure item; in the international definition, the amount of debt and of its servicing must be subtracted from both revenues and expenditures.

The second step is more complicated. There are in effect two budgets in the Chinese system. One is the conventional budget formulated on the basis of the

Chinese tax system, that is, on the basis of revenues collected by the Ministry of Finance and its local departments. The other is what is known as extra-budgetary revenues or expenditures (*yusuanwai*): these are revenues or expend-itures collected or dispensed through the government system but outside the fiscal channels of the Minisۃry of Finance. Both sources of revenues must be taken into account in assessing the total fiscal strength of the government.

Some may object to counting extrabudgetary revenues as part of govern-ment revenue; Wang Shaoguang (1994) has argued that the exponential in-crease in quasi-budgetary revenue is an indication of the weaknesses of the Chinese tax system. This view is rather misleading, as it suggests that the extrabudgetary revenue is completely dispersed. In fact, since 1986 the State Council has attempted to manage the extrabudgetary revenues and expend-itures more centrally, by adopting measures such as requiring the Ministry of Finance and its local departments to set up special accounts for the funds and by requiring the planning commissions to review the fund allocations (State Council 1987a [1986]); the Guangzhou tax bureau, for example, was already managing about 40 percent of the extrabudgetary revenue by 1986 (Xu Xu 1988).

Central as well as local government units finance provisions of some of the public goods out of the extrabudgetary revenues; these activities include roads and building maintenance, education, and scientific research – the activities that would have been financed from the government budget. For example, in 1991 the extrabudgetary expenditure on education was about 13 percent of the budgetary expenditure, as compared with 8 percent in 1979 (SSB 1994: 218). Thus it is at least arguable that the existence of an extrabudgetary rev-enue source in part obviates the need for a higher tax rate. According to a World Bank calculation based on data from the mid-1980s, extrabudgetary revenues in that period represented an increase in the enterprise income tax burden from about 49 percent to 67 percent (World Bank 1989a: 24). Both the adjusted and unadjusted consolidated revenues are presented in figure 2.1; the numbers refer to their GNP shares.

The main difference between the adjusted and unadjusted revenues is the portion of the extrabudgetary revenue that is clearly governmental. The extrabudgetary revenue consists of three components: tax supplements levied by the local tax bureaus, fees collected by the largely noneconomic units of government, and retained earnings shared between firms and their supervisory agencies. In the 1980s, the tax supplements declined continuously, from 9 percent in 1978 to 2.36 percent in 1992; the fees collected by the noneconomic departments rose from 13.36 percent to 22.97 percent. The bulk of the extrabudgetary revenue, at 74.67 percent in 1992, was shared between enter-

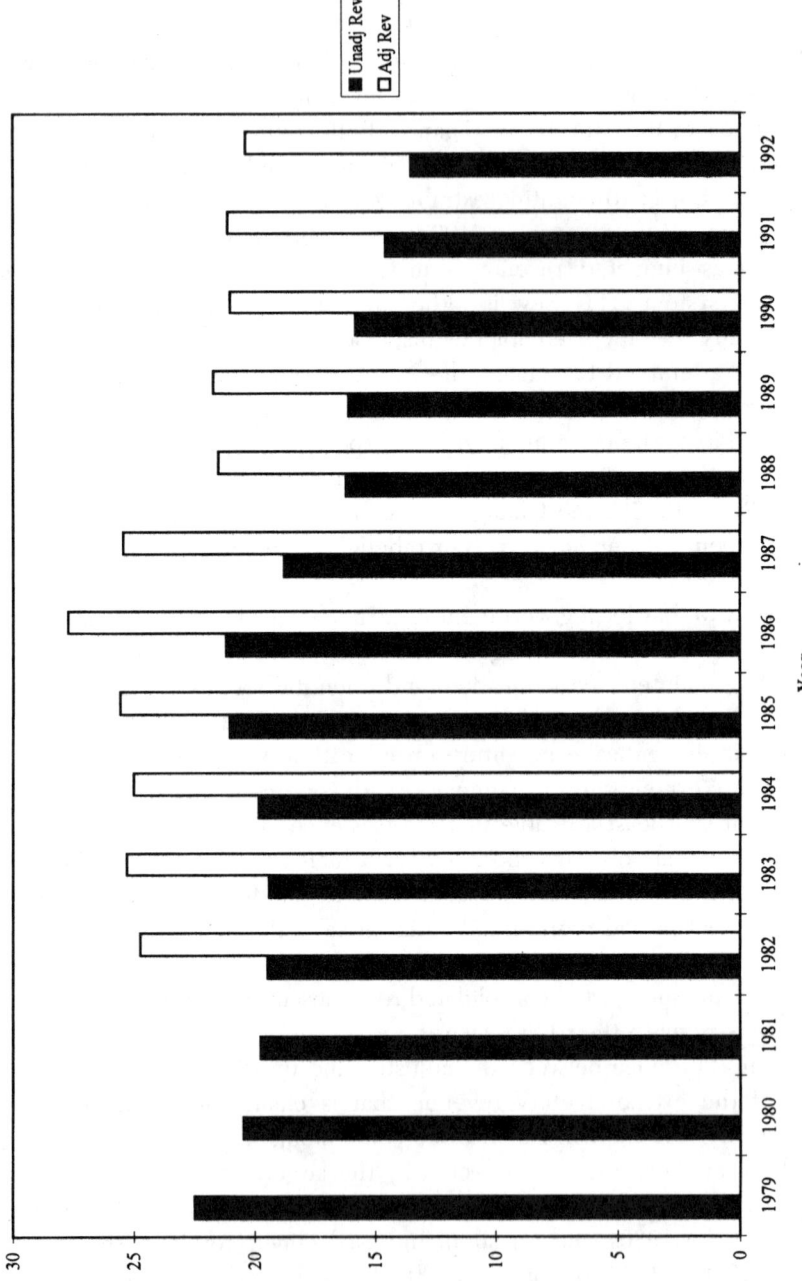

Figure 2.1 Consolidated revenues as a share of GNP, 1979–92

prises and their supervisory government departments.[27] Because retained earnings are not broken down between firms and supervisory agencies, the portion included in my calculation of the budget includes only the first two items, which are clearly governmental. This can cause a downward bias in estimating the actual resources available to the government equivalent to the amount that belongs to the supervisory agencies.[28]

Notice that a clear fiscal decline apparently began in 1988 when the government implemented tax contracts on a large scale. The tax contracts stipulated a fixed tax turnover quota, which reduced tax buoyancy when fully implemented. But, from figure 2.1, the tax share of the GNP experienced a one-time decline in 1988 but otherwise has managed to hold steady. There is also reason to believe that the structure of the Chinese budget enables the tax system to carry out macroeconomic management more than its level would suggest, as compared with the tax systems in developed countries. In most of the developed countries, the fastest-growing component of the budget has been transfer payments, such as social security and unemployment benefits. Transfer payments, as Alt and Chrystal (1983) have pointed out, are not an appropriate measure of the size of the public sector in market economies because they do not "crowd out" private consumption.[29] In the Chinese budget, the transfer component is near zero, and thus a larger proportion of the expenditures can be mobilized for macroeconomic and industrial policy purposes.

Have the revenue positions of the central government deteriorated during the reform era? Figure 2.2 presents central and local revenues as a percentage of GNP.[30] The first point to note here is that although the consolidated revenue is comparable to that in other developed countries, the share of central revenue in China is clearly smaller. The peak was in 1986, when the central revenue share was about 9.6 percent; in 1992 it stood at 6.2 percent. By international standards, the fiscal position of the Chinese government is clearly weaker. For low-income countries, the norm in the late 1980s was 15 percent in terms of revenue as a share of GNP; for developed countries, it was 24 percent (World Bank 1988). In the late 1980s Japan's central revenue share

27. These figures were calculated from the SSB (1994: 221).

28. See the appendix to this chapter on these reconfiguring steps.

29. In the United States, if the transfer payments are excluded from government expenditures, then the share of public expenditures as a proportion of the U.S. GDP declined from 37 percent to 29 percent.

30. Chinese sources on central–local budgetary breakdowns are incomplete. The central and local revenues are reconstructed by relying on the following simple assumptions. First, all the domestic debts are incurred by the central government; the breakdowns of external loans are given in SSB (1992c). Second, the clearly governmental portion of the consolidated extrabudgetary revenue also holds for central and local extrabudgetary revenues as well.

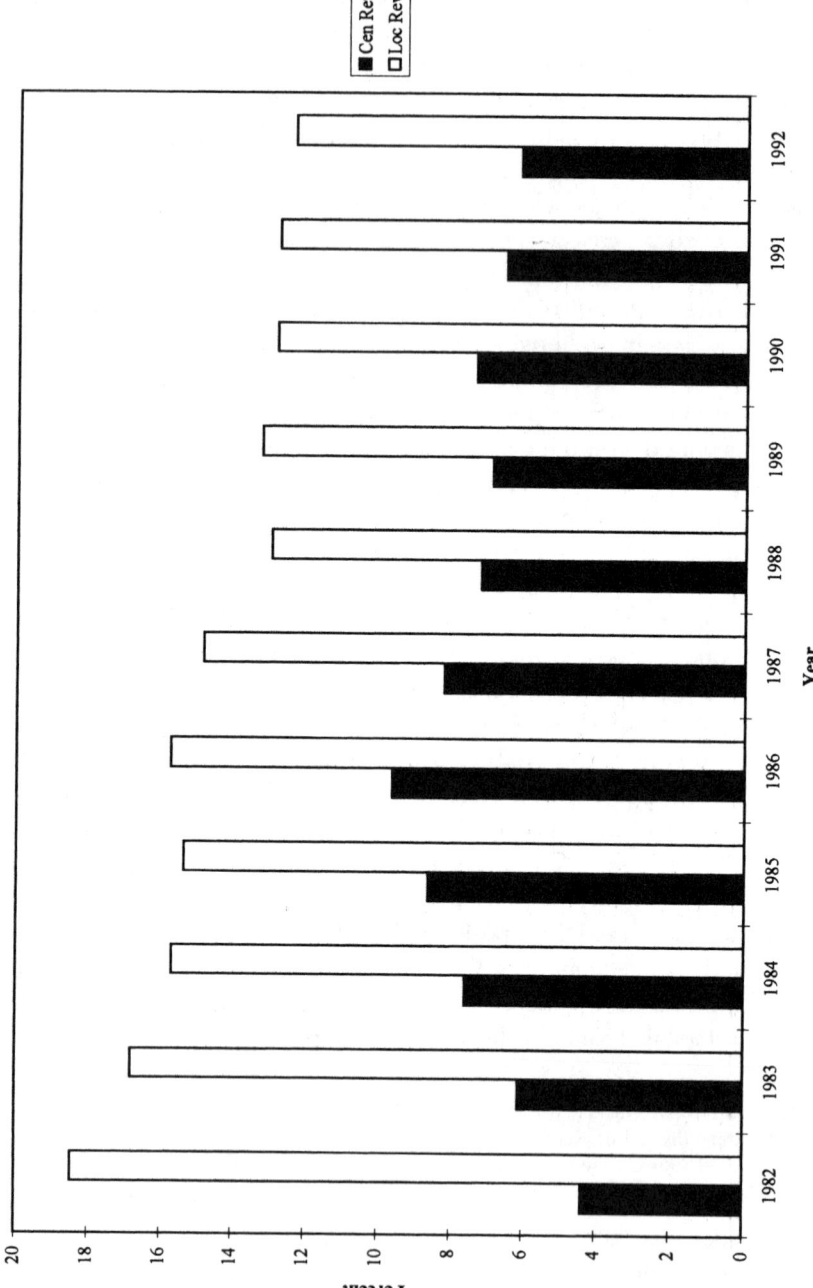

Figure 2.2 Adjusted central and local revenue as a share of GNP, 1982–92

was about 14 percent and India's was 15 percent. Second, the Chinese tax system in the early 1980s was much more decentralized than it was in the early 1990s. In 1982 the central revenue share of the GNP was about 4.4 percent, but it was 6.2 percent ten years later. The local revenue shares, on the other hand, have steadily declined, with the sharpest – and apparently one-time – drop in 1988.[31]

Another consideration in estimating the strength of central revenue collection is the budgetary transfer activities between the Center and the provinces. As a number of studies on the Chinese fiscal system have shown (Oksenberg and Tong 1991; World Bank 1989a), the central government supports its expenditure requirements not only from the tax revenues it directly collects but also from the revenue contributions that the localities make to central coffers. Unfortunately, the data on these transfer activities are extremely sketchy for our purposes; the reports by the minister of finance to the annual session of the National People's Congress have begun to reveal some of this information only since 1989.[32]

When provincial contributions are taken into account, the central revenue losses are not as severe as some have feared. In 1989, for example, the Center directly collected about 6.8 percent of the net material product (NMP) in taxes and another 2.8 percent directly from the provinces. The collection and contribution thus gave the Center a total revenue share of about 9.6 percent.[33] Very similar patterns prevailed in 1990 and again in 1991; altogether, provincial contributions have amounted to about 2.7 percent of the gross domestic product (GDP).[34]

31. We must be cautious in interpreting the Chinese budget. One of the complicating factors is the way Chinese budgetary revenue is defined, which includes domestic and foreign debt. However, the effort to calculate precisely budgetary revenues according to international definitions is difficult because Chinese statistical sources do not disclose the proportion of debt between the Center and the localities; what is known for sure is that debt, as a share of budgetary revenue, has increased, from 7.46 percent in 1982 to 16.12 percent in 1992. This implies, among other things, that at least a portion of the budgetary gains for *both* the Center and the localities was fictional. We also know that the central government borrows more foreign debt than the localities. In 1983, the localities borrowed about 2.3 percent of foreign debt; in 1991, this share rose to 8.5 percent (SSB 1992c). However, this refers to the contracted amount rather than the actual amount borrowed, although it is quite plausible that the share of foreign loans actually borrowed by the localities was quite small.

32. The details are reported in the appendix to this chapter.

33. Of course, the Center also grants tax subsidies to the localities. In 1989 such subsidies amounted to 3.52 percent of the GDP, a rather large sum in comparison with the provincial contributions. In this case, whether or not there is strong fiscal control by the Center critically depends on the degree that the central subsidies are discretionary. The more discretionary they are, the stronger the central fiscal control. At this point, we do not have the information to make this judgment.

34. These numbers do not include extrabudgetary revenues.

Provinces make two kinds of tax contributions to central coffers. One is the ex ante tax contribution, which is the tax contribution they agree to turn over to the Center as specified in the obligations laid out in the formal tax system. For example, between 1980 and 1985 Guangdong was formally required to turn over 1 billion yuan to the Center every year; Shanghai was required to turn over 10.5 billion yuan annually between 1988 and 1993. The other kind of tax contribution refers to the ex post contribution, which is the contribution the provinces make outside their formal obligations. To understand the distinctions between the two, it is necessary to delineate further the revenue-sharing arrangements between the central government and the localities.

The central tax base – from which the central government directly collects revenue – consists of income taxes from the centrally managed enterprises and an assortment of taxes, such as customs tariffs, special adjustment taxes, and energy and transport key project construction taxes. The local tax base consists of income taxes from the locally managed enterprises and an assortment of taxes such as agricultural and salt taxes.[35] These two tax bases constitute the fixed tax sources to the central and local governments, respectively. The second – and the main – source of revenue to the central and local governments consists of taxes that the local governments collect but share with the central government.

Two factors complicate this revenue-sharing arrangement. One is that the revenue-sharing base has been evolving almost continuously since the late 1970s. In the 1980s, there were two such bases. Under the 1980 system, the revenue-sharing base covered budgetary surpluses. That is, the central and local governments shared the difference between local revenues and local expenditures. This system is known as "revenue and expenditure classifications" (*huafen shouzhi*), since its core operating principle depends on how local revenue and expenditure items are classified. Since 1985, the prevailing system has been one of "tax classifications" (*huafen shuizhong*), because the revenue-sharing base shifted from budgetary surpluses to an assortment of taxes classified as shared taxes.[36]

Another complicating factor is that the formulas used to divide the shared revenues vary across provinces. Between 1980 and 1985, there were five different ways of calculating the shared revenue. Guangdong and Fujian, for example, instituted what is known in Chinese as the *dabaogan* system, under which the two provinces turned over a fixed amount of taxes to the Center

---

35. The specific tax categories have often changed; in the 1950s, for example, agricultural and salt taxes were central taxes (see Li Jinyuan 1991: 138).

36. Some examples of joint taxes include product tax, value-added tax, individual income tax, salt tax, and bonus tax.

every year. This was, in other words, a lump-sum tax system. Under this system, Guangdong was obligated to turn over 1 billion yuan while Fujian was obligated to receive 150 million yuan in subsidies; in addition, some of the central revenue sources were reclassified so that they would form part of the local tax base (*Dangdai Zhongguo Caizheng* 1988: vol. 1). Second is the so-called Jiangsu system, which fixes not the contribution base, as under the Guangdong system, but the tax rate (for five years). The third system is a sharing formula that divides the budgetary surpluses rather than the local tax revenue. The fourth system, mainly for ethnic minority provinces, fixes the amount of tax subsidies and the rate of the annual increase (at 10 percent); the fifth system, for Beijing, Tianjin, and Shanghai, adjusts the relatively high contribution rates on an annual basis.

The 1985 reforms essentially merged the five systems into three: the Fujian–Guangdong system; the Jiangsu system, which now covered most of the provinces, including Beijing, Shanghai, and Tianjin; and a system for the ethnic minority provinces. The 1988 reforms consolidated these changes by extending the *dabaogan* system to other provinces, most notably Shanghai, and by abolishing the 10 percent increase rate for the minority provinces.[37] More recently, at the Third Plenum of the Fourteenth Party Congress convened in November 1993, the Chinese leadership announced another major fiscal reform initiative. The gist of this initiative is gradually to phase out the current revenue-sharing arrangements and to federalize tax collection and expenditure responsibilities. This is to be achieved by imposing more or less uniform tax rates across provinces and by dividing taxes into central and local taxes. The intention is eventually to raise the central share of taxes from about 30 percent to 60 percent.

Apart from their formal tax obligations, provinces also make ex post tax contributions. Ex post tax contributions refer to provincial contributions not specified by the tax system that are a result of negotiations between the central government and the localities. Information on this source of provincial contributions is very sketchy, but it is clear that effective tax contributions – ex ante plus ex post contributions – may differ significantly from the formal tax contributions.

Under the formal system, tax contributions vary greatly across provinces

---

37. The above discussion is based on several sources on the Chinese tax reforms. In English, Oksenberg and Tong (1991), Tong (1989), and the World Bank (1990a) give a good overview of the tax reforms in the 1980s. For a discussion of the Chinese tax system during the pre-reform period, see Lardy (1978). The discussion also draws from the following Chinese sources: *Dangdai Zhongguo caizheng* (1988, vol. 1: 291–96, 367–77); Ministry of Finance (1984, 1989a: 11–15); Tian Yinong, Xiang Huaicheng, and Zhu Fulin (1988); and Wu Deming (1987: 65–81).

Table 2.4. *Provincial tax contributions as shares of provincial net material product, 1988 (percentage)*

Region	Formal contributions	Effective contributions
Guangdong	1.72	3.72
Jiangsu	6.43	3.68
Liaoning	7.55	4.15
Inner Mongolia	0.20	−14.40
Anhui	2.02	−1.42

Note: Formal tax contributions refer to revenues the provinces turn over to the Center under the central–provincial tax-sharing arrangements; effective contributions refer to tax payment minus central subsidies or, in the case of Guangdong, tax payment plus unserviced central borrowings.
Sources: Guangdong's tax figures are from Maruya (1992); figures for all other provinces are from Ma Hong and Fang Weizhong (1991). Provincial NMP figures are from SSB (1990).

when measured in terms of tax contributions to the Center as a percentage of provincial NMP (and thus controlling for the effects of differing economic development levels). In table 2.4 under the first column, for example, provincial tax contributions to the Center vary widely, from a high of 7.55 percent (Liaoning) to a low of 0.20 percent (Inner Mongolia). Rather remarkably, Guangdong's tax contribution, at 1.72 percent, is lower than that of Anhui (2.02 percent). However, the effective tax contributions – the tax contributions the provinces actually make – show quite a different pattern. For Guangdong, effective tax contributions are defined as tax contributions plus the unserviced central borrowings; for other provinces, effective tax contributions are tax contributions minus central subsidies. These figures are also shown in table 2.4. Interestingly, in the case of rich provinces, the large discrepancy in the ex ante contribution rates has disappeared. For example, Liaoning's tax contribution is about four times that of Guangdong under the formal system; the difference narrows to about 12 percent under the effective system.[38] Effective contributions from poor provinces are negative because they receive more central subsidies than they contribute to the central coffers (World Bank 1985).[39]

38. This calculation may bias downward the tax contributions from Jiangsu and Liaoning because we do not have data on central borrowings from these two provinces. It is unlikely that there were central subsidies to Guangdong because one of the reasons that Guangdong has a rather low formal tax burden is that it has nearly complete fiscal autonomy and responsibility.

39. Since the measurement used here already normalizes the differences in economic development, the fact that poor provinces have both lower tax contribution ratios and receive substantial subsidies might be due to the central government's pricing policies. According to the World Bank, Chinese energy and raw material prices are set low in relation to their economic costs. The

During the reform era, the Center has not only "borrowed" from Guangdong to cover its budget shortfalls; in 1981 it borrowed 154 million yuan from Fujian (Tong 1989: 19) and in 1987 it borrowed 236 million yuan from Tianjin (*Tianjin jingji nianjian 1988* 1989: 515). Usually, the Center does not appropriate this money in an outright manner; instead, it appropriates a significant portion by simultaneously reducing local retention and the collection base.[40] The central government inevitably comes out as a net winner, but how much retention and collection should be reduced is subject to bargaining. In Tianjin's case, the initial retention rate was 33.59 percent, compared with 39.45 percent stipulated in the 1985 tax reforms. Ultimately, Tianjin was able to negotiate the rate up, to 46.5 percent (See *Tianjin jingji nianjian 1989* 1990).

One aspect of the Chinese tax system that clearly works to the advantage of the localities is the existence of tax slippage – this refers to taxes that should be collected but are not. Although the data on tax slippage are necessarily scattered, figures that are available give a sense of the magnitude of the problem. In 1987 the government uncovered tax frauds or evasions in the amount of 7 billion yuan, which amounted to nearly 3 percent of the 1987 revenue (Wang Bingqian 1988). According to the World Bank, about 70 to 80 percent of enterprises engaged in some form of tax evasion (World Bank 1990b: 76). Interestingly, state-owned enterprises are the main offenders; in Sichuan province, for example, state-owned enterprises accounted for more than 54 percent of the revenue losses in the late 1980s ("Toushui loushui . . ." 1988).

The prevalence of tax evasions in the state sector suggests that they cannot be due entirely to the lack of skilled tax collectors and the lack of sophisticated internal auditing and examination. There seem to be perverse incentives to encourage tax evasions or not to enforce strict provisions against them. For the local governments, much of the tax slippage – in the form of excessive tax exemptions or reductions, or less than a rigorous enforcement of tax collection – can be recouped by their predatory practices. These predatory practices range from imposing ad hoc fees on enterprises to corporatizing governmental

---

price of heavy fuel oil is one-third that at the international level and coal is set at 60 percent of its long-run marginal production costs (World Bank 1985: 71). Administrative pricing affects the levels of tax revenues in different provinces: provinces with a large energy sector – many of which are located in interior regions – have a lower level of tax revenue because it is artificially depressed when their main products are set below their market values.

40. In 1988 the central government returned a portion of this money to Tianjin by excluding thirteen small taxes from being counted as local revenue and by excluding the loan as an expenditure item, as is customary in the Chinese tax system. In this case, the money appropriated by the Center equals the difference between Tianjin's loan and the value of these thirteen taxes. See *Tianjin jingji nianjian 1989* (1990: 539–40).

functions, such as financing schools or providing sanitary services in public areas in the vicinity of the enterprises. According to a survey conducted in the mid-1980s, about 5 percent of enterprise profits were appropriated as "fees" by the local governments (Zhao Yujiang 1986); the costs of other forms of predatory practices – such as enlisting labor contributions – are simply incalculable. Furthermore, to the extent that the formal tax system is the main channel by which localities contribute to the central coffers, giving excessive tax exemptions while appropriating the gains, directly or indirectly, amounts to a withholding of tax contributions to the Center (Huang 1990).

Conclusion

There is little question that local governments are critical actors in China's economic development process and that their role has become more important during the reform era. The Chinese political system formally acknowledges the considerable operational autonomy in the hands of local governments; this can be seen in the way bureaucratic ranks are classified, the documental transmittal process, and the divisions in the lines of command. Provincial economic bureaus have a high degree of operational autonomy from their corresponding ministries in Beijing in their day-to-day performance; the chain of command runs more from provincial governments than from central ministries.

The importance of local governments in the control of economic resources has increased as well. The considerable operational autonomy combined with increasing economic resources creates major coordination problems when it comes to macroeconomic control. The basic one is that macroeconomic control very often goes against the developmental imperatives of the local governments, yet the local governments are the very agents the central government relies on to carry out its austerity policies. This is the problem of "double identity" (*shuangchong shenfen*) often referred to by Chinese economists. As economists Shen Liren and Dai Yuanchen (1990: 14) put it:

The difficulty of controlling fixed-asset investment arises from the fact that, from the controller's point of view, the tasks of investment control have to be implemented by the local governments, but local governments are at the same time vested-interest entities (*liyi zhuti*); regional investment expansion, directly and indirectly, is related to local governments. Requiring local governments to perform surgery on themselves is not an easy task.

The economic power acquired by the local governments during the reform era should not be exaggerated. In the area of enterprise administration, the degree of decentralization was arguably deeper during the heyday of the Maoist period than during the reform era. Fiscal developments in recent years have been extremely complex, and it is inaccurate to argue that central control over tax revenues has declined to a dangerous level. There is little question, however, that the overall balance of economic control during the reform era has shifted in favor of the localities. Economic decentralization has accentuated local economic developmental urges, both during the Maoist era and during the reform era. Compared with local authorities in other CPEs, Chinese local governments traditionally enjoyed greater economic decision-making power and greater control over economic resources.

The reform era has brought three principal changes. First, there has been more economic decentralization along traditional lines; for example, output planning, except in the case of a few producer goods such as electricity and petroleum, has become completely decentralized. The growth of a parallel market also means that the physical availability of goods no longer constitutes an impediment to local economic ambitions, as long as adequate financial and fiscal resources are available. Second, the local governments have acquired new economic power, particularly in the realm of financial resources. Chinese banks have become active participants in the economic development process, and local governments have been able to stake their claim on the lending operations of the specialized banks.

The most profound change associated with the reforms, however, has been not so much in the balance of administrative control over economic resources between the central government and the localities, but in the *order* of economic control. During the Maoist era, the Center set the budgets and expenditures of localities and in effect had the ultimate say over the appropriation of resources. Although the local governments enjoyed a substantial degree of supervisory investment control, the investment returns were potentially or actually subject to appropriations by the central government via its revenue and expenditure-setting power. In both economic and administrative terms, the local governments could be considered simple extensions of the central government, with only subdued economic self-interests.

The reforms have given local governments the residual claim on investment returns, as is explicitly acknowledged in the tax contract system. The tax contract system itself, implemented gradually over the reform decade and extended from Guangdong and Fujian to other provinces, has contributed to this change, in that it is based on the lump-sum tax concept. Another factor is that the deepening of the economic reforms has made permanent what were shifting economic practices before the reforms. That is to say, the divisions of supervisory rights over enterprises are based on an implicit notion of shared property rights between central and local governments. Granick (1990) has found considerable empirical evidence for this hypothesis.

This change in the status of local governments has enormous implications.

As a number of studies have shown, China's local governments have in effect become an economic interest group *(liyi jituan)*, with its own policy preferences – which are often at odds with those of the central government – and a growing resource base.[41] Thus local governments cannot simply be considered an extension of the central government *in an economic sense*. This is a critical difference between the pre-reform and reform periods. The most unambiguous manifestation of the economic interests of the localities is their divergence from the central government in their investment preferences. This divergence is both systematic and quite permanent. Thus the asymmetry of economic control does not just imply that local governments command enormous economic resources; it also implies that local governments have economic interests systematically at odds with those of the Center.

The second implication has to do with connections between the political system and economic control. As pointed out before, the central government's share of revenue is small in relation to the size of China's consolidated revenue. Yet, the central government has been able to appropriate provincial revenues (that is why there are large discrepancies between the formal and informal tax burdens) and at the same time delegate significant financing responsibilities to the localities so as to reduce its own expenditure requirements. Largely because of this expenditure delegation, most of the provinces in fact incur significant deficits (see Wong 1990). As I will show in later chapters, the characteristics of the Chinese political system have a powerful influence on the macroeconomic outcomes.

APPENDIX

Central ministries and their provincial equivalents

One of the characteristics of China's unitary political system is that governmental structures across provinces are similar. The majority of Chinese central ministries have provincial bureaus in the provinces, and most of the provincial bureaus are under the administrative authority of provincial governments rather than under their ministries in Beijing. Table A2.1 presents the major provincial bureaus in charge of the economy,

---

41. Chinese economic and policy analysts do not disagree that the economic and policy autonomy of local governments has increased as a result of the reforms; they do disagree, however, on the normative judgment as to the benefits and costs of such autonomy. The negative view is that administrative decentralization has led to an economically wasteful arrangement known as "vassal economies": the economies strive for insularity by building a fully integrated industrial structure on a regional basis and by pursuing protectionism against interprovincial trade. On this view, see Shen Liren and Dai Yuanchen (1990). A more positive view is that many of the problems associated with vassal economies are in fact rooted in the way administrative decentralization is carried out, and it is possible to restrict the economic functions of the local governments to productive purposes such as cross-border trade and investment promotions.

Table A2.1. *Central ministries and provincial bureaus in different economic sectors, 1990*

Central ministries	Provincial bureaus
Ministries with provincial equivalents	
State Council Secretariat	Provincial Secretariat
State Planning Commission	Planning Commission
—	Economic Commission
State System Reform Commission	System Reform Commission
State Commission on Science and Technology	Commission on Science and Technology
State Commission of Science, Technology, and Industry for National Defense	Office of Science, Technology, and Industry for National Defense
Ministry of Supervision	Bureau of Supervision
Ministry of Finance	Bureau of Finance
Ministry of Personnel	Bureau of Personnel
Ministry of Labor	Bureau of Labor
Ministry of Construction	Construction Commission
Ministry of Energy Resources	Bureau of Coal
	Bureau of Petrochemical Industry
Ministry of Machine Building & Electronics Industry	Bureau of Machine Building & Electronics Industry
	Bureau of Machinery
Ministry of Metallurgical Industry	Bureau of Metallurgical Industry
Ministry of Light Industry	Bureau of Light Industry[a]
Ministry of Textile Industry	Bureau of Textile Industry
Ministry of Transportation	Bureau of Transportation
Ministry of Water Resources	Bureau of Water Resources & Hydraulic Power
Ministry of Agriculture	Bureau of Agriculture
Ministry of Forestry	Bureau of Forestry
Ministry of Commerce	Bureau of Commerce
Ministry of Foreign Economic Relations & Trade	Commission on Foreign Economic Relations & Trade
State Family Planning Commission	Commission on Family Planning
General Auditing Administration	Auditing Bureau
Ministries without provincial equivalents	
Ministry of Chemical Industry	—
Ministry of Geology & Mineral Resources	—
Ministry of Railways	—
Ministry of Post & Telecommunications	—
People's Bank of China	—

[a] In some provinces, there is also the Second Department of Second Light Industry.
Source: State Commission on Government Establishment (1990).

Table A2.2. *Central units with vertical leadership relationships, 1990*

Units with both leadership and professional relations	Primary control over professional relations
Ministry of Railways	Ministry of Supervision
Civil Aviation Administration of China	State Statistical Bureau
People's Bank	Auditing Administration
Construction Bank	Ministry of State Security
Agricultural Bank	Industrial & Commercial
Ministry of Geology & Mineral Resources	Bank
State Meteorological Administration	
State Seismological Bureau	
State Bureau of Oceanography	
State Bureau of Material Reserves	
Ministry of Post & Telecommunications	
Ministry of Water Resources & Electric Power	
General Administration of Customs	
State Administration for Tobacco Trading	

Source: "Buduan gaige . . ." (1990).

and the corresponding central ministry. There are also fourteen central ministries – in table A2.2 – that exercise vertical leadership over their provincial bureaus: these provincial bureaus are directly answerable to their ministries in Beijing rather than to their provincial governments.

China's tax system

The Chinese budget counts government debt as a revenue item and debt payment as an expenditure item. The extrabudgetary revenues, as defined by official statistical sources, have three components: (1) tax supplements collected by local tax departments, (2) receipts by other government units, and (3) retained earnings of the state-owned enterprises and receipts by the industrial supervisory bureaus. Reconfiguring the Chinese budget requires the following steps.

First, the debt should be subtracted from the budgetary revenue and the debt payments should be subtracted from the budgetary expenditure. Second, the tax supplements under the extrabudgetary revenue should be treated as budgetary revenue since they go through the formal tax system; thus the tax supplements should be subtracted from the extrabudgetary revenue and added to the budgetary revenue. Third, enterprise earnings should be separated from government earnings, and enterprise earnings should be subtracted from extrabudgetary revenues. Unfortunately, data are not available on enterprise earnings so this step cannot be carried out. Thus two definitions are given; the broader one includes the enterprise and government earnings and the narrower one excludes both enterprise and government earnings. Because of this problem, the broader definition overestimates the government revenue while the narrower definition underestimates it.

Table A2.3. *Reconstruction of Chinese budgetary data, 1991*

Reconfiguring steps	Budgetary data (100 million yuan)
Revenue	
Budgetary revenue	3,610.9
Subtract government debt	461.4
Add tax supplements	68.77
Add extrabudgetary revenue	3,243.31
Subtract tax supplements	68.77
Broad government revenue	6,392.81
Subtract extrabudgetary firm and	
government earnings	2,477.54
Narrow government revenue	3,915.27
Expenditure	
Budgetary expenditure	3,813.6
Subtract government debt payment	246.8
Add extrabudgetary expenditure	3,092.26
Subtract key construction contributions	189.84
Broad government expenditure	6,469.22

Source: State Statistical Bureau (1993b: tables 6–1, 6–5, 6–16, 6–17, 6–18).

Table A2.4. *Central revenue collections and provincial contributions, selected years*

Collection/contribution	1989	1990	1991[a]
Central collection[b]			
Amount (billions of yuan)	108.9	133.6	130.6
Share of GDP (%)	6.81	7.56	6.47
Provincial contribution			
Amount (billions of yuan)	44.7	48.2	52.99
Share of GDP (%)	2.79	2.73	2.63
Total central revenue			
Central + provincial (billions of yuan)	153.6	181.8	183.6
Share of GDP (%)	9.6	10.29	9.1

Note: These figures refer only to budgetary revenues and exclude extrabudgetary revenues.

[a] The 1991 budget data were government projections.

[b] The figures used here are preliminary, as presented in the reports of the minister of finance; they differ by a very small margin from the final published figures in the Chinese statistical sources. For example, the 1989 figure in the statistical yearbook is 110.6 billion yuan, whereas in the report of the finance minister it is 108.94 billion yuan.

Source: Wang Bingqian (1990, 1991); for GDP figures, SSB (1993b: tables 2–12).

Similar adjustment steps are necessary on the expenditure side. First, the debt payment should be subtracted from the budgetary expenditure. Second, key energy and transport construction contributions should be subtracted from the extrabudgetary expenditure because they appear as a revenue item on the central budget and therefore are a spending item on the budgetary expenditure. Third, government spending should be separated from enterprise spending, and enterprise spending should be subtracted from the extrabudgetary expenditure. Unfortunately, the available Chinese data are not sufficiently disaggregated to permit this adjustment step; as a result, only a broad definition of government expenditure – that is, inclusive of enterprise expenditure – can be derived. In table A2.3, I use the 1991 figures as an example to illustrate these reconfiguring steps; all figures are in 100 million yuan. As pointed out in chapter 2, the central revenue base consists of both taxes earmarked for central government and revenue turnovers by the provinces. Table A2.4 reconstructs the Chinese budget by incorporating the revenue contributions provinces make to the Center. It shows that when the provincial revenue contributions are taken into account, the central revenue share of the GDP increases.

3

Local bureaucrats as investors: The investment roles of local governments

Local governments are active and increasingly dominant investors in China. Their investment role is consistent with, and in part has been a result of, their substantial economic decision-making power, which is a unique feature of the Chinese planning system. This chapter provides an overview of the evolution of China's investment system, especially of the relationship between the central government and local governments in investment management. Three aspects of local investment are examined here: investment control shared between the central and local governments, local developmental imperatives, and the role of local governments in investment management.

The evolution of the Chinese investment system before the reform era

As in other areas of the Chinese economic system, investment management was highly centralized during the First Five-Year Plan (FYP) (1952–57).[1] Investment planning, for example, was a downward process whereby the Central Finance Commission (*Zhongcaiwei*) – the predecessor of the State Planning Commission – first issued annual investment control targets to government departments, which then formulated investment project plans on the basis of these targets and submitted them for approval. The State Council reviewed project applications in excess of 20 million yuan; the Central Finance Commission reviewed applications of 200,000 yuan to 10 million yuan. The LARs and provinces could approve projects under 200,000 yuan. During the First FYP, the central government directly supervised about 87 percent of the

1. The discussion in this section is based on the following works: Cao Erjie, Li Minxin, and Wang Guoqiang (1992), *Dangdai Zhongguo de guding zichan touzi guanli* (1989), Zhao Dexing (1989a), and Zhou Hanrong (1991).

total investment volume. Financing and material allocation were equally centralized. Ninety percent of investment was financed via budgetary sources, 70 percent of which came from the central government. The central government – that is, the SPC and the central ministries – controlled more than 1,000 production materials (*wuzi*); capital goods were allocated almost exclusively through the channels established by the line ministries.

The Great Leap Forward (1958–60) significantly undermined the centralized character of investment planning. First, the downward planning process was reversed; local governments and their enterprises now formulated investment requests and the central government had to achieve aggregate balances on the basis of these requests. The project approval process was simplified substantially. Local governments, when applying for a project above their approval limit, needed only to submit a project plan; financing plans and technical designs were no longer required for central review. Furthermore, if a project above the provincial approval limit did not have any links with the central government in terms of funding and material allocation, the provincial governments had the authority to review and approve the project. Investment fund management devolved from the Ministry of Finance to the construction units or to the government agency supervising the project. The Ministry of Finance no longer specified the precise investment expenditures, other than providing an aggregate fund-use quota; the fund-using units could appropriate the balance between their allotted funds and actual expenditures. In addition, 75 percent of the centrally allocated goods were turned over to the localities, and the central government removed a considerable number of supervisory procedures designed to ensure the quality and timeliness of project construction.

Excessive investment decentralization, carried out in an administrative manner, predictably led to large-scale imbalances in the Chinese economy. These imbalances – manifested as budget deficits of unprecedented magnitude, investment overheating, construction dispersion, and shoddy construction – occurred in the context of a steep fall in industrial and agricultural production. Chinese policy makers were forced to implement a series of corrective measures during the economic adjustment period (1961–65), most of which consisted of attempts to recentralize investment management.[2]

The first step was to enforce the approval procedures established during the First FYP. In 1962 the State Council issued three documents reimposing central review and approval authority on all "medium and large" projects and on projects above the provincial approval limits. Investment quotas were introduced for all projects, and the category of unplanned investment projects was abolished altogether. Fund management was recentralized by such measures

---

2. For a good account of the economic history of this period, see Zhao Dexing (1989a).

as authorizing construction banks – merged with the Ministry of Finance during the Great Leap Forward – to set up individual accounts for ongoing construction projects and monitoring investment expenditures according to detailed guidelines set forth by the Ministry of Finance. The Ministry of Finance also appropriated all the funds rolled over from the previous years in order to reduce aggregate investment spending. The SPC reissued and began to enforce administrative regulations and procedures to safeguard construction quality and completion schedules. Simultaneously, the central government began a drastic investment reduction program. In 1961 realized capital investment fell to one-third of its 1960 level, and in 1962 it was cut by another 44 percent.

Just as the economic planning system was resuming normal operation, the Cultural Revolution (1966–76) dealt another – and in many ways permanent – blow to the investment management system established during the First FYP. The most significant damage was to the central economic institutions in charge of coordination, monitoring, finance, and planning. The SPC, for example, had only fifty staff members in 1970 (Lee 1987); the State Statistical Bureau (SSB) was incorporated into the SPC as its statistical division.[3] The construction bank system was abolished and incorporated into the People's Bank of China (PBC); in 1969 the PBC had only 12 staff members in Beijing supervising investment fund management, and some 2,600 staff doing so nationwide, as compared with 17,000 before the Cultural Revolution. In effect, the central government completely lost its capacity to plan and structure investment programs at the local level in any meaningful sense. Indeed, for the three years between 1967 and 1971, the Ministry of Finance kept no record of local investment expenditures.

For ideological reasons, and for the simple fact that the central government lost almost all operational control over the economy, in the early 1970s it began to devolve a significant amount of investment decision-making power to the localities. A move to allow enterprises to retain depreciation funds – which were then used for technical renovation investments – was begun in 1967 and completed in 1971 (except in the Ministry of Second Machinery Building and in the Ministry of Hydraulic Resources). This measure amounted to fiscal decentralization as it reassigned depreciation fund management from the Ministry of Finance to enterprises and their supervisory agencies. Since there was a corresponding decentralization of enterprises, the local supervisory agencies benefited more than proportionately from this fund reassignment.[4]

3. There is evidence that the destruction of the SSB system was concentrated at the top of the system; for example, the scale of personnel reduction was much greater in Beijing than it was in the provinces. See Huang (1996).

4. In 1970 about 2,600 enterprises were turned over to provincial management. These included the Anshan Steel Works and the Daqing Oilfield (Zhou Hanrong 1991: 22).

With the rapid growth of depreciation funds, the localities were able to fund their own projects. The SPC, beginning in 1970, transferred many of the small and technologically simple investment categories out of its investment management portfolio. These categories included oilfield maintenance, capital construction for commercial distribution networks, and investment subsidies to rural industries, over which the localities assumed both financing and supervisory responsibilities. The growing importance of the localities is shown by the jump in capital expenditure on local projects from 14 percent in 1969 to 27 percent in 1975. In other words, it almost doubled its share in less than six years. In 1974, to recognize the increasing investment responsibilities of the local governments, the SPC formally drew up the so-called four-three-three plan for dividing up investment management. Under this arrangement, the central government managed about 40 percent of the investment portfolio; the central and local governments together managed about 30 percent; and local governments the remaining 30 percent.

Over the years, as the financing capabilities of the local governments grew, the central and local governments began dividing their investment responsibilities along sectoral lines. The central government has chosen to focus on certain economic sectors while leaving others largely in the hands of the local governments. It has done so in part because its resource base is shrinking, which makes it difficult to pursue a comprehensive investment objective. In part, this is also a deliberate economic strategy that reconciles investment decentralization with a rational division of investment responsibilities.

The decision to divide investment responsibilities on a sectoral basis dates back to 1964, and the economic adjustment program. The SPC and the Ministry of Finance stipulated that capital investment in nineteen nonindustrial sectors – such as forestry, education, health, local husbandry, and urban public utilities – should be the primary domain of the local governments. Gradually, the local governments acquired more investment authority over commercial distribution centers, local irrigation facilities, and some "small" industries (e.g., the small factories producing cement and fertilizer). These projects were financed via funds earmarked by the central government and channeled to the local governments without the Center specifying or enforcing any investment targets. In the mid-1960s these funds amounted to 20 percent of the annual capital expenditures; local governments also contributed matching investment funds and were responsible for allocating the capital goods used in these projects.

During the reform era, sectoral divisions were redefined. The main change was the demise of projects over which the central and local authorities had joint investment responsibilities. Since the early 1980s, this trend has continued; now the local governments are the predominant investors in the following sectors: agriculture, light and textile industries, construction industries, urban public utilities, environmental protection, commerce, and culture and education.[5]

Local investment controls and development imperatives

The excess demand for investment among local governments is fueled by two factors: the increasing share of control given to localities during the reform era, and the strong developmental imperatives felt by the local governments.

Investment control

The reformist leaders in the late 1970s inherited a decentralized investment system and a dispersed resource base. In fact, if one is to use the official definition for *difang touzi* (local investment), that is, the portion of investment activities that fall under the administrative supervision of the local governments, then the peak of local control was in 1958, when the localities administered 63.8 percent of state-owned capital construction. Changes in the balance of investment control between the central government and local governments during the reform era are best understood by examining investment control from two perspectives: the review and approval procedures, and the administrative supervisions.

Central control over investment activities rests on the government's ability to review and approve projects that have been proposed. Thus, even if the central government does not directly supervise and implement investment activities at the local level, its influence over nominally local investment programs remains substantial if it retains the power to approve or reject investment applications in accordance with its policy preferences. It was this realization that led to the decision in early 1990 to lower the provincial approval limit from thirty million yuan to ten million yuan as part of the central austerity program. Local control can also refer to administrative supervision over the life of an investment project; an investment project is local to the extent that the supervisory agency in charge is a local government office. As already mentioned, this is what the Chinese statistical agency means when it reports on local investment activities.

5. Unfortunately, Chinese statistical sources do not break down central–local investments sectorally and thus the patterns of divisions over investment responsibilities cannot be illustrated here. The discussion on investment responsibilities is based on Zhou Hanrong (1991), *Dangdai Zhongguo de guding zichan touzi guanli* (1989), and Zhao Dexing (1989b).

Table 3.1. *Measures of local control over investment activities, 1981–91*
(percentage)

Activity	1981	1982	1983	1984	1985	1986	1987	1988	1989	1990	1991
Approval											
SPC	41	34	40	36	32	31	32	30	32	33	—
Non-SPC	59	66	60	64	68	69	68	70	68	67	—
Supervision											
Fixed-asset											
investment											
Center	47.3	44.9	48.6	49.1	44.6	43.5	44.7	42.5	44.6	45.3	42.7
Locality	52.7	55.1	51.4	50.9	55.4	56.5	55.3	57.5	55.4	54.7	57.3
Capital											
investment											
Center	54.4	53.4	59.8	59.4	53.5	53.8	56.7	55.5	54.0	53.9	50.1
Locality	45.6	46.6	40.2	40.6	46.5	46.2	43.3	44.5	46.0	46.1	49.9

Sources: SPC and SSB (1992: 30), SSB (1987b, 1989, 1993b).

Table 3.1 presents figures for investments under these two kinds of control. Note, first, that the approval process remains one of the few and, in administrative terms, a fairly effective *short-term* policy tool with which the central government is able to assert control over investment growth and structure. This is a targeted tool in the sense that it can be exercised to solve a specific problem in investment policy. In contrast, other measures available to augment central investment control – such as reducing the funding capabilities of the local governments via changes in the tax divisions and the hardening of budget constraints and credit discipline – would necessarily involve substantial changes in the way resources are allocated and in the way the economic institutions are constructed. The point here is not that other measures are not invoked, but that they are unwieldy and less suitable to correct short-term investment fluctuations.

Second, it is more appropriate to measure control over investment activities in terms of ability to sponsor rather than ability to review and approve projects. The approval system works on a negative principle. That is, it grants power to the SPC to reject investment projects it does not like, but it does not give the SPC much power to design investment programs it favors. The weakness of this passive system is that few projects in priority sectors, as defined by the SPC, are proposed in the face of price distortions and policy uncertainties (Singh 1992).

Third, as explained in the next section, there are various ways for local governments and their enterprises to evade the constraints imposed by the approval system. For example, they can break a large project into separate components so that the project is subject to local review and approval.

Fourth, measurement of the non-SPC approved share is less precise because it includes all projects not requiring SPC approval and thus the figures contain ministerial projects as well.

Despite the differences in the magnitude of control in terms of the trends, the two measures used here (see the next paragraph) show a broadly consistent pattern: central investment control has declined over the years. The drop in the SPC approval share has been particularly sharp. At the beginning of the 1980s, SPC approval covered about 41 percent of the fixed-asset investment projects; by 1990, it decreased to 33 percent. The two measures of investment control, defined in supervisory terms, show a more modest decline in the central share; both show a decline of about 5 percent during the course of the 1980s. Another interesting pattern is that central supervisory control has not declined continuously but has fluctuated largely in tune with what is known about the ebbs and flows of the macroeconomic policies in the 1980s. In general, when an austerity policy was in effect in the 1980s the share of central investment control tended to rise, as in the years 1983, 1987, 1989, and 1990; otherwise the share tended to decline from the levels of the previous years. The years 1982, 1985, and 1988 are the most noticeable examples (for further details, see chapter 7).

In table 3.1, supervisory investment control is measured in two ways. One is central/local fixed-asset investments as a share of total fixed-asset investment; the other is central/local capital investment as a share of total capital investment. The difference between the two is the technical renovation investment (*gengxin gaizao touzi*), which is included in the fixed-asset investment share but excluded from the capital investment share. The two measures give very different estimates of the degree of central and local investment control. In terms of the fixed-asset investment share, local investment control is both significant and greater than central investment control; in terms of capital investment control, there is a nearly even split between the central and local governments.

There are substantive reasons to include technical renovation investment in our analysis of investment behavior. The local governments were responsible for about 72 percent of technical renovation investments in the early 1990s, up from 68 percent in the early 1980s; thus technical renovation investment is an overwhelmingly local investment activity and has become more so over the years. Provincial-level data also suggest the same pattern. In Hubei province, for example, the local share of the total technical investment volume was about 60 percent in 1976 and 63.5 percent in 1984 (Hubei Statistical Bureau 1985: 273); the share for Heilongjiang in 1986 was 61.6 percent (Heilongjiang Statistical Bureau 1987: 519); and that for Shandong in 1988 was 83.5 percent (Shandong Statistical Bureau 1989: 219).

Local developmental imperatives

There is considerable evidence that local governments are strongly motivated to develop local economies. This is readily translated into investment hunger because resources are not mobile across different regions; investment in local industrial capacity therefore often constitutes the only means by which to develop local economies. There is less certainty, however, about why these developmental urges are so strong. A number of Chinese scholars blame the way the performance of local officials is evaluated. According to this view, economic achievement is given heavy weighting in appointment and promotional considerations.[6] Thus career considerations drive local officials to achieve higher economic growth rates (Lou Jiwei 1992; Wang Liguo 1989).

Upon closer examination, this theory of "political motives" seems less plausible. The criteria for cadre promotions are highly sensitive to changes in the general political and ideological environment. During the Maoist period, the evaluative criteria heavily stressed ideological performance and deliberately discounted the value of economic performance. Although during the reform era economic achievement has become a dominant concern, the emphasis on it has not been consistent. The post-Tiananmen leadership, for example, has vigorously attacked Zhao Ziyang's approach, which is to promote cadres on the basis of economic performance, and has again made ideological purity a primary consideration in cadre evaluation. The high variability of promotional considerations makes it difficult for cadres in the Chinese system to have a stable set of expectations regarding their performance; in addition, the variability in the evaluative criteria fails to explain the fact that developmental and investment urges have been a constant phenomenon in the Chinese economic system, both before and during the reform era.

Economic motives are more powerful. Development projects require money;

---

6. Zhao Ziyang, in a speech on cadre evaluation, made the following remarks: "A cadre's and a region's work should be evaluated fundamentally in terms of liberation and development of productivity. . . . It is impossible for production to go up in those regions where their cadres are without any virtues" (Zhao Ziyang 1988a: 1).

for that reason, fiscal motives have often been linked with developmental urges at the local level.[7] The link between economic development and fiscal motives, however, can go either way in terms of the direction of causality: more money makes it possible for local governments to undertake more projects, but justifications for more development projects are often made on the grounds that they bring in more revenue. There is considerable evidence that local government officials often explicitly justify high economic growth in terms of fiscal considerations. Local officials usually seek to increase economic growth in two ways: by trying to achieve as high an economic growth rate as possible, and by making claims on the central government in order to secure more policy control.

The zeal of the local governments for economic development has often led to the overheating of the economy; when this occurs, an increase in the tax intake is partly illusory. But one can become a net gainer if the tax revenue rises at a higher rate than the national average level of inflation, and, by implication, one is a loser if the revenue growth is below the national average level of inflation. Knowledge of this dynamic provides an extremely strong incentive to Chinese provinces to increase their economic growth, not so much in relation to their past economic growth, but in relation to growth rates in other regions. This is what the Chinese refer to as *panbi*, or competitive spirals. A prominent Chinese economist, Xue Muqiao, revealed that Shanghai economic officials "felt a lot of pressure" (*gandao yali henda*) in 1983 because in the previous year Shanghai's industrial production increased by only 4.5 percent in a very inflationary environment, whereas "many regions were calculating how to double output" (Xue Muqiao 1983). Usually the well-to-do provinces cite their relatively advanced economic standing to justify their past growth policies. The Guangdong Statistical Bureau, in a report for internal distribution, listed its elevation from seventh place in 1978, in terms of share of the national gross value of output (GVO), to third place in 1986 as a major economic achievement. Furthermore, it attributed this achievement to the

---

7. Another plausible motive is to minimize administrative caprice in a shortage economy. Investment – especially investment that seeks to link industrial sectors vertically, either backward or forward – may be a function of concern for security, of the desire to avoid shortages, and of the desire to increase self-reliance in an economic system of considerable political and administrative caprice. The security consideration, on the other hand, does not explain the persistence of the investment urge with the deepening of the economic reforms and as an increasing number of goods have become available on the open market. Some economists have gone so far as to argue that planning has become virtually irrelevant in terms of guiding enterprise behavior. Byrd, for example, argues that profit incentives and prices have come to the fore, while planning mainly serves a redistributional function of reassigning rents in the system. See Byrd (1991).

fact that Guangdong's economic growth surpassed the national average by some two percentage points during the 1979–86 period (see Guangdong Statistical Bureau 1987: 8).

Backward provinces, however, often use their poor economic standings to make a case for faster economic growth. The argument is that they need to narrow the gap between themselves and the well-to-do provinces. He Zhukang, director of the Henan Planning Commission and later secretary of the Henan Provincial Party Committee, wrote in 1982 that Henan's standing in the provincial GVO was only twentieth in the country and on a per capita basis, the gross value of its agricultural and industrial output (GVAIO) was only 60 percent of the national average. To catch up, He Zhukang argued, Henan would need a faster growth rate than the national average. He suggested 9.4 percent, as compared with the national average of 7.2 percent (He Zhukang 1982: 19–20).

In addition to achieving high growth rates, local governments also strive for a greater policy-making role in order to realize their economic ambitions. Often local officials couch their requests for policy favors in terms of the contributions they make to the country as a whole and in terms of a sense of fairness or equity, but never in terms of self-interest. A report prepared by the Tianjin Statistical Bureau on the investment situation in Tianjin, for example, cited an impressive array of detailed statistics to show that between 1957 and 1981 Tianjin's economic contributions to the country as a whole depressed consumption and investment in the region; further, it called for an increase in investment to enlarge Tianjin's productive capacity so that contributions could be maintained at the same level (Tianjin Statistical Bureau 1989: 234–38). In another instance, Anhui economic officials made the following demand:

We suggest the Center compensate Anhui for the grain it ships out. In 1985, Anhui shipped out 3 billion jin of grain, equivalent to six million mu of grain output. If this six million mu had been used for economic crops, we would have earned 300 to 400 million yuan more. In the past, when the Center shipped grain out of Anhui, it made allowances for this via preferential allocation of industrial products. Now there are no longer such allowances; the peasants' incentives to grow grain have been hurt. (Anhui Economic and Cultural Research Center 1986: 54)

Another tactic is to couch policy favors in terms of the policy objectives of the central government. In 1985, when the central government announced its intention to move away from micromanagement of the economy to an emphasis on macroeconomic instruments, such as the interest rate and taxation, local governments seized the opportunity to demand more policy authority. Economic planning officials from Shanghai, Hangzhou, Chongqing, and Wuhan all asked for higher tax retention rates, more power to adjust tax rates, and more material-allocation rights to augment their macroeconomic control capabilities.[8]

Local officials openly vie for more policy autonomy. An analysis of position papers by mayors from twenty-three cities shows that eleven offered a vigorous argument for more economic policy authority.[9] The most common demand was to change central and local tax divisions in favor of the localities. Complaining about their financially strapped situations, these mayors advocated two solutions: an adjustment of the tax retention rates and the assignment of more enterprises to local control (Chinese Urban Economic Society 1988). In other instances, however, local officials have simply expressed their dissatisfaction with their limited economic power and made claims for more. Complaining about their limited power to set interest rates and adjust taxes, Shanghai Planning Commission officials have argued:

As far as bank credits are concerned, apart from working capital loans, all other interest rates are set by the Center; the localities have no power. As far as taxes are concerned, the localities cannot increase or reduce adjustment taxes and the authority to adjust other taxes is quite limited. As far as [the adjusting of] prices and wages is concerned, the localities have even less authority. (Shanghai Planning Commission 1986: 21–22)

Investment management

Managing investments is a highly complex affair. Numerous government agencies and enterprises are involved in investment approvals and construction, and there is no single administrative chain of command to compel all the actors to comply. The central government does not have detailed budgetary breakdowns on a project-by-project basis (Naughton 1987: 74). The shortage of information is compounded by the fact that at any given point in time there are a large number of ongoing investment projects. In 1985, 32,000 new investment projects broke ground, and in the first half of 1986, there were 11,000 new investment projects (Tao Zengyi 1988: 598). In 1986, a contractionary year, there were over 100,000 projects under construction (Shen Zhiqun 1988: 568).

The administrative complexities involved in investment management have often forced policy makers to centralize the review and approval processes in order to rein in investment growth. The SPC, and its various local bureaus, is

---

8. See Development Center of the State Council (1986).

9. The cities are Beijing, Shanghai, Chongqing, Wuhan, Shenyang, Guangzhou, Shenzhen, Dalian, Yantai, Fushun, Shashi, Changzhou, Taiyuan, Nanchang, Ji'nan, Zhengzhou, Changsha, Xi'an, Lanzhou, Qinhuangdao, Baotou, Daqing, and Baoji.

the paramount government bureaucracy in investment planning. Within the SPC system, there is a bureau of comprehensive planning for fixed-asset investment. Its principal tasks consist of enforcing the central government's industrial policies and structuring investment programs in accordance with these policies. The tools available to the SPC are mainly administrative in nature and include the authority to appraise project applications, a process that consists of feasibility review, site selection, and project design. Apart from these micro-level management responsibilities, the SPC formulates annual medium- to long-term investment plans, drafts investment policies and regulations, supervises investment policy implementation, and issues binding credit plans to finance specific investment projects. At the local level, many of these regulatory functions are performed by the local offices of the SPC.

In recent years, the SPC has also assumed a more active investment posture, moving away from its passive and purely regulatory role of project review and approval. The SPC's direct investment functions are carried out via six national investment corporations it set up in 1988. Each of these is mandated to invest in capital projects in six economic sectors: energy development, transport, raw materials, light and textile industrial machinery, agriculture, and forestry. These national investment corporations are charged with carrying out central investment programs.[10]

Local investment control has increased during the reform period, as measured both in supervisory terms and in terms of approval authority. As explained earlier, local investment control per se is not a new phenomenon. Recent economic reforms, however, have greatly altered the nature of local investment control in that they have given the local governments not only a greater share of managerial responsibilities but have enabled local governments to sponsor, organize, finance, and directly undertake investment activities. This newly gained investment autonomy is most significant in the areas of planning quotas, project review, and, most notably, project financing.

Investment planning quotas

Quotas are an important element in the Chinese investment planning process and a powerful instrument used by the central government to achieve its own macroeconomic and industrial policy objectives. Investment quotas are essentially SPC-imposed limits on how much local governments can invest in a given year. During the reform era, the central government has found it

---

10. The above discussion is based on World Bank (1990b) and Zhou Hanrong (1991).

necessary to revise the investment quota continuously in response to changing macroeconomic conditions. By and large, when the central government has sought to regulate investment activities at the local level through a fine-tuning approach, it has expanded or reduced investment quotas to make the system better serve its policy objectives.

In the early 1980s, the quota system only covered capital construction investments and investment activities undertaken by the state-owned enterprises. However, as the share of technical renovation investments and of nonstate investments increased as a result of the economic reforms, the central government gradually sought to bring these new investment activities under its overall investment planning process by imposing quotas on them.

At the same time, the central government has not attempted to impose a uniform degree of investment control. Nonstate investments, for example, are governed by "softer" and less binding "guidance" (*zhidao*) quotas, whereas more binding quotas operate on state units. In part, this differential treatment reflects the fact that state sector investments still account for the bulk of investment activities – 67 percent in 1992 as measured in terms of share of total fixed-asset investment. Targeting the state sector may adequately serve central macroeconomic and industrial policy objectives. This also reflects the fact that nonstate investments – much of them in housing – are beyond the immediate administrative orbit of the local governments.

At times, the central authorities have also reduced the coverage of the investment quotas as part of a deliberate policy to encourage local investment initiatives and drives. In 1985, for example, the central government announced the so-called five-exemptions policy, under which five investment activities were deliberately excluded from the investment quotas: capital expenditures on transport vehicles by transportation agencies; investments by the four Special Economic Zones and nuclear power plant construction in Guangdong; investments financed by the officially approved foreign exchange savings; construction of simple, nonproductive facilities; and investment categories specifically exempted by the State Council and the Central Financial and Economic Leading Group (SPC and SSB 1991 [1985]). Some of these exemptions were later reversed because they led to excessive investment expansions.

In general, investment planning proceeds in four steps. First, provinces and ministries aggregate investment requests from their subordinate units and submit these figures to the SPC. Second, the SPC assigns preliminary investment quotas to the provinces and to the line ministries, which in turn further disaggregate their allotted quotas to their subordinate units. Third, provinces and ministries translate the preliminary quotas into specific investment plans.

And fourth, a national planning conference sets interprovincial balances. The final result is then submitted to the State Council for approval.[11]

The determination of the size of the quota, however, is a highly contentious process, for two main reasons. First, a specific quota allotment carries with it a commitment of resources commensurate with the level of the quota; projects included in the investment plan can be guaranteed a degree of credit support because the plan is mandatory for banks as well (Singh 1992: 25). Thus the economic stakes are high. Second, the SPC does not have *independent* sources of information to make the quota determination; therefore its assessment of provincial investment demand almost exclusively relies on the requests submitted by the provinces, as well as on the levels of the previous year. However, both kinds of information are either directly structured or strongly influenced by the local officials themselves.[12]

Such influences can be exercised in several ways. One is to secure political interventions from powerful leaders to evade the SPC's control process. In investment planning, where the economic stakes are high and approval criteria are often flimsy and elastic, knowing the right people becomes a valuable asset to speed up the process or even to obviate the process altogether.[13] The SPC openly acknowledges this phenomenon and sometimes designs its control approach to accommodate it. In 1985, the SPC and the SSB (1991 [1985]) specifically exempted "projects approved by State Council leaders and leaders of the Central Financial and Economic Leading Group." Chen Yizi (1990: 51), a former economic adviser to Zhao Ziyang, made the following observation:

(Because investment projects increase revenues to local governments), when applying for approval, [local governments] deliberately underestimate project costs, exaggerate the technical levels of the projects, and falsify productivity. Then they use back doors – giving banquets and sending gifts to establish connections. Planning departments, on the other hand, have all sorts of nominally rational criteria; in fact they often make their decisions by looking up the connections of the applicants – whether or not they have

11. See Zhou Hanrong (1991: 45–46) for more details.

12. Contrast this situation with the Soviet investment planning process. Soviet planning officials usually had better information about investment demands, and indeed they used alternative versions of investment functions to estimate "genuine" investment needs. Although this did not eliminate bargaining, it implied that bargaining was conducted mainly in technical terms and that, everything else being approximately equal, the bargaining was less pervasive. On Soviet investment planning, see Gregory (1990) and Dyker (1983).

13. Political interventions are not a new phenomenon; Deng Xiaoping, in a 1962 speech on the work of the Construction Bank of China, commented (quoted from Zhou Hanrong 1991: 17): "The work of the Construction Bank is very important. It is a gatekeeper for the state and it should implement the state plan, i.e., it can only lend money to projects that are included in the state plan. For projects not included in the state plan, even if God approved them, money should not be lent. If it is lent, then it is a dereliction of duty."

powerful patrons. . . . In 1986, during the SPC's discussion of investment projects for the Seventh FYP (1986–1990), only two-thirds of the projects were actually on the table; the rest were so-called "decree projects" (*tiaozi xiangmu*) – those projects reserved for the central leaders' personal approval through decree issuance.

Overriding or evading the SPC's judgment is, however, by no means easy and requires help from politicians with very high stature, which suggests that this is probably not a widespread practice. Investment quotas are more commonly determined through bilateral negotiation between the SPC and the provincial governments. Officials in the State Planning Commission have described the annual investment review process as being full of "quarrels," and local officials have compared the process to "a good fight" (see *Dangdai Zhongguo de guding zichan touzi guanli* 1989). Bargaining does matter. Control quotas have sometimes been revised upward after consultations with provincial officials. In 1981, for example, the central government initially set the capital expenditure target at 30 billion yuan; later it revised the figure to 38 billion yuan. In 1986 the fixed-asset investment target was first set at 140 billion yuan, but after a governors' conference in June of that year, the target was revised to 150 billion yuan (Hei Aitang and Hu Ji 1988 [1985]).

Provincial officials also try to obtain favorable investment quotas by attracting investment flows from the central authorities to their regions. Central investment projects are desirable for two reasons, in particular. First, they are relatively large in size and therefore incorporating them into the provincial investment portfolio can increase the investment quota significantly. Second, central investments, in contrast to foreign investments, are more likely to be in sectors that the central government actively promotes and therefore are likely to guarantee more financial, material, and policy support than investments from other provinces or from foreign companies.

There is some evidence that poorer provinces tend to pursue central investments more aggressively than richer provinces because their ability to generate an investible surplus is rather limited. To begin with, they use fairly aggressive bidding strategies to lure central projects their way; Ningxia provincial authorities, for example, offered 2.7 million yuan for a sugar-processing plant when the Ministry of Light Industry was only asking for 1.8 million yuan; provincial leaders also instructed their departments to secure at least one large or medium project from the central government during the Seventh FYP. Each year, Yunnan province, a province in China's southwest, spends about 10 million yuan (about 1.3 percent of its total capital expenditures) on preparatory work aimed at attracting central projects (Zhong Chengxun 1993: 294–317).

The poorer provinces also appear to be motivated by the idea that good performance can be rewarded with more projects. When the central government became concerned that investments in nonproductive facilities (such as office buildings and apartments) would lead to shortages of funds for productive investments, for example, Ningxia province took the lead in issuing strict regulations on investment expenditures in the unproductive sectors. The Ningxia government also incorporated its extrabudgetary revenues and spendings into the budgetary channels, thus placing extrabudgetary funds under the direct purview of the Ministry of Finance and reversing the more common practice of funneling funds from the budget into extrabudgetary avenues (Zhong Chengxun 1993: 294–317). The Ningxia provincial leaders may well have calculated that central budgetary support exceeded their own ability to generate extrabudgetary revenues and therefore that it was rational to increase their fiscal dependency on the Center.

Investment review

The investment quota entitles a locality to a specific volume of investment; upon initiation, however, each specific project is subject to an investment review process, depending on the financing costs. Thus, whether an investment project can go forward or not hinges on at least two factors. One is the level of investment review and approval, and the other is an estimation of the financing costs. The investment review process refers to the process of appraising and approving investment project applications. Because review authorities come from both the central and local governments, the level at which review and approval are conducted significantly affects the probability of approval.

A local-level review is always more sympathetic since the local SPC bureaus, like the local governments, are highly interested in developing local industry, and, very probably, the local SPC officials know the enterprise managers and industrial bureau chiefs personally. Informal influences are much easier to exert than attempts to influence SPC officials in Beijing. In addition, more stringent criteria are applied at higher review levels. The SPC in Beijing, for example, may refuse an application to build a widget factory in Province X if it deems that the supply capacity at the national level is sufficient. But the SPC local bureau in Province X may argue from a different perspective. Province X needs a widget factory because transport problems have prevented the import of an adequate supply of widgets.

During the reform era, investment approval authority has been gradually decentralized. As is obvious from table 3.2, a feature of the Chinese

Table 3.2. *Changes in the provincial investment review and approval authority in the 1980s (millions of yuan)*

Investment type	1978–1984	After 1985	After 1990
Technical improvement	< 10		
Energy, transport, and raw materials		< 50	< 30
Other sectors		< 30	< 30
Capital construction	< 10	< 30	
Productive investment			< 10
Unproductive investment			< 5

Sources: Zhang Shaojie et al. (1986: 166), SPC and SSB (1992: 51), and Singh (1992: 23).

investment approval system is that capital construction investment review and approval is more centrally controlled than technical renovation investment. Furthermore, the review and approval authority in the 1980s was first decentralized and then recentralized. Before 1985, if a capital investment project involved an amount not exceeding 10 million, the project review and approval authority fell within the domain of the provincial authorities; otherwise authority rested with the SPC. After 1985, the threshold was increased to 30 million yuan. It was reduced again in 1990 to 10 million yuan for production-related projects and to 5 million yuan for nonproduction projects. The recentralization was instituted as part of the government's austerity program, in order to bring inflationary investment expansion under control.

What has been the effect of these changes in investment approval authority? One expected effect was the small coverage by the central government's review and approval process. Indeed, officials from the SPC and SSB estimate that among fixed-asset investments those requiring central approval dropped from about 41 percent in 1981 to 32 percent in 1987 and 33 percent in 1990 (SPC and SSB 1992: 30).[14] Thus, consistent with the expectation, the trend has been decreasing central control, although it should be noted that the SPC has tighter control over capital investment projects because of the lower investment threshold.

Another effect, according to Singh (1992: 24), has been the "miniaturization" of investment projects. There is an incentive to break large investment projects into smaller independent projects so that the applications can be

14. Singh (1992: 24) gives the higher figure of 42 percent for 1987.

reviewed at lower and more sympathetic local SPC bureaus. The current review and approval system places an administrative premium on small projects. Therefore there are many requests to launch small-scale and probably economically inefficient investment projects. These perverse incentives embedded in the current investment review process have in part contributed to greater industrial dispersion in China. The tendency now is for each province to have a "complete" industrial structure, including both downstream and upstream industries. As SPC and SSB officials (1992: 106–11) have pointed out, China now has 76 television enterprises (with 113 assembly lines) and 62 factories producing light vehicles.

Another bureaucratic strategy used to increase approval probability is to understate deliberately the cost estimates of the proposed projects. This lowers the review and approval requirement. Understating costs is in effect equivalent to overstating the economic and social returns of the project in the hope that approval will therefore be more forthcoming. According to a survey of 4,117 investment projects in 1991, the actual financing requirements for capital projects that year exceeded the originally stated financing requirements by a margin of 20.5 percent (31.4 percent for technical improvement projects). The margin was also greater for local projects than for central projects, 23.2 percent compared with 22.2 percent (SPC and SSB 1992: 92).[15]

Investment financing

Local governments can draw on a wide array of instruments to ensure financing of their projects. The most direct way, of course, is the budgetary capital expenditure, but this source has shrunk during the reform era. In Shandong province, it fell from 14.2 percent of capital investment in 1981 to 2.9 percent in 1987 (Zhong Chengxun 1993: 89). But much of the budgetary capital expenditure is not completely discretionary as it is largely used to finance the central investment projects under fund-matching requirements. Local governments usually have greater control over projects financed by extrabudgetary capital expenditure. In the 1980s, extrabudgetary capital expenditures accounted for 35 percent of the total extrabudgetary expenditure at the national level.[16] In the provinces, the share was even higher; in Shandong it amounted to 39 to 60 percent of the fixed-asset investment (Zhong Chengxun 1993: 92).

---

15. A variation of this strategy relates to the way the prices of investment inputs are calculated. Because plan prices are lower than market prices, one way to arrive at lower cost estimates is to use plan prices, even though there is prior knowledge that inputs will be secured through market channels. See Singh (1992).

16. Calculated from SSB (1993b: 231).

Bank credits have become a major source of project financing; most of the efforts of local government officials have been directed toward securing bank credits. One such way, as mentioned, has been to incorporate a targeted project in the investment plan, which guarantees credit financing because investment and credit plans are reconciled with each other. The administrative leverage over banks exercised by local officials, however, goes far beyond investment planning procedures. Provincial officials can call an economic development conference of the heads of industrial departments and the heads of regional specialized banks. Industrial departments often use such a forum to make direct credit requests of the banks; the banks, although administratively controlled by their headquarters, often find it difficult to refuse these requests because of the breadth of their relationship with local government agencies. If a bank branch should refuse a credit request by the specific order of its superior branch, local officials will often take up the case and directly lobby the officials of the superior branches.[17]

Local governments do not simply allocate bank credits by administrative fiat, however; they often pursue a set of policies that will create incentives or at least attenuate disincentives to the banks to make investment loans. They may pledge to be a guarantor to the banks and to safeguard its financial interests should the loans become uncollectible. Local governments assume the residual credit risks and subsidize bank losses with tax revenues. For example, local governments often demand surprisingly low profit-turnover targets in structuring the responsibility contracts with enterprises.[18] They also grant generous tax exemptions and amnesties to enterprises, especially for product and adjustment taxes. Other policies are motivated by similar considerations and aim at similar effects, as is the case for those that permit output prices to increase in conjunction with the ongoing project (which transfers some of the credit risks to the product user) and that permit debt servicing before taxes.

It is important to note that local governments bear only a portion of the revenue losses from excessive credit authorizations. Typically, local governments forgive the joint central–local taxes, and in so doing the central government in effect subsidizes the bank losses to the extent of its revenue-sharing

17. When he was the mayor of Shanghai (1988–91), Zhu Rongji often sought out division-level officials in the People's Bank of China in Beijing in order to impress upon them the need to allocate more bank credits to Shanghai. In that case, the bank officials usually relented as they found it hard to resist interventions from the Shanghai mayor (author's interview).

18. For example, an enterprise in an unnamed municipality reported a profit margin of 1.2 million yuan in 1986 but when the enterprise was planning a facility expansion for 1987, the municipal government signed a profit contract in the amount of 0.8 million yuan (Zhong Chengxun 1993: 251).

rates with the localities. Also, local governments do not lose as much as long as the revenue stays at the local level. As pointed out in chapter 2, there are nonfiscal means by which local governments eventually recoup some of the lost revenue.

Apart from the traditional funding channels (the budget, construction banks, and enterprise earnings), local governments have been able to develop some innovative instruments to mobilize investment funds: bond issues, the setting up of nonbank financial institutions, compensation investments,[19] and, increasingly important, attracting foreign direct investments. The first construction bonds issued by a local government came out in Shandong province in 1981. The Yantai Construction Bank raised about 100 million yuan for a 170 million yuan power-generation plant.[20] Because there was no bond market, they were issued to the end-users of the electricity generated by the plant, via relatively compulsory administrative means.[21] Other bond issues by local governments bore broad similarities to this in that they were all consumption-based. In Guangdong, for example, bondholders of a power plant received an entitlement to a "commodity quota," in addition to interest payments. In the case of compensation investments, investors were given entitlements to products in shortage that were typically under the allocation of the state plans (see World Bank 1990c: 18–20). The net effect of this kind of investment is to undermine central control as it reduces the dependency of the provinces on the state allocation of investment goods.

The main nonbank financial institutions involved in investment resource mobilization are TICs. In the late 1980s China had about 745 TICs, some of which were owned by the local governments; others were attached to specialized banks and were subject to the authority of local governments because of the latter's influences on the specialized banks. TICs receive funds from interbank lending and from governments and enterprises in the form of trust deposits (World Bank 1990c: 13). Recently, it has been alleged, many of the locally controlled TICs are beginning to trade in securities and invest in property development. The ostensible purpose of these financial operations is to raise funds for local governments to finance investment projects.

By far the most important nontraditional financial source has been foreign

---

19. This refers to payments-in-kind as investment returns to investors. In particular, this method is used for cross-provincial investments and for investments in facilities to produce upstream goods in shortage. Shanghai, for example, invested in cement facilities in Zhejiang in 1980; in return, Shanghai received 3,000 tons of cement from Zhejiang every year between 1981 and 1983 (Cao Erjie, Li Minxin, and Wang Guoqiang 1992: 326).

20. The Ministry of Water Resources and Electric Power put up the rest of the capital.

21. This is described in Cao Erjie, Li Minxin, and Wang Guoqiang (1992: 331–32).

direct investments (FDIs). In the early 1980s FDIs accounted for about 3 percent of China's capital formation; by the late 1980s the share had risen to 14 percent. Until recently, local governments operated under a number of central regulations designed to restrict foreign investment inflows. Some of the regulations were region-specific; for example, the Special Economic Zones (SEZs) in the coastal areas were given greater autonomy to devise tax incentives to attract FDI and to manage foreign investment projects. Many of the centrally imposed restrictions were also sector-specific; thus those provinces with a heavy concentration of the restricted sectors, such as strategic raw materials, were naturally at a disadvantage in comparison with those provinces specializing in manufactured goods. Typically, the sectoral investment restrictions unduly handicapped the interior provinces that have a large resource base but a smaller manufacturing base.

Partly because these policy restrictions have been steadily removed since the mid-1980s (and the pace of their removal has accelerated since the late 1980s), the share of FDI channeled regionally – that is, foreign investment made in local projects and negotiated with local governments – has increased sharply in recent years, as opposed to FDI channeled ministerially. In 1983, for example, the local share of realized FDI was about 63 percent. But in 1991 the share increased to 95 percent, and in 1992 the regionally channeled FDI, at 98 percent, accounted for almost all of the foreign direct investment volume. In some areas of China, the FDI is now a major source of investment capital. In Shenzhen, in the early 1990s, capital inflows exceeded 50 percent of capital formation; in Guangdong province as a whole, the contribution was about 25 percent (Kueh 1992). In the area of external loans, the role of the central ministries has traditionally been more dominant because a significant portion of these loans has come from international multilateral agencies and foreign government aid programs. But the local–central shares of external loans – or indirect foreign investments – also underwent similar changes. In 1983 the local share of external loans was 2.4 percent; in 1991 it went up to 8.5 percent.

Two other developments in FDIs over the course of the 1980s are noteworthy. One is that the average size of local FDI projects, in terms of capital commitment, has grown larger, indicating that the capital intensity of the local projects has increased. In 1983 the average investment per local project was US$0.14 million, compared with US$4 million for an average ministerial project; in 1991, the average local project was US$0.89 million, whereas the average size of a ministerial project decreased to US$1.38 million. Another development has been a geographic dispersion of FDI away from the SEZs and coastal provinces to the more interior regions. In 1984 the four SEZs –

Table 3.3. *Central and local controls over capital goods allocation, 1980 and 1987 (percentage)*

Good	Center		Localities		Firm (market)	
	1980	1987	1980	1987	1980	1987
Steel	74	47	n.a.	35.5	n.a.	17.5
Coal	54	30	n.a.	37.3	n.a.	32.7
Lumber	81	26	n.a.	41.3	n.a.	32.7
Cement	36	45.8	n.a.	34.6	n.a.	19.6

Note: n.a. = not available.
Source: SPC and SSB (1992: 42).

Shenzhen, Xiamen, Shantou, and Zhuhai – accounted for 38.7 percent of all the regionally channeled FDI; the other fourteen "open" coastal areas (such as Qingdao and Dalian) accounted for another 25 percent. In 1991 these two shares declined to 19.7 percent and 24.4 percent, respectively.[22]

Allocation of capital goods

Capital goods refer to factor inputs used in further production processes. In this context, capital goods specifically refer to what are called production materials in Chinese economic literature, such as the construction materials, steel, and machinery used in the capital construction process. As pointed out in chapter 2, although product allocation in general is considerably decentralized in China, the allocation of capital goods, as opposed to consumer goods, is somewhat more centralized. The central government uses the capital goods allocation process to pursue its industrial policy goals. For example, because capital goods carry plan prices and therefore embody administrative subsidies, the central government uses their allocation to motivate local governments to undertake priority projects. The costs of projects that use these goods are lower (and therefore their returns are higher), with the result that credit support commands a premium.

As in other areas, central control over capital goods allocation has declined during the reform era. Table 3.3 presents developments in the allocation of steel, coal, lumber, and cement in 1980 and 1987. The decline of steel and lumber is most dramatic; in 1980 the central authorities – mainly the SPC and

22. The statistics cited in the discussion on FDIs are from SSB (1992c) and SSB (1993b).

the central ministries – allocated 74 percent of steel and 81 percent of lumber, but in 1987 the shares declined to 47 percent and 26 percent, respectively. Although the 1980 data are not available for local governments and enterprises, it is quite plausible that the shares were smaller in 1980 than they were in 1987. By 1987 local control over capital goods was quite considerable. Coal and lumber allocation hovered around 40 percent. At issue is whether local control over capital goods allocation has impeded the development of market allocation. As shown in the last column of the table, market allocation by no means constitutes the dominant mode of allocation. It is at least arguable that the administrative decentralization of capital goods allocation has not created a fully functioning market for capital products in large part because local governments have usurped many of the allocation responsibilities.

Price liberalization also undermines central control by making capital goods more readily available through market channels. Today, 70 percent of the price of production materials is already liberalized; between 1986 and 1989 administered prices declined from 47 percent to 30 percent and market and semimarket prices rose from 34 percent to 45 percent and from 19 percent to 25 percent, respectively (Rajaram 1992). One of the consequences of parallel prices is that maintaining central control over product allocation is becoming increasingly costly, because enterprises that supply goods for central allocation receive lower-than-market prices, which reduces their profit streams and leads to large losses. Economic studies have shown that enterprise losses are concentrated overwhelmingly in sectors that are subject to central price controls (Rajaram 1992; Rohwer 1992). Eventually these enterprise losses become the fiscal or monetary burdens of the central and local governments because they have to be subsidized either out of the budget or, indirectly, through the nonpayment of debts. In the long run, the spiraling financial costs are likely to make product allocation increasingly unviable as an instrument of investment control.

Conclusion

The investment role of China's local governments, much like their general economic role, has traditionally been quite decentralized, with local officials performing many of the functions that normally belong to central ministries in a typical CPE. Chinese economic management had a strong local component even before the economic reforms of the late 1970s. The economic reforms, however, have deepened and varied the local roles in production, goods allocation, investment, and finance.

Indeed, at the end of the 1970s Chinese economic planners came to recognize a fundamental reality: that much of the economic management was decentralized and the costs of recentralization were prohibitively high. Because of the institutional destruction of the Cultural Revolution, China had very weak central planning capabilities on the eve of the reforms. When Chinese policy makers attempted to implement an investment program that required a high degree of supraministerial and provincial coordination, as Hua Guofeng did with his Ten-Year Development Plan, the result was massive macroeconomic dislocations. The main legacy of the political shocks of the Cultural Revolution and of the accompanying economic decentralization was that the post-Mao leadership was unable to reassert the kind of centralized investment management that they were able to resurrect in the early 1960s. In that sense, the economic reforms that the Chinese policy makers undertook in the late 1970s stemmed less from a grand vision of an ideal economic system than from the absence of a meaningful alternative.[23]

It is also important to note that years of decentralized investment management had created powerful bureaucratic and political vested interests concerned with maintaining the status quo. This means that it was politically difficult to completely reverse the existing institutional arrangements, in part because they conferred significant "rents" derived from local control over economic resources.[24] During the reform era, decentralized investment management withstood challenges from both central planners and reformers. The central government adjusted investment approval limits for the provinces a number of times as it attempted to contain local investment growth; however, the curing of the immediate macroeconomic symptoms only accentuated the demand for more local autonomy in investment management.

To a large extent, the tax reforms that have attempted to change the funding basis for decentralized investment management have yielded similar outcomes. From the very beginning, central policy makers recognized a fundamental flaw in the 1980 tax reforms: the administrative division of taxes, as they correctly anticipated, exacerbated interprovincial trade protectionism and the rush to build up local processing industries. The original intent was to phase out the administrative division of taxes in five years. Not only did the 1985 reforms fail to change the administrative nature of the tax divisions, but a host of

23. For a more detailed analysis along this line, see Huang (1994).

24. Rents here refer to the difference between the current value of a resource and its value derived from its next best alternate use. For a theoretical discussion, see Buchanan, Tollison, and Tullock (1980). On the distribution of rents via the product allocation mechanism, see Byrd (1991); for a general discussion on rent creation and seeking activities in China, see *Fubai* (1989).

economic reform measures were conditioned by the 1980 tax reforms, largely because the fiscal incentives of the localities had to be taken into account (Development Center of the State Council 1985: 25–28). An example includes Zhao Ziyang's coastal development strategy announced at the beginning of 1988. That strategy was to orient China's coastal areas to the world market, producing exports to pay for imported raw materials and energy, such that the coastal regions would not compete with the interior regions on the domestic energy, raw materials, and final goods market.[25] This is a far cry from his earlier emphasis on development along regional comparative advantages and was at least partially due to his recognition that the impulse to build vertically integrated industries had already become irreversible.[26]

All of this should not be taken to imply that the economic reforms have not had an independent effect on the character of investment management in China. The significance of the economic reforms lies in the fact that they have made local governments relatively *autonomous* economic actors and have created a diversified range of financing tools. Before the reforms, the local governments depended principally on the central budgetary allocations to carry out their investment programs. The main issue in policy discussions revolved around the amount of the budgetary grants and the stringency with which the use of these grants should be centrally monitored. During the reform period, the local governments have developed a wide range of financing tools, including bond issues, extrabudgetary revenues, nonbank financial institutions, and foreign direct investments. Some of these financing tools are intrinsically difficult to administer from Beijing, as some of the funding sources lie outside the administrative orbit of the central government. For example, the level of capital financing raised on securities and property markets can fluctuate quite widely; other sources, such as foreign direct investments, usually have a degree of protection written in the contract against the sharp edges of the central retrenchment policies.

In summary, to the policy makers in the late 1970s decentralized investment management was a given condition. They could modify it on the margin, but ultimately they had no choice but to accommodate to, and to design economic policies and reform programs in accordance with, the fundamental reality of

---

25. Zhao Ziyang (1988c: 6), in his talk about the "coastal development strategy," was explicit on this point: "The coastal region, in its economic development, should avoid competing with the interior regions for raw materials and markets; it should strive to export and import, transforming itself into an externally oriented economy."

26. For a political economy analysis stressing the political role of local officials to block institutional changes not in their interests, see Huang (1990) and Shirk (1989, 1990).

the powerful economic positions held by the local governments. The economic reforms, however, have turned the local governments into autonomous economic actors and have permitted the development of varied and nontraditional financing tools. How the central government is able to achieve its own investment objectives, despite the presence of independent economic interests and new sources of investment funds, is discussed later in the book.

4

The local officials in the bureaucratic hierarchy

Chinese local officials are first and foremost constituent members of one of the world's most centralized and well-organized political hierarchies. All of the top provincial officials are appointed by the Center, specifically by the Chinese Communist Party organs such as the Politburo and the Department of Organization (DOO). This personnel allocation power is the ultimate trump card that the Center can wield over provinces and it is a fundamental constraint faced by all Chinese local officials. Jiang Zemin, at a 1994 Central Party School conference attended by provincial Party secretaries and governors, reportedly cautioned: "Don't believe that because local economies are getting stronger and because you have more money you can bargain with the Center. I tell you that although you have money, the Party Center still has the power to select and fire personnel" (quoted in Zhong Xingzhi 1994: 8).

Thus local officials face not only normal economic or financial constraints in their investment behavior but also powerful political and bureaucratic constraints. Often economic and political forces pull local officials in opposite directions. Motivated by fiscal incentives and endowed with enormous economic resources, local officials on one hand want to expand investments; on the other hand, when their investment behavior harms macroeconomic stability, they are required to restrain investments by the central government. Local investment behavior is thus influenced by the economic interests (and resources) of local officials and by the structure of Chinese political and bureaucratic institutions. Focusing only on their economic roles but not on the political and bureaucratic constraints causes biases in our analysis.

To understand administrative governance in China it is therefore important to consider the institutional and formal aspects of Chinese administrative governance, including the cadre management system – especially the management of bureau-level (*ju*) cadres and administrative monitoring – the information channels, and the specialized government units that the central government employs to monitor the behavior of its cadres. Another factor to consider is the effect of the personnel reforms on the administrative relationship between the Center and local governments. All the evidence in these areas points to a decline in administrative localism during the reform era.

The cadre management system

In the Chinese system, cadre management (*ganbu guanli*) refers to the nomination, appointment, removal, and evaluation of cadres. The main units in charge of cadre management are the DOO under the Central Committee of the Chinese Communist Party and the Ministry of Personnel (MOP) under the State Council. "Cadre" is a broad term encompassing government officials, civil servants (such as heads of government bureaus), and technical personnel (such as college professors or factory technicians). Here, I use the term more narrowly to refer to *dangzheng ganbu* (Party and state officials). In the 1980s there was some decentralization in the system as the direct appointment power of the Party Center did not extend beyond ministerial and provincial posts. However the Party Center has developed various means to regulate and supervise bureau-level appointments.

The appointment system

One indication that the Party plays both an extensive and dominant role in personnel decisions is the explicitly political criteria by which cadres are selected and promoted. Every time a cadre is considered for a post, the nominating unit is required to report on the "political performance" (*zhengzhi biaoxian*) of the candidate. Political performance normally includes the candidate's activities during the Cultural Revolution and the Tiananmen movement, as well as his or her views (*taidu*) on the Four Cardinal Principles.[1]

Party institutions also play a role in personnel decisions. In the first half of the 1980s, three units shared primary responsibility for cadre management at the central level: the DOO, the Department of Propaganda, and the Department of the United Front. All three are arms of the Communist Party Central Committee and as such are distinct from the administrative units of the State Council (such as the MOP), which perform governmental functions. The division of labor among these three departments was approximately as follows:

---

1. Burns (1987b) shows that the limited implementation of civil service reforms has not diminished the role of the Party. The Party, for example, still determines the content of the civil service examinations.

the Department of Propaganda managed educational cadres; the Department of the United Front managed cadres dealing with Taiwan and the "democratic parties"; and the Department of Organization looked after the remainder (DOO and Department of Propaganda 1985 [1982]; DOO and Department of the United Front 1985 [1981]). In 1985, however, the DOO took over most of the cadre management functions from the other two departments (DOO, Department of Propaganda, and Department of the United Front 1986 [1985]).

Although "Party management of cadres" (*dang guan ganbu*) is said to be merely an organizational principle (Pu Xingzu 1990: 353), in practice the cadre nomination and evaluation procedures give the Party a prior and, in most cases, a monopolistic say over personnel decisions. For example, the procedure for transmitting documents is carefully laid out in such a way that the Party's organization departments, rather than their counterparts in the government, effectively exercise veto power over any appointment decision. A DOO memorandum concerning promotion and approval procedures stipulates that any personnel decision requiring State Council approval – that is, any decision regarding cadres working in the administrative units of the central government – must be reviewed by the DOO first; only after this review is completed can the State Bureau of Personnel, the personnel agency under the State Council, begin its own investigation (DOO 1984b [1980]). Because appointment and removal decisions regarding the heads of provincial bureaus are also required by law to be screened by the provincial people's congresses (National People's Congress 1985b [1979]: 134), to ensure Party control the provincial Party committees must seek prior clearance with the Party Center before going through the formal appointment and removal procedures (DOO 1985 [1982]).[2]

The DOO's monopolistic control over cadre management is evident from the relatively unimportant role the State Council plays in appointing its own cabinet members. The State Council has no say in appointment to ministerial posts; its appointment authority covers only the heads of the state bureaus directly under its jurisdiction (such as the State Statistical Bureau) and some major nongovernment units, such as the China International Trust and Investment Corporation and Peking University. And this authority was only granted in 1988 (State Council 1989a [1988]).

---

2. At least on paper, the local people's congresses had more power before the Cultural Revolution. As stipulated in the 1954 local organizational law, for example, the provincial people's congresses could directly elect governors and vice governors (National People's Congress 1985a [1954]: 127). The electoral authority of the local people's congresses was severely eroded during the Cultural Revolution when they did not convene, and by early 1967 when all provincial posts were effectively taken over by the military, the Center assumed power to appoint all provincial officials (Diao Tianding, Chen Jialin, and Zhang Hou'an 1989: 87–88).

In contrast to the decentralized nature of economic decision-making power, the Chinese cadre management system is still highly centralized. The authority to select, assign, and promote top provincial cadres in the Chinese bureaucratic hierarchy remains solely and unquestionably in the hands of the Center. Thus the issue being addressed in the administrative reforms is whether the second-tier officials, that is, the bureau-level officials in the ministries and in the provinces, should be centrally appointed.

As of 1979, the selection and appointment of bureau-level officials required the approval of the Politburo member in charge of organizational work and of the vice-premiers in charge of operations in the relevant sector, after an initial background investigation was completed by the DOO (see DOO 1984c [1980]: 156). In 1980 the DOO instituted the so-called two-level downward management system (*xialiangji guanli*), under which the central Party authorities were responsible for cadre management at the next two lower levels. Thus, for central government posts the Central Committee was in charge of ministerial and bureau-level officials; as for local government posts, the Central Committee was in charge of provincial and prefectural officials (DOO 1984a [1980]).

Prior to the 1980 decision, bureau-level appointments in the provinces were apparently listed in the local *nomenklatura* (DOO 1984b [1980]); thus the 1980 decision marked a major recentralization of cadre management. In part, this was a deliberate move designed to rid the provinces of the factionalism of the Cultural Revolution and in part it was aimed at solving the inherent problems associated with "one-level downward" management, such as nepotism and excessive localism when too many appointment decisions were made locally (Manion 1985).

In 1983, in a drive to streamline government, the two-level downward system was changed to the so-called one-level downward management system, under which Party authorities only manage cadres one level below them. The main criticism of the two-level downward management system was that it concentrated too much power at the top and that the number of cadres was simply too large for the Party Center to handle. Also, the central Party officials were said to have been too involved in detailed personnel decisions, while leaving little time for long-term policy planning and the formulation of principles (DOO 1986e [1983]).

The one-level downward system has largely prevailed since 1983. Under this system, the DOO manages ministerial and provincial officials; bureau-level officials within ministries and in the provinces are managed by the ministerial Party group or by the provincial Party committee. As a result of this change, the Party Center has, as of 1983, been directly responsible for the appointment and removal of seven thousand cadres, a reduction of some six

Table 4.1. *Provincial officials managed by the Department of Organization,* *1990*

Party	Government
Managed by DOO	
Secretaries and deputy secretaries, members of the Standing Committee	Governors and vice governors
Directors and vice directors of the Advisory Commission	Chairmen and vice chairmen of the People's Congresses
Directors and vice directors of the Discipline Commission	Chairmen and vice chairmen of the Political Consultative Conferences
	Justices and chief procurators
Report to DOO	
Heads of the Secretariat	Heads of the Secretariat
Heads of the Party departments	Heads of bureaus
President of the Party School and chief editors of Party newspapers	Deputy justices and deputy procurators
Leaders of Party groups in the People's Bank and specialized bank branches	Heads of the People's Bank and specialized bank branches

Source: DOO and MOP (1991 [1990]).

thousand from the previous system (DOO 1986e [1983]: 432). Table 4.1 lists those provincial positions managed by the DOO and those required to report to the DOO for the record, as of 1990.

Personnel regulation and supervision

Ever since it relinquished direct control over bureau-level appointments, the DOO has sought to improve its means of regulating and supervising bureau-level appointment decisions and to affect personnel decision outcomes by specifying the ground rules, imposing targeted direct control, defining the form and content of record reporting, and retaining veto power. These measures were designed to obviate the aforementioned problems commonly identified with the one-level downward system.

Bei'an system. The first such measure was adopted in 1984 when the DOO set up the system of reporting for the record (*bei'an zhidu*) to facilitate central monitoring of cadres whom the Center no longer appointed directly. This reporting system applies to the heads of bureaus in central ministries and to the heads of provincial bureaus; these authorities are required to report to the DOO basic information about cadres within their appointment purview every six months.[3]

These procedures were intended to ensure continuous monitoring by the DOO once it delegated the power to make bureau-level appointment decisions to ministerial and provincial Party authorities. This marked an effort to systematize the information collection process by laying down precisely what should be reported, by setting forth reporting schedules, and by requiring more detailed information. The standard information includes the candidate's name, age, length of Party membership, appointment or removal requests, and *kaocha* (scrutiny) materials. In 1985 a more stringent reporting rule was imposed whereby the records were to be turned over "soon after" the appointment or removal decision (DOO 1986e [1983]); in 1986, an even more precise schedule was devised whereby the relevant records were to be turned over fifteen days after an appointment or removal decision. The DOO also required additional information about appointment decisions, including the results of opinion polls regarding the relevant cadres and the number of votes garnered by the nominees in the deliberation process of the Party groups (DOO 1987 [1986]).

Even more detailed information is required of cadres on the central *nomenklatura*. In a 1991 circular, the DOO identified a number of problems with the record-reporting practices. Some units, for example, tended to be "abstract" (*chouxianghua*) when describing shortcomings of candidates; others failed to give the DOO enough lead time to consider their requests. To correct these problems, the DOO laid down specific guidelines regarding the kind of information that was to be reported. For example, apart from the standard package of materials, the minutes of the discussions in the Party groups must be turned over to the DOO. To ensure enough lead time for deliberations, all of these materials must reach the DOO two months before the convening of the relevant conferences, such as the provincial people's congresses (DOO 1992 [1991]).

Cadre evaluation. In 1979 the Chinese leadership established a cadre evaluation (*ganbu kaohe*) system (DOO 1980 [1979]). Over the years, there has been an effort to institutionalize this form of performance check by making it a regular and systematic operation. Like other aspects of administrative governance, the DOO at first only delineated a vague requirement for cadre evaluations; thereafter it defined the content and procedure of the process

3. See Huang (1995a) for more details on these developments.

in an increasingly detailed manner. The DOO imposed a cadre evaluation requirement on bureau-level officials in 1986 as a part of its attempt to regulate the appointment and removal of bureau-level officials. In its 1986 circular, the department stated that bureau-level officials were required to undergo a performance review (*gongzuo zongjie*) and that an opinion poll had to be conducted at year end; thereafter a comprehensive performance evaluation was to be written up (DOO 1987 [1986]).

In 1988 the DOO issued a circular outlining the procedures for performance evaluations of local Party and government officials (DOO 1989 [1988]). In 1989 it laid down similar procedures for bureau- and division (*chu*)-level officials in the ministries (DOO and MOP 1990 [1989]). These procedures have a number of characteristics in common. First, the evaluators are the immediate superiors of those being evaluated. In the case of bureau-level ministerial officials, the evaluation committee (*kaohe weiyuanhui*) consists of ministers and vice ministers, secretaries of Party groups, and heads of the Bureau of Personnel; for division-level ministerial officials, the evaluation committee consists of heads or deputy heads of the bureaus and the corresponding Party secretaries. For local bureau-level officials, the evaluation committee consists of top provincial and Party officials. Second, the same evaluation committees are also in charge of handling appeals from those being evaluated. Third, the evaluation results are not immediately transmitted to the DOO; they are put into the cadres' dossiers for future reference by the DOO when it makes appointment, removal, punishment, and reward decisions.[4]

It is difficult to determine the importance of these evaluations for decision making; their clearest function is probably to screen out candidates with questionable backgrounds. Cadre evaluation is thus somewhat akin to a security check used in the recruitment of government employees in the United States. For example, an evaluation of a deputy director of the System Reform Commission of an unnamed city, undertaken by the provincial DOO (probably for the purpose of considering a promotion), provides some details about his activities during the Cultural Revolution and during the Tiananmen events. The report notes that during the Cultural Revolution he was an ordinary member of a mass organization, "transcribing leaders' speeches." The report goes on to say that he was a factory technician during the "Repulse the Right Deviationist Wind to Reverse the Verdicts" movement (1975) and that his participation in that movement was purely perfunctory. During the Tiananmen events, the report reveals, he wrote to his daughter at college, "giving her an ideological education." The description of his recent job performance is quite

4. This discussion is based on DOO (1989 [1988]) and DOO and MOP (1990 [1989]).

detailed; however, his shortcomings are discussed in a pro forma manner (Chen Wenqing and Su Kai 1991: 112–14).

Although tenure typically runs for a number of years, evaluations are conducted every year and thus give the DOO an opportunity to make incremental changes in the leadership lineup. These changes may be necessary in light of the often shifting ideological emphasis. For example, a provincial DOO, after conducting an evaluation of the leadership structure of a provincial department, suggested recruiting a new deputy director of political affairs and moving the incumbent to a more operational position. Presumably, the department felt the need to strengthen political work; this new emphasis was quite consistent with the general ideological environment after the Tiananmen crackdown (Chen Wenqing and Su Kai 1991: 114–16).

Rule-setting and selective controls. In 1986, in another effort to impose some control over the management of bureau-level officials, the DOO specified a series of procedures for considering bureau-level appointments. These include a quorum rule that requires two-thirds of the members of the ministerial Party group to be present when discussing a nominee, a more detailed requirement regarding the information that ministries and provinces should report, and a prior approval procedure in a number of exceptional circumstances (DOO 1987 [1986]).[5] Also, the DOO still maintains control over the appointment of the heads of the crucial functional agencies, such as the personnel departments of provincial organizations. A 1990 DOO memorandum in effect gives itself veto power over bureau-level appointments; it stipulates that bureau-level appointment decisions must be reported to the DOO in a speedy manner; the decision stands only if the DOO does not veto the decision within one month (DOO and MOP 1991 [1990]).

Monitoring in the Chinese bureaucratic system

Because we are concerned with control problems, it is critical to examine the monitoring and supervision of local officials. When economic controls have been delegated and when there has been some administrative decentralization, there

---

5. If one of the following seven situations applies, then the appointment decision requires prior approval from the Department of Organization: (a) the nominee failed to secure majority consent in the opinion polls; (b) the nominee committed "errors" during the Cultural Revolution; (c) the nominee is considered for a promotion one rank above his current rank; (d) the nominee is considered for a position outside the quota; (e) the nominee is considered beyond his term of office; (f) the nominee is considered for a position created for a new unit; or (g) the nominee is a direct relative of the head of the department and is considered for promotion within the same department and system. See DOO (1987 [1986]).

is a greater need for the Center to monitor and supervise the performance of those cadres whose appointments it no longer controls. Several mechanisms are at its disposal to monitor the general administrative conduct of cadres, as well as their economic conduct.

Administrative monitoring

Three agencies are in charge of monitoring: the provincial general offices, the Central Discipline Inspection Commission (CDIC), and the Ministry of Supervision (MOS). The latter two agencies are able to collect information and act on this information to punish officials who engage in questionable behavior. Neither agency is directly involved in checking and enforcing the implementation of economic plans. They are included here because they contribute to a general atmosphere of administrative compliance. During the several austerity rounds, the central leadership has invoked Party discipline in its effort to curtail local investment growth.

This is not meant to be a complete list; other channels include the work team, the internal news bulletin, and the petition system (*xinfang zhidu*), all of which feed information to policy makers, although in a less regular and standardized manner. I have discussed the function and evolution of these channels elsewhere (see Huang 1995a).

Provincial general offices. There are two pivotal agencies in the provincial Party and government hierarchies: the *shengwei bangongting* (general office of the provincial Party committee) and the *shengzhengfu bangongting* (general office of the provincial government). The provincial general offices receive directives from the general offices of the Politburo and the State Council, control access to top provincial leaders, draft documents on their behalf, issue directives, and coordinate interdepartmental activities.[6] Recently, however, an additional function has been assigned – supplying accurate and timely information to the central general offices.[7] Jiang Zemin, in a speech at a conference on the work of the provincial general offices in January 1990, referred to the provincial general offices as "the intersection of upward and downward information transmittal" (Jiang Zemin 1991 [1990]: 4).

Policy makers apparently gained a deeper appreciation of the importance of acquiring accurate information in 1989, in large part as a result of the Tiananmen

6. For a description of the tasks of the provincial Party and government general offices, see MOP (1989: 5, 15).

7. This function is absent in the task description given in the document drafted by the MOP in 1989 (see MOP 1989).

demonstrations and the East European revolution. Jiang Zemin, for example, specifically singled out "the lessons of the Rumanian events and our own June 4th turmoil" (Jiang Zemin 1991 [1990]: 8) when referring to the importance of the general offices. The provincial general office is a natural place to collect information because it is a comprehensive unit and therefore is not allied with any departmental interests. Thus it is expected to be relatively free of bias. Yao Yilin (1991b [1990]: 18–19), the director of the General Office of the Central Committee from 1980 to 1982, signaled his unhappiness with the existing channels of information: "The most difficult thing for a leadership unit to do is to collect accurate information at the basic level. Various units also conduct their own investigations but their investigations sometimes have a departmental bias or partiality. . . . Now the reports from the localities are written after repeated deliberations and they have been perfected so that you cannot see anything in them."

Because of these concerns, Chinese policy makers may have wanted to develop a more reliable and forthcoming information channel that is somewhat independent of the provincial Party committees. Such a desire would of course have encountered immediate bureaucratic problems, since the provincial general office is a subordinate unit of the provincial Party committee, not to mention a morale problem, since it would mean instituting a separate monitoring device within the provincial Party establishment. Also, probably of greater concern to the central policy makers was not the reporting behavior of top provincial Party and government officials, whom they tightly control through the appointment process, but that of intermediate – that is, bureau- or lower-level – officials.

Yao Yilin demanded that provincial general offices conduct their own investigations, with the implicit plea that they avoid relying on various provincial units. After emphasizing that the relationship between the central and provincial general offices is not one of leadership, Wen Jiabao, director of the General Office of the Central Committee, urged that "communication" between the two be expanded and that traditional professional relations be strengthened (Wen Jiabao 1991 [1990]: 35). Li Ruihuan (1991 [1990]: 20) came closest to proposing a separate information channel by appealing directly to the heads of the provincial general offices – that is, the provincial secretaries general (*mishuzhang*) – over the leaders of the provincial Party committees:

The basis for central decision making is the materials supplied by the localities and bureaus; what kinds of materials are supplied, however, depends on the leaders of the provinces and municipalities and the various provincial bureaus. But as far as I know, you secretaries general are the most important factor. What is reported and what is not reported, how much is good and how much is bad, what to report, and what ways things are reported, all depend on you. From now on, we ask your help in supplying accurate and timely information to the Center.

Recognition of the informational function of the provincial general offices has led to a number of measures to strengthen that institution. First, the central General Office has emphasized not merely the task of issuing directives, but also that of overseeing (*ducu*) their implementation. To that end, the central General Office began publication of *Ducu jiancha qingkuang* (Supervision and oversight update) to monitor the progress of implementing Party directives, to check on "You have policies; I have counter-policies" tendencies, and to detect fraudulent reporting (Xu Ruixin 1991 [1990]). Attention has also been given to the treatment of staff, improvements in equipment, and other aspects of operations. Jiang Zemin, referring to the low pay and difficult working conditions for the general office staff, instructed the provincial Party committees to tend to "some of the practical problems" facing the general office staff (Jiang Zemin 1991 [1990]: 7). Qiao Shi (1991 [1990]) proposed holding national conferences on general office work more frequently than the current five-year interval. In addition, a national communication network (probably of an electronic nature) has been established within the system of general offices. General offices are also encouraged to be more comprehensive in their reporting, that is, to report both good news and bad news.

Central Discipline Inspection Commission (*Zhongyang jilu jiancha weiyuanhui*). The Central Discipline Inspection Commission and its various local units monitor the political performance of cadres. Political performance here refers to the observance of Party discipline and procedures and implementation of Party ideology. For example, a circular issued by the CDIC in 1986 singled out some examples of violations of Party discipline; these included using office power for private benefit, openly voicing opinions inconsistent with official Party positions, immoral personal behavior, deceit, and falsifying information to superiors (Central Discipline Inspection Commission 1987 [1986]).

Like many other local Party and government units, since 1980 the local discipline inspection commissions have been subject to dual leadership by the corresponding level of the Party committee and by the CDIC. Previously, they had been subordinate to the corresponding Party committee only. It may be that this change from single subordination to dual subordination (which augmented central control) was motivated by the same considerations that were responsible for instituting the two-level downward cadre management system. In practice, however, the Party committee at the corresponding level is probably the dominant unit in the dual leadership. This is because the heads of the provincial discipline inspection commissions are inferior in rank to the secretaries of the Party committees of the corresponding level.[8] In part, to overcome the inhibiting effect arising from this rank difference, the CDIC specifically authorized the local discipline inspection commissions to report to the superior levels of the discipline inspection commission without approval from the Party committee at the same level (Central Discipline Inspection Commission 1988 [1987]). In addition, the local discipline inspection commissions are able to initiate investigations of members of the corresponding Party committees without authorization from top Party officials at the corresponding level (Dai Qinxiang and Cai Yulong 1989: 289–90).

Ministry of Supervision (Jiancha bu). The Ministry of Supervision has had a rather uneven history. It was established in 1949, abolished in 1959, and restored in 1987. To some extent, the Ministry of Supervision can be considered the administrative equivalent of the CDIC; indeed, between 1955 and 1966 the CDIC was known as the Supervision Commission (see Discipline Inspection Commission of Heilongjiang Party Committee 1987). And the two units overlap considerably in their task descriptions; before the MOS was reestablished in 1987 there were no distinctions between violations of administrative discipline (*xingzheng jilu*) and those of Party discipline (*dangde jilu*). The divisions of responsibilities were set forth in a 1988 document issued jointly by the two units: the CDIC is now mainly concerned with Party members working in Party organizations, whereas the Ministry of Supervision is mainly concerned with administrative cadres – whether Party members or not – working in state institutions (Dai Qinxiang and Cai Yulong 1989: 65–66). This, obviously, is an administrative division and therefore the task divisions seem not to be as closely related to the nature of the activities as to the identity of the cadres involved.

The local bureaus of the MOS are subject to dual leadership by the MOS and the corresponding provincial government. The former has primarily professional relations with the local bureaus, whereas the latter exercises mainly authoritative relations, which means that the local governments have *nomenklatural* authority over local staff members of the MOS. As in the local bureaus of the General Auditing Administration (GAA) and the State Statistical Bureau, the appointment and removal of top officials of the local bureaus must first be cleared with the MOS, which is in charge of professional leadership relations. Because its principal task is to perform administrative

---

8. For a discussion of the CDIC, see Discipline Inspection Commission of Heilongjiang Party Committee (1987).

monitoring, the MOS has staff members working in other government units. Although these officials are on the *nomenklatura* of the Ministry of Supervision, which implies that the ministry controls their payroll, their administrative expenditures are controlled by their resident units (SCGE 1989 [1988]).

Unlike the CDIC, however, the MOS and its local branches seem to be more dependent on the support and cooperation of the corresponding administrative apparatus of the government than on the superior units of the MOS. For example, the MOS requires approval from the premier or the vice premiers in order to initiate an investigation case (*li'an*) involving ministerial- or provincial-level officials; an investigation involving bureau-level officials requires approval from the top officials of the relevant ministries or provinces. Interestingly, the MOS is able to initiate investigation cases of officials at the division or county level on its own (Dai Qinxiang and Cai Yulong 1989: 61–63). Thus if the degree of vertical authority and the natural difficulties of clearly differentiating administrative from Party discipline are any indication, the CDIC should be a more powerful agency than the MOS; in all likelihood it is more active in handling important cases concerning the conduct of local cadres.[9]

Economic monitoring

The Chinese central economic bureaucracy was devastated during the Cultural Revolution. The number of officials working in central planning agencies, such as the SPC, was extremely small and for a number of years the Center stopped collecting vital economic statistics at regular and frequent intervals. Chinese leaders were keenly aware of the inadequacies of their planning capacity. Oksenberg (1982: 187), in a study based on interviews with Chinese officials, observes: "Many officials believed China really did not have a capacity to develop reliable Five-Year Plans. Indeed, without a complex econometric model of the economy, many Chinese planners questioned their ability to make accurate, alternative projections one year into the future based on differing assumptions and different policies."

In the 1980s the central government attempted to improve its economic control capabilities by strengthening, both institutionally and technically, the existing institutions as well as creating new ones. Three agencies that received such attention were the SPC, the SSB, and the GAA.

---

9. One such case concerns Ni Xiance, the governor of Jiangxi province between 1985 and 1986. Ni was removed from his position and stripped of his Party membership for, apparently, having protected smuggler(s) in exchange for sexual favors. The CDIC handled the case (see Chen Wenqing and Su Kai 1991: 241).

State Planning Commission (*Guojia jihua weiyuanhui*). Like other central agencies, the SPC was hard hit by the Great Leap Forward and the Cultural Revolution. During the Cultural Revolution the number of personnel in the SPC was sharply reduced, to sixteen in 1968 (Lieberthal and Oksenberg 1988: 70) and only fifty or so in 1971 (Lee 1987: 104). For a number of years, the SPC did not have reliable and regular economic statistics to conduct systematic and detailed economic planning. During the Great Leap Forward, the State Statistical Bureau lost control over the definition of statistical norms and over statistical collection to local authorities, which made comprehensive planning difficult. Because of ideological opposition to technical expertise, the SPC was slow in developing input–output tables for planning. By 1982, it had developed an 88-by-88 input–output table, which only covered Shanxi province (Zhang Sai 1987); in the energy sector, the SPC only had a partial input–output table by 1984 (Lieberthal and Oksenberg 1988: 67).[10] Because it was technically underdeveloped, the SPC had to rely more extensively on the expertise of other government agencies and was compelled to serve more coordination rather than planning functions.

Since the late 1970s, the central government has launched a major effort to fully rehabilitate the SPC. First, as already pointed out, there were some efforts to develop input–output tables to assist planning. Second, the Center began to staff the SPC to a more adequate level. In 1987 the SPC employed about 1,255 officials, which made it one of the biggest agencies in the central government (Wu Peilun 1990: 167).

Probably most important, the SPC has developed into a more specialized and thus more focused agency. More and more short-term production planning and coordination functions have been turned over to agencies such as the State Economic Commission and other line ministries. Its core activities began to revolve around medium- and long-term developmental issues and macroeconomic control.

Investment planning has become one of the central tasks of the SPC. Its principal roles include formulating long- and medium-term investment targets, coordinating different ministries or provinces in large-scale investment projects, approving investment quotas, screening project applications above the provincial or ministerial approval limits, and enforcing investment reduction efforts.

The SPC, unlike most line ministries, is a comprehensive agency. Its ability to coordinate the activities of different units stems from the fact that its bureaucratic rank is a half grade higher than that of the line ministries and the

---

10. In sharp contrast, the Gosplan, the SPC's counterpart in the former Soviet Union, had a 73-by-73 product table by 1959 and a 110-by-110 table by 1972 (Gregory and Stuart 1981: 135).

provinces. Since the early 1990s, the SPC has been divided into a number of bureaus, ten of which are directly involved in investment planning. These include the Bureau of Fixed-Asset Investment Planning (*Guding zichan touzi si*), the Bureau of Technical Renovation (*Jishu gaizao si*), the Bureau of Coordination and Monitoring of Key Projects (*Zhongdian jianshe xietiao jiandu si*), the Bureau of Foreign Capital Utilization (*Guowai zijin liyong si*), the Bureau of Long-Term Planning (*Changqi guihua si*), the Bureau of Comprehensive National Economic Planning (*Guomin jingji zonghe si*), the Bureau of Industrial Policies (*Chanye zhengce si*), the Comprehensive Fiscal and Monetary Bureau (*Caizheng jinrong zonghe si*), the Bureau of Economic Regulation (*Jingji tiaojie si*), and the Bureau of Regional Economies (*Diqu jingji si*) (see Zhou Hanrong 1991: 57–58).

The SPC has also set up its own information supply network, in addition to the SSB channel. It controls the State Information Center and operates an Investment Research Institute. In 1982 it established China International Engineering Investment Consultancy Company, which performs feasibility studies for the SPC. Its reports, which are prepared by over 100 experts from fifty economic sectors, contribute to the technical sophistication of SPC decisions.

In recent years, the SPC has also transformed itself from a passive agency in investment planning concerned mainly with screening and approval to an active one directly involved in sponsoring, financing, and organizing investment projects. In 1988 the SPC established investment companies in six sectors that specialize in organizing investment projects in line with central industrial policy guidelines. The SPC also uses these six investment companies to influence the investment orientation of the localities through fund contributions.

State Statistical Bureau (*Guojia tongji ju*). The State Statistical Bureau conducts performance checks by collecting routine economic data that can then be used to evaluate plan fulfillment and policy implementation. Thus one of the bureau's main missions is to detect deviations from central policy guidelines. In 1985, for example, the State Council issued a notice criticizing the bonus policies adopted by the Gansu Department of Labor, the Department of Finance, and the provincial branch of the People's Bank. The State Council issued this notice on the basis of information supplied by the SSB (State Council 1986 [1985]).

This monitoring function is known as "statistical auditing" (*tongji jiandu*), as opposed to statistical collection and processing, which are referred to as "statistical services" (*tongji fuwu*). In recent years, while attempting to improve

Table 4.2. *Central statistical personnel as a share of total SSB personnel,
selected years, and personnel reductions at different administrative levels of
the SSB system from 1965 to 1976 (percentage)*

	Mid-1960s	Mid-1970s	Early-1980s	Mid-1980s
Shares of central personnel	6.73	0.59	1.64	1.04
	Central	Provincial	Prefecture	County
Personnel reductions from 1965 to 1976	97	74	56	64

Sources: Dangdai Zhongguo de tongji shiye (1990), Wang Yifu (1986: 213),
Zhang Sai (1992).

the SSB's technical and institutional capabilities to collect more and better
data, Chinese policy makers have begun stressing the statistical auditing function of the SSB. Li Peng (1990) and Yao Yilin (1992a [1988]; 1992b [1990])
have repeatedly mentioned the need to strengthen the SSB to enable it to
check on the performance of government bureaus and their enterprises.

However, the attempt to augment the auditing function of the SSB has run
into a number of obstacles. For one thing, the SSB is rather low in rank among
government agencies. It is a bureau-level organization directly subordinate to
the State Council; as such, it has an administrative rank somewhere between
that of a ministry and that of a bureau within a ministry, and it cannot directly
issue instructions either to ministries or to provinces, which have the same
bureaucratic rank.[11] In contrast, the Central Statistical Administration in the
former Soviet Union was of ministerial rank and in 1987 it was elevated to the
rank of state committee, above the other ministries.

Also, the SSB has had a history of decentralized operations and administration since the Great Leap Forward. Before the reforms, the local SSB staff
were effectively controlled by the local governments, although their administrative and operational expenditures were funded by supplemental funding
directly from the Ministry of Finance.[12] As seen in table 4.2, personnel reductions have been greater at the upper end of the SSB system. Between 1965
and 1976 there was a 97 percent personnel reduction at the headquarters of
the SSB, whereas reductions at the provincial, prefectural, and county levels

11. Between 1970 and 1978, the SSB was subordinate to the SPC (*Dangdai Zhongguo de
tongji shiye* 1990: 76 and 88).
12. The SSB was abolished in 1967; its personnel were taken over by the State Planning
Commission. It was reestablished in 1970 (Wang Yifu 1986).

were 74 percent, 56 percent, and 64 percent respectively. With the concentration of personnel reductions at the central level during the Cultural Revolution, the system grew lopsided: the number of employees at the headquarters are now just a fraction of the entire system; in the mid-1960s, central SSB personnel accounted for 6.73 percent of the total personnel; by the mid-1970s, they only accounted for 0.59 percent.[13]

In the 1980s central policy makers began to centralize some of the SSB local operations in part to provide the SSB with a degree of institutional power to conduct statistical auditing. Statistical researchers have argued that administrative subordination to the local governments, while enabling the SSB to provide statistical services, makes it difficult to audit government units. In 1982 Sun Yefang, a deputy director of the SSB in the 1950s and a respected economist, proposed that the SSB be made an independent agency, under the Standing Committee of the National People's Congress, and that it be infused with a degree of disciplinary authority by operating in conjunction with (*guagou*) the CDIC (Gao Zhongsheng, Yang Meilian, Fei Jianjun, and Zhang Hua 1988).

Although Chinese policy makers have not adopted such radical institutional changes, they have attempted to reclaim some administrative and operational control over the local SSB branches. In 1981, for example, the State Council granted the SSB veto power over the appointment of the directors, deputy directors, and the principal statisticians of its local branches (Wang Yifu 1986). In addition, the State Council made the decision in 1984 to include statistical employees at or above the county level in the central *nomenklatura* and to fund operating and capital construction expenditures centrally (State Council 1988 [1984]: 163); by 1986, the SSB reported that most provinces had completed these personnel and budgetary transfers (Yue Wei 1988 [1986]). However, administrative expenditures (*xingzhengjingfei*) – for example, on employee salaries – have continued to be funded locally (Zhang Sai 1987). Thus local governments still appear to command a great deal of administrative authority over the operations of the local SSB branches.

These institutional changes were obviously designed to move the SSB toward a more vertical chain of command to attenuate local political interference and to facilitate the SSB's effort to audit provincial performance. It seems that the political status of the SSB is still quite a sensitive issue, as Zhang Sai (1989: 54) intimated when he referred to the need for the SSB to establish a "detached" (*chaotuo*) status. But the Chinese leadership seems to have decided to emphasize policy changes rather than any fundamental institutional changes. In 1988 and 1990 Yao Yilin twice stressed the need for

---

13. For more details, see *Dangdai Zhongguo de tongji shiye* (1990) and Wang Yifu (1986).

independent statistical reporting procedures, and he stated that the SSB should have exclusive control over data checking, as opposed to data collection, which is also performed by other agencies (Yao Yilin 1992a [1988]; 1992b [1990]). The SSB officials, encouraged by the central leaders, repeatedly called for an augmenting of the statistical auditing function of the SSB (Zhang Sai 1992 [1989]; Zheng Jiaheng 1992 [1989]).

General Auditing Administration (Shenji shu). The General Auditing Administration was established in 1983. The same rationale that supported assigning more auditing functions to the SSB justified the establishment of the GAA. Chinese policy makers realized early on the need to improve the government's monitoring and auditing capabilities as the central government relinquished direct control over economic and fiscal resources and as economic conflicts between the Center and the localities and between the government and enterprises sharpened, as Tian Jiyun, a vice premier at the time, revealed in his speech at its opening ceremony (1990 [1983]). Two specific areas of concern were assigned to the GAA: investment and fiscal activities undertaken by government agencies and firms. The GAA is used largely to check the implementation of central rules on investment funding.

At the time the GAA was founded, some thought it should have a vertical leadership relationship with its local bureaus, and in 1990 a similar proposal surfaced again. But policy makers countered that it was simply unrealistic for the local auditing bureaus to perform their duties without active policy and logistic support from local Party committees and governments. To grant some degree of operational independence from the potential units to be audited and to enhance its stature, policy makers placed the GAA directly under the leadership of the premier, and the local bureaus of the GAA were put directly under the leadership of the provincial governors (Li Peng 1990; Wang Bingqian 1990 [1983]).

The local GAA bureaus are subject to dual leadership. That is, they are subordinate to the GAA in Beijing and also to the local governments. The division of labor is such that the GAA in Beijing exercises professional leadership, which in this case means that its local bureaus take precedence over local governments in the relevant professional jurisdiction and that the GAA can overturn decisions by its local bureaus if there are conflicts between them (GAA 1986 [1985]). Although local governments exercise leadership relations, the appointment, removal, transfer, and any discipline measures aimed at the top officials of the GAA by local bureaus require prior approval from the central office; however, local governments have the prerogative to appoint other staff members, and local GAA payrolls are in the purview of local budgets.

Auditing responsibilities are divided according to administrative subordination. The local GAA bureaus audit local government agencies and those enterprises under the supervision of local governments; the GAA itself audits the central units. For those central units located in the provinces, the GAA has established direct branches (*paichu jigou*) in thirteen cities; their operational and payroll expenses are funded by the Ministry of Finance, and their investment and material allocation needs are met by the SPC (GAA 1986 [1985]). In addition, the GAA has set up resident offices in all central ministries; although the GAA has *nomenklatura* authority over these officials, control of their administrative expenditures is in the hands of their resident units (SCGE 1989 [1988]).

Central administrative control during the reform era

These central institution-building efforts have had a number of important effects since 1983. Several rounds of personnel changes have taken place and administrative procedures have come under greater – albeit indirect – central control.

Personnel changes during the post-Mao period

The large-scale personnel changes and reforms undertaken during the post-Mao era had three somewhat overlapping objectives: (1) to purge Cultural Revolution followers or beneficiaries, (2) to rehabilitate Cultural Revolution victims, and (3) to create a professional corps more suited to the tasks of economic modernization and reform.[14]

As soon as the "Gang of Four" fell from power, the central leadership began in earnest a large-scale program of purges and, after a slight time lag, political rehabilitations. In Shanghai – Jiang Qing's political stronghold – the leadership was shuffled as early as October 1976; in 1977 the leadership in about half of the Chinese provinces was changed.[15] Rehabilitation was a somewhat thornier issue, because the Cultural Revolution beneficiaries headed by Hua Guofeng were not totally willing to negate the legacies of the Cultural Revolution, and through their control over key personnel positions they were able to stall the rehabilitation process.[16] The push for political rehabilitations got a boost when

---

14. The following discussion draws heavily from the following sources in addition to the sources cited in the text: Burns (1987a, 1989), Lee (1991), Manion (1993), and Zhao Shenghui (1987).

15. According to Zhao Shenghui (1987: 420), in 1977, 125 leadership cells (*lingdao banzi*) were "adjusted" both at the central and local levels; 1,300 cadres were removed or appointed.

16. For a general treatment of the conflicts between Hua and the Cultural Revolution victims, see Chang (1981, 1982) and Schram (1984).

Hu Yaobang replaced Guo Yufeng as the head of the Party's Organization Department in December 1977, and some leaders who had served as provincial officials prior to the Cultural Revolution were returned to their old provinces to occupy the top positions.[17]

This first phase of personnel shuffling was completed in 1982, when, according to a DOO document, "unjust, false, and wrong" verdicts for more than three million cadres were reversed (DOO 1986d: 42). While rehabilitating Cultural Revolution victims had been a tactical move on the part of Deng Xiaoping and Hu Yaobang to erode the power and reputation of Hua Guofeng, as soon as this objective was achieved, Deng and his protégés faced a new problem: the intransigent resistance by the rehabilitated officials to the implementation of Deng's ambitious economic reform programs.[18] To carry out economic reforms they had to remove the very cadres they had just helped install to leadership positions. Thus began the second phase of personnel changes and reforms, which turned out to be far more tortuous than the first and was to continue throughout the 1980s.[19]

The more reformist-oriented central leadership applied a two-pronged strategy to achieve their objectives. One was to push for reforms that would result in a leaner and a more efficient bureaucracy; the other aimed at changing the fundamental composition of the leadership such that it would be more technically competent and more educated. These two aspects of the strategy relied on the same measures of implementation: a mandatory retirement age and the active recruitment and grooming of younger people for future leadership positions.

In fact, the central leadership recognized the need for personnel reforms quite early on. A conference on personnel work, convened by the DOO in September 1979, identified three major problems plaguing the Chinese bureaucratic system: the low quality of Chinese officials, their advanced age, and the inflated size and inefficiency of the bureaucracy. In three years, according to a plan drawn up at the conference, the number of provincial Party com-

17. These include Song Ping of Gansu, Qiao Xiaoguang of Guangxi, Liu Guangtao and Yang Yichen of Heilongjiang, Mao Zhiyong of Hunan, Xu Jiatun of Jiangsu, Tie Ying of Zhejiang, and Wang Xian of Shanxi.

18. An example of this sort of resistance is provided by Yang Yichen of Heilongjiang province. Yang, a Cultural Revolution victim, was appointed Party secretary in December 1977 and was removed in February 1983. Part of the reason for his removal was his delay in implementing the agricultural reforms. The Heilongjiang Party Committee, as pointed out by his successors, had intervened to suspend implementation of the household responsibility system in 1981 and 1982 and, stressing the special conditions in Heilongjiang, had limited reform to "poor and technologically backward" regions, despite the fact that such a system had been affirmed by the Center repeatedly in the early 1980s. See Zhang Xiangling (1989: 422–23).

19. For a detailed case study of personnel reforms at the provincial level (Zhejiang province), see Forster (1986).

mittee members was to drop from 30–40 to 7–13 and the number of vice governors from the low teens to 5–7 (Zhao Shenghui 1987: 425–26).

During 1981 and 1982 the second phase of personnel reforms was carried out within central government agencies; in 1983 this was extended to the provincial level. In November 1982 a working group under the Secretariat was set up to supervise the leadership selection process and, as an indication of the difficulties encountered in such a large-scale shuffling, 300 retired central officials were mobilized and dispatched to the provinces to assist in the implementation work (DOO 1986b: 187). The Center also issued a series of "hard" criteria for new leaders: one-third had to have a university education or equivalent, and the candidates had to be under the age of fifty-five (Central Committee 1986 [1982]).

In an evaluation of the 1983 reforms, the DOO expressed general satisfaction with the results, although, it noted, the age of top officials was still rather advanced (DOO 1986a: 210). The hard criteria laid out to guide the reforms leave little doubt that the Center was quite successful in changing the composition of the provincial leadership: the average age was reduced from 62.2 years to 55.5 years after the 1983 adjustment, and the percentage of officials with a university education jumped to 40 percent, compared with 20 percent before 1983 (Zhao Shenghui 1987: 446). After the major leadership shake-up in 1983, progress continued in reducing the age of the leadership and in increasing their educational level. Following a detailed statistical analysis of a select group of Chinese local officials, Li and Bachman (1989) concluded that as of the latter half of the 1980s the Chinese local leadership had undergone a technocratic transformation; current leaders were selected and promoted primarily on the basis of their educational and managerial credentials rather than exclusively on their ideological views.

In addition, there is little question that the scope of the personnel changes was massive. Figure 4.1 shows the average percentage of secondary provincial officials – deputy Party secretaries and vice governors – replaced and appointed every year during the 1976–92 period. Altogether, six peaks can be identified, in 1978, 1980, 1983, 1985, 1988, and then in 1990. As indicated earlier, the 1983 personnel adjustment was far-reaching; as shown in figure 4.1, almost 80 percent of the provincial officials were removed from office that year, and about 60 percent of the officials were newly appointed.

The second largest personnel adjustment took place in 1978, when more than 55 percent of the officials were either removed or appointed. The other three rounds, in 1985, 1988, and 1990, were less drastic; removals and appointments hovered between 25 to 30 percent. Figure 4.1 also suggests the constancy of such changes. Even in trough years, such as 1979, 1981, 1984, 1986, 1989, and 1991, between 5 and 10 percent of provincial personnel were

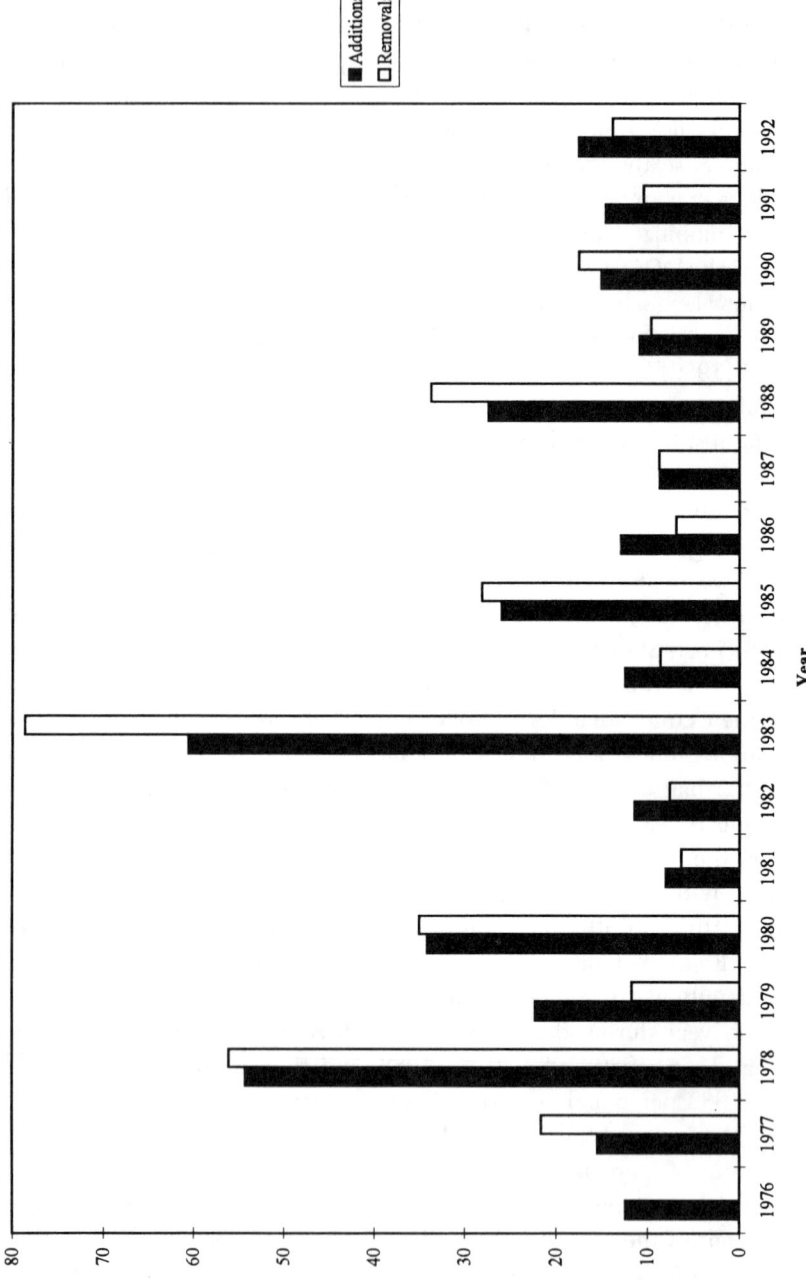

Figure 4.1 Removals and additions of secondary provincial officials as percentages of total officials, 1976–92

reshuffled. Similar patterns are seen in the appointments of provincial Party secretaries and governors. Figure 4.2 illustrates the number of secretary and governor appointments made between 1976 and 1992. The cycles of peak and trough years roughly coincide with the reshuffling at the level of deputy Party secretaries and vice governors, especially in 1980, 1983, 1985, and 1990. Again, the 1983 reshuffling was the most drastic; twenty-two governors were re-placed, while there were seven turnovers of Party secretaries.

Interestingly, the timing of the appointments of Party secretaries and gov-ernors appears to coincide over the years. In 1977 and in 1978, for example, the number of secretary and governor appointments was exactly the same. This should not be surprising given the fact that the same persons often held both posts in many provinces during the Cultural Revolution and in the late 1970s. Gradually, however, the number of appointments for the two positions began to diverge; in general, except for 1984, 1985, and 1991, more governors were appointed than Party secretaries. This is easily seen in figure 4.2: the lighter bar – representing governor appointments – tends to be taller than the darker bar. Furthermore, before 1986 the appointments for the two posts tended to correlate with each other systematically. That is, the peak and trough years for the two appointments tended to coincide. This began to change after 1986, when the two bars moved in different directions. This is an indication that the two appointments began to be treated separately from each other and that in the second half of the 1980s there was more independence between the two processes. This might have arisen from the efforts to separate Party functions from governmental functions under the leadership of Zhao Ziyang since 1987.

Personnel changes and central administrative control

The scope, manner, and frequency of personnel changes in the provinces are all indicative of the strong hand of the central government at work in engin-eering these far-reaching adjustments. For example, as figure 4.1 shows, personnel appointments and removals nearly perfectly coincided with each other in terms of timing. This suggests that each round of personnel changes would require a significant amount of coordination on the part of the central Party authorities so that new appointments would match the positions being vacated by the removals. Second, there seems to be a cycle of two to three years in duration. That is, the peak years – 1978, 1980, 1983, 1985, 1988, and 1990 – were either two or three years apart. This is prima facie evidence that provincial personnel adjustments have been a regular feature of China's *nomenklatura* system and may have become an institutionalized practice.

A number of scholars have argued that administrative localism has become

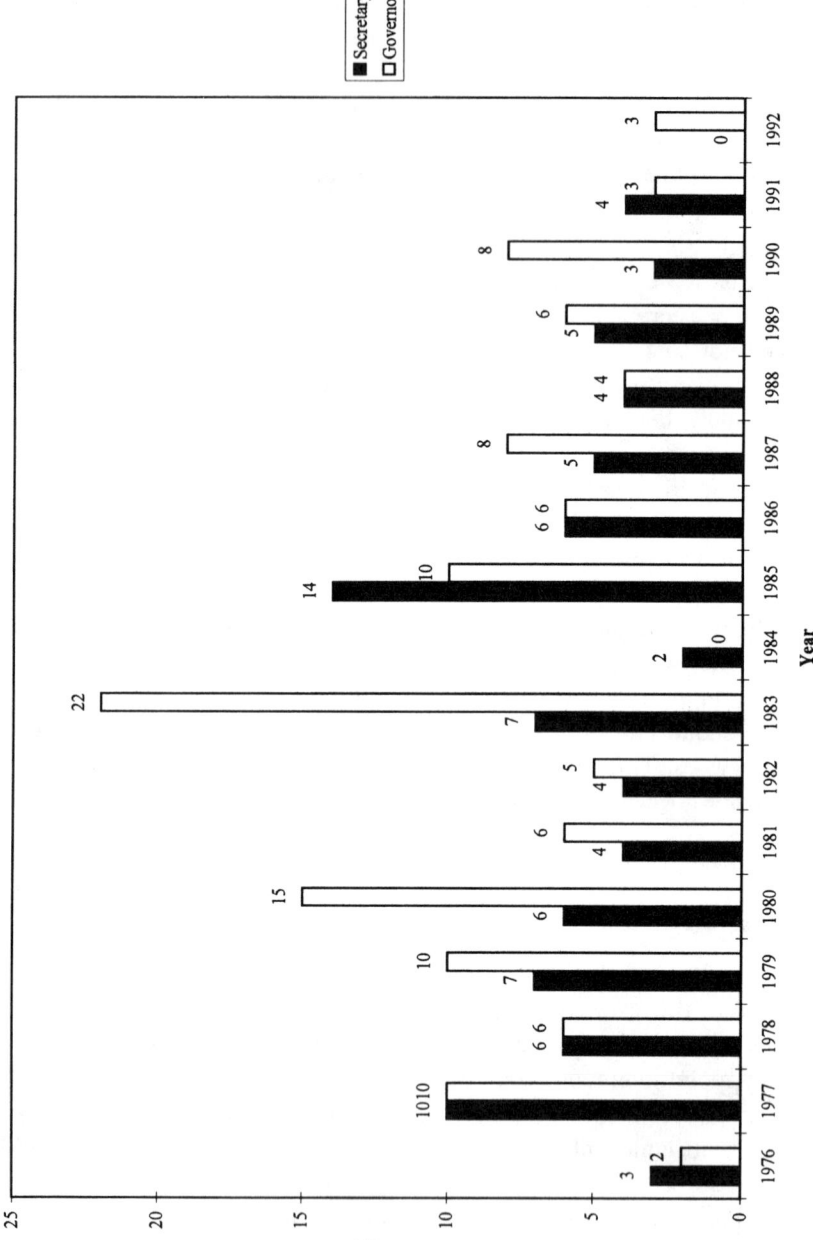

Figure 4.2 Appointments of provincial Party secretaries and governors, 1976–92

more entrenched in China during the reform era (Li and Bachman 1989; Zang 1991). Data on provincial personnel changes cast doubt on this view. If anything, central administrative control has increased and, to the extent that central administrative control and localism are symmetrical, the increase in central administrative control is equivalent to a decline in localism.

Evidence of this enhanced central control – and therefore the attenuation of localism – is found in three aspects of the administrative system. First is the degree of uniformity among Chinese provinces in a number of important administrative characteristics. All else being equal, the more uniform the Chinese provinces have become, the more likely that administrative control has become centralized. Second is the length of tenure; entrenched localism is associated with long tenures of local officials; conversely, shorter tenures are prima facie evidence that localism has abated. The third telling feature is any systematic correlation between the tenure length of Party officials and that of government officials: a high level of positive correlations suggests strong localism. This is based on the intuitive notion that administrative localism tends to become stronger when local officials are able to interact with one another over a long period of time.

The uniformity index – standard deviations – is applied to assess tenure length and the number of positions in local government and Party establishments. Uniformity increases if the standard deviations of these values decrease over time; 1983 can be taken as the watershed year because of the personnel changes effected in that year and because of personnel reforms introduced since 1983. Administrative uniformity is an indication of central control, because it suggests control occurs not by accident but by design and by supra-provincial coordination. The results appear in table 4.3.

With only one exception – the tenure of deputy Party secretaries – all indicators show that administrative characteristics have become more uniform across provinces since 1983 as compared with the period preceding 1983. For example, the average difference in terms of the number of positions in the local Party establishment was 4.71 before 1983; after 1983 the value was cut by more than one half, to 2.02. A similar decline took place in the number of local government positions, from 3.36 to 1.17. This finding suggests that since 1983 provincial Party and government institutions have become more similar in structure despite the inherent heterogeneity among the Chinese provinces and despite the increased economic and administrative autonomy accorded to the local governments during the reform era. Similarly, the decline in cross-sectional differences in length of tenure suggests that factors affecting tenure duration have become more systemwide and less idiosyncratic to particular provinces.

Table 4.3. *Standard deviation values of local Party and government positions and of tenure length, before and after 1983*

	Before 1983	After 1983
Positions		
Party	4.71	2.02
Government	3.36	1.17
Tenure		
Party secretaries	2.35	2.20
Governors	2.70	2.10
Deputy secretaries	1.21	1.34
Vice governors	1.49	1.40

Source: Database.

As in the case of the appointment of provincial-level officials, the positions of Party and government establishments (*bianzhi*) are centrally defined and enforced.[20] Streamlining of the structure of government institutions (*jigou gaige*), including the standardization of establishment positions, was part and parcel of the administrative reforms and has been a continuous process since the early 1980s. In 1979 the DOO and State Commission on Government Establishment (SCGE) issued a directive requiring local governments to stream-line ad hoc agencies and to reduce the intermediate administrative layers; in 1980 the Center froze government hirings across the board; and in 1981 the State Council reissued the nationally uniform code of establishment positions for provincial and subordinate government agencies. In 1983 the central Party authorities not only made large-scale personnel changes, but they completely redefined and stipulated the number (or a range) of local government agencies and their associated positions.

These measures have affected provincial Party and government establish-ments in three ways. First, the 1983 reforms led to a leaner bureaucracy, as shown in the drastic reduction in the average number of establishment posi-tions. Second, regional variations in the size of the bureaucracy decreased sharply, an indication that bureaucratic structures had become more similar across provinces. Third, the annual fluctuations in the size of the bureaucracy

---

20. The following discussion is based on the following sources: Central Committee and the State Council (1986 [1983]); DOO and Ministry of Labor and Personnel (1986 [1983]); State Council (1984 [1980]); and State Commission on Government Establishment (1990).

were smaller after 1983, an indication of increased bureaucratic stability. These three trends are shown in more detail in the appendix to this chapter.

Tenure length of provincial officials also confirms the impression that cadre appointments are still tightly controlled by the Center and that appointment procedures favor Party institutions in personnel decisions. The legally specified term of office for governors is five years; in reality, the term of office does not even approach that number. Only governors from three provinces, Beijing, Guizhou, and Neimenggu (Inner Mongolia), have approached five years; all other provinces have fallen far short. The average tenure length is slightly below four years. On average, since 1979 the tenure for Party secretaries has been only 3.44 years; for governors, it has been even shorter, around 2.85 years. Secondary officials have slightly longer tenures; Party officials, on average, have stayed in their offices for about 4.04 years; government officials for about 3.73 years. Chinese top provincial officials do not hold on to their posts as long as their Soviet counterparts. According to Bunce (1981: 149), the average tenure for first Party secretaries of the Soviet republics during the 1955–70 period was 7.59 years; for lower-level officials, however, the tenure was about 4 years.

Since 1983 there has not been a uniform trend in the changes in tenure. For top provincial officials, the average period increased; for secondary officials, there was no uniform trend. Before 1983 the average for Party secretaries was 3.34 years; after 1983 it was 3.52 years; for governors, it was three years before 1983 but 3.12 after 1983. The average tenure for secondary Party officials declined from 4.24 years before 1983 to 3.95 years after 1983; for secondary government officials, it rose from 3.74 years to 3.89. Both the small magnitude of these changes and the lack of a uniform direction suggest that over time changes in tenure length since 1983 have not been significant and, to the extent that administrative localism is associated with the prolonging of local tenure, administrative localism does not appear to have increased after 1983. Remember, too, that provincial personnel went through several rounds of large-scale adjustments; for that reason there are some a priori reasons to believe that the somewhat short tenure durations before 1983 were a result of rather extraordinary personnel adjustments associated with the central leaders' political objectives at the time.

Consider, now, the systematic correlations between the tenure of provincial Party officials and that of government officials. The hypothesis is that overlapping tenures between Party and government officials fosters administrative localism. This can happen in several ways. The network of connections becomes more entrenched when people work together and interact for a long period of time. Patronage or collusion tends to be stronger among people who are close for a long period of time than it is among people who interact for a shorter period of time; as joint tenures lengthen, local officials may come to share more common interests.

There are standard practices in China's bureaucratic system to curb this kind of administrative localism. One such practice is what is known as the *ganbu jiaoliu zhidu* (the cadre rotation system), whereby provincial (or sub-provincial) officials are routinely rotated to equivalent positions in other provinces. This practice forces the rotated officials to work with new officials and in new environments. Chinese leaders have often stressed the importance of this administrative practice to curb localism. As Chen Yun (1986 [1982]: 396) commented in 1982, "The rotation system is good. It is not good to have an official work in a locality for a long period of time because it gives rise to factionalism." More recently, Lu Feng (1991), the director of the DOO, gave three reasons to explain why cadre circulation should be made a standard administrative practice, one of which was to break up the local "network of connections."[21] Since the late 1970s, central Party authorities have stepped up the use of this practice; it is applied not only to intraprovincial rotations but also to interprovincial rotations (MOP 1991a: 25–31).

The structure of the data on provincial personnel allows us to analyze systematic correlations, if any, between the tenure length of government officials and that of Party officials. Positive correlations indicate that tenure durations for government and Party officials tend to be similar and that their services tend to overlap; long tenures of one are associated with long tenures of the other (or short tenures of Party officials are associated with short tenures of government officials). Negative correlations imply that tenure durations for government and Party officials are different from each other. That is, long tenures of one are associated with short tenures of another, or vice versa. The evidence for localism thus pertains to both the direction and the strength of the correlations between the tenure of Party and government officials. Administrative localism is obviously less severe when the correlations are negative because government and Party officials overlap to a lesser extent; positive correlations, on the other hand, are prima facie evidence for localism. Changes in localism can be assessed by examining changes in the strength of the correlations: Localism becomes weaker if correlations decline in amplitude; otherwise it means that localism has increased.

A simple statistical model can be used to determine whether administrative localism has increased or declined: The tenure of the government officials

---

21. The other two rationales are to gain work experience and to fill vacant positions.

Table 4.4. *Regression of tenure of government officials*

Dependent variable: $Tenure_{(gov)}$	Top officials	Secondary officials
Intercept	−1.16*	0.53*
	(0.376)	(0.287)
Time	0.30*	0.17*
	(0.035)	(0.031)
$Tenure_{(party)}$	0.64*	0.47
	(0.052)	(0.048)
$Tenure_{(party)} \times period_{(1983)}$	−0.52*	−0.17*
	(0.061)	(0.058)
Adjusted R^2	0.29	0.24
Number of observations	464	464
D-W statistic	1.54	2.02

Notes: Standard errors are in parentheses. Significance tests are two-tailed. Explanation of variables: $Tenure_{(gov)}$ is the tenure of government officials measured in years; $Tenure_{(party)}$ is the tenure of Party officials measured in years; $Period_{(1983)}$ is a period dummy where the 1976–82 period is coded 0 and the 1983–92 period is coded 1. Time is a trend variable where 1976 is 1, 1977 is 2, 1978 is 3, and so on.
* $p < 0.05$.
** $p < 0.1$.
Source: Database.

($Tenure_{(gov)}$) is regressed on the tenure of Party officials ($Tenure_{(party)}$). It is hypothesized that the tenure of government officials is related to the tenure of Party officials in the same province. To test if there were changes in localism, I create a dummy variable for the post-1983 period ($Period_{(1983)}$) and allow the tenure coefficient for Party officials to vary with it. A time variable is included to represent any effect arising from the time trend. Table 4.4 presents the results from the regression analysis from this model.

In interpreting these results, one should refrain from attributing causal relationships to the variables included in the model. Regression analysis itself cannot establish causality; causality is established by theory or prior studies. The purpose here is not to argue that the tenure of government officials depends on the tenure of the Party officials. Rather, it is to determine if administrative localism has increased or declined; thus the only concern is the direction and the strength of the relationships between different tenure variables.[22]

22. Another way of making the same point is that our dependent and independent variables are perfectly interchangeable. That is, it makes as much sense to treat the tenure of government officials as the dependent variable as it does to treat the tenure of Party officials as the dependent variable.

Because the a priori hypothesis here does not indicate how the independent variables are related to the dependent variable, a two-tail significance test is applied. All the coefficients are statistically significant, and the two models for top and secondary officials explain about 29 percent and 24 percent of the variance of the tenure of government officials. Consistent with the knowledge that the late 1970s and early 1980s were associated with large-scale personnel shifts, personnel stability increases with time. The time variable has a coefficient of 0.30 for top officials and 0.17 for secondary officials. This means that as time increases by one year, the tenure of government officials increases by about three months (30 percent of one year) for top officials and by about two months (i.e., 17 percent of one year) for secondary officials.

The evidence for administrative localism before 1983 is strong. The term $Tenure_{(party)}$ measures the effect of the tenure of Party officials on that of government officials before 1983. It is strongly positive; for top officials, the coefficient is 0.64 and for secondary officials, it is 0.47. The coefficient 0.64 means that on average if a Party official's tenure increases by one year, the tenure of a government official increases by about eight months (i.e., 64 percent of one year). Armed with this knowledge, one can calculate the typical amount of time government and Party officials overlapped in their respective posts. As noted earlier, the average tenure for a Party secretary was 3.34 years before 1983; suppose a governor assumed office in the same year, this implies that a Party secretary would work with the same governor for roughly about two out of 3.34 years.

The evidence for localism in the post-1983 period is a different matter altogether. The effect of the tenure of Party officials on that of government officials for the post-1983 period is given by: $Tenure_{(party)} + Tenure_{(party)} \times Period_{(1983)}$. This formula gives 0.12 (0.64 − 0.52) for top officials and 0.3 (0.47 − 0.17) for secondary officials. Thus the strength of the correlations between the tenure of Party officials and that of government officials has declined drastically since 1983. An increase of one year for a Party secretary would only increase the tenure of a governor by about 1.44 months instead of the eight months evident before 1983. A one-year increase for a secondary Party official is associated with an increase of four months for a secondary government official, instead of the six months before 1983. Both from the model and from the calculations done earlier, it is known that tenures for provincial officials have with time increased to some extent and thus the finding that the coefficient for the Party tenure is smaller after 1983 suggests, among other things, that Party secretaries and governors overlap to a lesser extent in the post-1983 period. And if our theory about the connections between joint tenures and patronage and the informal network of connections is correct, the fact that government and Party tenure durations have become more asymmetrical is evidence for declining localism and, by inference, for greater central control.

Conclusion

The reform era has witnessed a number of important institutional developments in the areas of personnel management and administrative and economic monitorings that, on balance, have given the Center a greater degree of control. Chinese central authorities have retained a firm grip over the vital aspects of personnel allocations: selection, promotion, and removal. They have been able to do so for two reasons. One is that the Party's principle of management stresses ideological conformity and gives the Chinese Communist Party dominant procedural control over appointment decisions. For example, the cadre evaluation process, although not necessarily always able to select the best people in a technical sense, weeds out those with questionable backgrounds by placing a premium on political performance. The process also ensures a continuous role for the DOO in making personnel adjustments.

The second reason is that cadre management is centralized. Even under the one-level downward management system, the reach of the Center is both extensive and deep. Not only does the Center directly control the top ministerial and provincial officials, but it retains appointment authority over secondary officials who preside over vital functional units, such as the provincial bureaus of the DOO and MOP. Furthermore, it retains veto power over the appointment of bureau-level officials and aggressively collects data and develops reporting procedures about those appointment decisions it no longer controls directly. This selective and strategic approach is bound to enhance central administrative control over the localities because it reduces the number of people the Center has to pay attention to while it sharpens the policy attention that the Center gives to those officials occupying strategic positions.

Is the Chinese system of administrative monitoring effective? Although there is no way to answer this question definitively, it is clear that a major institution-building effort to improve administrative monitoring has been under way. This effort includes both the establishment of new institutions or the resurrection of old institutions, such as the GAA and the MOS, and the strengthening of existing institutions (most notably, the SSB) and the systematized reporting requirements and procedures. The latest attempt to assign some information-collection responsibilities to the provincial general offices is also part of this effort. Although these measures may not be sufficient to make the monitoring system effective in an absolute sense, they have helped improve the central government's ability to collect information, as a number of scholars have pointed out (Halpern 1992; Naughton 1992a).[23] These institutional developments should lead to a decline in administrative localism. This conclusion is consistent with evidence indicating increased uniformity in a number of critical administrative characteristics among provinces and in the apparent attenuation of local patronage ties and the network of connections. By and large, the tenure of provincial officials and the number of positions of the provincial Party and government establishments have become more similar across provinces.

The findings here raise a significant question about how to assess the power of the central government during the reform era. Although the question warrants far more systematic attention than it can be given here, two broad points should be mentioned. First, although administrative localism at the provincial level has clearly declined, it is quite plausible that administrative localism at the levels of prefectures and counties has increased, if only through a "generational succession." Between 1949 and the 1980s the subprovincial Party leadership throughout the south and southwest was dominated by former PLA officers born in Shanxi, Shaanxi, Henan, Hebei, and Shandong. In the 1980s their replacements rose mainly through local ranks.[24] The implication of this development, however, is the growing importance of the provincial-level appointments as an integrative mechanism. Second, note that fiscal and economic decentralization has taken place in the context of a continued central hold over cadre appointment and of some improvement in the Center's administrative capabilities. If these elements are overlooked, one is likely to exaggerate the power of the local officials and their ability to act independently of the wishes of the central government.[25]

Of course, the improvement in administrative capabilities is fraught with problems. Probably the most significant factor inhibiting the effectiveness of administrative monitoring in the Chinese system is that most information

---

23. My description concentrates on the formal side of the Chinese administrative system. Although it is quite legitimate to criticize this approach as failing to describe "how the Chinese system really works," it is also important to recognize that topics such as personnel control, evaluation, and internal information channels remain the most secretive aspects of the Chinese bureaucracy. In general, outsiders do not have access to documents that address specific persons, issues, or events. The most we can get is information on procedures and processes. In addition, I argue that focusing on the formal and institutional features of the system enables us to form stable expectations about behavior, a critical element in any social science modeling effort.

24. I owe this observation to Michel Oksenberg.

25. Naughton (1992b) makes a similar point in discussing investment and macroeconomic controls in the 1980s.

channels and specialized agencies perform, in essence, a self-monitoring function. As an arm of the local governments, the local monitoring units probably have few incentives to monitor the behavior of local governments aggressively, given their shared interests. In addition, there is a rank difference between those doing the monitoring and those being monitored. The heads of the local branches of the CDIC, MOS, GAA, and SSB are equivalent to or lower in bureaucratic rank than the heads of the local governments or their subordinate bureaus. This rank and administrative subordination prevents efficient parallel monitoring. The Chinese themselves clearly recognize this problem. Li Peng (1990: 13–14) stressed the need to appoint high-ranking auditors in the GAA; otherwise "they would ignore you" (*renjia bu mai chang*). The same considerations have led the SSB to try to upgrade its local branches from division-level to bureau-level organizations (Wang Yifu 1986: 56–64).

What has prevented the Center from creating an administrative monitoring system completely independent of the localities? In part, the answer lies in the fact that there may be mechanisms in the Chinese system that constrain a full-blown divergence of interests between the Center and the localities. There is a systematic relationship between a divergence of interests and the need for objective monitoring. The more divergent the interests are, the greater the need for monitoring. Indeed, the recognition of this relationship justified strengthening the SSB as a monitoring agency. Zhang Sai (1992 [1989]: 294), the current SSB director, makes the case for statistical auditing functions in the following way,

[Because of the economic reforms], the contradictions and conflicts between individual, collective, and state interests, between local, departmental, and state interests, between partial interests and the interests of the whole, and between current interests and long-term interests have become very complex and even quite sharp. Therefore it is inevitable that in certain regions, bureaus, and units there is a tendency to pursue self-interest at the expense of the interests of the state and to adopt a "when you have policies, I have counter-policies" stance. If this tendency is not checked immediately, microeconomic operations will divert from the trajectories of the macroeconomic policies and there will be chaos in the national economy.

The nature of the appointment system is the key to central control. So far, I have treated cadre management and administrative monitoring as two more or less separate processes. In reality, the two are closely linked. The centralized and Party-dominated cadre management process may have alleviated some of the problems associated with self-monitoring to the extent that the process is successful in weeding out those candidates who may pursue self-interests excessively. In other words, the cadre management system may have narrowed, to some extent, the divergence of interests between the central authorities and their local officials. The appointment system performs ex ante monitoring functions. That is to say, when detailed, micro-level supervision of specific tasks is difficult, it pays to direct supervisory attention to the persons who perform the tasks. Personnel selection and supervision act as a filtering process: reliable and loyal cadres are chosen, and these cadres take the interests of the Center seriously, even when they are left unsupervised in their job performance. Internalized norms, as Manion (1993) argues, reduce the demand for elaborate external monitoring and control.

APPENDIX

The drastic reduction in the size of the bureaucracy occurred in 1983, when the number of Party establishment positions declined from about twenty to twelve, the number of government establishment positions from thirteen to six. Bureaucratic stability, as measured by the annual fluctuations in the size of bureaucracy, has also increased since 1983. The number of positions fluctuated within a much narrower band on an annual basis after 1982. The biggest fluctuation, in the number of positions on the Party committees, was from 1988 to 1989 and from 1989 to 1990. The number increased from about eleven in 1988 to fourteen in 1989, then back to eleven in 1990; the lines between 1983 and 1992 are relatively flat in comparison with the previous period. Figure A4.1 demonstrates these two developments, bureaucratic streamlining and stability.

Enhanced central control is also shown by the reduced variations in bureaucratic size across provinces. Similar bureaucratic structures across provinces do not occur by accident but by supraprovincial coordination. Thus increasing similarities are a sign of increasing central control. This is shown in figure A4.2, which records coefficients of variation of Party and government establishment positions across provinces. Although there have been fluctuations, the predominant trend is a gradual decline.

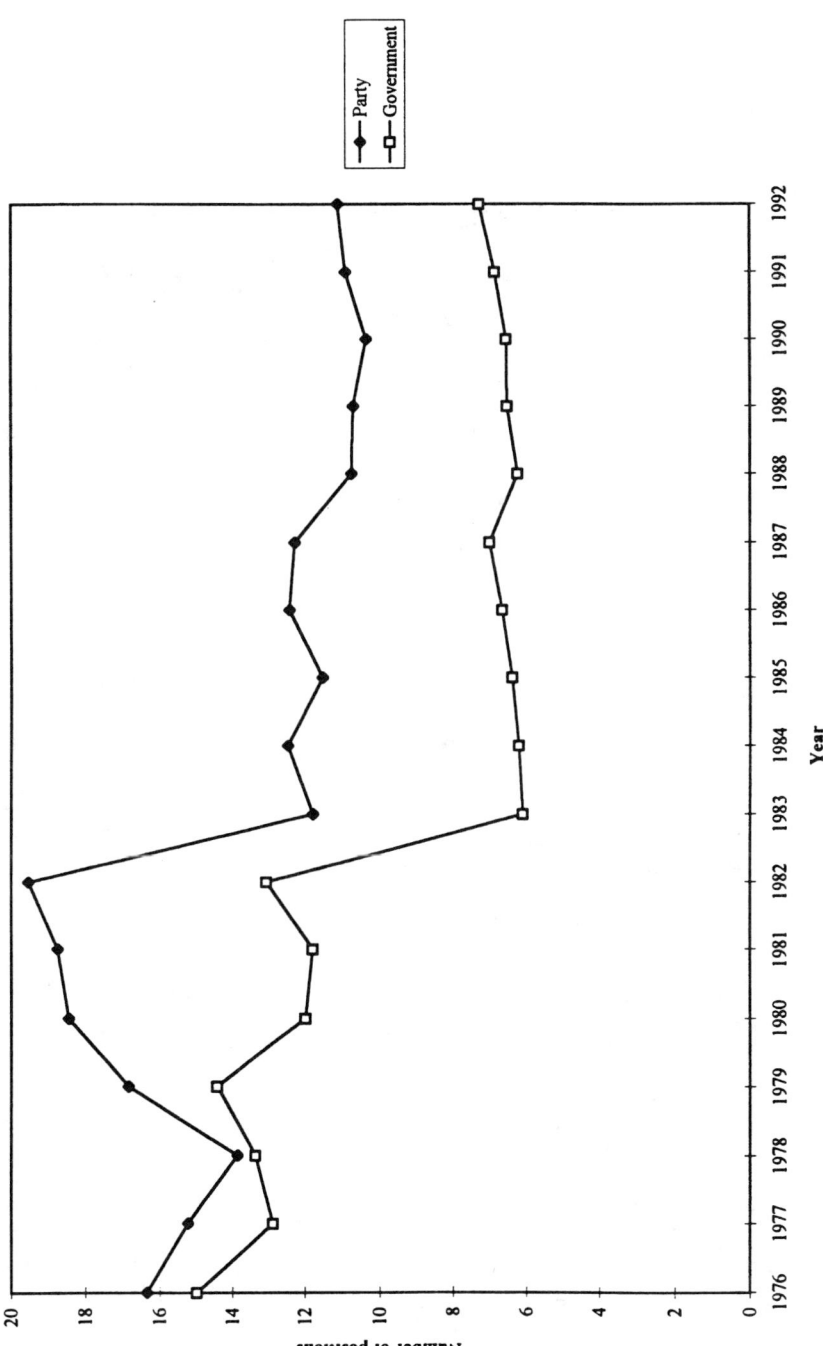

Figure A4.1 Number of positions of Party and government establishments, 1976–92. *Source:* Database

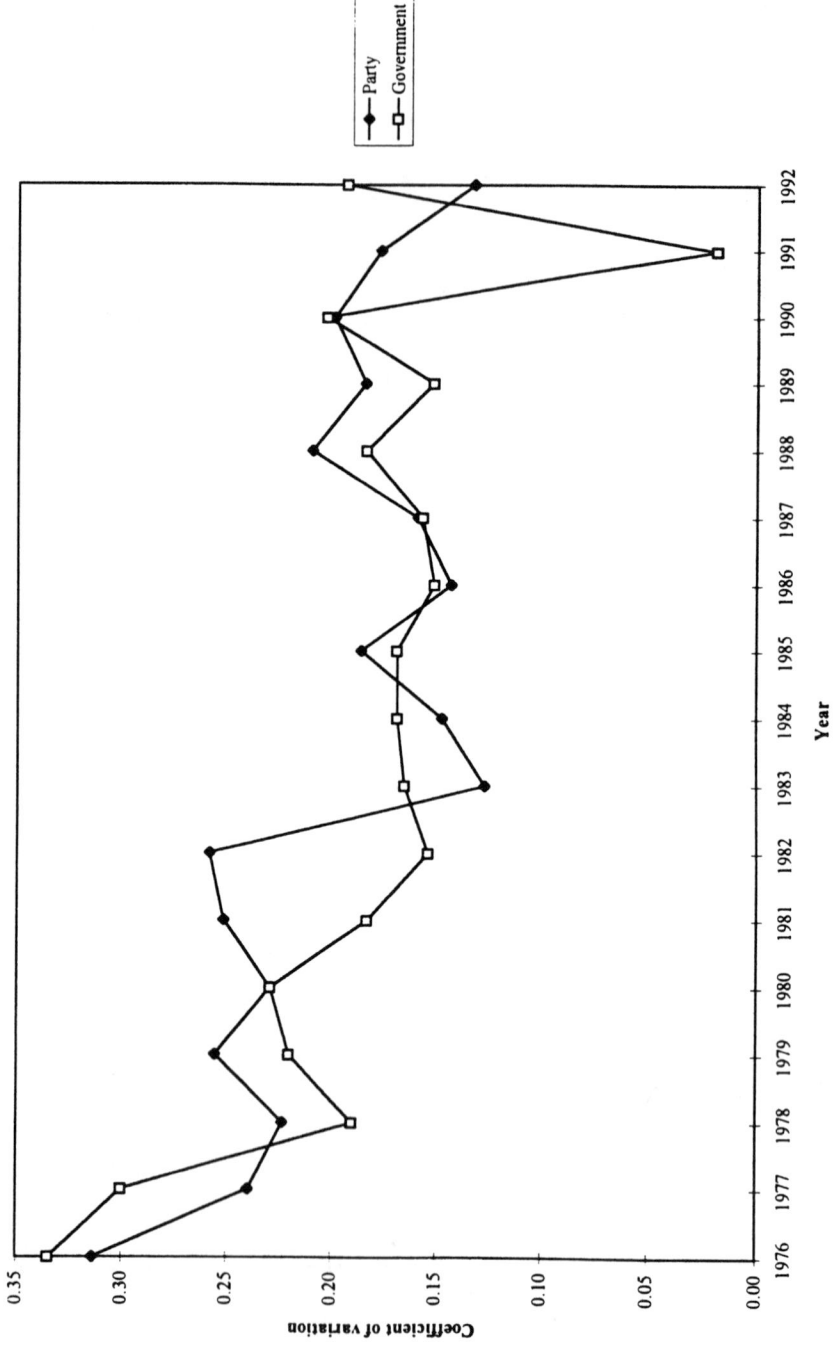

Figure A4.2 Coefficients of variation for the Party and government establishment positions, 1976–92. *Source:* Database

Part II

Macroeconomic policy developments during the reform era

5

Excess investment demand and austerity policies

During the reform period, Chinese economic policy makers focused their attention on two investment concerns: the inflationary consequences of China's runaway investment, and the effect of an expanding investment volume on the country's industrial structure. This chapter examines the common origin of these two policy concerns – excess investment demand in the Chinese economy – and the austerity policies designed to contain that demand.

Investment demand is said to be in excess when the demand for investment projects by firms or their supervisory agencies constantly exceeds the level permitted by existing investment resources, such as capital, labor, land, and foreign exchange. The concept of excess investment implies that the demand for investment projects and the supply of investment resources tend to be in a permanent disequilibrium.[1] As explained in chapter 1, inflation in centrally planned economies is often a consequence of excess investment demand when such demand is combined with lax macroeconomic control; conversely, austerity policies in all instances are aimed at curbing excess investment demand.

Excess investment demand in China

The excess demand hypothesis is more easily inferred than empirically demonstrated, in part because of the lack of a well-developed investment theory.[2] Most econometric approaches take for granted the existence of excess demand and build that assumption into the model specification to test some other

1. There is some controversy in the economic literature as to the sources of price inelasticity. One school of thought holds that prices are inelastic because they are set below the market-clearing level and are rigid; the other contends that firms in CPEs simply are not sensitive to price signals (Zhang Jun 1991). Both views are consistent with a finding of this study, namely, that investment demand is elastic with respect to other indicators such as bureaucratic commands.

2. This is especially true if the objective is to demonstrate economy-wide disequilibrium. As Kemme (1989: 87) notes, "The evidence of chronic excess demand at the aggregate level presented by adherents of the model is limited and indirect."

propositions. This study is no different; yet I believe that some description of excess demand, even if somewhat simple and indirect, coupled with a discussion of the reasons for excess demand, can make the hypothesis more plausible.

Several indices can be used as prima facie evidence for the existence of excess investment demand. The first approximate measure is the unfinished investment capacity; it refers to the share of investment resources tied up in unfinished (and therefore nonproductive) investment projects. Two considerations underlie the rationale that this is an approximate measure of excess investment demand. First, as pointed out earlier, CPE firms are interested in project commissioning more than project completion. Thus the time lag between project inception and project completion is typically long. Second, planning officials often use the unfinished capacity rate as a rough gauge of whether investment is overheating. One of the effects of the maximal strategy described above is an elongation of the gestation period and a delay in the commissioning of new projects on account of the dispersal of investment resources. Unfinished investment projects draw resources away from purposes that are either economically or socially productive, such as current production and wages. Thus unfinished investment exacerbates shortage and, after an implicit threshold is reached, invites decisive actions from central policy makers to embark upon retrenchment.[3]

Figure 5.1 presents the unfinished investments as a share of total investments and the net material product. Clearly, unfinished investments account for a sizable proportion of China's economic activities. In 1976, the highest year in the series, 41 percent of that year's investment and about 6 percent of the country's net output went into unfinished projects, projects that neither formed a part of the country's capital stock nor a part of its consumption.[4] By comparison, excess demand in the former Soviet Union was less extreme. The highest ratio, in relation to total investment, was 14.1, and the average figure for the 1950–83 period was 5.97 (Harrison 1985), which was far lower than the ratios of 27.3 and the 25.1 in China for the periods 1950–82 and 1976–90, respectively.

Alternatively, excess investment demand can be shown by tracking the peaks and troughs of unfinished investment over the years. Scholars working on comparative economics have long proposed an investment cycle hypothesis (Bauer 1978; Winiecki 1982; Grosfeld 1987; Imai 1994). According to this

---

3. For a fuller discussion, see Harrison (1985).

4. Historically the highest ratio was in 1968, when unfinished projects claimed 54.1 percent of that year's investments (Zhou Hanrong 1991: table 5–3–2, 1067).

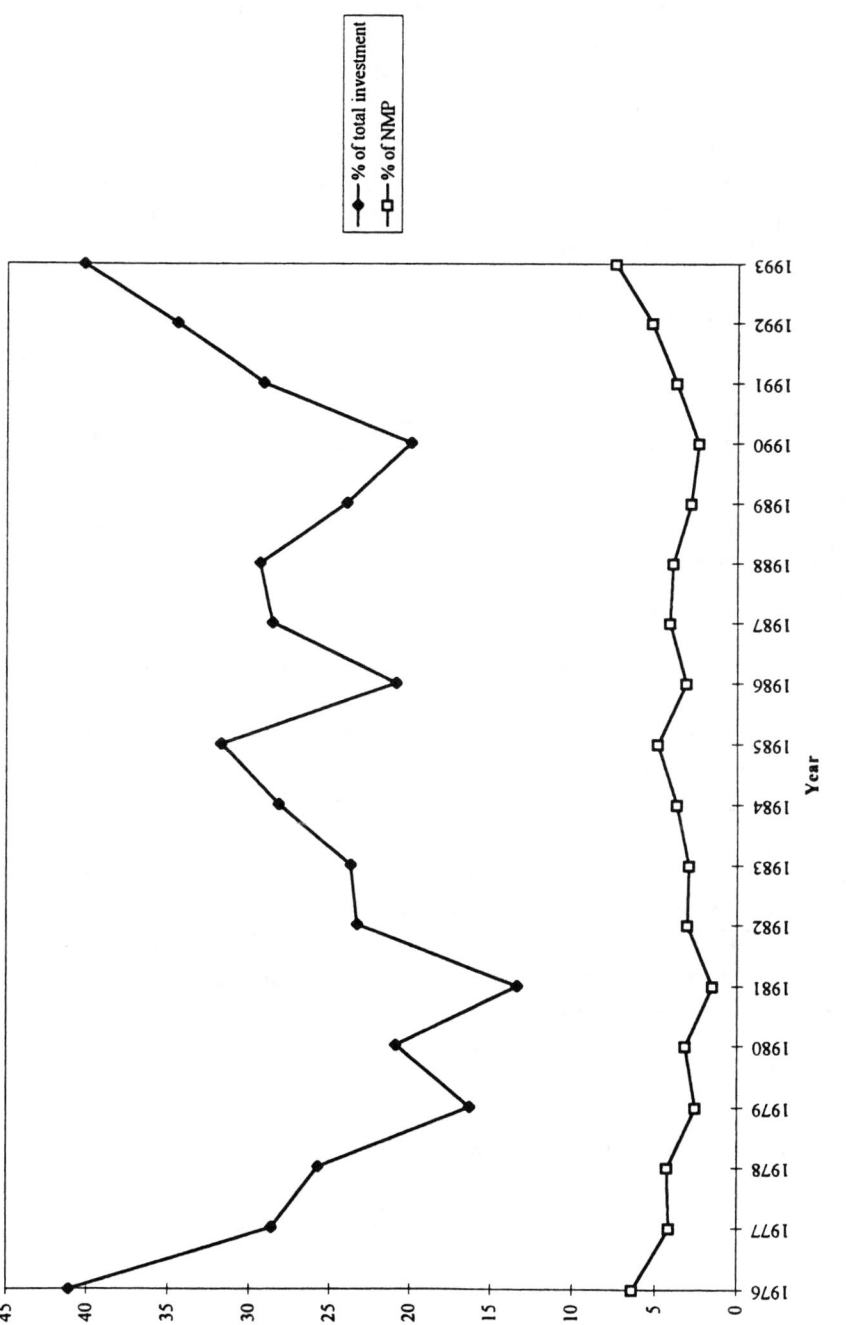

Figure 5.1 Unfinished investments as a percentage of total capital construction investments and net material product, 1976–93.
Source: Based on figures published in SSB (1993b, 1994)

hypothesis, investment fluctuates in a clearly cyclical manner; the reason is that planners react to investment performance retrospectively. When a set of shortage indicators, such as the supply and demand situation for consumer goods and labor markets or trade balances, reaches a certain threshold on account of overheated investment, planners will take action to reduce the annual investment commitments. In particular, planners will attempt to reduce or even prohibit altogether the initiation of new projects in order to mobilize resources to finish the existing projects. During the next period, planners will relax some of the screening and approval restrictions as the macroeconomic situation improves, ushering in another round of high investment growth. Thus, investment demand is less excessive in the first period than in the second.

Figure 5.1 also shows the cyclical nature of Chinese investment performance since the mid-1970s. All the trough years – 1979, 1981, 1983, 1986, 1989, and 1990 – were years when the central government pursued a restrictive investment policy; the peak years, on the other hand, coincided with a more reflationary policy.[5] The difference between the peak and trough periods is roughly equivalent to the impact of administrative restrictions on investment demand.

Another way to identify the existence and the significance of excess demand in the Chinese economy is to compare a number of investment characteristics with other economies in which the causes of excess investment demand are presumed to be absent. This, at best, is an imprecise measure because the comparison is not adequately controlled; yet persistent and sizable differences do indicate the effect of systemic features.

Table 5.1 shows investment characteristics in a number of CPEs compared with those in some market economies. In all the CPEs, China included, investment as a share of GDP is higher, sometimes significantly so, than the equivalent statistic in the market economies. Columns two and three show the GDP growth rates in relation to the investment growth rates. A comparison of the two statistics roughly indicates the degree of capital investment dependency of economic growth. In the case of the market economies, the ratios between investment and GDP growth rates are uniformly lower than those for the CPEs, as demonstrated by column four. Investment and economic growth have roughly a one-to-one relationship in the market economies, whereas in the CPEs they have a two-to-one relationship. Significantly for our purpose,

---

5. The year 1976 was probably an exception. The runaway character of investment growth for that year resulted from the political and bureaucratic chaos prevailing at the time.

Table 5.1. *Investment characteristics of selected countries, selected years*
(percentage)

Country	(1) Investment shares of GDP 1980	1988	(2) GDP Growth 1950–79	(3) Investment Growth	(4) Ratios (3)/(2)
CPEs					
China	**24**	**32**	**6.65**[a]	**15.96**[b]	**2.40**
Soviet Union	30	30	4.95	8.02	1.62
East Germany	24	27	3.77	8.52	2.26
Hungary	29	21	3.64	8.85	2.43
Poland	25	23	4.12	9.70	2.35
Market economies					
West Germany	23	20	4.85	5.69	1.17
Italy	24	22	4.92	4.79	0.97
Netherlands	21	22	4.58	5.10	1.11
United States	17	17	—	—	—
India	24	22	—	—	—

[a] Net Material Product for the 1953–79 period.
[b] The 1953–79 period.
Sources: Adapted and calculated from Kornai (1992: tables 9–1 and 9–2, 166 and 168). Chinese NMP growth is calculated from SSB (1991c: table 7–1, 34). Investment growth is calculated from Zhou Hanrong (1991: table 5–1–2, 1030). All the calculations are deflated by the consumer price index.

China has the next highest ratio (2.40) after Hungary, compared with every other country in the table.

It should be noted that the above figures denote realized or ex post investment characteristics and therefore are an imprecise measure of notional or ex ante demand, which the concept of excess demand tries to capture. In addition, there are two cross-cutting statistical biases, which, without any knowledge of their magnitudes, make a straightforward substantive interpretation difficult. First, in the market economies capital utilization is by and large more efficient than it is in nonmarket economies. The main impediment to an efficient utilization of capital in a nonmarket economy is a low marginal substitution rate between capital and labor. This leads to a lower level of output than otherwise possible with an additional unit of capital deployment. Thus a higher investment/GDP ratio may simply reflect inefficient capital utilization rather than investment hunger, as posited by the excess-demand hypothesis.

The second bias, however, cuts the other way. China, compared with almost all the other countries in the table, is abundant in labor in relation to capital. Thus China's capital-prone economic growth pattern across a number of indices suggests an inefficient pricing of capital or the presence of noneconomic investment motives. Both, of course, are completely compatible with and, indeed they make plausible, the excess-demand hypothesis.

The logic of excess investment demand in CPEs

Although economists debate whether there is chronic excess demand for consumer goods in CPEs, the consensus is quite solid that such is the case for the investment sector (Grosfeld 1989: 361).[6] The causes of excess investment demand fall into two distinct categories. One has to do with firms' positive incentives for bidding or claiming investment resources, the other with negative incentives for not doing so. Both sets of incentives need to be discussed in order to demonstrate that excess investment demand is not only a function of the systemic features of CPEs but is also unique to CPEs.

The first cause pertains to the motives and actions of central policy makers that give rise to insatiable investment demand in CPEs. One such motive is ideological in nature. Leaders of socialist countries often embark upon a full mobilization of resources – via an artificial depression of rural income and other compulsory savings schemes – to achieve, in short order, economic progress in general and industrialization in particular. This economic strategy, known as a "forced-growth" strategy, is attributed to their desires to catch up with the developed countries and to use economic performance to demonstrate the superiority of the socialist system.

It has also been suggested that central decision makers want to use the investment drive to overcome information problems in the CPEs. According to this argument, CPEs are plagued by an asymmetrical distribution of information, since planners typically have less information than the lower-level agents, bureaucrats, and managers about the latter's capabilities to fulfill plans.[7]

---

6. See Kemme (1989) for a review of these controversies.

7. Various reasons are given for the existence of the asymmetrical distribution of information. One, as argued by Hayek (1974), lies essentially in the nature of economic information itself. Economic information is inherently complex; consumer preferences, for example, are atomistic and unique to "circumstances of place and time" and, above all, are ever changing. On the production side, the same problem arises from the heterogeneity of products and production processes. Thus central economic bureaucrats are unable to command more accurate information than economic agents. Another argument points to the nature of bureaucracy. Bureaucracy, Assar Lindbeck (1971: 51–52) notes, consists of a hierarchy of several administrative layers; losses and distortions of information are inevitable in the filtering process. Informational asymmetry is also caused by incentives that lead lower-level agents not to supply truthful information. Because the assignment of future targets feeds on the information conveyed in the form of current performance, lower-level bureaucrats and managers have an incentive deliberately to underperform. This is a classic problem in socialist planning. See Berliner (1957); for a more recent application, see Gorlin (1985).

"There must be something hidden, [the planners] reason, and pressure will compel it to emerge" (Nove 1986: 97). In the former Soviet Union, taut investment planning – deliberately overauthorizing investment projects – amounted to an administratively convenient way to uncover hidden and potentially new reserves that would otherwise remain untapped, since it forced local officials to improvise and utilize their own resources (Gregory 1990: 107).

Investment drives are by no means confined to central policy makers, as many comparative economists point out. Although ideological motives for investment expansion have declined over time and informational considerations may vary across CPEs, a more sustained cause for excess investment demand in CPEs lies in the incentive structures facing the lower-level agents. Three incentives, in particular, are said to be responsible for investment drives. One is simply "empire-building" – the desire to enlarge the size of the firm to capture the prestige and the financial rewards that are associated with an enhanced organizational status. In the former Soviet Union and in China, a larger firm belongs to a higher level of *nomenklatura* than a smaller firm, and in general it enjoys higher priority in the allocation of resources (on the former Soviet Union, see Gregory 1990: 104–6; on China, see Zheng Hongliang 1992).

The second incentive is inherent in the planning process. In a typical CPE, managerial performance is evaluated as well as rewarded in terms of plan fulfillment, a fact that shapes managerial objectives profoundly. Managers strive to maximize the ease with which the plan targets can be fulfilled. Two strategies are available. One, as mentioned before, mainly aims at attaining easy targets from planners, often via deliberately understating one's productive capacity to influence target-setting. The other strategy is to maximize one's productive capacity in relation to the assigned plan targets. The second strategy requires investment, and investment viewed in this sense is equivalent to building up a buffer stock.[8] In extensive interviews, Soviet economic officials have attributed investment overbidding mainly to the expectation that plan targets would be ratcheted up annually (Gregory 1990: 106).

Concerns over supply security are an additional incentive to expand investment, in response not to the formal operation of the planning process but to some of its by-products. Central planning, as many comparative economists

---

8. Obviously some combination of the two strategies is a rational course of action for managers. If planners can instantaneously adjust to the increased productive capacity by ratcheting up plan targets, there is no net gain with the second strategy. Interestingly, Polish economist Bartlomiej Kaminski has argued that the second strategy is used to enhance the effectiveness of the first one. Investment, according to this logic, has the effect of changing constantly the labor/capital ratios of the firm. These changes, in turn, make it more difficult for planners to determine the "true" production possibility. "The paradox," he remarks, "is that stagnation makes the task of central planning easier because central planners are more likely to overcome information indeterminacy when the productive structure of the economy is stable" (1991: 85).

have pointed out, often fails to allocate goods consistent with the firms' requests; either the wrong goods are assigned, or the requested goods are simply not supplied. This supply uncertainty gives rise to a strong incentive to engage in backward integration, that is, to invest in plants and facilities to produce inputs for the production of final goods.[9]

Although some of the aforementioned causes can be said to be unique to CPEs (especially overauthorizing investment as an informational strategy and overbidding to achieve the ease of target assignments), others are not. For example, the wish to catch up with developed countries is quite common among developing and late-industrializing countries, irrespective of the nature of their economic systems. The belief that capital formation was the key to economic development in the 1950s and 1960s was then supported by the powerful voices of the multinational aid agencies.[10] Nor is bureaucratic empire-building necessarily unique to CPEs; Parkinson's law was invented in and applies with equal force to capitalist countries.

The unique existence of excess investment demand in CPEs depends not so much on the presence of the aforesaid positive incentives as on the absence of a set of negative incentives that would act as self-enforcing constraints on investment demand in a typical market economy. There are two kinds of negative incentives. One consists of the incidence of costs and benefits associated with investment activities; the other consists of financial constraints.

In a typical CPE, there is a fundamental asymmetry in the incidence of costs and benefits associated with undertaking investment activities. Benefits – enhanced reputation and higher financial rewards – accrue to the investors either exclusively or proportionately in relation to investment volume; investment costs, on the other hand, are borne by the society at large, as Kornai (1992: 163) has noted: "Expansion drive is a fact of life for the bureaucracy. And because this system has only bureaucrats and no real owners, there is an almost total lack of internal, self-imposed restraint that might resist this drive."

This situation is analogous to the presence of "negative externalities" in market economies, and the consequences are similar: the costs of the affected

---

9. The investment expansion motives for the subnational administrative hierarchy are discussed extensively in Bauer (1978), Gregory (1990), and Harrison (1985).

10. A report from the United Nations (1984 [1960]: 219) declared: "If any one scarce factor associated with underdevelopment should be singled out, it would be capital. . . . [Entrepreneurship and training of workers and public administrators] are seldom possible without some increase in the stock of capital. Therefore capital accumulation may very well be regarded as the core process by which all other aspects of growth are made possible." Also see Wade (1990) for a discussion of the emphasis on capital formation placed by Korean and Taiwanese leaders. For an argument as to why late industrializing countries should stress capital accumulation, see Gerschenkron (1984 [1962]).

activities are lower than is socially optimal, and therefore the incentives to undertake these activities are stronger than when the external costs are taken into account.

The second characteristic that may distinguish a CPE firm from its market counterpart is the budgetary environment in which it operates. Socialist firms are said to face "soft-budget constraints," which refer to bureaucratic readiness to provide financial assistance and, ultimately, to prevent bankruptcy.[11] In essence, soft-budget constraints imply zero risks for the investment activities undertaken by a CPE firm and are the second reason why restraint on investment demand is not self-enforcing in CPEs.[12] Grosfeld (1989: 364) makes the following observation: "Softness of the budget means that there is no danger of a forced exit. Even if enterprises have to repay credits (which is not always necessary) insolvency is not a real threat; they can always rely on subsidies, price adjustments, tax facilities, and so on."

The logic of excess investment demand in China

Excess investment demand can be attributed to two kinds of causes. One kind can be called top-down causes: they emanate from higher-level bureaucracies and filter down through the layers of the system. The other kind are bottom-up causes, and they work in the opposite direction: the original pressures originate from the lower bureaucracies or the enterprises under their charge. As in other mature socialist economies, excess investment demand in China is not a result of top-down pressures from policy makers; rather, the causes relate to the incentive structures facing Chinese firms and bureaucrats alike and the objectives that they pursue.

The two top-down motivations – ideological motives and the desire to use taut planning to extract information – apply in only limited degree to Chinese

---

11. For households, however, the story is very different. In a CPE, households purchase goods and services in much the same way as their Western counterparts, except that their purchasing power is curtailed by administrative rationing. The degree of that curtailment depends on the difference between the monetary purchasing power and the supply of consumer goods. Before the reforms, China was what is known as a "low-wage-and-low-consumption" economy, meaning that money constrained household consumption in a real sense (Cao Erjie 1988). For a more general discussion on the behavioral differences between households and firms in CPEs, see Kornai (1980 and 1986a).

12. One may object by pointing to a similar phenomenon in market economies: savings and loans institutions in the U.S. economy. But this observation is a mere restatement of the same point. Savings and loans institutions are federally insured and hence face a similar budgetary environment as a normal CPE firm. How reckless their behavior is then depends critically on the degree of government supervision; if the government supervision becomes lax, as it did in the 1980s, the behavior tends to be reckless.

investment practices during the reform era. In the case of the first motivation, catching up with the developed countries in short order, two conditions must be met to drive investment growth. First, the leaders must have such a desire or policy goal. Second, the leaders must believe that an economic strategy with an emphasis on investment growth is appropriate for accomplishing such an objective.

Both conditions have been absent during the post-Mao period, the second condition in particular. During much of the period, the Chinese leadership's commitment to high rates of economic growth has not been consistent, ranging from Hua Guofeng's "Ten-Year Development Plan," comparable to the Great Leap Forward in terms of its impetuousness and ambition, to the several retrenchment rounds in the 1980s that stressed control and stability. During the reform era, Chinese economic strategy has not relied on investment as "an engine of growth" but on a more efficient utilization of existing capital and labor stock. Furthermore, to the extent that an investment strategy has been used to stimulate economic growth, it has been the result of initiatives of local governments rather than those of the central government.

The post-Mao period can be divided into two phases according to the leaders' economic objectives. During the first phase, the traditional, forced-growth strategy was intensified; the second phase, roughly since 1979, has alternated between moderately ambitious economic goals and those that stress stability and control.

The fall of the Gang of Four in October 1976 ushered in an era known as the Great Leap Outward in Chinese economic history. The name derives from Mao's Great Leap Forward of the 1958–60 period; the resemblance between the two economic initiatives lies in the forced growth embodied in both strategies.[13] In the Ten-Year Development Plan announced at the Fifth National People's Congress in February 1978, Hua Guofeng (1992 [1978]) set forth a number of extremely ambitious economic objectives to be achieved by 1985, including the construction of 120 large-scale industrial projects.

The plans based on this vision quickly collapsed, first of all because the Chinese bureaucracy was no longer capable of implementing and coordinating large-scale economic activities (Naughton 1991b). Another factor was the sheer ambitiousness of the targets. The capital cost of the 120 projects envisioned in the Ten-Year Development Plan, for example, was equal to the total capital outlays for the previous twenty-eight years (Riskin 1987: 289). The collapse

---

13. Indeed, the leadership openly declared that the Great Leap Forward was their model (see "Sudu . . ." 1992 [1977]).

of the Ten-Year Development Plan effectively discredited the forced-growth strategy and ended Hua's political leadership. In April 1979 the Chinese government, upon strong urging from Chen Yun, the architect of China's planning system and a vice premier in charge of the economy in the 1950s, formally adopted the program of "adjustment, reform, rectification, and improvement" (*tiaozheng, gaige, zhengdun, tigao*). The central purpose of this program was to stabilize the macroeconomic situation and to set the economy on a more moderate and realistic growth path. This marked the beginning of the second phase.

The moderation of the economic strategy during this second phase is seen in the relatively conservative goals adopted by the leadership. Here conservatism means consistency between economic goals and the historically relevant performance, as seen in the economic objectives of the Sixth (1981–85) and the Seventh (1986–90) Five-Year Plans. The emphasis on economic stability is apparent during these two FYPs. For example, the targets for the annual average growth rates for the gross value of agricultural output (GVAO), gross value of industrial output (GVIO), and net material product (NMP) were set at 4.0–5.0 percent for the Sixth FYP and at 4.0 percent, 7.5 percent, and 6.7 percent, respectively, for the Seventh FYP. The actual performance surpassed them by wide margins.[14] Although the Chinese economy significantly outperformed the Sixth FYP's projections, lower targets were set than those actually achieved during the previous period. On the surface, there is little evidence that the Chinese leaders have attempted to push the economy toward its full capacity by administrative fiat.[15]

The FYPs, however, provided medium-term directions for the economy rather than specific and binding instructions for annual economic planning. The actual economic behavior and, by extension, the cumulative long-term economic impact, are driven mainly by short-term Party and government policies and programs that are only loosely constrained by the FYPs. For example, the goal of the Twelfth Party Congress, concluded in September 1982, was to quadruple agricultural and industrial output by the year 2000. The implicit annual growth rate was 7.2 percent, a figure much higher than the Sixth and the Seventh FYPs permitted.

Furthermore, during most of the reform era, the Chinese leadership has

14. Between 1981 and 1985, for example, GVAO grew at 8.1 percent annually; GVIO at 12.2 percent; and NMP at 10 percent.

15. Sixth FYP figures are from Zhao Dexing (1989b: 441); Seventh FYP figures are from SSB (1991a: 13). GVAO, GVIO, and NMP growth figures are derived from SSB (1991c: tables 2–37 and 2–15, 56, 34). All calculations are based on constant prices.

been quite divided over the appropriate pace of economic growth. This is reflected in the formulation of the Sixth FYP. Initially, the growth targets proposed by the SPC for the NMP, GVAO, and GVIO were 4 percent; however, after an expanded Politburo meeting to discuss the SPC's projections in connection with formulating the Sixth FYP, the target was changed to "4 percent but striving for 5 percent" (Zhao Dexing 1989b: 441).

The main factor seems to be pressures from Chinese provincial officials for higher growth rates, as well as from Deng's support for such a position.[16] The pressures for high growth rates were tempered, however, by the resistance of Chen Yun and Li Peng, which led to the stop–go cycles that characterized much of economic life in the 1980s. In addition, investment growth in the 1980s was fueled in large part by the local governments; the central government alternated between a permissive and a contractionary macroeconomic policy environment rather than directly initiating and organizing these investment activities, as discussed in chapter 3.

Consider now the leadership's view of the role of capital formation in economic development; overemphasis on capital formation is the second condition for centrally driven excess demand for investment. The leadership's view of this role departed markedly from that of previous periods and has shaped China's investment strategy during the reform era.

Its strategy before the 1980s was based, implicitly or explicitly, on an "extensive" concept of economic growth. In that concept, the relationship between economic growth and capital stock is a linear one. That is to say, a higher rate of growth requires, first and foremost, a larger capital stock. Zhou Enlai (1984 [1954]: 132) summarized this notion in a 1954 speech: "Our country's economy used to be very backward. If we do not build up a powerful modern industry, a modern agriculture, a modern transport industry, and a modern defense, we cannot shake off backwardness and poverty and our revolution will be unable to attain its aims."

The extensive approach to economic growth cannot be divorced from the

---

16. Zhao Ziyang referred to this change in a speech to the National Industrial and Transport Work Conference in March 1982. He said that the reason for the "4 percent but striving for 5 percent" target was to take into account (*kaolu dao*) "provincial planned growth rates." See Zhao Ziyang (1982a: 1184). There is only indirect evidence of Deng's position on the Sixth FYP. In Zhao Dexing's account of the Sixth FYP formulation, Zhao Ziyang is said to have voiced support for the SPC's 4 percent target "numerous times before the expanded Politburo meeting in October 1980." But at the meeting, according to Zhao Dexing, Deng Xiaoping and Zhao Ziyang proposed that the target should be "4 percent but striving for 5 percent" (Zhao Dexing 1989b: 440–41). This interpretation is consistent with Deng's later and better-known disagreement with Li Peng and Chen Yun over the appropriate pace of economic growth.

overwhelming emphasis placed on the producer goods sector or, in Chinese planning parlance, on heavy industry.[17] This is because the producer goods sector, compared with the agricultural and consumer goods sector, is more capital intensive. As some Chinese economists have pointed out, investment resources claimed by the producer goods sector between the First FYP and the reform era far exceeded the highest level in Soviet history. Except during the First FYP and during the 1963–65 adjustment period, on average about 50 percent of investment resources went into the producer goods sector, compared with 39.8 percent in the former Soviet Union during wartime conditions; for the consumer goods sector, it hovered around 5 percent during the same period (Liu Hui, Li Qun, and Qi Mingqun 1983: 411–12).

An alternative concept – the one that is often associated with Chen Yun – stressed not so much the size of the capital stock but the efficiency with which capital is deployed to promote growth.[18] Although this view, known as the intensive growth perspective, does not necessarily repudiate the extensive growth perspective, it does recognize that there can be fundamental choices between policies that stress additional investment and those that stress the quality of investment, and it sharpens the trade-offs between these two policy choices.

China's investment strategy during the reform era has by and large attempted to adhere to efficiency considerations, although by default investment efficiency slipped periodically when central supervision became lax.[19] The clearest indication of the leaders' acceptance of the efficiency rationale is their effort to reform the economic system. Economists have often equated reforms, in China as well as in other socialist countries, with a change from an

---

17. The justification for stressing the producer goods sector at the expense of the consumer goods sector is ideological in that it often links the strategy with the nature of the socialist system. As a Soviet economist once put it: "The law of priority growth of the production of the means of production . . . is a necessary condition for ensuring the uninterrupted advance of socialist production" (quoted in Ellman 1989: 140).

18. Three concerns are often voiced in the central investment planning process: concern that investment can "crowd out" consumption and therefore can reduce living standards; concern over the macroeconomic implications of investment growth; and concern over investment efficiency. To different degrees and at different times, Chen Yun has been identified with all three of these concerns, especially the latter two. For example, during the First FYP, when the Chinese leaders almost unanimously concluded that large-scale capital construction was justified by the country's "poor and blank" conditions, Chen Yun pointed to the surplus capacity in the economy and argued that investment should be reined in and the emphasis should be on a fuller utilization of existing facilities (see Chen Yun 1984a [1954]: 268).

19. A partial indication of this can be seen in figure 5.1 when the unfinished investment rate fluctuated along with the ebbs and flows of the macroeconomic policies.

extensive growth strategy to an intensive growth strategy (Dernberger 1986; Szelenyi 1989).

A more immediate indication, however, is the shift away from the capital-intensive producer goods sector and, by implication, away from the single-minded pursuit of the growth of the capital stock. Relatedly, the new approach urged that the existing productive capacity be deployed to meet production goals and at the same time discouraged expansion drives. Zhao Ziyang (1982b [1980]: 621–22), in a speech that set the tone for the retrenchment program to be implemented in 1981, summarized both the trouble with the old approach and the gist of the new approach:

For a long period of time, we stressed capital construction investment at the expense of production and high accumulation at the expense of efficiency; we craved for capital construction, mobilizing a huge amount of resources to establish new plants, especially those with high capital requirements and long gestation periods in heavy industry. . . . We should find another way, one that relies on the existing enterprises and one that increases social production through technical upgrading, lowering energy consumption, and improving quality and efficiency, rather than on an ever increasing investment scale and the consumption of energy and raw materials.

Taut investment planning motivates excess demand to obviate the asymmetry of informational distribution between planners and firm managers. In CPEs, this "informational motivation" allegedly leads to excess investment demand. Yet there is little evidence that Chinese planners have systematically resorted to taut planning either before or during the reform era. Taut planning requires, first and foremost, that the plan targets be ratcheted up periodically, that is, that planners adjust the target for the year$_t$ closely, according to the achieved performance in year$_{t-1}$.[20] The achieved performance is the best information available to planners, and if, as posited by this hypothesis, their motive is to extract additional information, then the target-setting needs not only to be ratcheted up but to be taut as well. In other words, plan targets are set at a level above that set by ratchet planning.

To distinguish ratchet from taut planning would be impossible without detailed data about the planners' intentions. Fortunately, in the case of China such an exercise is not necessary. If one can show that ratchet planning is by and large absent, one can simply infer that taut planning is absent as well because the existence of the latter is predicated on the existence of the former.

One way to test for the existence of ratchet planning is to study the records of plan fulfillment. If firms persistently overfulfill their plan targets, the plan

---

20. For a detailed discussion of this practice and its effect on firm behavior, see Berliner (1957: 77–78).

targets are not ratcheted up. Otherwise the null hypothesis – that there is no ratchet planning – is rejected. Plan fulfillment is calculated by dividing the actual investments by the investment targets for the relevant years. Figures larger than unity denote plan overfulfillment; those smaller than unity denote underfulfillment. Such calculations show that Chinese investment plans are overfulfilled, sometimes overwhelmingly. Nationally, the largest overfulfillment occurred in 1982 for capital construction and in 1985 for technical renovation. These ratios were 1.46 and 1.68, respectively, meaning that the plans for those years were 46 and 68 percent overfulfilled. The magnitude of performance/ plan deviation contrasts sharply with that in the other CPEs. In Poland, for example, the worst deviation occurred in 1972, when actual investment exceeded the plan by 13.4 percent (Portes et al. 1987).

Granick (1990) has conducted a systematic analysis of Chinese firm behavior based on a sample of enterprise-level data from twenty Chinese state-owned enterprises in the production sphere. His conclusion is closely congruous with our finding in the investment sphere, namely, that Chinese planning is not ratcheted up. One-third of the Chinese enterprises in his sample overfulfilled the output plan by more than 10 percent. Further, he observes (1990: 87): "During 1979–82, one-fourth of all enterprise-years represented more than 20 percent overfulfillment of the final plans for value of output, one-half of such years in the case of profits, and one-tenth for physical output. There is no indication in these data that planners aimed to set plans that just matched enterprise potentialities."[21]

There is also evidence that Chinese planning has become more "slack" since the onset of the reforms. Using the same sample that Granick analyzed, Byrd (1991: 110–11) calculated that during the 1965–78 period enterprises overfulfilled output value targets by at least 2 percent or more roughly 65 percent of the time; between 1979 and 1984, this figure increased to 83 percent of the time. By comparison, fewer enterprises in the European socialist countries overfulfilled plans, and when they did, they did so by smaller margins. In one study, about 12 percent of Soviet enterprises were found to overfulfill their sales plans by 6 percent or more; in East Germany, the incidence of overfulfillment was even lower than or at about the same level as the Soviet

---

21. Although Granick (1990: 89–91) did find evidence for ratchet planning in situations in which enterprises relied exclusively on the allocation bureaucracy for input provisions, the larger substantive conclusion should not change because of the smaller number of such enterprises in the Chinese economy. A group of Chinese researchers found that the mandatory planning in 1984 covered about 20 percent of input allocation for intermediate goods; the rest was either under "guidance planning" or procured from the market. The coverage for raw materials was significantly higher, around 70 percent, and the rest were under guidance planning (see Zhang Shaojie and Zhang Amei 1986: 66).

record. In Rumania, 27 percent of the enterprises overfulfilled their production plans in the data covering the 1969–70 period.[22]

Indeed, very often the question posed is not whether Chinese firms operate in an environment of taut planning but whether they operate in an environment of any sort of planning at all. Chinese managers' own evaluations reflect an "atrophy of planning" in the Chinese economy. In a survey conducted in the mid-1980s, managers responded to the question "Which aspects have the greatest impact on your decision making?" by ranking state plan targets as only fourth in overall importance: market pressures, however, were cited as the number one constraint (Yang Guansan et al. 1986: 286). The managers' attitudes were closely matched by the economic reality. In the mid-1980s, state mandatory planning covered about 26 percent of the industrial output in a sample of 429 enterprises; guidance planning covered about 27 percent, and the market covered the rest (Zhang Shaojie and Zhang Amei 1986).[23]

The empirical evidence presented so far strongly suggests that "top-down" causes do not serve as systemic pressures leading to excess investment demand. During the reform era, the central policy makers did not launch the kind of investment drives one finds in other socialist countries or drives similar to the First and Fourth FYPs in China. This was principally because of the shift away from an extensive growth approach to an intensive growth approach and because of the recognition that excessive investments entailed significant economic costs. Also, there appears to be no evidence of a deliberate attempt to extract informational value by making plans taut. Actual investment performance has consistently exceeded investment targets, often by wide margins. Enterprise-wide data show the same pattern in the production sphere.[24] Ratchet – and, by implication, taut – planning is thus ruled out as a systematic policy instrument exercised by Chinese economic bureaucrats.

Bottom-up causes emanate from local government officials and from firm managers. The pressures for investment expansion can in turn be divided into negative incentives, those incentives that tend to constrain investment demand, and positive incentives, incentives that induce investment demand.

---

22. All the figures cited are from Granick (1990: 76–78).

23. Guidance planning formally means that the targets are nonbinding. In reality, some local governments have turned guidance planning into a form of mandatory planning. However, such a practice varies across regions. See American Economists Study Team (1984).

24. Another piece of evidence is the date of receipt of the production plans from the bureaucracy. In Granick's sample (1990: 83), 33 percent of the enterprises received their production plans in December prior to the plan year; the rest received output plans in January or after (26 percent of this group received their plans between April and August).

Negative incentives. The first negative incentive, asymmetry of cost incidence, is said to encourage investment demand because the costs of investment accrue to the investor less than the benefits he receives. In the Chinese context, this is due to the financing arrangements of Chinese firms. Everything else being equal, a firm that invests out of its own resources or incurs real costs in raising external funds is more likely to be cautious in investment choices and behavior compared with one that finances its investment out of zero-interest budgetary grants.[25]

During the pre-reform period, Chinese firms financed almost all of their investments through budgetary grants; during the reform era, budgetary sources have declined continuously and drastically in relation to other sources, such as bank loans and retained profits. In 1977 the government budget accounted for about 78 percent of investment financing, and what the Chinese call "self-raised funds" (mainly in the form of depreciation allowances) came a distant second, at 18 percent. By the late 1980s, there were major shifts in investment financing. Self-raised funds, now consisting of retained profits as well as depreciation allowances, were the most dominant source, at 43 percent; the previous negligible domestic bank loans reached 21 percent and by 1989 surpassed the government budget (13.9 percent) (based on SSB 1987a, 1991b).

Su Sijin (1993) has argued that reliance on self-raised funds has compelled Chinese managers to be careful in their investment choices. This is too simplistic. Whether diversified investment financing can impose curbs on investment demand by instilling financial discipline depends entirely on the firmness of the firms' debt or other obligations. If these obligations are not stringent, then the problem with "negative externality" will persist and the firms' behavior will remain fundamentally the same irrespective of the diversity of the funding sources. Indeed, the increasing reliance on bank financing has apparently increased enterprise investment appetite as local officials overauthorize investment approvals while urging banks to fund them (see Imai 1994: 194).

The nature of the loan obligations requires a word here. Foreign loans should be the most binding. Foreign capital constituted about 9.9 percent of total capital construction investment financing in 1993 (as compared with 6.8 percent in 1985), a portion of which was in fact allocated through the state budget (*guojia tongjie tonghuan*) (calculated from SSB 1994: 146). The impact of this portion of foreign capital should be the same as that of the state budget.

---

25. I will relax the ceteris paribus condition when I discuss the absence of the second negative incentive in the Chinese economy, the soft-budget constraints.

This portion, however, has declined in a fairly dramatic fashion throughout the 1980s. In 1977 all the foreign-funded investments were allocated through the state budget; in 1985 it was about 55 percent, and by 1989 it had declined to only 17.8 percent (calculated from SSB 1987b: 59, 1991b: 53). Once the budget allocations are subtracted, foreign loans constituted, on average, only about 4.23 percent of investment financing between 1977 and 1989, a rather inconsequential source of investment funds.

Domestic loans have been a far more important funding source, accounting for more than 20 percent of investment financing since the late 1980s. Originally, the introduction of credit-based financing was meant to instill caution and responsibility in enterprise investment behavior; however, a lack of effective stringency of loan obligations and a number of administrative features of the Chinese banking system have made it difficult to achieve this goal.[26]

First, investment loans still retain strong budgetary characteristics. Nominal interest rates are set very low and in 1980 and again in 1985 and in 1990, the real interest rates were negative.[27] Low or negative interest rates encourage excessive borrowing because opportunity costs are either low or negative. Furthermore, a portion of the loan repayments is in fact borne by the state in the form of a reduced tax base because principal and interest repayments for investment loans are deducted from income before the product tax is assessed.[28] Second, loan obligations are not stringent, as indicated by the high percentage of overdue loans; by 1985 over 50 percent of bank loans were overdue (Zhang Xun-hai 1992: 66). Furthermore, either as a matter of policy or via negotiations between banks and firms, repayment deferrals are granted frequently; taxes are often forgiven to avoid defaults, in effect turning loan obligations into transfers between the government's tax department and its bank.[29]

---

26. Starting in 1979, the Chinese government converted all budgetary investment grants into "loans" intermediated through branches of the People's Construction Bank of China (PCBC), a process known as *bogaidai* (literally "grants changed to loans"). See SPC, MOF, and PCBC (1991 [1985]). The change in name did not, for all intents and purposes, produce any changes in the nature of these financial obligations; the Ministry of Finance allocates funds to the PCBC as budgetary grants; lending decisions are made by planning rather than bank officials, and loans are paid back in the form of taxes and profit turnovers. See Lin Song, Liu Huirong, and Ma Chunfeng (1989: 120–23).

27. For a general survey on banking reforms, see Dittus (1989b) and De Wulf and Goldsbrough (1986).

28. In their study of Chongqing Clock and Watch Company, Byrd and Tidrick (1992) find that depreciation charges or taxes on fixed assets are diverted to loan repayments, and whenever these are not sufficient, industrial-commercial taxes are used for the same purpose. Another enterprise-level study, of Changchun Bicycle Factory, reveals that the Changchun municipal government bailed out the money-losing factory in 1983 by exempting all of its tax obligations for 1983 and 1984, in addition to granting a subsidy of 3 million yuan in 1983. The factory was able to take out a new loan of 4.8 million yuan from the same bank. See Zhang Xun-hai (1992: 66).

29. Walder (1992) describes how this process works at the local level.

Third, the problem with the attenuated loan obligations is compounded by the way credits are allocated. Banks often cannot make credit decisions solely on the basis of profitability. The misalignment of prices between energy and raw materials on the one hand and the finished goods on the other means that sectoral lending is done on an administrative basis and that those bodies in charge of the country's industrial policies, such as the SPC, have the prerogative to allocate credit. The SPC routinely overrules the banks' lending decisions and directs resource flows according to its own priorities list regardless of profitability considerations. The Chinese have described this situation vividly: "The SPC orders dishes; banks pay for them" (quoted in Liu Hongru 1987: 206).

If the banks' sectoral lending is heavily constrained by industrial policy concerns, the ability to fund projects within the same sector is limited by the weak political and bureaucratic positions of banks with respect to local government officials. Local officials have a strong incentive to keep capital immobile because the rent derived from the creation of a local industrial base is larger than any interest income they can receive. They exert enormous pressure on banks to lend to local projects; this can be direct pressure (e.g., making a phone call or issuing a decree), or it can be more subtle (e.g., visiting a project site or making speeches praising certain projects).

The Chinese administrative system facilitates the exertion of such pressures. Unlike the regional branches of the U.S. Federal Reserve, regional branches of the PBC overlap with the Chinese administrative jurisdictions; PBC officials in essence belong to the same *nomenklatura* as other local government officials, and the appointment of PBC personnel requires the approval of those officials. As discussed in chapter 2, the power local government officials have over job allocations and educational opportunities informally accentuate their influence over banks (Zhou Mubin 1988). Last, Chinese banks have yet to become full economic entities; their profits continue to be remitted to the government, and their operational losses are borne, ultimately, by the central bank. In that respect, Chinese banks are not fundamentally different from other state-owned firms: weak financial discipline combined with positive inducements – such as prestige and financial rewards associated with size expansion – act as a powerful incentive to engage in credit expansions (Zhou Mubin 1988). This occurred in 1984 when Chinese banks competed to make credit available in order to establish higher lending quotas for the next year.

Now let us turn to the remaining funding source, self-raised capital. The purpose is to see if firms are motivated to economize on the use of their retained funds in their investment behavior. Both the operational features of Chinese firms and the more direct evidence suggest, however, that the increasing use of retained capital is not a sufficient constraint on investment demand. The principal factor inhibiting economizing investment behavior is the persistence of "soft-budget constraints" in the Chinese economic system, especially in the state-owned sector. Soft-budget constraints, a concept made famous by the Hungarian economist Janos Kornai, refer to the ability of firms to continue operating despite chronic losses (Kornai 1980, 1984). There are two major reasons for soft-budget constraints in a socialist economy. One is the largely bureaucratic as opposed to market environment in which state-owned firms operate; the other, relatedly, is the implicit or explicit guarantee that firms will not go bankrupt.

The bureaucratic environment is most prominent in the area of managerial appointments and promotions. According to an enterprise survey conducted in 1985, an overwhelming majority, about 90 percent, of Chinese managers were promoted through bureaucratic channels (CIRES 1986a: 273); more recent data reflect a slightly less bureaucratic profile of Chinese managers. In a survey of 769 enterprises conducted in the late 1980s, about 77 percent of the managers were appointed by supervisory authorities (Zheng Hongliang 1992: 27).

However, bureaucratic interventions go well beyond the formal power of appointment and promotion into a wide range of enterprise operations. As already mentioned, decisions over credit allocation and over sectoral or project funding require heavy bureaucratic involvement; tax forgiveness and deferrals of loan repayments are routinely negotiated between bureaucrats and enterprise managers. Although in general bureaucratic arrangements for input provisions have declined in importance, bureaucratic assistance is indispensable when firms attempt to obtain inputs at plan-based prices.

A deeper reason for the persistence of soft-budget constraints is the lack of a credible threat of bankruptcy. Although the Bankruptcy Law of 1986 and the Chinese Enterprise Law of 1988 have laid out formal provisions for bankruptcy, to date the application of bankruptcy has remained extremely limited and has been carried out in a highly administrative fashion.[30] Summarizing China's reform experience in the 1980s, a World Bank paper points out that the main achievement in the area of enterprise reforms has been an enhancement of positive inducements for improving efficiency and output, but the negative consequences of failure remain fundamentally unclear (Harrold 1992).

Positive incentives. In the absence of negative incentives, excess investment demand arises only when there are benefits to be derived from investment expansion. As mentioned at the beginning of this chapter, three

---

30. Some descriptive evidence suggests that the credibility of bankruptcy does make a difference to investment behavior. Collective firms in China, which face constant threats of bankruptcy, are found to be relatively cautious and restrained in borrowing loans to finance capital investment. See Zhang Xun-hai (1992: 189).

investment motives are common in CPEs: empire-building, plan fulfillment, and supply uncertainty.

In China, empire-building usually stems from the desire to capture those tangible benefits that confer on size. Chinese authors, without proof, allude to empire-building as an investment motive (Zhao Suying 1986: 17; Zheng Hongliang 1992: 25–26). The tangible benefits cited in these studies include enhancement of prestige, status, and material rewards (*mingwang, diwei, he daiyu*), or of assigned administrative ranks (*xingzheng jibie*), along with capacity expansions. Although these motives are difficult to evaluate directly, indirect evidence suggests that they play a significant role in the Chinese economic system.

A World Bank study, for example, finds an "engineering" motive to be strong among enterprise managers (Byrd and Tidrick 1987: 64). An engineering motive can refer to a desire to produce excellent products or to adopt the most modern technology. The benefits are not merely psychological; they are often quite tangible. A system of ranking enterprises and varying bonus, wage, and credit treatments according to their technological sophistication accentuates investment motives to the extent that investment is intended to upgrade technology to qualify for a higher ranking and for the associated benefits.[31] Lu Dong (1992: 261), a vice minister and then minister of the State Economic Commission in the 1980s, criticizes those managers who "crave for investments and for new projects" (*rezhongyu zheng touzi shang xiangmu*) as a way to upgrade technology rather than seeking better management.

The second and third postulated motives – plan fulfillment and supply uncertainty – are less important in China. Plan fulfillment cannot act as a powerful incentive for investment expansion because investment planning, as shown before, is not taut and Chinese enterprises routinely overfulfill their targets. There is some evidence that although output targets are not important, financial targets can be a motivational factor. A survey conducted in the late 1980s of managers of 769 state-owned enterprises reveals that an overwhelming majority, 91.6 percent, ranked "fulfillment of profit and tax quotas" as the most important justification for initiating a new investment project (Zheng Hongliang 1992: 26).

It is, however, very difficult to interpret these data in a straightforward manner. First of all, they may not represent the true motives of managers; rather, the justification of investment projects on the basis of profit and tax quotas reflect the motives of the supervisory bureaucrats who are in a position

---

31. Chinese enterprises are ranked as belonging to special, first, and second classes at the national level and advanced class at the provincial level. See "Guowuyuan guanyu jiaqiang gongye qiye guanli ruogan wenti de jueding" (1990: 1618–19).

to approve new investment projects. Managers may simply tailor their applications to bureaucratic preferences. Second, financial targets are not binding and therefore managers can and often do negotiate with supervisory authorities to reduce targets rather than increase capacity to fulfill the targets, as the plan fulfillment hypothesis implies.[32]

The third motive – supply uncertainty and investing in backward integration processes as a buffer stock – is quite incongruous with Chinese economic reality during the reform era. Bureaucratic underallocation of inputs is more pervasive in China than in the European socialist countries, but it is also deliberate and coincides with the reform measure to allow enterprises to market their own goods. Except for electricity, Chinese enterprises are able to obtain most of their inputs from a combination of three sources: central allocation, local allocation, and the market. Thus, as a World Bank study concludes, supply problems do not constrain Chinese industrial output (Tidrick 1987: 186–90) and there is no reason to believe that supply constraints motivate investment expansion.

Three positive inducements are specific to China: the welfare of enterprise employees, the presence of "supernormal" profits on account of misaligned prices, and the administrative division of taxes. Employee welfare drives investment demand to the extent that size expansion is associated with improved working and living conditions and with a larger labor force (Zhao Yujiang 1986: 16–17). To show that employee welfare has such an impact, it is first necessary to establish that maximizing employee welfare constitutes an important managerial objective. There are a number of such indications. Chinese enterprises, for example, allocate retained profits overwhelmingly into the employee bonus funds and at a level far exceeding government stipulations;[33] other managerial behavior is also consistent with this motive, such as giving out excessive bonuses to workers and paying workers in kind when the government restricts monetary bonus payments.

In addition, several features of Chinese enterprise operations make maximizing employee welfare a *plausible* motive. Most Chinese managers are promoted from inside the enterprise, or when appointed from the outside they spend a long period of time in the same enterprise; in such circumstances strong identification with workers' interests is likely (Byrd and Tidrick 1987:

---

32. A World Bank study finds, for example, that profit retention is highly sensitive to enterprise performance unidirectionally. When profits are rising, the correlation index between profits and retained profits is 0.66; when profits are falling, the same index drops to 0.15. This observation indicates a degree of stickiness with retained profits. See Tidrick (1987: 206).

33. A study by Chinese economists shows that the actual bonus fund to retained profit ratios can exceed government regulations by some 40 to 50 percent (CIRES 1986b: 24).

62). Another feature is the absence of worker dismissals, except for the most egregious cases. A study of ten large enterprises in Sichuan finds that personnel matters are controlled most tightly by supervisory bureaucrats; only 8.5 percent of the enterprise managers in the sample believed that they had the authority to fire workers (Zheng Hongliang 1992). Some have suggested that excessive bonus-giving practices arise from a managerial desire to induce labor discipline.[34]

The second positive incentive, the desire to capture supernormal profits, is shared by both managers and local government officials. Supernormal profits refer to those profits in excess of all the opportunity costs a firm incurs in order to be engaged in its current activity. In China supernormal profits are concentrated in the manufacturing sectors because of the government's price-setting policies. Partly as a result of the labor theory of value, prices for extractive industries – raw materials and energy – and for the capital-intensive intermediate goods sector are set low in relation to the prices of manufactured goods because capital and land costs are not fully incorporated in the prices. This distortion in prices can be shown in two ways. One is to take international prices as the point of reference; such a comparison reveals that washed coal in China, as of the mid-1980s, was priced at 45 percent of international market prices, crude oil at 30 percent, cast pig iron at 70 percent, and plain carbon steel at 60 percent (Wu and Zhao 1987: 313–14). A more direct indicator is the relative returns from different sectors; the returns, measured as returns on the fixed assets, are concentrated in light industry, such as food-processing, textiles, and clothing; within heavy industry, "daily use" items command very high returns.[35]

Supernormal profits in the consumer manufactured sectors have two consequences bearing on investment. One is that these highly profitable sectors tend to draw investment resources to them and at times do so at the expense

---

34. See Jefferson and Xu (1991: 54) and Wiemer and Liu (1991: 117). Not all economists agree that maximizing employee welfare is a dominant managerial motive. One Chinese economist (Ma Jiantang 1992) shows that profit increases are the number one objective of managers and that the growth of workers' income is their number three objective. These survey results must be treated with caution. Maximizing profits is consistent with bureaucratic preferences while maximizing workers' income is not, a fact that may have colored these responses. Also, profit-seeking and maximizing workers' income are not mutually exclusive goals; the former may well be used for the purpose of the latter via the allocation of retained profits. In addition, because workers cannot be dismissed, labor costs are essentially fixed and therefore long-run profits do not depend on labor costs.

35. Divergence in sectoral returns has declined over time. Profit equalization indicates an improvement in allocative efficiency, as increased supply diminishes the profit margins of the previously profitable sectors. For a more detailed analysis and an empirical testing of this proposition, see Jefferson and Xu (1991).

of the intermediate goods or raw material sectors. This is a particularly serious problem when the investment policy is expansive; in 1985, for example, the supply of investment in the metallurgical industry fell short of demand by 207 percent (Research Group 1986: 32). This creates what the Chinese call "imbalances in the investment structure." That is, a large portion of total investment volume goes to finance light industry projects. This strains the supply of energy, raw materials, and intermediate goods both because the derived demand for them increases with investments in the consumer goods sector and because financial resources are diverted away from their development.[36]

The other consequence arising from the concentration of supernormal profits in the consumer goods sector is excess investment demand. This is because higher returns from finished goods production induce firms and supervisory agencies to engage in "forward integration activities." In other words, they are led to invest in downstream production processes to capture accounting profits. This is one of the important reasons why energy-producing regions with a comparative disadvantage in manufacturing also strive to build up energy-using manufacturing industries. The evidence here is scattered and anecdotal; the information that is available suggests that industrial dispersion has increased during the reform era and that areas producing raw materials have been establishing processing industries. Shanghai and Shandong, for example, manufactured 7 percent and 11.4 percent of the total production of cigarettes, respectively, in 1979; their shares fell to 4 percent and 9 percent in 1984, while the tobacco-producing provinces, such as Yunnan and Hunan, increased their shares of cigarette production by some 3 percent (World Bank 1990b: 209).

The third motive – the desire to increase tax revenues – applies mainly to government officials: investment enhances the local tax and revenue base because of the administrative nature of tax divisions. The Chinese system divides profits and taxes administratively: the central government's profit and tax base consists mainly of revenue streams from central enterprises; the provincial profit and tax base consists of revenue streams from provincial enterprises. Although Chinese enterprises are nominally owned by the "whole people," the immediate supervisory agencies exercise many ownership rights, including the right to income and to control over personnel in the enterprises

---

36. This is exactly the opposite situation from other CPEs, as portrayed by Kornai. Kornai (1980) argues that shortages in the consumer goods market arise mainly because the "insatiable" demand for producer goods diverts resources away from the manufacture of consumer goods. The fact that an opposite pattern has been observed in China indicates the distance that China has departed from a typical CPE; relative price differentials have played a meaningful allocative function in China.

under their charge. Investment, according to the doctrine "Whoever builds and manages the enterprise has the right to use its output" (quoted in Wong 1985: 260), has become in effect a purchase price and a principal means of acquiring de facto ownership rights. Granick (1990), in his study of ownership patterns of Chinese state-owned enterprises, has found strong empirical support for the notion that ownership in Chinese industry is a function of past investment patterns.

This system is unique among the CPEs. It evolved from a circular issued by the State Council in March 1951, "The Decision to Establish a Tax Division System for 1951," which has since shaped the basic contours of revenue-sharing practices between the central government and local governments (Wu Deming 1987: 55–57). This circular modified the fiscal system set up a year earlier, which gave Beijing tight control over local expenditures and collection procedures. The 1951 tax reforms created a three-tier system of budgetary administration: it consisted of central government, LARs, and provinces, and it introduced the principle of revenue-sharing (Lardy 1978: 49–60). Although the specific formulas for revenue-sharing changed a few times, the principle embodied in the 1951 tax reforms has remained constant: the fiscal and revenue base of the central government is the central enterprise, and that of the local government is the local enterprises.

This principle implicitly acknowledges the status of supervisory authorities as de facto residual claimants of the income generated by enterprises under their charge. This recognition was illustrated by an interesting case in 1980, when, as if to compensate for the transfer of supervisory authority, the central government agreed that the original "owners" – in this case the provincial governments – would still claim 20 percent of the income tax revenue generated by enterprises previously under their supervision (Wu Deming 1987: 68). Furthermore, the benefits from investing in an enterprise under one's own jurisdiction go beyond formal tax revenues. Supervisory officials possess a host of policy tools over enterprises under their charge that they can use to their own pecuniary advantages. In the mid-1980s, about 5 percent of enterprise profits were collected as "fees" by local governments (Zhao Yujiang 1986: 118).

Central investment concerns during the reform era

Central decision makers have two principal investment policy concerns. One is the aggregate volume of investment (*touzi zongliang*) in a given year; this is a policy concern because of the connections between investment expansions and inflationary pressures in the economy. As argued in chapter 1, investment activities in CPEs account for a large portion of the national economy and contribute to open or repressed inflation more than household spending. The other concern is the structure of investment (*touzi jiegou*). The central government complains that local governments tend to steer resources into projects producing manufactured goods with high profit margins at the expense of those projects that produce vital infrastructural facilities and energy for the national economy. This is the industrial policy concern, since it is about the *sectoral* allocation of investment resources. Because the macroeconomic and industrial policy concerns are closely related, there tends to be an industrial policy component in the central austerity and investment reduction policies. During the reform era, macroeconomic policy concerns have motivated every investment reduction round, and industrial policy concerns have played a major role in the last three austerity rounds (1983, 1986–87, and 1989–91).

The macroeconomic concerns must be understood against the background of China's long-term macroeconomic stability, from the early 1950s on. Up to the late 1970s, China had been enjoying price stability for a considerable period of time. The quest for economic stability in China began immediately after the communists seized power in 1949 and was widely successful. In Shanghai, for example, wholesale prices rose less than 20 percent in 1951, just after a sixfold increase between July and December 1949 (Eckstein 1981: 171; Tsakok 1979). Thereafter, except for brief periods of relatively mild inflationary pressures in 1953, 1956, and 1960, China enjoyed near complete price stability until the late 1970s, which was sustained via a mixture of involuntary savings, rationing, and administrative price controls (Chen and Hou 1986: 811–12; Eckstein 1981: 171–76). Price stability, at least before the reform era (1979–92), was touted as one of the major policy achievements of the communist regime.

Inflationary pressures intensified quite sharply after the unleashing of the reform program in the late 1970s. Four inflationary surges can be identified between 1980 and 1993. The first one was in 1980, when retail prices rose 6.0 percent, compared with 2.0 percent in 1979; in 1985, retail prices rose 8.8 percent, compared with 2.8 percent in 1984; and in 1988 retail prices jumped 18.5 percent from 7.3 percent in 1987 (World Bank 1990b: 35); in 1993, retail prices reached double-digit growth once again and jumped to 14 percent. These numbers contrast sharply with the indices of inflation for the 1950s and 1960s. Between 1952 and 1962, retail prices rose at an average annual rate of 1.5 to 2.0 percent (Eckstein 1981: 171).

Price stability, however, is only a partial measure of inflation in a centrally planned economy where prices are controlled administratively. Economists who study the Soviet Union have focused on symptoms of "repressed inflation" – queues, waiting lists, and the size of involuntary savings – as indicators of the extent of inflationary pressures (Gregory and Stuart 1981: 363–64). It is quite possible that the Chinese economy also experienced repressed inflation, or shortages, while nominal price stability reigned.[37] The use of prices to map a statistical course of inflation in China during the reform era is justified on two grounds. First, price changes have political significance and therefore acutely influence the leadership's perception of the extent of the crisis. In commenting on the economic situation in 1980, Zhao Ziyang, the premier at the time, expressed alarm that rises in retail prices could wipe out the gains peasants had made from the rural reforms. "This is not only an economic issue," he remarked; "political stability will also be affected" (Zhao Ziyang 1982b [1980]: 609). Second, in a reforming centrally planned economy prices lose some of their original rigidity, either because of officially sanctioned price movements in response to changes in underlying forces in the economy or because of the creation of a formal market sector. Price movements have thus become meaningful indicators of inflation.[38]

Several indices are available to show the extent of inflationary pressures in China. Theoretically, the most comprehensive indicator is the national income deflator – the price index that differentiates changes in the monetary values of the national income from those that result from changes in output. A number of problems arise when national income deflators are used to measure inflation. The valuation of national income is based on nonmarket prices, and the Chinese definition of national income excludes the service sector. Since the service sector has been growing faster than any other sectors in the economy since the onset of the reforms, assessments can systematically underestimate true changes in the economy (Chen and Hou 1986). To solve these measurement problems, other indexes can be used, such as those of retail prices, market prices, and the urban cost of living. The retail price index is a more flexible and reliable measure as it incorporates, to some extent, the effect of market prices (Chow 1985). The course of inflation in China is mapped in figure 5.2.

The three measurements of inflation are consistent both in trend and in

---

37. A minority view among Western economists takes issue with the conclusion that China actually experienced price stability during the 1950s and 1960s. See Peebles (1986).

38. In China, considerable price flexibility in the state sector was introduced in 1985 when the "double-track" price system was established. This system mandates the sale of producer goods produced within the production plans at state-set prices but allows goods produced above plan targets to be sold at market prices. At first, a 20 percent floating band was imposed, but soon this restriction was relaxed. As a result, sizable premiums – the difference between state and market prices – accrue to some of these producer goods. In 1985, for example, the ex-factory price of #6.5 steel wire was 610 yuan per ton, but its market price was between 1,500 and 1,600 yuan (see Wu and Zhao 1987: 313).

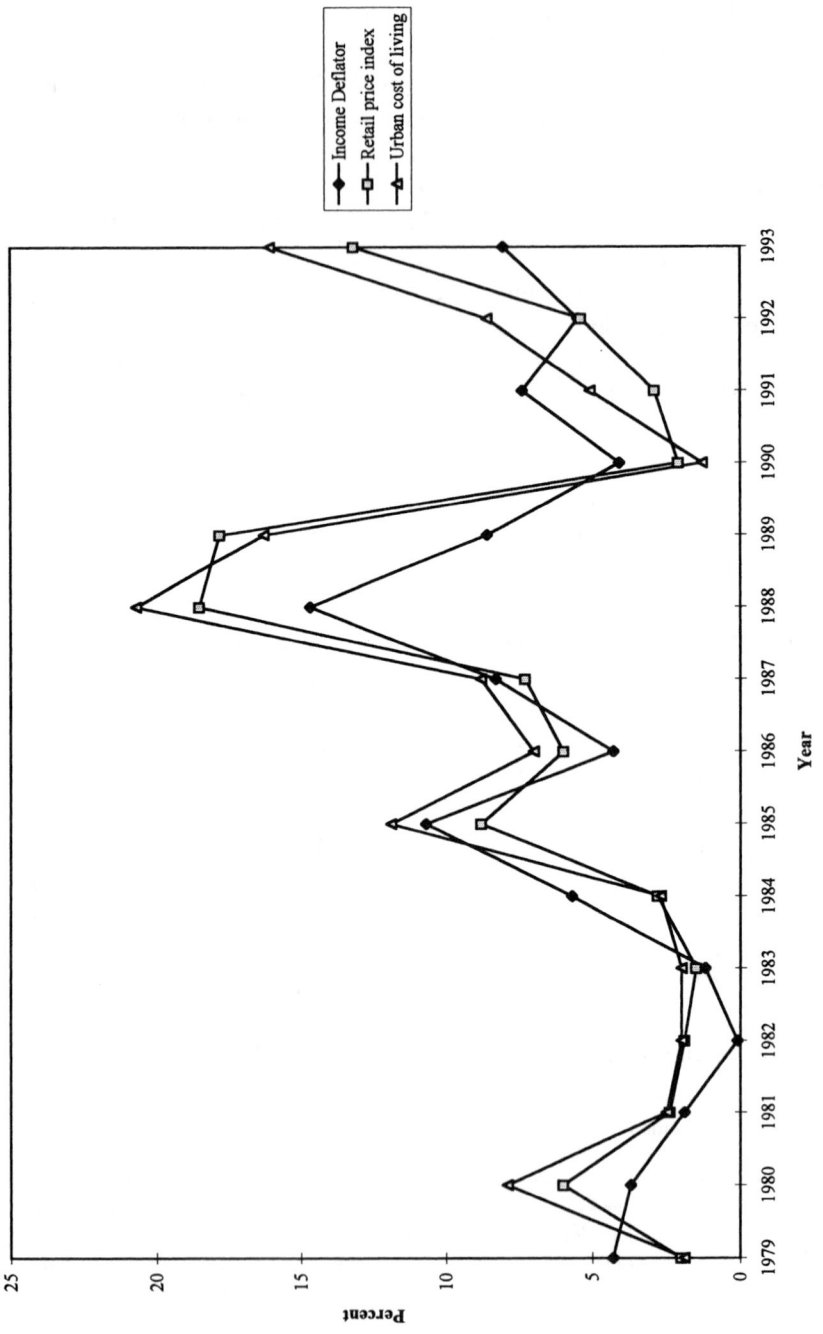

Figure 5.2 Macroeconomic developments in China, 1979–93. *Note*: Chinese statistical sources do not disclose national income deflators directly. Implicit deflators are calculated using national income figures measured in current prices and national income indices measured in constant prices, which are available.

scope. It is clear that inflation in China, even in the peak years of 1980, 1982, 1985, 1988, and 1993, has been quite modest by international standards. During 1965–80 and 1980–86, for example, the average annual inflation rate for low-income countries, excluding India and China, was 11.3 percent and 19.1 percent, respectively, and at no time did China approach the hyperinflationary level of Brazil – 157.1 percent – in the 1980 – 86 period (see World Bank 1988: table 1, 222–23). However, the low levels of inflation belie its fundamental political importance. First, inflationary expectations in the 1980s were low, both because of the long period of price stability and because the central importance that the Communist Party attached to a low inflationary stance. Second, those who bear a disproportionate burden of inflation tend to be vocal urban elites – civil servants, intellectuals, and retirees – because they live on fixed incomes. A partial indicator of this burden is shown in the rise of the urban cost of living. Thus the political reaction to inflation, as pointed out in chapter 1, is stronger than its level would suggest.

Third, as Charles Maier (1985) has commented on the politics of inflation in advanced market economies, it is not so much the rate of inflation but the rate of its acceleration that is politically significant. By that criterion, the potential for inflation in China is enormous. In August 1988, for example, price inflation reached an annualized rate of 80 percent; in June 1993 the cost of living rose by an annualized rate of 36 percent. Inflationary acceleration can also be calculated by taking the ratios of price increases between two time periods. Three acceleration surges can be detected. The first one began in 1980, when retail prices rose three times faster than prices in 1979. The second occurred in 1985, when the retail price increase rate was 3.14 times the level in 1984. In 1988 inflation accelerated at a rate 2.5 times over that in 1987. Furthermore, inflation in the second half of the 1980s accelerated at a rate roughly three times faster than that of the first half of the decade. Similar trends are exhibited by the two other measures, the urban costs of living and the national income deflator.

Industrial policy concerns

The macroeconomic and sectoral issues are, in fact, closely related. From the point of the view of the central government, the structure of investment is particularly unsatisfactory in cases of investment overheating, when projects with high accounting profits – usually those in the processing sectors – tend to "crowd out" those in less profitable sectors such as agriculture, transport, and energy. Here the investment preferences and behavior of local governments are arguably the most important contributing factor, as observed by Gui Shiyong (1992: 2), a vice chairman of the SPC:

By the end of August this year [1992], only 44 percent of the 161 priority projects sponsored by the SPC have been completed, a decrease of 5.5 percent compared with last year. Although capital expenditures have increased so much, the completion pace of the state's priority projects has slowed down. This is mostly because localities failed to deliver the funds [*zijin bu daowei*] and diverted the funds to their own projects. In August alone, local capital expenditure increased by 55 percent.

The gist of the problem, from a central point of view, is that in an environment of investment overheating investment resources are not sufficiently concentrated in the "strategic sectors" – agriculture, transportation, energy, and the like – in other words, in those sectors that feature prominently in the central priority investment program. The problem with this "crowding out" effect is twofold. One is that too high a level of resources flows into the local consumer goods sectors, creating, in the process, a dispersed industrial structure or a wasteful arrangement, which the Chinese refer to as "duplicate construction" (*chongfu jianshe*).[39] The other problem is that the concentration of investment resources in the downstream industries exacerbates supply constraints in the upstream industries because of the high input demands for transport, energy, and raw materials in these sectors. Thus an uninhibited resource flow into the profitable processing sectors acts like a two-edged sword in that it not only draws resources away from the strategic sectors but causes further shortages of transport, energy, and raw materials.[40]

The central government's concerns over the sectoral allocation of investment resources are shown in the reports prepared by the State Statistical Bureau assessing the implementation of the Sixth FYP. The Sixth FYP (1981–85) called for the completion of 400 medium- and large-scale projects, but only about 59 percent were finished on schedule. Capital commitment also fell short of the targets. The Sixth FYP called for 38.5 percent of capital investment funds to be allocated to the energy and transport sectors ("Zhonghua Renmin Gongheguo Guomin Jingji . . ." 1983); in reality, only 34.4 percent were so allocated ("Woguo Guomin Jingji . . ." 1986). This outcome, as a World

---

39. Evidence for industrial dispersion is largely anecdotal. A World Bank report (1990b: 153) points out that all but two of the Chinese provinces produce washing machines; there were 700 automobile factories in China as of 1991, and except for the First and the Second Automobile Works, only ten of these firms have a production capacity in excess of 10,000.

40. This analysis, it should be emphasized here, represents an official view on the issue and is not necessarily shared by all economists. A World Bank economist, Inderjit Singh (1992), for example, makes the case that shortage in the transport, energy, and raw materials sectors is a short-term phenomenon caused by unforeseen high rates of economic growth and by relative inefficiency in the user industries. As reforms deepen, enterprises are expected to economize on their use of energy and raw materials both because of an enhanced cost consciousness and because of higher input–output price ratios on account of price adjustments.

Table 5.2. *Official assessments of investment performance, selected years*

Year	Statistical criteria	Qualitative assessments
1982	Completion rate of priority investment only 65% Energy investment share reduced by 3% from the 1981 level	Excessive investment volume; dispersed investment structure
1985	Growth of local projects higher than that of central projects by 49.4% Growth of nonproduction projects higher than production projects by 33.3%; energy and transport investment shares shrank by 4.6% from the 1984 level	Excessive investment volume; low investment completion rate
1988	Less than 20% of fixed-asset investment in energy, transport, and key raw materials	Investment growth too fast and a skewed investment structure
1992	Investment shares of energy and raw materials decreased by 4.2% from 1991; only 44% of the SPC projects completed on schedule by August Nonproduction investment share rose by 0.9%	Investment in priority sectors lagged behind downstream sectors

Sources: Gui Shiyong (1992); Ma Hong and Sun Shangqing (1993); SSB (1992a, 1992b); State Council (1989c [1988]).

Bank (1990b: 91) report points out, was quite remarkable given the fact that the Sixth FYP was not drawn up until 1982–83. Implementation of the Seventh FYP was by and large more satisfactory on account of an augmented effort by the central government, although new rail construction lagged behind the planned level by some 36 percent in terms of the projected length of new tracks (SSB 1991a: 57).[41]

The central government's concerns over investment structures were sharper on a year-to-year basis. In the annual assessment of the economic situation prepared by the SSB, usually one section is devoted to the completion record of priority investment projects. This information is presented in reduced form in table 5.2 for the two years deemed especially unsatisfactory, 1982 and 1985. For 1992, the information is drawn from the works of Chinese economists in

41. The SSB (1991a: 60) notes that investment in the raw materials, energy, and transport sectors increased by 5.5 percent compared with the Sixth FYP level.

the central government and the quarterly reports of the SSB. The assessment criteria and the conclusions reached are briefly noted.

In 1985 the SSB noted the high growth of investment in local projects and in "nonproduction" projects. In general, local projects are more heavily concentrated in the downstream sectors producing consumer durables than central investment projects, and thus the central government's concern over the growth of local investment is the same as its concern over the diversion of investment resources away from the bottleneck sectors. Nonproduction projects refer to office buildings, housing, urban construction, and other social infrastructural projects. Chinese government officials and economists alike have become concerned about these "prestige" projects, such as investing in the construction of high-quality office buildings and recreational centers (Xu Gang 1986). Chinese economists have also found an increasing concentration of resources in the nonproduction sector at the lower end of the administrative ladder of the government. In 1984, for example, about 6 percent of the self-raised funds were invested in city construction at the national level; at the city level, however, the share was about 23 percent (Xu Gang 1986: 184). Local projects are thus more heavily concentrated in the nonproduction sectors than those projects sponsored by the Center.

Austerity policies

The official definition of the periodization of the austerity policy rounds is adopted in this discussion. This is not to suggest that the intensity of austerity does not vary across the years in which an austerity policy is in effect. Indeed, later in this chapter, the austerity policy periods are divided into firm and soft subperiods and reasons are given for the wavering policy commitment to an austerity stance. By this definition, there were four austerity rounds between 1977 and 1992: in 1979–81, 1983, 1986–87, and 1989–91.

Austerity programs

By and large, the central austerity program has entailed both a reduction in investment volume and an adjustment in the investment structure, and it has embodied a mixture of administrative and economic measures, with a heavy emphasis on administrative measures in the earlier rounds and a gradual reliance on economic measures in the later rounds. The first round, between 1979 and 1981, is known as the program of "adjustment, reform, rectification, and improvement" (*tiaozheng, gaige zhengdun, tigao*), which formally became central government policy in April 1979. Mainly for political reasons (discussed in the next section), the implementation of this program was not rigorous in 1979 and 1980, but once political consensus was secured at the top level, the retrenchment program began in earnest in 1981. The new premier, Zhao Ziyang, announced a three-pronged approach. The first consisted of a set of fiscal measures: budget-financed investment was cut from 24.2 billion yuan in 1980 to 17 billion yuan in 1981, and the investment target for 1981 was set at 30 billion yuan (later revised to 38 billion yuan), an 86 percent cutback from the actual investment level in 1980. Eight billion yuan was transferred to central coffers from the provinces via "central borrowings," and 5 billion yuan of treasury bonds were issued.

Second, the strategy also aimed at strengthening monetary discipline to control the money supply. This was the purpose of the central borrowings from the provinces, which avoided using bank overdrafts to finance central spending. In addition, measures were taken to augment the administrative authority and the vertical control of the People's Bank of China, China's central bank, by prohibiting local officials from authorizing loans. There is no evidence, however, that an adjustment of interest rates was used to curb credit demand. Third, the Center tightened investment approvals and imposed price controls (Zhao Ziyang 1982b [1980]: 612–17). Furthermore, the State Planning Commission, the State Capital Construction Commission, and the Ministry of Finance drew up detailed guidelines for investment approval criteria, banning investment projects in ten categories (SPC 1987: 558–60).

The result of the 1981 retrenchment was quite impressive. Realized capital investment was 44.3 billion yuan, about 16 percent above the planned target. The budget deficit was cut to 2.55 billion yuan, an 80 percent reduction from the level of the previous year. Price rises were contained. Retail prices and the cost of living rose by 2.5 percent, as compared with 6.0 percent and 7.5 percent, respectively, for 1980 (SSB 1986: 446, 595, 623).

The second austerity round was in 1983. Only a year after the 1981 retrenchment program was declared a success, the Chinese government was hit by another economic shock. This time the problem was a steep increase in investment and, from the central government's point of view, a deterioration in the structure of investment.

After the 1981 decline, in 1982, investment quickly recovered and climbed to 55.5 billion yuan, which was close to the 1980 level of (55.9 billion yuan). This represented a 25 percent increase over 1981. This steep increase made investment growth in 1982 the fourth largest ever in PRC history. (The other three times were 1958, 1970, and 1978.) The investment target for 1982, initially set at 38 billion yuan and later revised to 44.5 billion yuan, was surpassed.[42] In addition, the authorities became concerned about the structure of investment – the sectoral distribution of investment resources. Chinese planning authorities were particularly alarmed by the declining shares of resources claimed by the "strategic" or bottleneck sectors. The strategic sectors were usually given top priority in central investment plans. But, according to the SSB's (1983) assessment of the economic situation in 1982, all priority sectors, except telecommunications and transport, experienced declines in investment shares.

The diversion of investment resources from the priority sectors meant that the central government had difficulties completing many of its projects on schedule. According to the SSB, 35.6 percent of the projects in the national plan that were to be finished in 1982 were not completed. The completion rate for investment projects – often used as a measure of investment efficiency – also declined as a whole; as a result, the completion rate was 74.4 percent as compared with 86.6 percent in 1981 (SSB 1983: 2).[43]

The official explanation for, and Chinese economists' analyses of, the 1982 investment expansion attributes it in part to the alleged residual influences of "leftist" ideology among Chinese economic officials. Some also point to the fact that administrative decentralization had undermined central financing capabilities and that local economic officials had vested interests in developing industries within their jurisdiction.[44] None of these is a *sufficient* explanation, however, as they all merely identify a set of constant factors that had been present for a long period of time rather than those events specific to 1982.

---

42. The original investment target was given by Yao Yilin (1982: 2), a vice premier and minister of the State Planning Commission, in his report on the 1982 plan. The revised target was in the State Statistical Bureau's report on the 1982 economic performance (SSB 1983: 2).

43. For a Western economic analysis of investment completion in China and the Soviet Union, see Harrison (1985).

44. Leftist ideology is traditionally blamed for the investment expansions during the Great Leap Forward. Economic leftism maintains that material and financial balances are not necessary for and indeed are harmful for growth. Such an analysis stems very much from a planner's perspective: it views investment expansion as a function of defective planning rather than as a product of the planning system itself. For an example of this kind of analysis on the 1982 investment expansion, see Bo Yibo (1983). Bo, a vice premier at the time and China's first minister of finance (1949–53), as well as the first chairman of the State Economic Commission (1956–66), is often associated with the central planning school in China. The argument that surrendering resources from the Center to the localities created economic instability is another variant of this view, as it does not take into account the institutional context. For an example of this view, see Li Kaixin (1983) and Zhou Shulian (1983). The view that investment expansion is motivated by the self-interests of local officials is a major departure from the planning perspective in that it identifies a systemic cause, namely, that the system allocates benefits and costs of investment expansion asymmetrically. This view has been put forward by an influential Chinese economist, Xue Muqiao (1983).

What distinguished 1982 from the previous year seemed to be a shift in central policy away from exclusive concern with the macroeconomic situation. In a way, the success in 1981 contributed to this shift, as indicated by the authorities' declaration in the annual plan for 1982 that there could be "an appropriate increase" in investment in the latter half of 1982 (Yao Yilin 1982: 2). This was a signal to local economic officials that they could anticipate a relaxation of investment control later in the year. Another contributing factor to this policy shift, less palpable at the time than the first factor, but probably with more lasting impact on later investment-reduction decisions, was a shift in the leadership's emphasis from "stability" to reforms. Zhao Ziyang, in his speech at the National Industrial and Transportation Work Conference on March 4, 1982, which laid down the basic guidelines for economic work in 1982, contended that the main effect of economic overheating was the loss of economic efficiency. To improve efficiency in a way that departed from orthodox central planning edicts required "recognition of (*chengren*) and consideration to (*zhaogu*) local interests" (Zhao Ziyang 1982a: 2). Zhao Ziyang argued that economic stability was to be achieved via some harmonization of interests between the central government and local governments, rather than by a suppression of local interests, as central planners have often stressed. The year 1982 witnessed the very beginning of what later evolved into a major policy issue in the debates among the top decision makers – concerning the appropriate pace of reforms with respect to the appropriate level of the rate of growth and, by extension, to the degree of appropriate economic decentralization.

The central authorities reacted to the investment expansion in 1982 in the same way as they did in 1981 – by scaling down the investment target and imposing more stringent administrative controls. There were three important differences this time, however. First, probably reflecting the aforementioned reservations Zhao had felt about traditional control mechanisms, the authorities initially relied, to some extent, on indirect economic levers to regulate investment activities. In March the SPC and the State Economic Commission (SEC) issued "Provisional Regulations on the Economic Contract System in Construction of Capital Investment Projects," which aimed at introducing cost consciousness in project construction and improving investment efficiency by further clarifying benefits and costs in investment projects, rather than by imposing direct administrative controls (SEC 1986: 496–97). In addition, with Zhao's approval (SEC 1986: 505), construction taxes were levied. According to Naughton (1988), this use of taxation to regulate enterprise behavior signaled a more sophisticated approach to macroeconomic control.

Second, the cutback was much less drastic than in 1981; the investment target for 1983 was set at 55.07 billion yuan, which was 8.6 percent less than the actual investment level in 1982. This reduction, compared with 86 percent in 1981, signaled a much less alarmed reaction by the leadership, as well as a different objective for investment reduction in 1983. Although in 1981 the central government had sought a reduction in all categories of investment, the primary central objective in 1983 seemed to be an adjustment of the investment structure. Thus a major cut was sought in the local governments' projects; central projects, on the other hand, were not affected to the same degree.[45]

By mid-1983, however, it became apparent to the authorities that these measures were not sufficient to contain investment growth. After a Central Committee Work Conference in June, efforts to control investment escalated. First the authorities began to move away from "indirect economic levers" and to stress instead control techniques of a more administrative nature. At the end of June, work teams from the State Council were dispatched to different localities to investigate their investment-reduction efforts. At the same time, ministries and provinces were ordered to review sources of project financing in their jurisdictions (State Council 1987b [1983]: 576). Furthermore, the State Council issued a directive that held governors, ministers, and heads of banks directly responsible for investment excesses in their areas (State Council 1987b [1983]: 576–77).

The second indication was the increasingly political connotation attached to investment control in the latter half of 1983. Between July 8 and August 19, *Renmin ribao* printed six editorials exhorting Communist Party members, because of their ideological and organizational obligations, to implement the policies of the Central Committee. Invariably in these editorials, support for the "priority projects" designated by the central government was touted as one such obligation. Similar articles appeared in the Party's other publications, such as the theoretical journal *Hongqi* and the economic daily *Jingji ribao*.

The third austerity round was ushered in in 1986. In 1984 and 1985 capital investment had surged ahead. In 1984, the growth rate was 25.1 percent over the previous year; in 1985, it reached 44.5 percent, one of the highest in PRC history (SSB 1986: 446). Then signs of macroeconomic instability began to surface. Retail prices rose 2.8 percent in 1984, the highest rate since 1981, and in 1985 they rose by another 8.8 percent. Market prices in 1985 rose by 16.9 percent, a marked increase over 1984 (0.3 percent), 1983 (4.1 percent), and 1982 (3.5 percent). In addition, China's current account position deteriorated massively: the trade deficit was US$14.9 billion (SSB 1988: 721).

Two related factors apparently contributed to this somewhat lax management of aggregate demand. The first was that the Chinese leadership at this

---

45. Statistics in this section are taken from Yao Yilin's report on the 1983 plan (Yao Yilin 1983: 3).

time had become preoccupied with economic reforms, rather than devoting its time and energy to demand management. By the mid-1980s, the reformist leaders, Hu Yaobang, Zhao Ziyang, Wan Li, and Tian Jiyun, had consolidated their positions and were pushing reforms aggressively on the government's economic agenda. A document that proved to have far-reaching repercussions, "The Resolution of the CCP Central Committee on Reform of the Economic System," was passed by the Third Plenum of the Twelfth Party Congress on October 20, 1984. Although the document did not contain a specific blueprint for the reform program, it provided a sense of direction for reforms and a much-needed ideological justification for the entire reform program. The goal of the reforms was to build "a socialist commodity economy" and to seek to integrate market mechanisms with central planning. This was a significant departure from Chen Yun's planning orthodoxy that relegated market functions to a residual role in a socialist economy.[46] Even before the adoption of this document, however, large-scale reforms had already been unfolding. These reforms included the opening of fourteen coastal cities to direct foreign investment, the granting of autonomy to enterprises, banking reforms, and foreign trade reforms. The cumulative effect of these measures was a transfer of substantial economic decision-making power from the central government to the localities.

The second cause is more complex and is related to the controversy surrounding the appropriate measures to control investment demand. As mentioned before, reformist leaders were reluctant to resort to direct administrative measures to restore macroeconomic equilibrium. This reluctance explains a number of policy initiatives in 1984 in the area of investment management. In his report on government work for 1984, Zhao Ziyang outlined an approach for reforming the investment management system that would introduce a degree of market discipline to regulate investment activities. The measures he proposed included placing project completion on a contractual basis and converting budgetary grants to investment loans with positive interest rates (SEC 1986: 536). Later in 1984 these ideas were formulated into a set of specific regulations by the SPC, the Ministry of Finance, and the Construction Bank (SSB 1987a: 19–48).

Another of Zhao's ideas that probably contributed to the character of the macroeconomic policies at this time was his belief that a rapid rate of growth could be compatible with economic stability and that a moderate level of inflation was necessary to facilitate economic growth. This belief grew stronger in the 1987–88 period and, as will be illustrated next, led to a policy split

---

46. For a good analysis of this document, see Lin (1989).

between Zhao and Li Peng in 1988. The expansive fiscal and monetary policies in 1984 and during the better part of 1985 were the result of Zhao's economic beliefs. In the investment arena, this policy posture was reflected in the high investment targets set for 1984 and 1985. In 1984 and 1985, for the first time since 1978, the investment target was set at a higher level than the actual level achieved the previous year. This move indicated a degree of laxness toward investment control.

In the end, the overambitious economic targets proved to be unsustainable. The acceleration in the increase in the general price levels and the taut supply situation in the latter half of 1985 compelled the government to make a "hard landing." Provincial governors' conferences were convened twice, once in June and once in September, to discuss specific methods of controlling investment growth and to ensure provincial compliance with central investment policies (Tian Jiyun 1986: 1). In August 1985 the State Council issued a circular announcing that the investment quota was not to be raised and ordering further investment cuts. The circular also ordered regional branches of the People's Construction Bank to freeze savings deposits and to halt lending to projects not included in the investment plan (SEC 1986: 663). In his report on the Seventh Five-Year Plan (1986–90), Zhao declared the onset of a contractionary phase in macroeconomic policies that would last two years, during 1986 and 1987 (Zhao Ziyang 1985). Predictably, the investment target for 1986 was revised downward from the actual investment level achieved in 1985, from 107.4 billion yuan to 90.5 billion yuan, a reduction of 15.7 percent (Song Ping 1986: 2). This ushered in the third round of investment reduction.

The fourth round of investment reduction, between 1989 and 1991, was put into effect in the wake of the deepest macroeconomic crisis in ten years. In 1988 inflation in China entered the double-digit range; retail prices rose by 18.5 percent and the climb in the urban cost of living was even steeper, around 20 percent. By the third quarter of 1988, price rises reached an annualized rate of 50 percent (Naughton 1992a). Exacerbating the situation was an ill-timed announcement for a major price overhaul in May 1988. Together, these developments caused unprecedented panic runs on banks and shops. This was clearly of grave concern to the leadership. A carefully worded communiqué released by the SSB revealed that for the first three-quarters of 1988 the rise in the official cost of living resulted in "a decline of real incomes for substantial numbers of residents" (*Renmin ribao* October 19, 1988: 1).

In an emergency atmosphere, the CCP convened the Third Plenum of the Thirteenth Party Congress between September 26 and 30, 1988. Many components of the retrenchment program aimed at reversing the economic decentralization effected during the reform era. The plan to overhaul China's price structure was shelved indefinitely. Price controls were reimposed on some of the industrial goods whose prices had been liberalized; the State Council, in its notice on price controls, specifically mentioned that there were to be no exceptions for Guangdong, Fujian, and Hainan in this regard (State Council 1989b [1988]: 180). Li Peng, in his address to the State Council, gave a virtual blank check to local governments to impose administrative price ceilings (*Renmin ribao* October 13, 1988: 1). The state monopoly over the marketing of a number of key raw materials was reimposed, and many of the trade corporations were ordered to shut down (*Renmin ribao* October 14, 1988: 1).

Investment expansion was viewed as a major contributor to inflation in 1988. By July of that year Li Peng had already raised the specter of investment expansion (*Renmin ribao* July 18, 1988: 1). For this reason, Li Peng and Yao Yilin wanted to project an image of firm commitment to investment reduction as part of the retrenchment program. In a move to centralize the investment approval procedure, a "regulatory committee" was established to review project applications and to remove approval authority from individual government officials (*Renmin ribao* September 16, 1988: 1). Li Peng himself headed the interagency leadership group within the State Council to preside over investment reduction work. As a sign that the State Council was assigning the highest priority to investment reduction and as a signal to the localities that their disobedience would carry disciplinary consequences, this group not only consisted of economic agencies, such as the SPC, PBC, MOF, and SSB, but also of the State Council Secretariat, the GAA, and the MOS. Each central ministry and each province was required to establish such a leadership group, and ministers and governors were required to head it (State Council 1989a [1988]: 32–33).

The investment reduction target was quite drastic. Yao Yilin (1991a [1989]) announced that the capital investment target for 1989 would be 22 percent lower than the 1988 level, and in an attempt to preempt any anticipation of a more relaxed macroeconomic policy course later in the year, he strongly reproached those regions that had a "wait-and-see" attitude and were dragging their feet in implementing central investment reduction measures. The State Council also drew up a long list of projects that were to be suspended. Unlike the previous rounds, which relied mainly on local governments themselves to decide which projects to cut (as long as they did not exceed the control target), this list was both long and extremely detailed. The list contained five general categories of projects, and within each category between twenty and thirty products were banned categorically (State Council 1989a [1988]: 35–43). This was to leave no room for subjective interpretation at the implementation stage.

To curtail local investment, the State Council in essence abolished the authority of the localities below the provincial level to approve new project applications for 1989 and 1990. Approval authority at the provincial level was reduced in part; projects in excess of 10 million yuan were still approved by the provincial governments, but the decisions had to be reported to the SPC for record keeping. Although the investment control approach was overwhelmingly administrative in nature, some indirect macroeconomic levers were also applied. In particular, the central government raised interest rates on deposits and indexed them to inflation to stop the flight from financial assets. Lending rates on fixed-asset loans were raised sharply; explicit quotas were assigned to local banks for investment lending separate from quotas for other lendings in order to minimize slippage in the use of funds. The local branches of the PBC were also required to report to the head office every month (World Bank 1990a: 11–16).

In 1989 and 1990 the central policy response to the macroeconomic crisis that had been fermenting since the mid-1980s was more sweeping in part because the inflationary situation was more severe and in part because the economic decentralization had created countervailing forces in the localities against central policies; thus a more forceful posture was required to bring about the same amount of investment reduction. There was also a political angle. The entire debate on macroeconomic policy was engulfed in a power struggle between the reformist wing of the leadership (headed by Zhao Ziyang) and the more cautious, central planning wing headed by Li Peng. The lack of political consensus hampered the effectiveness of a central macroeconomic policy stance.

Political commitment and central policy credibility

Austerity policies varied in their severity. There were two contributing factors. One was the conflicting policy signals from the central government and a wavering macroeconomic policy course. Conflicting policy signals are a sign that the central leaders are divided on the austerity policies, or they are unwilling to bear the full economic and political costs of the austerity program they adopted. The other reason was the political or policy conflicts among central policy makers. Severe policy conflicts among central leaders – whether these conflicts are related to the immediate economic issues at hand – weaken their commitment to the adopted austerity policy either because their attention is occupied elsewhere or because they cannot reach a consensus as to the importance of the program or as to how to implement the specifics of austerity policies. Of the four investment reduction rounds chronicled earlier, political conflicts intensified in 1979 and 1980 (the first round) and in the first half of

1989 (the fourth round), whereas conflicting signals were a factor in 1987 (the third round) and in 1991 (the fourth round).

In 1979, the retrenchment program was adopted to deal with the macro-economic disequilibria created by the ambitious development strategy put in place by Hua Guofeng, Mao's immediate successor. Hua's development strategy, embodied in his "Government Report" to the National People's Congress convened in February 1978 and in the State Council's "Ten-Year Plan for the National Economy, 1976–1985," stressed the primacy of China's heavy industrial sectors and viewed mobilization of resources for investment as a basic engine for economic growth. As a result, the investment target was set at an unrealistically high level, in relation to the availability of financial and material resources. Between 1977 and 1978 the capital investment target was raised to 41.7 billion yuan, which represented an increase of 33.7 percent, and at the National Planning Conference held in September 1978, the investment target for 1979 was again revised upward, to 45.7 billion yuan, which represented an increase of 15.7 percent from the already inflated 1978 target (Zhao Dexing 1989b: 386–89). Because domestic production could not keep up with demand, the ambitious investment targets required large-scale imports. As a result, China had a trade deficit of US$1.14 billion in 1978, the highest until that year.

At the beginning of 1979, a number of top leaders became alarmed by the potential economic dislocations from Hua's economic development strategy. Deng Xiaoping, in a speech on January 6, 1979, urged scaling down investment in some of the giant steel plants (Fang Weizhong 1984: 614); on March 14, 1979, two of China's most senior economic planners, Chen Yun and Li Xiannian (1982: 72–73), wrote a letter to the Politburo, warning of "serious economic imbalances" in the making, and argued vigorously for a retrenchment program of two to three years to correct the situation. In April 1979 retrenchment was adopted as the official policy at a lengthy Central Committee Work Conference attended by provincial governors and other central Party and government officials. Li Xiannian gave the keynote speech, in which the doctrine of "adjustment, reform, rectification, and improvement" was formally announced. The conference also agreed to a much scaled-down economic plan for 1979 (Zhao Dexing 1989b: 413–14). The investment target was revised down to 36 billion yuan from the previously announced 45.7 billion yuan (Xue Muqiao 1983).

The central commitment to investment reduction in 1979 and 1980, however, remained in doubt. A critical impediment to an effective retrenchment policy posture was the increasing conflict among central leaders concerning both political and economic issues. Politically, there was a fierce power struggle between what MacFarquhar (1993) calls "Cultural Revolution victims" such as Deng Xiaoping and Chen Yun and "Cultural Revolution benefactors" such as Hua Guofeng. Ostensibly, the debate revolved around a proper evaluation of Mao Zedong and of the Cultural Revolution in the history of the CCP.[47] Chinese commentators refer to remnants of ultraleftism within the CCP that continued to stress rapid expansion and favored an extensive approach to economic development. Also, many government officials apparently were not fully convinced of the necessity of a major investment reduction; some argued that the adjustment program would "cause delays in the realization of the four modernizations" (see Zhao Dexing 1989b: 421–24; Cao Erjie, Li Minxin, and Wang Guoqiang 1992: 284–85).

In 1980 the succession struggle and the attendant economic conflicts were resolved in favor of the Deng Xiaoping and Chen Yun faction. At a Politburo meeting on December 5, 1980, Hua was forced to resign from both the chairmanship of the Central Committee and the chairmanship of the Military Affairs Commission. Deng Xiaoping, in a speech to a Central Committee Work Conference on adjustment policies in December 1980, openly blamed the weak policy consensus ("differences within the Party leadership") for the lack of progress in 1979 and 1980:

After the Third Plenum of the Eleventh Party Congress, Comrade Chen Yun was put in charge of financial and economic work and he proposed the principles for the adjustment programs. The Central Committee Work Conference last April also made a decision in this regard. But because of significant differences of understanding within the Party and because the understanding [of the problem] was not sufficient, implementation was ineffectual. Only now has the situation changed. (Deng Xiaoping 1982 [1980]: 627)

The third round, in 1986–87, was characterized by conflicting policy signals, especially in 1987, about whether the Center really meant to pursue the zero-growth goal. Between July 1986 and March 1987, the State Council flip-flopped in devising its investment control procedures. Second, the monetary policy in 1986 and 1987 remained relatively permissive, which was incongruent with the official goal of achieving zero-growth investment.

In July 1986 the State Council issued the document, "Provisions for Controlling the Scope of Fixed-asset Investment." The document expanded the government investment plan to cover collective, private, and foreign firms. The State Council also tightened the approval requirements, placing small projects – requiring up to 3 million yuan – under the auspices of the provincial planning commissions. But less than nine months later, in March 1987, the

---

47. For accounts of this period, see Harding (1987) and Wang Hongmo (1989).

Table 5.3. *Quarterly monetary course, 1986–87 (percentage)*

Quarters	1986			1987			
	2nd	*3rd*	*4th*	*1st*	*2nd*	*3rd*	*4th*
Reserve money growth	18.9	26.6	23.2	19.0	14.2	12.5	12.9
Growth of money and quasi money	24.2	28.1	28.9	33.2	30.6	31.6	24.2
Excess reserves as % of required reserves	106.0	95.8	98.7	106.0	107.9	83.9	78.7

Source: World Bank (1990a: 46).

State Council issued another document, "Notice about Expanding Approval Authority and Simplifying Approval Procedures," the gist of which was that administrative approval authority should be delegated. For example, the threshold for SPC approval was raised from 30 million yuan to 50 million yuan; the document also gave approval authority for below-threshold projects to the investment agencies themselves.[48]

The wavering policy stance can be seen in the monetary policy course of the PBC. Since bank lending financed between 23 and 24 percent of the state fixed-asset investment, a detailed examination of China's monetary course in 1986 and 1987 on a quarterly basis sheds light on the wavering commitment to economic contraction and reveals a largely accommodating monetary policy during this period. China's monetary course during these two years is presented in table 5.3.

The degree of laxness in monetary policies can be gauged in several respects. First, although the growth of reserve money – central bank lending to specialized banks – from the third quarter of 1986 slowed somewhat, it sustained a high level, hovering around 20 percent, until the second quarter of 1987. Second, and very important, the growth of broad money was steady until the fourth quarter of 1987, when it experienced a decline. Third, withdrawals of deposits by the specialized banks from the central bank increased throughout both 1986 and 1987. This is indicated in the last row of the table, which shows that excess reserves – the amount of deposits in the central bank above the reserve requirement set by the central bank – fell continuously. This contributed to more liquidity in the hands of the specialized banks and therefore helped increase the money supply.

Similar tendencies can be detected on the policy side. Monetary contraction, from the last quarter of 1985 through the first quarter of 1986, was eased

48. For a detailed discussion of these two policy documents, see Guo Shuqing (1992: 83–84).

by Zhao's announcement in April 1986 that there should be "flexibility within contraction" (*jinzhong youhuo*) (see Naughton 1988). In a speech to officials of the Agricultural Bank, Chen Muhua (1987), the governor of the PBC, charted the monetary policy course for the second half of 1986 in terms of "seeking flexibility within stability" (*wenzhong qiuhuo*). Another development at this time was the lowering of the reserve requirements for the PCBC from 30 percent to 10 percent in January 1987 (World Bank 1990b: 46). This reduction of the reserve requirements enabled the bank, which was officially in charge of disbursing investment credits, to increase its line of credits to finance investment.

China's monetary policy became tight again in the fourth quarter of 1987 with the announcement of "dual contraction," meaning both fiscal and monetary contractions. Several policy measures were then introduced to achieve monetary stringency. Reserve requirements were raised from 10 percent to 12 percent, thus reducing the reserves in the specialized banks; interest rates that the PBC charged to the specialized banks were raised to 7.2 percent from a previous range of 4.68 percent to 6.84 percent. Credit quotas were tightened and lendings to rural enterprises were frozen at the level prior to the fourth quarter of 1987 (Naughton 1988: 23). The third retrenchment round persisted until the first quarter of 1988, when the policy of "dual contraction" again dropped out of the official media.

There were two reasons for this wavering policy commitment. Politically, by the mid-1980s the direction and pace of the economic reforms had created two clearly identifiable groups within the Chinese leadership: the reformist leaders and defenders of central planning. Although much of the debate concerned the pace and direction of the reforms, macroeconomic issues were inevitably involved in the leadership disputes because macroeconomic policies could not be separated from such issues as economic and fiscal decentralization and enterprise profit retention. Macroeconomic issues were also relevant because central planners used the emergence of macroeconomic instability following the launching of the urban reforms in the 1984–85 period to attack the reformers (Sullivan 1988). As early as January 1984, Song Ping, the chairman of the SPC (1983–87) and an official schooled largely in the central planning tradition, in a speech at the Central Party School, warned of impending macroeconomic tensions and repeatedly quoted the concerns of an unnamed central leader – most probably Chen Yun – regarding investment expansion and the resultant losses in investment efficiency (Song Ping 1984: 1–7).

Although the political dominance of Zhao Ziyang brought Song Ping in line at the time, as indicated by Song's optimistic assessment of the economic situation in the annual report on economic planning in May 1984 (Song Ping

1984: 2), criticisms of the reform program prompted Zhao Ziyang into a defensive posture. On January 12, 1986, his close assistant, Vice Premier Tian Jiyun (1986), made a lengthy speech to a conference of cadres in central Party and government departments (*zhongyang jiguan ganbu dahui*) offering a vigorous defense of the basic soundness of the reform program. He argued that a few problems were inevitable in the process of the reforms and should not detract from the overall success of the reform program. In addition, he assured the audience that corrective measures had been taken, and that they were effective in ameliorating stresses in the economy.

The effect of the conservatives' assault on the economic reform program, however, was an increase in the political costs of a contractionary policy posture. On the one hand, the fact that the conservatives factored the economic reform program into the macroeconomic debate meant that instituting a contractionary policy posture could amount to an admission of defeat for Zhao and shake his political power base. On the other hand, the intensification of conservative criticism accentuated Zhao's need to placate his political allies – provincial officials in particular – by not retrenching the economy too severely.[49] There were economic considerations as well. The wavering monetary and investment policy course in 1987 coincided with the introduction of enterprise reforms in industrial enterprises. The hope then was to achieve a "soft landing" by infusing more financial discipline into enterprise incentives. That is to say, the government wanted to achieve macroeconomic stability not via a restrictive monetary and investment policy but via microeconomic reforms (see Guo Shuqing 1992: 181–82).

Of the four austerity rounds, the fourth round was probably the most politicized. It began in September 1988 amidst political and policy conflicts between Zhao Ziyang and Li Peng. During its implementation, between April and June 1989, massive student protests mounted the most serious challenge to the authority of the communist regime since the founding of the People's Republic of China. In the end, the bloody Tiananmen crackdown decidedly ended the leadership conflicts in favor of the conservative central planners. Zhao Ziyang was ousted in June 1989 and Li Peng and Yao Yilin seized near complete control of the central government. For the rest of 1989, and to a lesser degree in 1990, Li and Yao pursued a tight retrenchment program that not only tamed inflation but overshot its objective by bringing on the most serious recession the Chinese economy had experienced since the inception of the reforms.

The economic policy conflicts between Zhao and Li can be traced to the

---

49. For an argument that provincial officials largely supported Zhao Ziyang, see Shirk (1989, 1990).

beginning of 1988 when Zhao, as the Party general secretary, pressed for a faster growth rate and relatively reflationary fiscal and monetary policies. He argued that because of the implementation of economic reforms – notably the enterprise reforms of 1987 – economic performance in 1987 was at a turning point in that the economy had entered a "virtuous circle" whereby sustained growth could be achieved in conjunction with a reasonable level of economic stability. The task for 1988, Zhao declared in his speech to the Second Plenum of the Thirteenth Central Committee in March 1988, was to "maintain relatively fast and sustained growth" (*Renmin ribao* March 21 1988: 1–2).

Li Peng viewed the 1987 economic situation with alarm and concluded at the beginning of 1988 that the economy was already "overheating." Contrary to Zhao's optimistic assessment of the effect of the reforms in 1987, Li argued that the Chinese economy still operated under the constraints of the traditional system, that there was an inevitable trade-off between speed and stability, and that the system, if left alone, would gear toward investment expansion. Li pressed for a cautious economic policy course for 1988 and set economic stabilization as the main task for that year. These points were made repeatedly in Li's speeches, once at the Spring Festival celebration, another time in his mid-year assessment of the 1988 economic performance (Li Peng 1988).

In his capacity as the Party general secretary, Zhao continued to intervene actively in economic affairs, contributing further to the friction between himself and Li Peng. According to a Chinese economist, the PBC received two conflicting policy directives at the beginning of 1988, one from the office of the Party general secretary instructing the PBC to loosen monetary control and the other from the premier instructing the PBC to tighten credit.[50] Zhao's perspective prevailed. Between January and July, the money supply increased by 22.7 billion yuan over the same period in 1987 (this amounted to an increase of 18.3 billion yuan in 1988 and a withdrawal of 4.4 billion yuan in 1987), even though the increase target for the whole year was 20 billion yuan. This forced the monetary authorities to revise the 1988 target by almost doubling the money supply target for 1988.

The strains in the economy worsened considerably in the second and third quarters of 1988. By the summer, prices were rising at an annualized rate of 50 percent, which, together with an ill-timed announcement of a major price reform program, brought about panic runs on banks and shops. Li Peng and Yao Yilin took advantage of the severe macroeconomic situation to attack

---

50. Author's interview. In January 1989, after a full-scale retrenchment program had been adopted, Yao Yilin "absolved" the PBC of any responsibility for having pursued a loose monetary policy by pointing to the "lax overall economic management" in 1988 (*Renmin ribao*, January 21, 1989: 1).

Zhao. At the Third Plenum of the Thirteenth Central Committee held in late September 1988 to launch an economic retrenchment program, they demanded Zhao take personal responsibility for the price rises, which Zhao steadfastly refused.[51] They also wrestled economic decision-making power away from Zhao. In March 1989, in a move to augment the State Council's economic authority, the State Council issued a directive to news organizations placing the Research Office of the State Council in control of economic propaganda (*Jingji ribao*, March 10, 1989: 1).[52] Zhao, in an interview with the American publisher, Frank Gibney, also revealed that he was no longer involved in economic management.

The open political rift between Zhao Ziyang and Li Peng marked not only the initiation of the 1988 retrenchment program, but also its implementation. As late as April 1989, Zhao still insisted that the administrative measures adopted were temporary and second-best options, and that they were necessary only because they could win time and bring about a more stable environment for further reforms (*Renmin ribao*, April 12, 1989: 1). This view of the relationship between retrenchment and reforms contrasted sharply with that of Li Peng. In his annual "Report on Government Work" presented in March 1989, Li argued that the goal of the economic reforms was to help stabilize the economy, not the other way around (Li Peng 1989). This apparently innocuous semantic maneuver enabled Li Peng to define what was normally considered centralization as "reform."

The nominal leadership unity after the Tiananmen crackdown enabled Li Peng and Yao Yilin to impose tight limits on bank credits and investment in 1989 and 1990. However, the central planners overshot their stability objective by issuing excessively stringent investment targets, having failed to realize that the high inflation rate in the first half of 1989 had already eroded the purchasing power of households and enterprises. By 1990 China had already entered into a recessionary phase unprecedented in the reform era. The most tangible cost of the recession was a significant jump in unemployment. In 1989, 4 million jobs were lost in the private sector and another 3.5 million were lost in rural industry (Naughton 1992a).

High unemployment raised the specter of political and social instability. The Rumanian revolution had an impact on the Chinese leadership, and there was great concern about the possibility of unrest among urban workers in China. Thus in 1990 the leaders began to modify the austerity program. First,

51. Author's interview.
52. The Research Office of the State Council was a new agency established in late 1988, reportedly to eclipse Zhao's economic think tanks (Lam 1989).

they eased working capital credits to increase current production and to keep workers employed. They also revised upward the investment target – originally set at the realized level in 1989 – although investment control remained tight. Because of soft consumer demand, however, output recovery was still painfully slow.

In 1991 the leadership moved further away from the austerity program. Investment and credit controls were eased. For the first time in three years the investment target set at the beginning of the year mandated an increase from the actual investment volume of the previous year. More important, the leadership began to distance itself from some of its openly antireform rhetoric it had adopted in 1989. As explained earlier, Li Peng had argued that reforms should serve the needs of economic stabilization in March 1989; in November 1989 the Communist Party Central Committee adopted the "39 points" that called for a substantial increase in central control over commodities and the abolition of the two-track price system, although none of these "39 points" was actually implemented (Naughton 1992a).

At the end of 1990 and the beginning of 1991, more positive endorsements for the reforms began to appear in the Chinese press and in the leaders' speeches. In December 1990 the CCP adopted an outline for the Eighth FYP that in essence amounted to an explicit refutation of the 39 points (Naughton 1992a). Also in December 1990, at the National Planning Conference, Li Peng gave a speech stressing the "great achievements of the ten years of reforms," and in February 1991, in his speech at the National Economic Reform Conference, he again praised the economic reforms and called for "increasing the scale of the reforms" ("Jiushi Niandai Zhonggong Jingji Gaige Zouxiang Ji Wenti" 1992). Enterprise and housing reforms were put on the government agenda (see SCRES 1992). In November 1991 a government report proclaimed that the three-year austerity program had been a success in terms of stabilizing the economy ("Jiushi Niandai . . ." 1992), thus indicating that the austerity program had outlived its usefulness. In March 1992, the government formally ended the austerity program (Jefferson 1993).

Conclusion

Like all CPEs, the Chinese economic system is noted for its lack of negative incentives, which in a market economy would act as self-enforcing constraints on capacity expansions. This lack of negative incentives is the result of a socialist planned economy – the state ownership of investment resources and assets. Because the state is an abstract entity and cannot be reduced to a specific person, there is a fundamental asymmetry in the way costs and benefits of investment activities are allocated. Benefits accrue to specific investors – firms or government agencies – whereas costs, in the form of financial or social costs resulting from project failures, are borne diffusely. Furthermore, because of the bureaucratic environment, the firms' budget constraints are soft; bureaucratic assistance and bailouts are frequent and form a part of managers' operational mentality. These two factors combined imply that investment activities carry zero or very low risks to the investors and therefore, when combined with positive incentives, feed investment expansion.

Excessive investment expansions result in inflationary pressures and a deterioration in investment structure. When central policy concerns over inflation coincided with those over the investment structure, austerity policies were adopted to restore macroeconomic stability and to achieve a desirable sectoral balance. There were four such austerity policy rounds between 1979 and 1991. Common to these four rounds was an effort to reduce investment growth, especially investment growth of projects controlled by the localities. At the same time, the investment reduction effort sought to direct resource flows to bottleneck sectors. In that sense, the promotion of central and production projects was an effort to achieve a more appropriate balance in China's investment structure.

Macroeconomic and, to some extent, industrial policies are closely interwoven with politics. Thus the austerity policy rounds varied in their severity because the political commitment behind the austerity stance was by no means solid. In 1979, 1980, 1987, and 1991, a "soft" austerity policy regime was in place either because the leaders were preoccupied with political issues or because the leaders were reluctant to bear the full costs of their retrenchment policies. As explained in chapter 7, the firmness of the austerity policy stance affected the decision of local officials whether to implement central investment reduction policies.

Part III

Analyzing local investment behavior

6

Explaining local investment behavior

Local investment behavior can be analyzed from both the demand and supply sides. Investment demand here refers to the preferences of local governments and the firms under their charge for a certain level of investment volume. Investment demand in the Chinese economy is often said to be "excessive." That is, preferences for new projects constantly exceed the level permitted by the existing investment resources, such as money, land, foreign exchange, and capital goods.[1] One of the implications of the excess investment demand hypothesis (chapter 5) is that the notional investment demand can never be fully realized; by arithmetic necessity, however, the actual level of investment supply must be equal to some level of investment demand.[2] Thus one way to think about this issue is to argue that the actual level of investment is, a fortiori, a function of investment supply. Supply constraints are imposed by the limits of physical resources. Houses cannot be built indefinitely because the supply of land is fixed; in the short run, there are fixed supplies of energy, technology, or even foreign exchange that impose a form of "ultimate" constraint on investment demand.

Another way to think about this process is from the demand side. Here, the supply constraints are taken as given and then the actual investment levels are interpreted as a function of demand management. Because the notional or natural investment demand is always excessive (i.e., exceeds the potential supply), demand management means reducing the notional demand to a level at which the existing supply constraints can potentially accommodate it or a degree of slack is created. Typically, this is exactly what an austerity policy attempts to do.

1. Labor can be a source of constraints, although this is a lesser problem in China.

2. The controversy arises over the duration of this equality between demand and supply. The excess investment demand hypothesis naturally posits that such an equilibrium is only fleeting because of the strength of the underlying demand. This is called the permanent disequilibrium hypothesis. For an analysis, see Grosfeld (1989).

I take the second approach in this book. I posit that investment demand management is a bureaucratic process and resource constraints impinge on a firm's investment behavior via the force of bureaucratic decisions. When resource constraints are tight, bureaucrats approve fewer investment applications or even act to cut investment projects; when resource constraints are loose, bureaucrats are more generous in granting approvals. The decisions by the government therefore constrain or expand investment demand and the decisions by the central government constrain or expand local investment demand. Because supply constraints are taken as exogenously given (i.e., as a constant), variations in the actual investment levels are then attributed to variations in bureaucratic demand management. The analytical task of this book is to explain why bureaucratic demand management varies; the empirical task is to demonstrate how variations in bureaucratic constraints are related to variations in investment behavior.

The explanation provided here has two components. The first part is an analytical framework borrowed heavily from institutional economics. It focuses on two variables that allegedly have an impact on actors' behavior: monitoring and interest divergence. The second part consists of a number of specific hypotheses about local investment behavior in China. Because the explanation focuses heavily on incentive structures and constraints facing local bureaucrats, I call it a "bureaucratic model of investment behavior."

An analytical framework

The analytical framework provided here must satisfy the following three concerns. First, it must be applicable to interactions between two actors under a condition of hierarchy. Second, it must address the issue of how self-interested actors structure their behavior because of such intangible factors as informational distributions or monitoring. Third, it should focus on the strategic aspects of the actors' behavior. These three concerns lead to a principal and agent model.

A principal and agent relationship covers a broad range of human activities and it arises each time when one party, the principal, enters into an arrangement with another party, the agent, with the expectation that the agent will take actions consistent with the interests of the principal. Agency literature has two quite separate theoretical focuses. One concentrates on factors inhibiting optimal behavior by the agent from the principal's point of view and explains agent behavior given the presence of these factors. This is the so-called positive theory of agency. The other, more normatively oriented, explores possible constructions of principal–agent arrangements so as to reduce suboptimal behavior by the agent and evaluates and compares the costs of different schemes in terms of some definition of welfare.[3] The application in this study falls into the first category of agency literature: the task is to apply agency literature as an analytical tool to see if it helps explain Chinese provincial investment behavior. The first step will be to outline some of the core features of agency literature and then discuss its relevance to and limitations on political economy analysis.

The principal–agent model originates from institutional economics, a branch of economics that disputes mainstream economists' claim of a firm as a black box and as a unitary entity maximizing profits. Institutional economics approaches the business firm as a contractual unit and argues that the goals a firm pursues do not result from an exogenously given utility function; rather, the goals are determined by an equilibrium process internal to the firm, just as prices are formed competitively in the market.[4]

One important contractual relationship in this equilibrium process within a firm is the relationship between stockholders and managers.[5] Stockholders, the principal, delegate some control rights (such as the right over resource use) to managers, the agent, to perform tasks in the expectation that the managers will maximize the stockholders' utility. Whether managers actually do so critically depends on the presence or absence of a group of factors that often renders a principal–agent relationship problematic.

The first factor is a divergence in interests. Jensen and Meckling (1976: 312–13) give the examples of managers pursuing a "nonpecuniary" consumption of perquisites out of the firm's resources and risk-averse behavior to avoid uncertain, albeit potentially profitable ventures because of their unwillingness to sacrifice their leisure and effort. Both of these managerial activities are at the expense of the stockholders' interests in maximizing the returns on their equity.

The second factor that compounds the difficulties related to the divergence of interests is the "information asymmetry" between owner and managers. Managers, in general, have superior information about the tasks assigned to

---

3. In general, positive agency literature is less mathematical and is more empirically oriented. Normative agency literature is more interested in developing mathematical models and as a result is less empirically oriented. See Jensen (1983).

4. Economists use the term "equilibrium" to denote both the process by which a price is formed on the basis of the intersection of demand and supply and the situation in which stability is such that individuals have no incentive to change their behavior. It is the former usage that is relevant here. For seminal works on firms as a competitive process, see Alchian and Demsetz (1972) and Coase (1937).

5. The discussion is drawn mainly from the following sources: Eggertsson (1990: 40–45), Jensen and Meckling (1976), Moe (1984), and Ross (1973).

them, either because of the technical details attached or their proximity to the tasks, and about their own abilities and preferences. The net effect from the presence of these two factors is managers' "shirking" or "opportunistic" behavior: managers will maximize their own interests, whether in leisure or in non-pecuniary consumption, because the costs of these activities are disproportionately borne by the owner and the costs of being detected are small owing to the unobservability of their actions. Jensen and Meckling (1976: 308) posit the control problem in the following way:

> If both parties to the relationship are utility maximizers there is good reason to believe that the agent will not always act in the best interests of the principal. The principal can limit divergences from his interest by establishing appropriate incentives for the agent and by incurring monitoring costs designed to limit the aberrant activities of the agent. . . . However, it is generally impossible for the principal or the agent at zero cost to ensure that the agent will make optimal decisions from the principal's viewpoint.

As pointed out before, the logic of the principal–agent relationship is applicable to a broad range of human activities beyond the economic realm. There have been attempts to adapt the principal–agent model to political and bureaucratic analyses. Weingast and Moran (1983), for example, use a principal–agent perspective to analyze congressional-bureaucratic relations in the American political system; Holmstrom (1982) applies the framework to study Soviet incentive schemes; and a recent effort by Granick (1990) employs an explicit principal–agent model to examine management issues of Chinese regional enterprises.

The relevance of the principal–agent model as an analytical tool in studying Chinese provincial investment behavior derives, first and foremost, from the structure of analysis in the principal–agent framework. Principal–agent analysis is about two parties, interacting with each other under a given arrangement and in a hierarchical setting. The policy conflicts over investment control in China take place between two political and bureaucratic hierarchies, the Chinese central government and provincial officials. Second, provinces gain their decision-making rights or parameters of such rights over investment approval, goods and credit allocations from the central government. Furthermore, the central government makes personnel allocation decisions, at least as far as appointments and promotions at the top level of a province are concerned. In this sense, the Chinese central government possesses certain "ownership" rights over provincial officials and delegates to or, as has happened several times, reclaims certain decision-making rights from the provinces.

Third, during an episode of inflation control, there is a conflict of interest between the central government and the provinces. The central government desires economic and political stability and deems investment control as a mechanism to achieve this objective. Provinces have incentives to expand investment, as the benefits of reduced inflation are not fully recouped, but returns from an expanded tax or revenue base accrue to the provincial coffers. The divergence in preferences, compounded by informational asymmetry and asymmetry of economic control, leads to abundant opportunities for "agency problems" in the Chinese political economy. A specific manifestation of the agency problems is "shirking," a situation often modeled by theorists of agency.

Last, a principal–agent relationship between the Chinese central government and the provinces is simultaneously a gaming relationship. A gaming relationship arises when one party takes certain actions given the constraints imposed by the other party and in full consideration of the possible responses of the other party. The structure of expectations one player has about the actions of the other player has an impact on the actions of the first player (Schelling 1980). This study is concerned with how provincial leaders calculate their relative tenure security in the system and what impact this calculation has on provincial investment behavior.

There are, however, limitations to applying an agency framework to political analysis. These are not intrinsic to the Chinese setting per se; rather, they are germane to political analysis as a whole and reflect critical differences between political and economic research. The first such limitation pertains to intrinsic differences between a bureaucracy and a corporation. The most obvious difference is that a bureaucracy is not profit-maximizing. Bureaucrats often pursue slack or expansions or other economically inefficient goals; this is because they are not subject to the process of natural selection in the marketplace that selects out inefficient firms. "Bureaus," Moe (1984: 762) observes, "survive by securing political support – from congressmen in committees, the institutionalized presidency, interest groups – sufficient to veto life-threatening legislation by enemies; and they expand the scope of their activities by building on this base of political support."

A further difference between corporate and bureaucratic organizations relates to the methods of internal control. Top managers control their subordinates through both administrative means (such as promotion and firing) and monetary remunerations. Bureaucrats, however, rely more heavily on administrative means and do not use monetary remunerations extensively for control purposes. In part, this is a result of the difficulty of measuring bureaucratic performance precisely to construct a workable reward schedule; in part, this is due to the fact that the relationship between a bureaucratic superior and his or her subordinates is more authoritative in nature, and administrative compulsion is more likely to elicit compliance than it is at a firm. Analytical attention in this case should, therefore, be directed to the ways subordinates are appointed, selected, and promoted more than to the usual economic analysis of institutions.

The second limitation involves specifications of goals. In an important way, a relationship between two political hierarchies is not a pure agency relationship in that there is a "multiplicity of goals" in politics. Unlike the interactions between stockholders and managers, where the division of interests can be neatly reduced to returns on the owners' equity and to the effect on the owners' returns from various actions taken by the managers, a political relationship between two hierarchies is infinitely more complex. Politicians maximize different and often conflicting goals simultaneously, and their preferences change over time. The political process is competitive rather than static; coalitions supporting a given policy may shift quickly and unpredictably. In short, a literal treatment of a government as a unitary and coherent unit known as a "principal" may miss the political reality.[6]

Related to the multiplicity of goals is the problem of the multiplicity of tasks. Bureaucrats, more than corporate managers, are multitask agents. That is, they are expected to perform many tasks, and the performance of one task may diminish that of others. The slogan in the company boardrooms, "the bottom line is profits," is seldom heard in government corridors, and for a very good reason. Although tax bureaucrats try to collect as much money as they can, welfare bureaucrats try to spend as much as they can to subsidize the poor and the needy. In China, top local officials, for example, are essentially put in charge of the entire economic performance of their regions; agriculture, industry, urban development, education, and population control all compete for their attention, not to mention the implementation of political tasks such as propagandizing the Party line and eradicating spiritual pollution.

When there are multiple tasks, it is generally undesirable to devise an incentive scheme that rewards the performance of only one of the tasks; doing so would direct excessive attention to the particular task to which the incentive scheme is linked. This issue is illustrated in the debate in American education about the wisdom of linking teachers' pay with their students' test scores. Although proponents argue that the scheme will make teachers work harder on raising test scores, opponents point out that the scheme will discourage creative thinking and intellectual curiosity – qualities not easily captured by

---

6. Another complication is that there are no "ultimate" principals or agents. This concern is especially relevant to an analysis of Chinese provinces. Each provincial leader is simultaneously an agent and a principal. First, some provincial leaders are also Politburo members and therefore are both policy makers and implementors. Second, provincial leaders, while being agents with respect to the central government, become principals when they deal with county governments and enterprises under their subordination. Thus another set of constraints between principals and agents must be introduced.

test scores.[7] The upshot of this analysis is that multiple tasks deter the use of one incentive scheme to clearly measure performance, and the lack of such a scheme, in turn, may lead to the possibility of control problems. To put it another way, in the presence of multiple tasks, reliance on one incentive scheme produces adverse consequences.

These complications make a rigid application of the principal–agent model difficult. The model is still useful, however, since it vastly simplifies the analytical task at hand. In essence, we make inferences about local investment behavior on the basis of two variables: how information about local investment activities is distributed (i.e., monitoring) and how the investment preferences between the Center (the principal) and the localities (the agent) diverge. Under this analytical scheme, many of the problems identified above can be respecified as factors that either affect the distribution of information or the divergence of investment interests. For example, it is plausible to argue that personnel control is a form of monitoring; instead of monitoring the specific tasks that local officials perform, the central government carefully monitors political and professional credentials when they make personnel selections. Many of the institutional developments discussed in chapter 4 are devoted to this form of monitoring. I call it ex ante monitoring.

The multiplicity of tasks is not a problem for this analysis; in fact, it is directly germane. Local governments engage in different investment activities and when the central government strives to monitor one form of investment activity, the result is an increase in shirking behavior in other categories.[8] Chapter 7 examines this form of strategic behavior in great detail. Also there is no need to insist that central or local policy investment preferences always be internally consistent; the only requirement is that central and local officials, *on average*, hold different policy preferences, and that they hold one set of policy preferences more consistently and more stably than they hold the other set. Similarly, I do not require unanimity in the central position to enforce investment reduction or unanimity in the local position to resist investment reduction. The multiplicity of goals among central policy makers, for example, can be modeled to affect the credibility of the central investment policy as it calls into question the degree of policy commitment behind an austerity stance; on the other hand, the absence of unity among local leaders gives rise to variations in the divergence in investment preferences between central and local policy authorities.

7. For an analysis of these issues, see Holmstrom and Milgrom (1991).
8. Here, monitoring of one activity is functionally equivalent to devising an incentive scheme that is tied to the performance of that activity. Monitoring implies actions taken either to reward or to penalize on the basis of information gathered in the monitoring process.

A bureaucratic model of investment behavior

Chinese provincial officials are not only responsible for economic affairs in their jurisdictions; they carry out a host of intrinsically political functions ranging from implementing central political lines (e.g., the launching of the antibourgeois liberalization campaign in 1987), propaganda work, and enforcing Party discipline to personnel appointment and management. In short, top provincial officials, the Party secretaries and governors, are "generalists" at the provincial level.[9] Nor is the management of economic policies considered strictly an economic affair. The central government in the 1983 investment-reduction drive invoked Party discipline to put pressure on provincial officials in order to ensure that central investment policies that gave precedence to central projects were enforced. This prompted Hunan officials to declare that controlling investment was "a concrete manifestation of our step-by-step compliance and our political agreement with the Party Center" (*Hunan ribao*, June 20, 1983: 1).

The importance of political institutions needs to be explicitly considered. In essence, a bureaucratic model of investment behavior views that behavior not purely as a function of the familiar economic variables but also as a function of bureaucratic variables. As far as local investment behavior is concerned, the bureaucratic status of local officials can be said to shape their investment behavior to the extent that bureaucratic status affects the incentive structures of local officials and the ability of the Center to supervise and monitor their performance.

From the above discussion, it appears that investment-shirking behavior – evasion in implementing investment reduction – in China is a function of two factors: the ability of the central government to monitor local officials and the degree that investment preferences diverge between central and local authorities. Although monitoring and interest divergence obviously do not cover everything that affects local shirking behavior, monitoring and interest divergence can be proxies for many other factors as well. One can then further infer that *variations* in shirking behavior can be attributed to *variations* in monitoring capabilities and to *variations* in the degree that investment preferences diverge.

Two kinds of variations can be identified. One relates to variations over time (time-series variations); the other relates to variations taking place across different provinces (cross-sectional variations). Although the research method used here permits a direct testing of the cross-sectional variations, it is more difficult to test time-series variations. The main difficulty is that time-series changes in the independent variables – in administrative monitoring and interest

---

9. Generalists have a wide range of policy responsibilities, as distinct from *functional specialists*, who are responsible for issues in specific functional spheres (Lieberthal and Oksenberg 1988: 36–37).

divergence – are intrinsically difficult to operationalize. Thus in the case of time-series variations, our hypotheses take the form of a number of expectations about the patterns of local investment behavior during one period as compared with another (i.e., patterns of the dependent variable are compared at different times). In the case of cross-sectional variations, the hypotheses are about relationships between bureaucratic variables with local investment behavior. In part because more empirical data or more scholarly discussion are available to lend to the effort to specify a direct relationship between our independent variables and the dependent variable, it is important to discuss this relationship in more detail as compared with our speculation about time-series variations. Indeed, this discussion is unavoidable. Because past scholarship gives conflicting directions about this relationship, our specifications are necessarily open-ended.

Hypotheses regarding time-series variations are discussed in chapter 7, and cross-sectional variations in chapter 8. Both kinds of variations are examined here by relying heavily on data analysis. In the appendix to this chapter, I explain the sources and probable problems that arise from such a reliance on Chinese data.

Time-series variations

My first hypothesis is that investment-shirking behavior is a function of the ability of the central government to monitor the actions of local officials. Monitoring can refer to general administrative checks on performance or to specific checks on investment performance. The stringency of monitoring may vary in two ways. First, central monitoring capabilities can change over time as a function of institutionalization, improvement in bureaucratic design, and greater technical sophistication. As noted in chapter 4, during the reform era there has been moderate and incremental progress in all of these areas. If our hypothesis is correct, then shirking behavior should not increase over time despite economic decentralization, or at least it should not increase to the extent predicted by those who only look at the effect of the economic reforms.

Another reason for the monitoring variations is that the central policy authorities traditionally monitor some investment activities more closely than others; historically, for example, the SSB has collected more complete and more regular series on capital construction activities whereas its efforts to collect renovation series began only in the mid-1980s. The monitoring variations across different investment activities provide a way of examining the hypothesis that investment behavior is a function of central monitoring. Accordingly, one should expect to see moral hazard conduct, that is, more shirking behavior in those activities where monitoring is weak and less in those activities where monitoring is strong. Furthermore, because there has been a general improvement in the monitoring capabilities of the central government, one should expect to see a decline in moral hazard conduct over time.

Interest divergence between the Center and the localities can also vary over time. This may occur through variations in the Center's commitment to investment reduction. As pointed out in chapter 5, the central government has oscillated between "soft" and "firm" policy stances for political or policy reasons. Central policy commitment to an austerity stance is soft when an austerity program is formally in place but the Center is not certain about how seriously to enforce it. For example, a declaration of a reduced investment target accompanied by a liberal credit policy sends mixed and conflicting signals about central policy intentions. A soft austerity policy commitment can be thought of as a conceptual equivalent to either weak central monitoring or to a lesser degree of interest divergence (or both). When the policy commitment is weak, for example, there will be only an attenuated attempt to perform checks on how well local officials implement central investment directives. Or when the soft policy stance is induced by differences among central policy makers about the necessity of the austerity program, then we can argue that interest divergence is less sharp than the limiting case in which central policy makers are united in their position. By implication, effective monitoring and sharp divisions in investment preferences will characterize some austerity rounds more than others and shirking behavior should vary, in some systematic way, according to the characteristics of the austerity rounds.

Cross-sectional variations

Although it was pointed out in chapter 1 that there are some systematic factors leading to consistent differences between central and local preferences for different mixes along the Phillips trade-off curve, it is important to remember that this describes the *typical* policy preferences at both levels. The reality is often more complex. Some central leaders could be sympathetic to local investment preferences as was Zhao Ziyang; or some local leaders might interpret things closer to central policy preferences. Rather than delve into the possibility that central leaders act on local interests, this discussion focuses more closely on the consequences of the narrowed central–local interest divergence.[10]

For analytical tractability, I assume that cross-sectional differences in the

10. In part, this analytical focus is justified by the fact that I already take into account the possibility that central leaders are sympathetic with local interests. I model this possibility as a factor driving divisions among central leaders and thus inducing a soft policy commitment. Second, it is never the case that *all* the central leaders take the side of local interests. Historically, leaders such as Zhao Ziyang have always been checked and balanced by others who stress central planning (such as Li Peng, Yao Yilin, and Song Ping), not to mention the positions of the central bureaucracies.

ability of the central government to perform administrative and economic monitoring (such as collecting data on technical investments) are minimal and therefore do not give rise to investment performance differences among Chinese provinces. Instead, I focus on the possible differences in supervision and interest among China's provinces and view any such variations not as a random event but as a systematic consequence of the differences in the bureaucratic status of the local officials. Bureaucratic status refers to two characteristics of local officials. First, it refers to the institutional relationship between local officials and the Center. Although all provincial officials are appointed by the Center, they vary in their relationship with the Center in a number of ways. At the one extreme, some provincial officials serve in concurrent central government posts (they may be members of the Politburo); at the other extreme are local officials who have served in local posts throughout their professional career. Second, bureaucratic status refers to the tenure considerations of local officials, such as the tenure security with which local officials actually govern or expect to govern their regions; it can also mean leadership stability (i.e., the rate of bureaucratic turnovers in a given year).

Bureaucratic integration. Political power also affects central–local relations. Political power is denoted by a "bureaucratic integration" variable, which measures the degree to which a provincial official is incorporated into the central political or bureaucratic machinery. Because there are many secondary officials – vice governors or deputy provincial Party secretaries – and because background information about these officials is incomplete, the bureaucratic integration variable covers only top provincial officials, namely, Party secretaries and governors.

The bureaucratic integration variable has four dimensions. First, an official can serve concurrent central and provincial posts. The most common central posts include a back seat on the Politburo or a position as a state councilor. Those provincial officials who serve concurrent central posts are most closely incorporated into the central political machinery. The seat on the Politburo is a case in point. As in all other socialist countries, the Politburo in China is the highest governing body, at least in a formal sense. Although it is possible for some Politburo members who are in political disgrace to retain their seats with only nominal power and it is possible for some leaders to enjoy preeminent power without occupying Politburo seats, it is safe to say that most Politburo members are powerful politicians in the Chinese political system.[11] Usually,

11. Chen Yonggui, Wu Guixian, and Hua Guofeng in the late 1970s and the early 1980s are examples of leaders with only nominal power. After his fall from power in early 1987, Hu Yaobang retained his Politburo seat without much decision-making responsibility. Most of the first-generation revolutionaries, such as Deng Xiaoping and Chen Yun, are examples of leaders with real power, although without the formal position.

Politburo members are given specific areas of responsibility, and collectively they are responsible for "resolving major bureaucratic conflicts and deciding upon major policy issues" (Lieberthal and Oksenberg 1988: 36). Obviously, making decisions on retrenchment policies and overseeing the implementation of central investment guidelines fall into this category of activities.

Since the late 1970s, fourteen officials have occupied a seat on the Politburo while serving primary administrative functions in the provinces: Wu De and Li Ximing from Beijing, Wei Guoqing from Guangdong and Guangxi, Li Ruihuan, Ni Zhifu, and Tang Shaowen from Tianjin, Jiang Zemin, Peng Chong, and Su Zhenhua from Shanghai, Zhao Ziyang and Yang Rudai from Sichuan, Seypidin from Xinjiang, plus the Party secretaries of Guangdong and Shandong, who were added to the Politburo roster at the Fourteenth Party Congress (1993). This makes up the largest provincial representation on the Politburo in the history of the PRC.[12] Compared with the republics of the former Soviet Union, Chinese provinces have traditionally been less widely and less continuously represented on the Politburo, despite a larger pool of provinces. Under Khrushchev and Brezhnev, six out of fifteen republics gained Politburo representation, in a marked departure from the Stalin era, when only officials from Russia and the Ukraine were regularly represented on the Politburo (Bahry 1987: 27–28).

The second dimension to the bureaucratic integration variable has to do with career backgrounds. Before assuming their current provincial posts, some bureaucrats worked in central government agencies in Beijing; others served in other provinces in equivalent positions; and still others climbed to the top exclusively from within the provincial ranks.[13] For example, Jiang Zemin, now the Party general secretary, was the minister of the electronics industry before becoming mayor of Shanghai in 1985; Zhao Ziyang, the first Party secretary of Sichuan province in the late 1970s, had served in similar positions in Guangdong and Neimenggu. These three types of provincial officials represent different degrees of bureaucratic integration, with those having a central government background being the most integrated and those having an entirely local background being the least integrated.

Counting those provincial officials serving in central posts simultaneously,

---

12. There are also other officials who were Politburo members and served in the provinces. But they are excluded because they were made secondary provincial officials as a relatively gracious way of purging them. Examples include Chen Yonggui in Shanxi and Wu Guixian in Shaanxi.

13. The criterion I use emphasizes career trajectory rather than place of birth or residence. For example, an official born in Shanghai can still be classified as a "centralist" if he spent the majority of his career working for the central government. Jiang Zemin, for example, is classified as a centralist even though he was born in Shanghai. For operationalization details, see the appendix to this chapter.

I thus divide top provincial officials into four distinct categories: concurrent centralists, centralists, outsiders, and insiders. To denote the differences among provinces in the extent of bureaucratic integration, I assign a value of four to the concurrent centralists, three to centralists, two to outsiders, and one to insiders. Figures 6.1 and 6.2 show the annual average political integration scores for the twenty-nine provinces and the balance between the four types of provincial governance between 1976 and 1992. For simplicity, a composite index of political integration values has been arrived at by taking the averages of the bureaucratic integration scores for Party secretaries and governors.

From Figure 6.1 it is immediately apparent that Beijing (BJ) and Shanghai (SH) belong to a class by themselves: They have extremely high integration values in comparison with other provinces. If integration values between three and four are taken to mean concurrent central governance, Beijing and Shanghai, both with an integration score of 3.06, show the greatest integration with the central political apparatus. The next tier finds Guangdong (GD), Henan (HN), Sichuan (SC), Tianjin (TJ), and Xinjiang (XJ), all of which have a bureaucratic integration score of between two and three, which means that, on average, they have been governed by centralists. The rest of the provinces range from one to two in bureaucratic integration scores, which indicates that on the whole these provinces were presided over by outsiders during the 1976–92 period.

The wide distribution of integration scores suggests that personnel assignments are treated very differently from province to province. The integration scores for Beijing and Shanghai, for example, are almost twice as large as those for Guangxi (GX), Heilongjiang (HLJ), Jiangsu (JS), Liaoning (LN), Shandong (SD), Yunnan (YN), and Zhejiang (ZJ). Because figure 6.1 shows the composite index for Party secretaries and the average scores for the entire 1976–92 period, it masks the considerable variations among provinces from year to year and the variations between Party secretaries and governors. Some provinces have been continuously governed by officials from the inside track; on the Party side, an insider presided over Guangxi and Hunan for fifteen out of the seventeen years; on the government side, an insider governor led Guangxi, Heilongjiang, and Hunan for fifteen years and Zhejiang for sixteen years. At the other extreme, between 1976 and 1992, Beijing, Fujian, Neimenggu, and Xizang (Tibet) never had an insider Party secretary, and Shaanxi never had an insider governor.

Figure 6.2, which breaks down the four types of provincial governance by years, makes it possible to track both the distribution of the four types of governance in a given year and their developments over time. Each bar is divided into four segments representing, respectively, the number of provinces

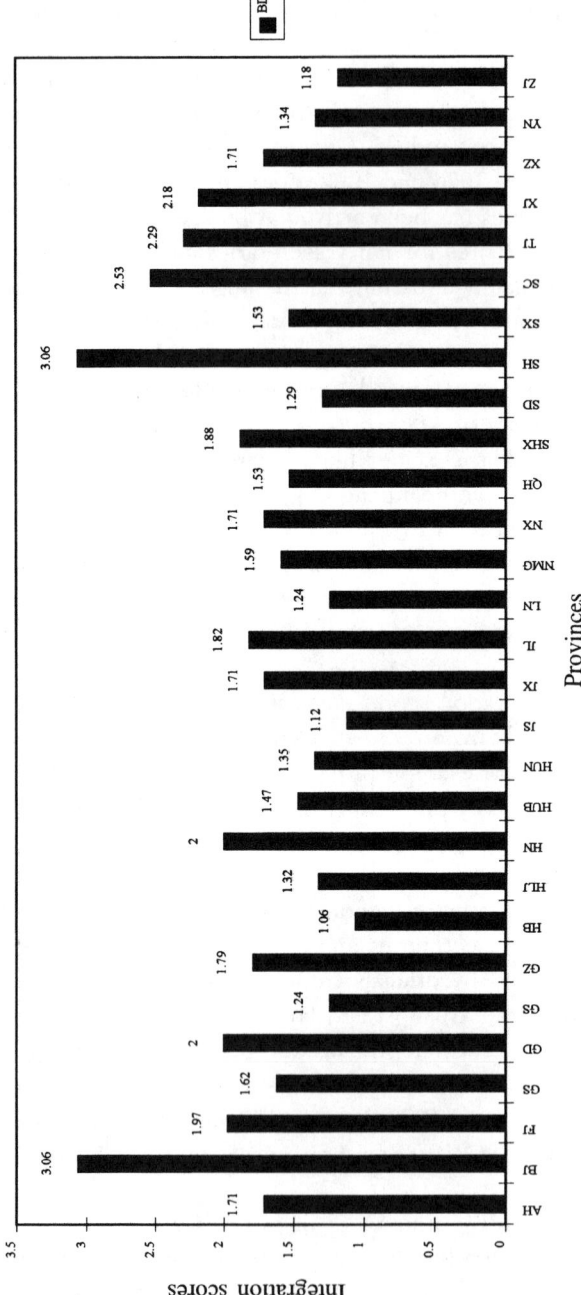

Figure 6.1 Bureaucratic integration by provinces, 1976–92

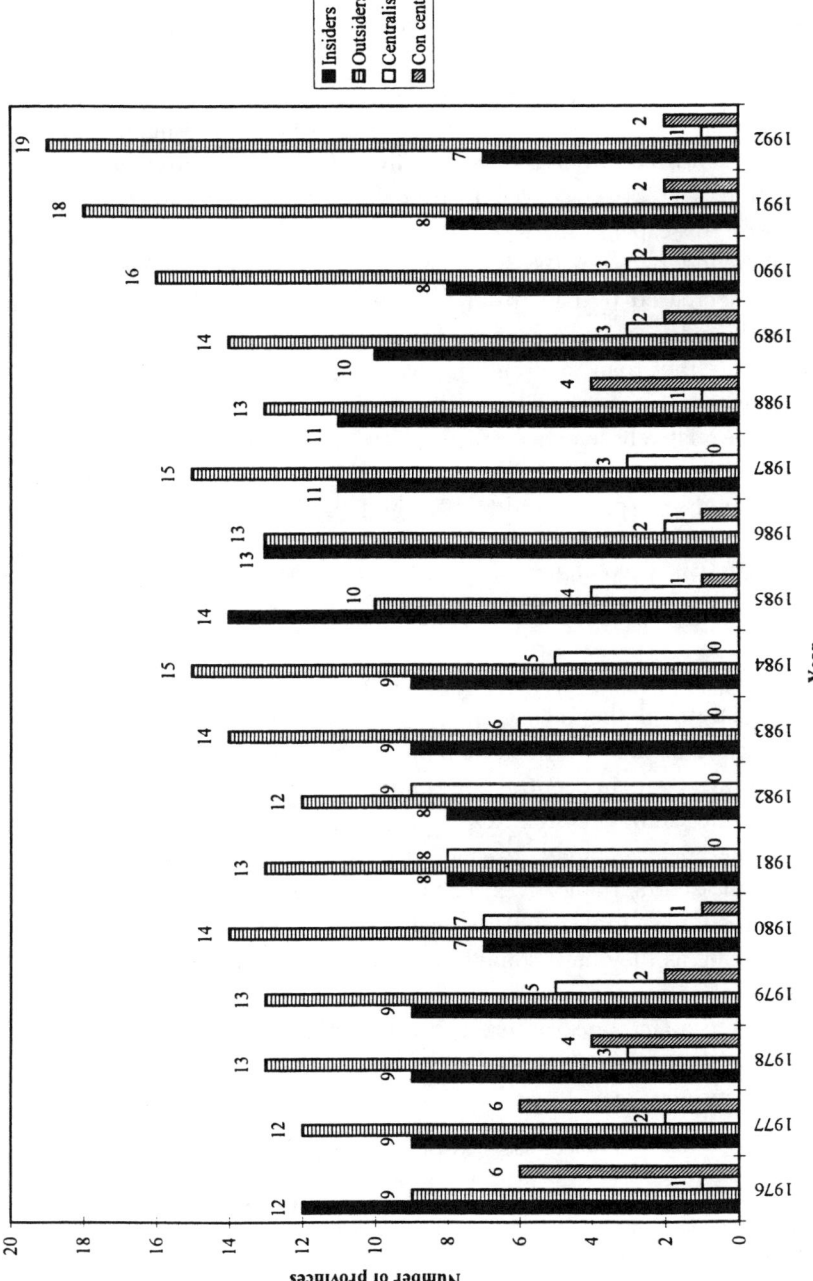

Figure 6.2 Four types of provincial governance, 1976–92

characterized by concurrent central governance, central governance, outsider governance, and insider governance; each bar totals to twenty-nine.[14] On the whole, the largest block of provinces consists of those characterized by outsider governance (except for 1976 and 1985, when there were more insider provinces). As noted in chapter 4, there has been an increase in the use of "the cadre circulation system" to curb administrative localism; as a result, the number of provinces controlled by outsiders steadily expanded since the early 1980s. In 1982 there were twelve such provinces; in 1992 there were nineteen. Furthermore, this expansion has occurred mainly at the expense of the insider governance mode; between 1985 and 1992, the number of provinces governed by insiders decreased by half, from fourteen to seven. This trend, like the increase in the outsider governance mode, was steady and represented a chronic development, rather than random fluctuations. These findings reveal that the use of concurrent centralist and centralist governance modes to rule Chinese provinces is a relatively selective practice. Very few provinces have been governed by concurrent centralists, and in the 1981–84 period there were none; the largest number, six, occurred in 1976 and 1977; since the late 1980s, the number has stabilized at two. The centralist governance mode was relatively important between 1979 and 1985, but since 1985 the number has fluctuated between one and three.

Investment hypotheses about the effect of bureaucratic integration. Given the centralized nature of the management of those provincial cadres who are within the scope of this study, the mix of provincial personnel can provide a meaningful way of gauging central policy intentions regarding the allocation of personnel in the Chinese system. Of course, such an exercise rests on a fundamental belief that personnel decisions are not made randomly, but purposefully, to advance certain objectives. For the purposes of this discussion, these objectives do not have to be explicitly related to investment or macroeconomic concerns as long as they have something to do with some aspects of central–local relations.[15]

However, the main concern here is not to explain the patterns of political integration but their effect. The assignment of concurrent centralists, centralists, outsiders, or insiders may affect local investment behavior in tangible ways.

14. For 1976, the total was twenty-eight because of missing background information on Tang Chirui, the Party secretary and governor of Yunnan province.

15. When this belief turns out to be erroneous, a supplemental assumption says that certain practices are found to be less useful, and leaders will change their practices in time. It is therefore the persistence of the practice and the degree to which the practice is widespread that gives us confidence in the substance of the belief. Again, this is another justification for studying a relatively large number of cases over a sufficiently long period of time.

What is infinitely more difficult, however, is to explain the direction of the connection between them. What is the effect of sending concurrent centralists and centralists to run provinces with large economic or fiscal clout? Does this enable the Center to control them better, or does it give them a greater voice in economic decision making? Depending on one's basic assumptions, extremely different, if not opposite, predictions can be made about local investment behavior.

Official Chinese sources do not give any clues to why some provincial leaders are made Politburo members and why some have a more substantial background in central ministries. It may be because of political sensitivity or because of their lack of interest in the subject.[16] In marked contrast, Western scholars have devoted a significant amount of attention to understanding this issue. One view is that organizational integration to the Center is a control instrument in that central personnel in the provinces are able to suppress local interests; by implication, the Center should be better able to implement its policies in the more integrated provinces as compared with the less integrated ones.

Teiwes (1971: 128–29) shows that the Chinese Communist Party assigns outsiders to top provincial posts to curb localism.[17] Vogel (1980 [1969]: 93–94, 118–19) describes battles between Guangdong's native cadres and central deputies stationed in Wuhan and argues that central cadres were harsher and more determined in implementing the locally unpopular land reform measures than were the Guangdong cadres. Chamberlain (1972: 288–98), in his study of three municipalities – Wuhan, Guangzhou, and Tianjin – finds not only that outsiders occupy top posts, but that they are also predominately represented in positions with control and coercion functions. Oksenberg (1969), in his study of rural China, arrived at a similar conclusion. Solinger (1977: 136), in her study of the gradual integration of China's southwest provinces after the communist takeover, argues that top officials assigned to run these provinces perceived it to be in their self-interest to carry out central policies when those policies were at odds with local interests. She argues that Central Committee

---

16. I scanned the 1988 and 1989 issues of *Zhongguo xingzheng guanli* (*China Administrative Management,* published by the China Administration Society) and *Zhengzhixue yanjiu* (*Studies in Political Science,* published by the China Academy of Social Sciences), and a sample of recently published books on cadre management (Diao Tianding et al. 1989; Huang Daqiang and Liu Yichang 1988; Wang Zhigang 1988; Liu Kegou 1988; Zhang Quanjing 1988; and Zhao Shenghui 1987). Not one of the articles or books referred to provincial leaders' Politburo membership or to differences in other aspects of bureaucratic integration.

17. Teiwes (1971: 128) quotes Shandong's governor, Zhao Jianmin, as saying: "I am a native of Shantung [Shandong], I am for the people of Shantung [Shandong], and the cadres of Shantung [Shandong]."

membership helps shape local loyalty to the Center; as for Politburo member-ship, Goodman (1986: 179) speculates that the elevation of Sichuan's gover-nor, Li Jingquan, was "a symptom and symbol" of Sichuan's position as an integral part of China.

Despite an impressive amount of data and materials, the studies cited above do not give a clear idea of the design of the appointment system. One problem is that most of them focus on the years immediately after the birth of the People's Republic, which raises some methodological issues. During a period of power consolidation, when a country is faced with external and internal threats, it is quite natural for the Center to emphasize integration rather than regional autonomy. Thus it is rather difficult to disentangle the effect arising from policy emphasis from the effect arising from personnel mix. This prob-lem is compounded by the fact that most of these studies are based on single cases and by the absence of counterfactuals. In other words, they fail to show that provinces without the kind of personnel mix thought to matter in fact failed to comply with the central government.

Second, it is not entirely clear whether the mix of personnel results from a well-defined central desire to shape local policy implementation or from happenstance. Recall that most of these studies focus on the period immedi-ately after the People's Liberation Army (PLA) drove out the Nationalist forces. This fact alone might have heavily affected staffing decisions at the time. Deng Xiaoping (1986: 6), who led the army that liberated China's southwest regions, recalled many years later: "When we drove into the Southwest, there were so few local cadres that some platoon leaders became county Party secretaries, so did some company political commissars and some battalion and regiment officers." Given the scarcity of local personnel, the fact that outsiders occupied top positions should not come as a surprise and, furthermore, cannot be used as evidence to show a conscious manipulation of personnel.

Later years are therefore more appropriate for such studies, and in that context one plausible hypothesis is that bureaucratic integration tends to bring about compliance in local conduct in general and to reduce shirking in local investment conduct in particular.[18] There is some direct evidence for this line of reasoning. As Chen Yun (1982: 1060) remarked in 1981 after stressing the need for the Center to appropriate foreign exchange earned by the provinces: "Comrades in the localities say that Beijing people speak Beijing dialect. I am

---

18. Curiously, more recent studies on Chinese provinces, in politics or political economy, have largely abandoned the approach of emphasizing different degrees of integration as an explanatory variable. Chang (1978) and Goodman (1984) have focused on provincial leaders as a single, unified group, rather than exploring their differences; Wong (1985, 1987), on the other hand, examines economic resources in the hands of provincial leaders without dealing with their political status.

a Shanghainese but I speak Beijing dialect. Some comrades say that since Comrade Ziyang came to Beijing, he started speaking Beijing dialect. I think this is true; Comrade Ziyang governs the whole country now."

Why is this hypothesis plausible? The traditional line of reasoning points to the organizational strength, ideological coherence, and discipline of the Chinese system. Schurmann, for example, portrays the Chinese Communist Party as an organization armed with a coherent ideology that provides both "a unified and conscious world view" and a set of ideas that are "rational instruments of action." Furthermore, the Party has developed detailed procedures, rules, and formal organizational structures for daily operations (Schurmann 1968).[19] Other analysts, such as Lewis (1963) and Barnett (1967), also marvel at the organizational capacity of the Chinese Communist Party and portray the Chinese system as hierarchically organized and vertically integrated from the top leadership down to the most basic level of Chinese society. In the traditional line of research, then, bureaucratic integration reduces the political independence of local officials. According to this logic, local investment compliance occurs as a result of the suppression of self-interests via a well laid-out socialization process.

The empirical research on which this volume is based casts some doubt on this argument, at least as far as its applicability to the reform era is concerned. There is considerable opportunism in local investment behavior and investment compliance is conditional: it depends on the stringency of supervision and monitoring. Self-interest is not absent but it can be defined very differently, or the benefits and costs of attaining its objectives may vary. Thus my own argument, although leading to the same conclusion as the traditional view, stresses strategic calculations of this kind. Provincial representation at the Center or a central presence in the provinces helps reduce the divergence of investment interests between central and local policy makers. Highly integrated officials, for example, may calculate that their long-term career prospects lie with the Center rather than with the provinces they are assigned to govern. The real principals are not the industrial bureaus or factory heads in the provinces but the central policy makers in Beijing. Thus highly integrated officials tend to maximize central interests more than less integrated officials.

Alternative but closely related reasoning points to the distinction between those with "encompassing interests" and those with "narrow interests." Those with encompassing interests have a substantial stake in the welfare of the society as a whole, whereas those with narrow interests are only concerned

19. Whereas Schurmann (1968) stresses the fundamental differences between the Chinese communist system and its traditional antecedents, John King Fairbank has long argued that there are important continuities. For an exposition of his view, see Fairbank (1987: especially 271–368).

about the welfare of the groups they represent. Group size separates those with encompassing interests from those with narrow interests: the bigger the size of the group, the more encompassing its interests are. An implication of this logic is that those with encompassing interests are motivated to provide public goods because they reap a substantial portion of the benefits of providing the public goods.[20] This analysis is directly relevant to our story. Highly integrated officials develop encompassing interests because they become principals themselves. Inflation control in CPEs, as noted earlier, is a public good in that the economic and political benefits and costs are distributed very unevenly between the central government and local governments. A specific implication is that for highly integrated provincial officials compliance is said to be "incentive-compatible," because they are appropriately motivated to control inflation.

Equivalently, it is also possible to hypothesize that the distribution of benefits and costs varies systematically with bureaucratic integration. For example, highly integrated officials are more easily monitored by the Center than less integrated officials. It would be harder for a provincial Party secretary to explain investment intransigence in his province when he has to sit in on the Politburo meetings than it would be for someone who does not have to do so. Thus local officials calculate the benefits and costs of their actions according to the probability that their pursuit of local investment interests will be detected. High probability of detection increases the costs of attaining local investment interests; conversely, low probability increases benefits of doing so. Because this hypothesis views bureaucratic integration as accentuating central control, it can be called the "control" hypothesis.

Is it reasonable to suppose that bureaucratic integration with the Center can actually have the opposite effect from what the control hypothesis predicts: that is, are the more closely integrated provinces actually more able to realize their own interests and, by implication, their investment preferences? The answer depends entirely on one's prior conception of the nature of the Chinese political system. For example, if it is assumed that the formal system cannot have the kind of socializing impact posited by Schurmann, Lewis, and Barnett, then a priori expectations about the connections between bureaucratic integration and local investment behavior would be entirely different.

One contrasting view stresses the informal nature of the Chinese political system. Here, it is said that power resides not so much in the formal positions leaders occupy as in the informal network of patron–client relationships.[21]

---

20. This discussion is based on Olson (1982).

21. There are different views as to why the Chinese political system is clientelist. Lucian Pye argues that clientelism is a product deeply rooted in Chinese political values that long anteceded

Proponents of this view can point to the role Deng Xiaoping plays in contemporary Chinese politics; although Deng holds no formal position on the Politburo or on the Military Affairs Commission, he still calls the final shots because he commands a vast network of personal loyalties permeating the Chinese system, forged through decades of past common experiences and collegial associations. The importance of the personal network in Chinese political and policy processes during the later period of Mao's rule has been noted by Michel Oksenberg (1982: 167):

> Chains or networks of personnel linked leaders in Beijing to provinces, counties and even basic level units (*dan-wei*). The cement holding these networks together was the Chinese concept of *guan-xi*, meaning a relationship or an interconnection. A sense of loyalty, mutual obligation, and, given the atmosphere of the times, shared vulnerability bound clusters of people together.

Walder (1986) and Oi (1989) have provided the most systematic analyses of Chinese society and politics from a clientelist perspective. A clientelist system, Walder (1987: 47) observes, is "one in which individual members of subordinate social groups pursue their interests not by banding together for coordinated group action, but by cultivating ties based on the exchange of loyalty and advantage with individuals of higher status and power."[22] If such a description is fairly accurate, two inferences can be made about the connections between bureaucratic integration and local investment behavior. One is that bureaucratic integration is simply irrelevant to local investment behavior. Bureaucratic integration does not tell where the real power lies, and, to the extent that informal networks of connections drive the real political and policy dynamics, bureaucratic integration does not shape the incentive structures of local officials, as previously alleged.

The other inference is that closer integration to the Center actually advances local investment interests. It may create access to top policy makers or secure powerful patrons at the Center. Personal connections can be an expedient way of "getting things done." It should be to a province's advantage to have help from a leader of national stature. To the extent that securing

---

the rise of communism (Pye 1968); Oksenberg also stresses the primacy of "the Chinese concept" in giving rise to the persistence of clientelist ties. Others, such as Walder (1986) and Oi (1989), offer a more structural and functional explanation: clientelist ties exist in the Chinese political system, they say, because they perform vital functions that the system is otherwise unable to provide. Thus, according to this view, informal channels of interest articulation, cultivation of personal ties to obtain scarce goods and services, and mutual obligations based on an exchange of loyalty stem from the very design of the system, which does not allow formal opportunities for participation and interest articulation (Oi 1989: 9–10).

22. For sophisticated treatment of the role of connections and the efforts to cultivate them, see Walder (1986) and Oi (1989). For general expositions on clientelism, see Schmidt (1977).

investment approvals and funds requires weaving through China's myriad bureaucracies, having "friends in high places" can be tremendously helpful, and, when push comes to shove, can provide needed protection against the sharp edges of retrenchment programs. Because this hypothesis views bureaucratic integration as an enormous bargaining asset on the part of localities, it can be called the "bargaining" hypothesis.

Appointments and tenure durations. Two aspects of provincial governance are examined here: leadership succession patterns and the stability of their tenure. Provincial cadres include secondary provincial officials, defined as anyone who is a member of a provincial standing committee in the Party hierarchy or is a vice governor in the government hierarchy. They are important cadres who usually are assigned a specialized area of responsibility, and they are also appointed by the Center.

Succession is a straightforward concept. Succession occurs when there is a change in leadership. Because all provinces have the same number of top officials (one Party secretary and one governor), for top officials, the succession variable simply records that change; for secondary officials, it is necessary to take into account the number of secondary officials and thus for them, the succession variable denotes the percentage of new officials in a given year.

Leadership stability is first and foremost understood in terms of the length of time an official is able to serve in his current post. Obviously, an official who has served in a particular position for a long time can claim more tenure stability than an official who has served for a short time. Thus tenure is measured by the number of years an official serves in a given post. Needless to say, this measure is not able to capture some of the more qualitative aspects of "leadership stability." For example, an official may be stripped of his decision-making powers without formally losing his position; this is exactly what happened to Hua Guofeng. At a critical Politburo meeting held in November and December of 1980, Hua was asked to resign from his chairmanships of both the Central Committee and the Military Affairs Commission, while Hu Yaobang and Deng Xiaoping were put in charge. These personnel shifts, in compliance with the Politburo decision of the same meeting, were not formalized until the Sixth Plenary Session of the Eleventh Party Congress (held between June 27 and June 29 the next year) and were deliberately kept secret from the Chinese public (Zhao Shenghui 1987: 443).[23] Although in that situation, our measure

---

23. The absence of a formal decision, while Hua's power was in a clear decline, led to the erroneous impression that Hua was launching a counterattack to resist his demise. Clarke (1987: 37) asserts that Hua refused to resign, and he was "bolstered by Ye Jianying and other disgruntled PLA leaders."

would inevitably cause an upward bias in our estimate of leadership stability, the extent of this bias is in all likelihood small, and the bias itself is randomly distributed among the twenty-nine provinces over the 1976–92 period.

Investment hypotheses about the effect of appointments and tenure. In a unitary political system tenure duration and control can be linked in a number of ways. Here the discussion is drawn from literature on the theoretical and empirical aspects of this issue. The purpose, as before, is to clarify the complexities of the issue by pointing out that, on empirical as well as on theoretical grounds, our hypothesis is by no means determinate and, given this indeterminacy, there is a need for rigorous empirical testing.

An overwhelming number of the studies on cadre appointments in China or in other communist countries focus on one of the two following subjects: (1) changes in recruitment criteria, and (2) how changes in recruitment criteria bring about new outlooks and attitudes among leaders and, consequently, produce profound changes in the character of the communist regime. On the changes in recruitment criteria, for example, Burns (1987b), Li and White (1988), and Lee (1991) have carefully documented the shifts in the Chinese Communist Party's cadre policies during the history of the People's Republic. Lee (1991), in his recent book, has meticulously shown that in a personalized political system, such as China's, the "elite's idiosyncrasies" matter tremendously in shaping the political system.

Many studies on the impact of changes in recruitment criteria focus on the transition from the so-called revolutionary mobilization stage to a period that places a high premium on economic development and modernization. Such a transition, it is argued, has a strong impact on the communist polity. Lowenthal (1970: 110–11) expresses this chain of reasoning most clearly:

In the conflict between the revolutionary veteran elite and the post-revolutionary expert elite, a victory of the experts leads, in one form or another, to a major change in the Party's composition, and hence in its outlook. In the conflict over the role of moral and material incentives, a victory for economic man leads to a growing acceptance of materialist values, and in due course to a major decline in the role of coercion, a corresponding decline in the political and economic power of the security police, and the disappearance of mass terrorism as an instrument of polity.

There is no denying that recruitment criteria and their changes constitute important subjects of analysis, but they do not tell the whole story. First of all, as a number of writers have made clear, changes in recruitment criteria generally follow from or are directly attributable to leadership changes at the very top of the Chinese political system. Clarke (1987), for example, links the spurts of personnel reforms in the late 1970s and early 1980s to the rise of the post-Mao leadership and argues that the reforms were Deng's attempts to mold a more hospitable environment for his economic reform programs. Similarly, the ascent of a "technocratic" or managerial elite in the former Soviet Union was linked, respectively, to the successions of Khrushchev and Brezhnev to leadership posts.[24] To the extent that changes in recruitment criteria have any tangible political impact, they are, at best, an intermediate variable heavily dependent on succession issues. Thus the deeper force at work seems to be the political dynamics surrounding the succession process. What, for example, explains the desire to carve out differences with predecessors and what explains the success of one policy vision as opposed to another?[25]

Second, analyzing recruitment criteria or their changes alone has precious little relevance to the issue of concern here. On theoretical grounds, one cannot expect recruitment criteria that stress ideological purity and conformity to reduce shirking more than those that stress technical expertise, administrative rationality, or procedural predictability, or vice versa. On empirical grounds, as noted in previous chapters, local investment expansion above the level the Center deems appropriate has been a long-standing problem in the Chinese economy and seems historically unrelated to the wide oscillations in bureaucratic recruitment criteria. Whether they are appointed or promoted because of their ideological outlook or because of their technical skills, Chinese local officials are driven by fiscal incentives and are strongly motivated to expand investments.

Third, changes in elite recruitment criteria, as an independent variable, better explain the convergence rather than the divergence of behavior and longitudinal rather than cross-sectional differences. Because changes in recruitment criteria are a *systemwide* phenomenon, there is no reason to believe that this change should impinge on different provinces differently. If one argues that officials recruited because of their technical competence place economic modernization ahead of ideological work and therefore should engage in more investment expansions, then it becomes difficult to explain why some officials expand investments more than others. To explain differences in behavior that are observed during approximately the same time period, one should focus on incentive structures and on the calculation of costs and benefits that inform agents' behavior. Quite plausibly, officials recruited on the basis of similar criteria may nevertheless behave differently if different windows of

---

24. Hough (1980), for example, argues that great differences existed among the generations of Soviet leaders in terms of their attitudes toward the role of the military in the society, the conduct of foreign policy, and the way to manage the economy. Given these differences, generational gaps and successions would produce conflicts as well as opportunities for reforms.

25. This line of inquiry can be found in Bunce (1981).

opportunity for gains or losses are presented to them. In fact, in the aforementioned admittedly stylized scenario, recruitment criteria drop out as an explanatory variable; constancy does not explain things that vary.

What are the factors that may explain cross-sectional differences in Chinese provincial officials' investment behavior? My hypothesis is that some provinces experience more leadership instability than others, and this difference gives rise to different incentives to engage in investment expansions. This obviously begs the question of why.

Why *should* succession matter? Should it matter only when succession brings in someone with entirely a different policy perspective or character, or should it matter simply because the role-player has changed? The answer is, succession per se matters because it affects the mindset of the officials involved. That is to say, a new official characteristically thinks and behaves differently from others just because he is new. What is the mindset of a new leader? An accurate and full answer to this question would have to be sought in the circumstances under which he rose to power and even in his personality traits. Since information on these aspects is difficult to come by, one can only strive to formulate some general expectations as to the likely state of mind of an official assuming a new post, abstracted from historical specifics.

One line of thinking says that local personnel decisions are a result of intense bargaining between the Center and the localities. In this scenario, a candidate who is chosen is someone who has won the support of other local officials. Thus a new official is always a localist. For another thing, a new leader may expect "windfall gains" of some kind to be associated with the new appointment. A new leader typically has a lot of energy, fresh ideas, and, more important, enjoys a "honeymoon" period when his actions are less critically scrutinized.[26] Bunce (1981), in her statistical studies of Soviet republics' budgetary allocations, has found evidence to show that a new first Party secretary tends to shift budgetary priorities quite drastically, but once the new priorities become set and defined, departures from them are incremental. What then is a Chinese official likely to do during a "honeymoon" period? If he is rational, he should use this period of time to placate local interests and to establish rapport with his local colleagues. To establish one's reputation and support base among his local subordinates or colleagues, it is necessary to show that the appointed leader is "one of them," and to launch investment projects that confer rents on local government agencies. If the above description is accurate, one should expect to see a boosting effect of local interests immediately

26. This part of the discussion draws from the works of Bunce (1979, 1981). In her comparative studies of socialist states and democratic systems, Bunce draws the conclusion that succession has a significant impact on public policy outcomes in both types of systems.

following the succession of a new leader. This hypothesis is the "bargaining" hypothesis.

Of course, an opposite scenario is also possible. Although it is unlikely that an extremely unpopular official at the local level is always selected over one who is popular, given the centralized appointment procedure, it would be equally, if not more, unlikely that an official's propensity to comply with the Center is not a factor in his favor.[27] It may be that new local leaders operate under strict policy and ideological constraints; a new leader may be timid and inexperienced but will usually toe the line laid down by his superiors. To be sure, he may want to defend local interests, but only after his position has become secure; willingness to challenge central policy comes with time and experience. Another possibility points to the role of administrative monitoring. Each selection of officials requires an extensive process of screening and checking of backgrounds of the officials under consideration; for this reason, the personnel selection process is analogous to ex ante monitoring. If this description is right, then one can argue that new officials are more closely monitored than old officials and therefore new local officials should shirk less in their investment conduct. This is the "control" hypothesis.

Why should tenure length matter one way or the other? Downs (1967), in his classic study of bureaucratic behavior, asserts that high personnel turnover rates, in contrast to a situation of personnel stability, are likely to enlarge what he calls the "performance gap": the gap between what is being done and what ought to be done.[28] The critical problem, in this case, is how to define "performance gap": given the fact that there are dual constituencies for any given provincial official, whose judgment of the "performance gap" counts more in this calculation? In certain situations, a provincial official may well assign weights to competing judgments on the part of his superiors and his local clients.

Consider first the possibility that a longer tenure causes an official to value local interests more than central interests. Most investment projects do not produce instantaneous benefits; typically, there is a time lag between the commitment of resources and the actual yielding of tangible economic or fiscal dividends, because the completion of projects and the sales of products both take time. Obviously, an official who expects to step down quickly would behave differently from one who does not have such expectations: he will not be around to reap the benefits. As George Shultz, when remarking on the

---

27. This can be partly inferred from the leadership selection process. According to Manion (1985), detailed negotiations take place between central officials in charge of organizational work and local officials to ensure the collegiality of the appointee under consideration.

28. Downs (1967: 192) also acknowledges that there can be varying opinions as to what constitutes the performance gap, but in his analysis he largely omits this issue.

American economy in the 1980s, mused, "The economist's lag is the politician's nightmare" (quoted in Simmons 1990: 7).

A further consideration accentuating the impact of tenure is a possible shift in loyalty. This occurs in a number of ways. First, to the extent that appointments are equivalent to ex ante monitoring, long service tenure is then associated with less frequent ex ante monitoring. Second, because of the centralized appointment and promotion procedures, one may naturally expect willingness to comply with the Center, even for a local candidate, to play some role in the selection process and eventually rule out alternative candidates. But as years of service in one province increase, leaders will begin to identify themselves with or be captured by local interests, and the Center will begin to experience control problems. When specific information about these control problems themselves is costly to gather, as indeed is the case for investment control, adjusting the length of personnel tenure is a relatively efficient control method. Kaufman (1960: 155–56), in his study of the management of the American forest service, argues that personnel turnovers check policy deviations because no matter how successfully a ranger can hide his practices from his superiors, he cannot do so with his successor.[29] To extend this logic, one can argue that frequent turnovers – and thus shorter tenure length – improve information distribution for the Center and this improvement should reduce shirking.

As usual, there are countervailing scenarios. Consider the career trajectory of a typical top official at the provincial level. His average tenure is less than four years. At the end of his tenure, he faces three possibilities: (1) he may be purged or retired, (2) he can be moved to an honorary post within the same province, such as the head of a provincial advisory commission, or (3) he may be promoted to a central post or be moved horizontally to serve in another province. Statistics show that after leaving their current posts a substantial proportion of top provincial officials are either promoted to serve in the central government or are transferred to similar positions in other provinces. In 1977 and 1989 there were altogether eighty-five replacements of Party secretaries and of these, forty-six (54.12 percent) were either promoted or moved to other provinces. There were 108 governor replacements and forty-seven (43.52 percent) were promoted or moved to other provinces.

To the extent that such a pattern can affect provincial officials' career

---

29. There are in fact many similarities between an American forest ranger and a Chinese local official. Both have a high degree of autonomy and operate quite independently; in addition, they both must reckon with powerful local interests, which from time to time pull them in a direction inconsistent with that of their respective superiors. Kaufman (1960) argues that there should be considerable centrifugal forces that fragment the forest service and the fact that it is not fragmented shows the success of the design of the management system.

expectations, one may hypothesize that a provincial official's modus operandi is tied not so much to how long he is associated with a given province but to how long he expects to interact with the Center during his entire career. If, for example, he only expects a temporary association with a province and his long-term career path lies elsewhere, he may calculate that an optimal strategy is to strive to please his superiors rather than to advocate interests on behalf of his local subordinates, in which case tenure length may not have a significant effect on investment, or it may even be negatively related to local investments. A second reason is that local investments may actually benefit from short-tenure expectations. Recall that local investments, because of their smaller scale and less technological complexity compared with central investment projects, have shorter gestation periods, and, as posited in chapter 3, a shorter gestation period provides an incentive to local officials to eschew committing resources to central projects.

Conclusion

The analytical framework presented here focuses on the two variables that are hypothesized to have an effect on local investment behavior. One is how the central government monitors local officials; the other is the degree to which investment interests differ between central and local policy authorities. These two factors, in turn, are a function of a number of other significant variables. My main proposition is that investment patterns tend to be closer to the central government's macroeconomic and industrial policy concerns when the central government can closely monitor the investment activities or when there is less divergence between central and local investment interests. This proposition can be tested by (1) demonstrating that these two variables take on different values over time, across different investment activities, or across different provinces, and (2) hypothesizing that these variations produce variations in local investment behavior in some systematic way.

Our bureaucratic investment model departs from many existing studies in two ways. First, our model attaches great importance to the bureaucratic nature of intergovernmental relations rather than simply focusing on the economic aspects. Taking into account the personnel allocative monopoly of the Center, this explanatory framework does not automatically equate asymmetry of economic control with weak central power. The only sensible explanation seems to be that local investment behavior is a function of cross-cutting political and economic forces. The argument will become biased if either economics or politics is omitted from our analysis. For example, if one looks only at the economic side, one is tempted to believe that local officials have gained economic and fiscal resources and control to such an extent that they may defy those central economic policies that harm their interests. If one looks only at the political side, one may arrive at the opposite view. I have consistently followed an integrated approach that explicitly takes into account the joint effect of economic and political or bureaucratic variables and that models the role of political institutions as alleviating coordination problems created by economic decentralization.

Our explanatory framework departs from the traditional research in a methodological sense as well. Our explanatory framework stresses the effect of "incentives" in motivating compliance; traditional research stresses the effect of coercion in punishing noncompliance and in suppressing self-interests. Roughly, this difference corresponds to a crude difference between political science and economics: traditionally, political scientists tend to stress "power," while economists tend to stress "interests" in their research. My emphasis on incentives is a result of adopting the institutional economics approach, which is concerned with both understanding and designing "incentive-compatible" arrangements.[30] Substantively, the assumption is also consistent with many established facts about the operations of the Chinese system during the reform era. Local officials are known to possess considerable operational autonomy and economic self-interests at variance with those of the Center. Over time, changes in administrative and economic monitorings and improvement in the abilities of the Center to supervise the personnel process should lead to an attenuation of investment-shirking behavior. This expectation contradicts the conventional wisdom in the field, which is that central macroeconomic control has been steadily declining during the reform era. A full account should incorporate the effect of declining administrative localism. Because changes over time are difficult to capture in explicit measurements, one can only speculate about their effects descriptively, as shown in chapter 7. Cross-sectional variations provide more direct evidence by which to assess the plausibility of the hypotheses presented here. I propose two broad categories of bureaucratic status that vary across provinces and that are hypothesized to lead to cross-sectional variations in local investment behavior. One involves the degree to which a local official is organizationally and bureaucratically integrated to the

---

30. The traditional research is similar to the "organic view" of organizations in which the primary role of leaders is to inspire subordinates to transcend narrow self-interests. The alternative approach in the studies of organizations (which I adopt) is "mechanistic": it views organizational control as primarily a problem of designing incentive structures. For these two contrasting views, see Miller (1993). A good example of the "mechanistic" view of organizations is Alchian and Demsetz (1972). Alchian and Demsetz argue that the solution to the problem of monitoring in team production is to give team leaders a stake in the residual income so that they have an incentive to monitor production accurately.

Center; the other involves a set of tenure considerations. I also propose two alternative ways these bureaucratic attributes may affect local investment behavior. One hypothesis stresses the control character associated with these attributes; the other stresses their bargaining character. Chapter 8 turns to the conflicting hypotheses about the effect of bureaucratic variables.

APPENDIX

Sources of Chinese data

The qualitative information used in this study comes from three main sources. One is provincial newspapers, which publish speeches by provincial officials. Particularly useful are those speeches given by the heads of the provincial planning commissions and by the heads of provincial finance bureaus. These speeches contain valuable information about investment and other economic plans. The second source is the provincial almanacs published in a number of provinces. These usually provide detailed information about changes in personnel and the implementation of economic policies, and in a number of cases they contain open complaints about central investment policies. The third source is the interviews I conducted between 1989 and 1992 in Jiangsu, Guangdong, and Beijing. My goal in these interviews was to learn about the rules of operation in investment planning and the enforcement of investment reductions.

The quantitative information consists of two principal kinds; economic data, such as investment and tax levels, and political and administrative data detailing the characteristics of Chinese provincial governance. National economic data are readily available in the annual statistical yearbooks that the State Statistical Bureau has published regularly since 1981.

Provincial data are more difficult to gather and come from more varied sources. The main source of economic data pertaining to the provinces is *Quanguo gesheng, zizhiqu, zhixiashi lishi tongji ziliao huibian* (Collection of historical data of Chinese provinces, autonomous regions, and directly administered municipalities) compiled by the State Statistical Bureau (1990). This is probably the most complete and comprehensive collection of Chinese provincial data to date, and since the comparability of data is a key requirement for this study, it is important to rely on that volume, rather than on statistical yearbooks published by individual provinces, in order to reduce any errors that might result from nonstandardized reporting procedures and from using different definitions of norms. In addition, as supplemental sources I have used the statistical series known as *Zhongguo guding zichan touzi tongji ziliao* (Statistical materials on fixed-asset investment in China) (SSB 1987b, 1989, 1991b, 1993a), covering the 1950–85, 1986–87, 1988–89, and 1990–91 periods, respectively. More disaggregated data can be found in *Zhongguo tongji yuebao* (Monthly bulletin of Chinese statistics) compiled by the SSB. I have drawn some fiscal data for a few provinces from *Zhongguo caizheng tongji* (1950–1988) (Statistics on Chinese finance [1950–1988] (Ministry of Finance 1989b). For some of the data series for Guangdong, provincial yearbooks were used. *Quanguo gesheng, zizhiqu, zhixiashi lishi tongji ziliao huibian* does not provide the breakdowns between provincial and central investments, nor do the various volumes of the Guangdong statistical yearbook. To arrive at an estimate, I used the sectoral breakdowns for the 1977–85 period given in *Zhongguo guding zichan touzi tongji ziliao (1950–85)* and counted some sectors as local investment and others as central investment. Provincial investment since 1985 is provided for in *Zhongguo tongji yuebao*. Also, for Guangdong province, *Quanguo gesheng, zizhiqu, zhixiashi lishi tongji ziliao huibian* does not give budget breakdowns and therefore I had to use provincial yearbooks for figures on investment spending.

Political and administrative data – for example, those concerning provincial leaders' tenure and turnover rates – come from two main sources. For the top provincial leaders, the Party secretaries and governors, their dates of appointment are recorded in *Zhongguo gongchandang zhizheng sishinian* (Forty years of rule by the Chinese Communist Party) (Ma Qibing and Chen Wenbing 1989) and in various issues of the *China Directory* (published by Radiopress, Inc., in Tokyo); for information on lower-level provincial officials, I used *Zhonggong nianbao* (Yearbook on Chinese communism) (between 1977 and 1993), compiled by the Institute for the Study of Chinese Communist Problems in Taipei, Taiwan, which publishes the names of all provincial officials on an annual basis. Background data on the provincial officials are found in the three editions of *Who's Who in the People's Republic of China* (1981, 1987, and 1990), compiled by the German scholar, Wolfgang Bartke. Supplemental information on the Chinese leadership is found in *Who's Who in China: Current Leaders* (1989) published by the Foreign Languages Press in Beijing and Liu Jintian and Shen Xueming, eds., *Lijie Zhonggong Zhongyang Weiyuanhui renmin cidian* (Biographies of the Chinese Communist Party Central Committee members) (1992).

Issues in using Chinese data

My reliance on data in official Chinese sources raises an obvious question: Can one trust conclusions based on Chinese data? It is widely agreed that the Chinese data-collecting apparatus is quite backward and therefore its data are bound to be incomplete and inaccurate. The other point concerns the motives of those who collect the data; since they operate under an authoritarian regime, they can only present the "rosy pictures" by overreporting political and economic achievements.

It is, by and large, easier to deal with the first concern. Proxies can usually be found or created when data are missing. Data inaccuracy in fact *justifies* the use of the statistical method, because, as King (1989: 3) points out, reliable data showing clear relationships require little if any statistical analysis. Biases arising from the motives of the data collectors are more troubling, especially when such motives correlate in some systematic manner with the motives of the researcher. In the face of problems of this nature, there are usually two lines of defense. One is the assumption, or the hope, that the bias or the degree of the bias, is not *systematically* correlated with the objects of inquiry. In the present study, for example, this would mean that some provinces do not *always* overreport (or underreport) their data or do not *always* over- or underreport their data by a consistent margin. In a separate study, I have found that the main problem with Chinese data is random errors; systematic biases are averted in part because Chinese economic data have not been used extensively for planning purposes (Huang 1996). Of course, systematic biases cannot be assumed away for certain years, for certain provinces, and for certain statistical series; in that case, the hope is that this study will at least provide some grounds to falsify the results when new and better data come forward.

The second justification in using the data even when it is known that they contain problems is that the statistical method has a number of solutions to such problems. One solution is to enlarge the sample size in the hope that the biases will be canceled out to some extent when there are many cases. This is known as the normality assumption – it states that deviations from the mean tend to be normally distributed around the mean level as the sample size increases. The data collected for this study cover seventeen years (1976–92) and twenty-nine provinces, generating about 493 observation points (twenty-nine times seventeen), a respectable sample size.

Coding of political and bureaucratic variables

Political and bureaucratic variables do not exist in standard format and they have to be created in a way that suits a given analytical purpose. To measure the bureaucratic standing of local officials vis-à-vis central Party and government authorities, I created a bureaucratic integration variable (BINT). For each province, there are two values for the BINT, one for the Party secretary and one for the governor. To assess the degree of bureaucratic integration, I assigned values from one to four to provinces, depending on the applicability of a set of criteria.

The BINT values are

4: A concurrent centralist – a provincial official who holds a provincial post while also serving in a central government position,
3: A centralist – a provincial official with significant past service in central ministries,
2: An outsider – a provincial official with significant service in other provinces,
1: An insider – a provincial official with significant service in that province.

Concurrent central posts include Politburo members and alternate members, members of the central Party Secretariat, state councilors, or vice chairmen of the National People's Congress Standing Committee. Significant service is defined as service of at least more than three years. Also, service that has a higher rank counts more. For example, a county position compared with a provincial or national position should count less, even if an official spent a longer time in the county position. Outside provincial positions should be approximately equal in rank to the current position, that is, at the provincial level. Thus a prefectural position would not count as an outside position unless that is the only position the official held. In some cases, a province is given a value of one even though the official came from an outside position before assuming the provincial post. This is because the person in question had a very long term of service in that province. An example here is Xie Xuegong of Tianjin, who served in Tianjin between 1968 and 1977, even though before 1967 he served in Hebei.

In a case where a person has had mixed experience (as did Han Peixin of Jiangsu), then the duration and the rank of the positions should be taken into account. For example, ministerial rank should count more than a provincial post, other than Party secretary or governor. Between the ministerial rank and Party secretary or governor, the duration of service should count. Only the work experience after 1949 is relevant. In the case of some of the earlier officials in our sample, their career tracks were interrupted by the Cultural Revolution and therefore their careers before the Cultural Revolution are also taken into account even though the service was not continuous.

Military appointments were especially prominent in 1976 and 1977. They are treated the same as provincial appointments because during the Cultural Revolution many provincial posts were taken over by the military, and it would be inaccurate to characterize all military positions as central positions. However, distinctions between outsiders and insiders still exist. Sources of background information for the coding of the bureaucratic integration variable are Bartke (1981, 1987, 1990a, 1990b), *Who's Who in China* (1989), and Liu Jintian and Shen Xueming (1992).

The appointment variable is a dummy variable for top officials (APPTOP) that takes the value of one when an appointment occurs and of zero when there is no appointment. September is the dividing line. If a person enters office in or before September, then his characteristics apply to that year; if he enters office after September, his predecessor's characteristics apply. The assumption is that investment will be harder to control with only three or four months left in the year; appointments made after September are credited to the next year. For secondary officials, the appointment variable is the ratio of new officials in any given year (TENSEC). The tenure variable is simply the number of years a provincial official served in his post. For top officials, the tenure variable is a composite index for secretaries and governors; for secondary officials, the tenure variable is the average tenure length in that province.

The appointment dates for top officials up to 1989 are given in Ma Qibing and Chen Weibing (1989); for the 1990–92 period, I rely on recent issues of the *China Directory*. For secondary officials, I compare name lists for provincial Party and government establishments for each year of the 1976–92 period; the names that appear for the first time are then counted as new appointments. The name lists appear in *Zhonggong nianbao* (Yearbook on Chinese communism) (1976–93), published annually by the Institute for the Study of Chinese Communist Problems in Taipei, Taiwan. The length of service is then determined on the basis of the appointment dates. A slight complication arises in the determination of tenure for secondary officials. In the late 1970s most provincial officials at the secondary level were appointed before the sample period (1976–92) and thus their tenure began before 1976. In the late 1970s there were, on average, between twenty and thirty secondary Party and government officials in one province, which gives between 580 to 870 secondary officials for the twenty-nine provinces altogether. Precise information about when these officials started and ended their services is incomplete. Thus the year 1970 is the cutoff point for all secondary officials and therefore is coded as the first year of tenure. New provincial leaderships in all provinces were installed in 1970, after the Ninth Party Congress in 1969. Thus such a coding strategy produces a reasonable approximation of the actual tenure of the secondary officials.

7

Strategic investment behavior during austerity

The discussion now turns to the evidence of local investment behavior, beginning with the impact of monitoring. That impact can be seen in the over-time investment performance of local governments. The intent here is to determine if central control over local investment behavior has declined owing to greater dispersion of economic and fiscal resources during the reform era against a background of improved administrative capabilities over time. The second aim is to determine how the central government controls local investment when it commands poor information and how informational distribution affects investment behavior, with a view to explaining the implementation of investment control outcomes at the local level.

The story of implementation is complex. For one thing, local officials have considerable operational autonomy. Some of this autonomy is rooted in the way the Chinese system divides the lines of command between ministries and provinces; some of it is de facto control, arising from the superior command of information by local officials. There are also strong disincentives to comply with the central government's aggregate and distributional policy objectives. Investment reduction slows down economic growth, with adverse implications for revenue collection and employment creation. The costs are specific and tangible. On the other hand, the benefits of investment reduction – a stable macroeconomic environment and the alleviation of shortages – are diffuse and the tragedy-of-the-commons characteristic of the situation causes local officials to shirk adjustment costs. The distributional objective of central austerity programs also hurts local interests. The local industrial base is the main source of tax revenues and of employment to local governments; local investment projects, by concentrating on high value-added commodities, are also more profitable. And because administrative price controls are imposed on key raw materials, energy products, and transport, whereas prices of consumer commodities respond more flexibly to underlying economic trends, the discrepancy in the profit margins between central and local projects grows in an inflationary environment, at least in nominal terms.

Quite apart from these disincentives, the enormous information asymmetry between the central government and local officials is another hindrance to an effective implementation of investment reduction. Central planners in Beijing simply know less about the specific investment programs in the localities than do the local officials in charge. The technical complexity of managing tens of thousands of projects in a given year and the lack of a vertical administrative chain of command to compel compliance imply that central planners cannot issue direct and detailed directives about which projects to cut and how to steer resources sectorally at the local level. When monitoring is a problem, there is a high probability of evasion.

Nevertheless, central investment reduction programs appear to have had a significant impact both on the level of investment and on the direction of investment at the local level. In general, the investment growth rate slows down considerably under the impact of austerity policies, and the investment activities that the central government discourages – such as local projects – slow down considerably more than those activities the central government promotes. The overall evidence does not support the prevailing view that the central government has lost control (*shikong*) of local investment behavior because of the decentralizing effect of the reforms. Rather, central control has declined in some areas but has been strengthened in others. The strengthening of central control, despite the wide-ranging economic reforms, is consistent with my hypothesis that there has been an improvement over time in the central monitoring capabilities. This improvement is associated with an increase in compliance.

In a way, the overall success of the central government in achieving local compliance with its investment policies is a puzzle. The economic resource base under central control has been slipping steadily during the reform era and, as this chapter shows, central planners only have poor information to make their decisions in enforcing investment plans. Typically, compared with local officials, the central government has less knowledge about the local investment projects that it seeks to suspend and about local financial and economic conditions. This is by no means a new finding; Chinese planning officials themselves are keenly aware of the information shortage. Indeed, the economic reforms have been explicitly justified by the need to economize on the use of information. Consider the following paragraph from the reform declaration adopted by the CCP Central Committee in 1984:

Because social demand is complex and changes constantly and because conditions in enterprises are different and the economic links between enterprises are intertwined in complex ways, it is impossible for any state institution to know fully the whole situation and adjust to the situations. If the state directly manages all the state-owned enterprises, subjectivism and bureaucratism will be inevitable and incentives and the vigor of enterprises will be suppressed. (Central Committee 1992 [1984]: 288)

The distribution of information affects both the approaches with which the central government seeks to control investment activities and the calculus of local officials on whether to comply with central investment policies. The overall record of investment compliance should not belie the fact that local officials often try very hard to evade central control, as indicated by their different responses to the different levels of central policy commitment. But because strategic motives are not directly observable, it is a challenge to demonstrate how their posited motives actually affect their investment behavior.

Aggregate impact of austerity policies

The economics and administrative mechanisms of investment reduction are fairly straightforward. Central policy authorities respond to surges of inflation by adopting contractionary monetary and fiscal actions. The first effect of this is that financial resources available for building new plants and factories are reduced. Here the administrative nature of the contractionary policies means that regional branches of the specialized banks are given tighter credit targets, are prohibited from making loans to banned projects, and are ordered to collect payments on existing debts. Thus the gist of the contractionary policies is not so much to increase the costs of borrowing to investors (which, in any case, may not be sufficiently constraining given the soft-budget constraints) as to make investment loans physically unavailable.

Monetary or fiscal policies alone are seldom relied on to combat inflation; administrative measures are invoked in tandem with economic policies. Typically, investment approval authority is recentralized. Projects previously under review at the county level are then required to be submitted to provincial authorities; projects previously under review at the provincial level then require screening from the SPC. Reduction of investment volume, however, is only half of the coin; the other half concerns investment structure. Local officials are required to devote financial resources, manpower, and their policy attention to completing projects designated by the central government as priority projects, and usually these are the projects under the control of the central ministries. In a contractionary policy environment, it is a zero-sum game: an increase in the resource flow to central projects means a decrease in the resources available to local projects. This has distributional consequences. To examine the implementation of investment reduction, it is necessary to

Table 7.1. *Central investment objectives during rounds of austerity policy*

Central objectives	Purpose of central objectives	Predicted effect
Growth	To reduce overall investment growth	Lower annual growth averages
Sectors	To shift resources from local and nonproduction projects to central and production projects	Lower growth in the discouraged sectors relative to protected sectors
	To speed up project completion and to slow down commissioning of new projects	Negative correlation between discouraged and protected sectors
Equity	To promote sharing of adjustment costs among provinces	Convergence in the growth rates among provinces

operationalize austerity objectives in ways that are conducive to data analysis, as explained in the next section.

Central investment objectives and their operationalization

In order to examine the systematic effect of austerity policies on local investment behavior, one first needs to specify exactly what the central austerity policies seek to accomplish. Furthermore, these objectives must be stated in a way appropriate for data analysis. Therefore these objectives need to be operationalized into specific indices. Table 7.1 presents three central investment objectives during an austerity policy period in summary form together with the investment categories that are relevant to central policy objectives.

The selection of these policy objectives and their categories is based largely on the discussion in chapter 5. Reducing investment growth is probably the most straightforward objective during an austerity period. Investment expansion exacerbates aggregate demand and supply balances and is a direct contributor to the buildup of inflationary pressures in the economy. Thus investment growth rates during an austerity period, as compared with investment growth rates during an inflationary period, are a proxy of the effect of the austerity programs. Reduction of investment growth is not the only goal of the central austerity policies; there is a sectoral consideration as well. Central policy authorities invariably seek to reduce investment growth in certain sectors and promote investment in other sectors. Quite apart from a desirable aggregate level of investment, there is the issue of the sectoral distribution of investment resources. During an austerity policy period, the central government seeks to promote central projects (which are concentrated in bottleneck sectors) and production projects, and it also aims to speed up project completion.

At the same time, central policy authorities hope to discourage growth in local, nonproduction projects, and to slow down the commissioning of new projects during a period of general resource stringency. This amounts to a shift of resources from the investment activities the Center discourages to those that the Center favors. To examine this impact, one must compare the relative growth rates between the discouraged and favored sectors, as well as determine the nature of the association between the investment activities in these two sectors. The intended policy effect is that they should be contrarian in nature. That is, an increase in the growth of one activity should be accompanied by a decrease in the growth of the other.

For the lack of a better word, I call the third policy objective the "equity" objective. This is often implied rather than explicitly stated in the central austerity programs. It refers to the requirement that investment reduction across provinces be relatively uniform. In the language I have adopted in this book, it is an effort to get every province to bear a portion of the adjustment costs and to minimize shirking behavior. Thus, in addition to investment level and trade-offs, investment dispersions – the differences in the growth rates among provinces – are the third criterion I use to assess the impact of the central austerity policies.

Unless otherwise noted, the data used throughout this book all refer to the provincial level. The mean growth rates, for example, refer to the average annual growth rates of the twenty-nine provinces included here. The data run from 1976 to 1992; when growth rates are calculated, the data run from 1977 to 1992. This gives a maximum number of observations of 464 (twenty-nine provinces times sixteen years) for most of the statistical series; some series, however, fall short because there are missing data, especially for the earlier years. Investment growth rates are measured in real terms: that is, the differences between the nominal growth rates and the retail price index (previous year = 1).[1] Although the economic data are organized by provinces, they also encompass subprovincial economic activities. For example, the Guangdong investment level not only includes investment activities controlled by the Guangdong provincial government but also prefectural and county activities. Thus, consistent with the stipulation laid out in chapter 1 and to

---

1. A more appropriate deflator is the investment goods price series, which is not available. The use of the retail price index would be a problem if it systematically misrepresents the investment goods price index. However, there is no indication that this is the case.

avoid confusion, they are referred to as local investments rather than as provincial investments.

Investment variables can be measured in two ways. One is the unweighted series, which assigns an equal weight to each province in the calculation. Implicitly, the weight is 0.035 (1/29); that is, each province has an equal weight as one of the twenty-nine provinces included in this study. As such, this measurement captures *administrative* investment behavior. The second measurement is the weighted series. Here each province is weighted by its share of the national net material product, in recognition of the fact that provinces may have vastly different impacts on the macroeconomy even if their investment growth rates are similar, due to the differences in their economic size. Bigger provinces should be counted more than smaller provinces in calculating the average growth rates.[2]

Using two different measurements for the same variable also has substantive implications. Because these two measurements are designed to represent the same underlying phenomenon, they should not behave too differently from each other, except in cases where economic size specifically matters. In order to claim that the austerity policy has an alleged effect – say, reducing investment growth – prudence makes it necessary to see if these two measurements agree in showing this effect.[3] Thus consistency in the findings is an important criterion to assess the reliability of any inferences drawn from the data analysis. Such prudence is especially warranted in situations where one may not have full confidence in the quality of the data.

Aggregate impact

When the incentive not to comply is strong and when monitoring is problematic, one should expect many instances of noncompliance. In reality, cases of outright noncompliance are rare. There is no evidence of massive and pervasive noncompliance; instead, the evidence is quite strong that Chinese provinces,

---

2. In order to capture the notion that economic size is a stationary concept, I use the moving averages of provincial and national NMP as the provincial weights. The following benchmark years are used: 1976–79, 1980–83, 1984–87, and 1988–92.

3. Ideally, we also want to see if there is consistency in all three investment categories included in this book. This is a difficult requirement, however. Production and nonproduction projects and completion and commissioning are not broken down centrally and locally; thus we cannot directly show central–local investment behavior. The project completion and commissioning category encounters an additional problem: during austerity, the Center often categorically bans project commissioning, but it also tries to suspend ongoing projects. Thus, unlike central–local projects and production–nonproduction projects, the two are not completely contrarian. For these reasons, I rely more on the central–local project category to derive our substantive interpretations.

when confronted with a contractionary policy, by and large comply with the central government by reining in investment growth and by steering resources in ways compatible with central industrial policies. Noncompliance, which is analyzed later in this chapter, is mainly strategic in character. That is, local officials disobey the central government when they deem that they can get away with it. This section focuses on indicators of implementation success.

There are two ways to measure success. The first is to examine the actions or the processes in which the Chinese local officials engage when they implement central investment policies. This is what Lampton (1987b) refers to as the "procedural approach" to assess successes and failures of implementation; its virtue, as Lampton (1987b: 7) points out, is its simplicity: "If procedures were followed, it was successful by definition."[4] The second approach focuses on the outcomes of implementation; the evidence here is more quantitative. The appendix to this chapter shows how the procedural approach can be used to describe the policy actions some of the local governments took to reduce investments; here, the focus is on the statistical measures of the implementation outcomes.

Impact on investment growth and on trade-offs

In order to make a claim that central investment policies have an impact, it is necessary to specify a baseline scenario to which one can compare the alleged impact of the central investment policies. The baseline scenario in this case is the investment performance during an inflationary period. Any inferences one draws about the impact of central investment policies should be based on an explicit comparison between the two policy periods. The 1977–92 period can be divided into two subperiods according to the characteristics of the macroeconomic policies at the time. The years 1977, 1978, 1982, 1984, 1985, 1988, and 1992 were years in which an inflationary macroeconomic policy regime was in place and are thus labeled inflationary periods. The years 1979, 1980, 1981, 1983, 1986, 1987, 1989, 1990, and 1991 were under a relatively disinflationary macroeconomic policy regime and are labeled austerity periods.

The most direct measure of the impact of an austerity policy is the ratio of the level of actual investment to the planned investment targets, but a number of problems arise with this measure.[5] I thus mainly rely on actual investment figures to measure local investment behavior to compare investment behavior among provinces. The norm is the average performance among the twenty-

---

4. This measures what Lampton (1987b) calls "congruence between outcomes and intentions."
5. For a detailed discussion of this measure, see the appendix to this chapter.

Table 7.2. *Average provincial growth rates by investment categories among Chinese provinces under two macroeconomic policy regimes (two measurements, percentage)*

Period	Central projects	Local projects	Nonproduction projects	Project commissioning
Austerity				
Unweighted averages	6.32	1.75	6.60	1.83
Weighted averages	7.45	3.81	8.29	2.43
Inflationary				
Unweighted averages	22.40	25.63	28.53	22.36
Weighted averages	18.26	24.29	29.25	20.12

Note: Weights refer to the provincial shares of national NMP.
Source: Database.

nine provinces. Although this is a less intuitive measure of performance vis-à-vis policy intentions, there is some evidence that individual provinces do compare their performance with that of other provinces. Henan province noted that although its 1987 investment growth exceeded the level allotted by the central government, it was "much lower than the national average" (Henan Local History Editorial Committee 1987: 206).

The details of the findings are presented in table 7.2. The patterns of behavior are remarkably clear. All the figures during the inflationary period are in the double digits, and some are as high as 29 percent (the weighted average for the nonproduction projects). Because all the figures are deflated by the previous years' prices, the growth figures are in real terms. During the austerity period, however, provinces switch their behavior quite dramatically. All the figures are then in the single digits. In an aggregate sense, there is simply no question that the central government is able to enforce its investment preferences, and the provinces, by and large, comply.

Is there a resource shift between central and local projects or between production and nonproduction projects, as mandated by the austerity policies? As noted before, during the austerity period the central policy authorities pursue macroeconomic and industrial policy objectives simultaneously. The macroeconomic concern calls for a reduction of the aggregate investment level; the industrial policy concern, on the other hand, seeks to suspend some projects while trying to steer resources toward other projects. In general, from the viewpoint of local officials, the macroeconomic concern is easier to attend to than the industrial policy concern. Because the macroeconomic concern aims at restoring aggregate demand and supply, theoretically speaking at least, local governments can simply issue uniform investment reduction quotas to their subordinate agencies, which do not affect the relative welfare of different bureaucratic agencies and the enterprises under their charge. The industrial policy concern, on the other hand, necessitates an interdepartmental transfer of resources. As a result, the implementation of the industrial policy concern is a more strenuous test of the willingness or the capability of the local governments to comply with the central government. The reflection of the vice chairman of the Henan Planning Commission on the 1983 investment control drive illustrates this point well (Yao Ruxue 1984: 258):

> Compared with the two previous investment reductions [1979 and 1981], which aimed at big projects and preserved the small projects, this time it is to scale back those small but numerous projects so that the state's priority projects can be preserved. Quite a number of regions and departments would rather see an investment reduction, but they do not want to suspend the existing projects. They are still hesitating and have adopted a wait-and-see attitude.

Provincial officials explicitly use the ratios between central and local projects as a yardstick to assess the implementation of central investment policies. Henan province, for example, made note of its achievement in this regard. Its share of central projects in the total investment portfolio increased from 63.8 percent in 1983 to 69.9 percent in 1984, while its share of local investment projects decreased from 36.2 percent in 1983 to 30.1 percent in 1984 (Henan Local History Editorial Committee 1985: 382). To raise the visibility of central projects, in 1983 the Party secretary and governor of Henan personally inspected the sites of central investment projects.[6]

I use two measures to gauge the distributional impact of austerity policies. One is relative growth differentials, which are the differences in the growth rates between an austerity policy period and an inflationary policy period. Thus a negative growth differential indicates that the growth rate during the austerity period is smaller than it is during the inflationary period, and the larger the value the greater the difference between the two policy periods. The other is the Pearson correlation value between the two investment categories that are being compared. The Pearson correlation measures the direction and strength of the relationship between the two variables. A negative Pearson coefficient implies that the two variables move in opposite directions; a positive

6. They also attempted to solve concrete and urgent problems faced by these projects. For example, the commissioning of a number of priority projects was delayed because the local residents bargained hard for land acquisition fees. With the intervention by provincial leaders, these deals were quickly settled, apparently on terms favorable to the Center. The provincial Party committee and government also publicly censured, through newspapers, TV, and radio, some of the local residents "who refused to relocate in order to extract exorbitant benefits from the state." On this incident and the discussion in the text, see Yao Ruxue (1984).

Table 7.3. *Resource shifts among investment categories during austerity and inflationary policy regimes (unweighted measures, percentage)*

Investment categories[a]	Growth differentials[b]	Austerity, Pearson correlation (1) & (2)	Inflation, Pearson correlation (1) & (2)
(1) Central projects	−16.08	−0.10	0.06
(2) Local projects	−23.87		
(1) Production projects	−19.16	0.13	0.43
(2) Nonproduction projects	−21.93		
(1) Project completion	−16.32	0.11	0.21
(2) Project commissioning	−18.78		

[a] Investment category (1) is favored by the central government and investment category (2) is discouraged during an austerity policy period.
[b] Growth differentials = average growth rates$_{(austerity)}$ minus average growth rates$_{(inflation)}$.
Source: Database.

Pearson coefficient implies that they move in the same direction.[7] A larger value of the Pearson coefficient indicates a stronger relationship between the two variables than a smaller value. This distributional impact is examined in table 7.3.

The trade-off hypothesis says that certain investment categories are contrarian in nature; for example, during an austerity policy period, central investment growth rates should accelerate in relation to local investment growth (and vice versa under an inflationary environment). The same logic should also apply to production or nonproduction and existing or new project categories. Table 7.3 presents mixed evidence that there is a trade-off relationship between different investment categories as a result of austerity policies. The growth differentials between the austerity and inflationary periods are all negative, which means that growth rates are lower during the austerity period across all investment categories, whether they belong to the categories the central government seeks to protect or to the categories it seeks to cut. The austerity policy, however, has cut deeper into those projects that the central government discourages; for example, the growth differential for central projects is about −16 percent, as compared with about −23.9 percent for local projects. Another

7. This point is best illustrated by the following example. Suppose that both the central and local investment growth rates are initially set at 2 percent and that central investment is to grow to 3 percent. In that case, a −0.10 Pearson value means that local investment should decline by 0.10 percent, to 1.9 percent. In contrast, a 0.10 Pearson value would add 0.10 percent to the local investment growth rate, to 2.1 percent.

way to tell the same story is to compare the first and second columns of table 7.2. During an austerity policy period, invariably across different measurements, central investment grows at a faster rate than local investment; the situation is completely reversed when an inflationary policy regime is in effect.

In contrast, the growth differentials between the other two categories are not that pronounced; in fact, a difference of means test shows that the differences can be due to chance as much as to the impact of the austerity policies. The Pearson correlation values further confirm the notion that there is a resource shift from central to local projects, whereas a similar resource shift is absent in the other two investment categories. During the austerity policy period, the Pearson value for the central–local project correlation is −0.10, which indicates that every 1 percent of gain in the growth of central investment in a typical province is achieved at the expense of one-tenth of 1 percent of local investment. That central investment does grow at a faster rate during austerity indicates that resources that otherwise would have been assigned to local projects flow to central projects, just as the central policy authorities have intended. In contrast, such a trade-off relationship is entirely absent in the production–nonproduction and in the completion–commissioning categories. The Pearson values are positive during both policy periods, which indicates that a change in the macroeconomic policy regime does not have a tangible effect on the direction of the resource flows between different categories. Rather, the investment categories that should be contrarian in nature actually grow or decline together.

Impact of reforms

Some Chinese policy makers and analysts blame investment overheating on the economic reforms. Reforms, they argue, have decentralized economic decision making, transferred economic resources downward, and diversified investment funding sources. These developments reduce policy, financial, and economic leverage on the part of the central government over local investment conduct. The long-run impact of economic reforms is an erosion of the central capacity to affect both the level and direction of investment activities in the localities.

My own expectation of local investment conduct during the reform era differs from this conventional interpretation. Although it is true that reforms have reduced central leverage in a number of important aspects, a reduction in central leverage has not been the only development during the reform era. There has also been a moderate improvement in the ability of the central government to monitor local officials; the central government, through its personnel policies, has attempted to limit economic localism. Although these reforms are not expected to countervail completely the offsetting changes in the economic area, they do work to ameliorate some of the effects.

The erosion of central policy leverage is now almost taken as conventional wisdom. Yet there have not been many systematic and appropriately designed studies evaluating this claim empirically and critically. One of the common flaws in the existing analyses is the lack of sufficient research control. The World Bank (1990b), for example, shows that decentralization has caused investment to overheat at the local level and argues that the gap between central investment commitments and central control over resources is one of the major factors leading to macroeconomic instability. This study only looks at time-series data and changes in the level of local investments during the reform era. But during this period many other things have changed, including the tolerance on the part of the central policy authorities for local investment expansions. In the mid-1980s, for example, policy makers such as Zhao Ziyang and his policy advisers believed that actively reducing central economic control was the only right approach to reform central planning; in fact, they encouraged local policy initiatives, sometimes at the expense of central policy objectives. To argue that the central government has lost investment control because of resource dispersions one must hold constant central tolerance for local investment overheating. This can be done by holding constant the macroeconomic policy regime while varying the surrounding reform environment under which the austerity policies are in effect. This is done in table 7.4, which presents local investment behavior during the respective austerity policy periods.

Although economic reforms have not always been continuous and linear – the most recent and arguably the most serious reversal was in 1989 – there is no question that over the 1977–92 period the Chinese economy became considerably more liberalized and reforms have achieved remarkable successes.[8] For example, by 1992 more than half of China's industrial output was coming from the nonstate sector of the economy, and foreign trade constituted a sizable portion of the Chinese economy.[9] Closer to the subject of this book, Chinese local control over key production products and tax and bank operations and the ability of local governments to raise funds for investment projects have been considerably enhanced during this period.[10] A logical implication arising from these profound changes in the Chinese economy is that central investment control should decline over time and, by inference, later austerity

---

8. Lardy (1991) argues that many of the measures the Chinese leaders took in 1989 and 1990 – such as closing down village enterprises and cracking down on trade corporations – aimed more directly at restoring macroeconomic stability than at reversing the economic reforms. Naughton (1992a) points out that much of the initial antireform rhetoric was in fact never acted on.

9. For an excellent and a highly readable review of the Chinese economic reforms, see Rohwer (1992).

10. For more details, see chapters 2 and 3.

Table 7.4. *Annual mean growth rates, standard deviations, and investment trade-offs under an austerity policy, before and during the economic reforms (percentage)*

Period	Unweighted measures		Weighted measures[a]	
	Austerity	Inflation	Austerity	Inflation
Pre-reform (1977–83)				
Central projects				
Mean growth	6.21	34.32	8.47	26.32
Standard deviation	43.05	49.27	24.30	23.92
Local projects				
Mean growth	−0.95	18.39	1.56	15.61
Standard deviation	33.17	22.77	17.59	13.91
Correlations in growth between				
central and local	−0.23	0.10	−0.33	0.29
Reform (1984–92)				
Central projects				
Mean growth	6.40	13.41	5.72	11.85
Standard deviation	27.53	27.63	11.40	11.87
Local projects				
Mean growth	3.77	31.09	6.11	30.43
Standard deviation	24.77	29.58	10.32	15.42
Correlations in growth				
between central and local	0.11	0.18	0.22	0.29

[a] Weights are the moving averages of provincial shares of national NMP.
Source: Database.

policy rounds should have a smaller impact on local investment behavior than earlier austerity policy rounds. The three criteria for assessing the impact of central austerity policies (investment growth, trade-offs, and dispersions) can now be used to evaluate the impact of the reforms.

In table 7.4, the 1977–92 period is divided into two subperiods: the pre-reform period of 1977–83, and the reform period of 1984–92. Although most China analysts take the year 1978 as the beginning of the reform era, it is important to recognize that the industrial reforms did not commence until 1984, when the Central Committee issued "The Decision on the Reform of the Economic Structure," which ushered in a series of reforms in industry, trade, banking, and education. The year 1984 was a watershed year in that the reforms since 1984 have focused on the urban sector, whereas the reforms prior to 1984 were mainly concentrated in the agricultural sector.[11]

11. For a good account of the history of reforms, see Harding (1987).

The overall evidence does not support the conventional belief that there has been an across-the-board decline in central policy leverage; rather, it suggests that central policy leverage has increased in some areas but declined in others. The clearest and the most consistent indication that local investment compliance has declined over time can be seen in the sectoral shifts of resources. During the pre-reform period, the association between central and local investments was moderately negative, at -0.23 for the unweighted series and -0.33 for the weighted series (row 3). A negative association and the faster growth rates registered by the central projects imply that there was a clear resource shift from local to central projects during the pre-reform period when an austerity policy was in effect. In general, when central investment increased 1 percent, local investment declined by one-fifth to one-third of 1 percent in a typical province. In many ways, this should be the ideal situation for central policy authorities: an overall investment reduction falls disproportionately on local projects and the resources freed from the local investment reduction are then transferred to those projects the central government seeks to promote.

During the reform era, the signs for both the unweighted and weighted series reverse to positive. A positive Pearson value means that the two investment categories grow or decline together. Substantively, this means that when a typical province accelerates (reduces) central investment growth, it also accelerates (reduces) local investment growth by an amount equal to the Pearson correlation coefficients. Prior to the reforms, a change in the macroeconomic policy environment had a clear impact on the nature of the relationship between central and local investments: they were contrarian during austerity periods, and they became complementary during inflationary periods. Thus during the reform era, the sectoral effect of the austerity program has clearly dissipated; during both austerity and inflationary periods, central and local investments are positively related. There is no indication that local governments are sacrificing their own projects in order to complete more central projects. This finding is entirely consistent with the argument that the decentralization of investment approvals has weakened the ability of the Center to pick and choose projects.

In and of itself, a positive association between central and local projects during an austerity period does not mean that the central government is unable to implement its industrial and sectoral policies. It does mean, however, that the Center can only achieve its policy objectives at greater costs; the two central policy objectives during an austerity period are more incompatible than they were during the pre-reform era. Because the central government is less able to steer resources in a targeted manner and shift resources between different projects, the costs of the austerity programs are higher. The Center has to choose between its inflation and industrial policy objectives; achieving both of them at the same time is more difficult. The resource "stickiness" implies that a sectoral reallocation is a less feasible industrial policy strategy; the Center may be forced to relax its credit squeeze to ensure adequate funding of its own projects, rather than depending on local governments to sacrifice their own investment interests. This consideration played some role in credit relaxation in 1987 and 1991. In short, central industrial policy objectives require a less austere austerity program and conversely overly ambitious austerity objectives make the attainment of the industrial policy objectives more costly. This is a dilemma the Center did not have to face before reforms, and it is one of the most important factors contributing to inflation acceleration in the recent years.

The two other criteria used to assess the impact of austerity programs provide little evidence that the central government has become powerless during the reforms. To be sure, the local investment growth rate during the austerity period was higher during the reform era (it rose from −0.95 percent to 3.77 percent for the unweighted series and from 1.56 percent to 6.11 percent for the weighted series); once the greater tolerance for inflation during the reform era is taken into account, however, this jump in growth rates is less remarkable. In fact, the magnitude of investment reduction during the reform era – that is, the difference in the growth rates between the austerity and inflationary periods – is about one-third more than the level achieved during the pre-reform era (−27.32 percent compared with −19.34 percent).[12] Arguably, this is an indication of an enhanced ability on the part of the central government to control the level of investment volume, a finding that completely contradicts prevailing views on this issue. In addition, before 1984 the reduction of investment level came about mainly because of contractions in central projects; since 1984, local projects have become the main target of the austerity programs and the contractions of local projects far exceed the contractions of central projects (−27.32 percent compared with −7.01 percent).

In this book, investment dispersions are used as a proxy for shirking behavior. By this criterion, there is unambiguous evidence that shirking behavior has attenuated during the reform era. Table 7.4 contains several indications to this effect. Under both measurements, and especially during the austerity regime, the size of the standard deviation values has declined over the 1977–92 period

---

12. These figures are derived by subtracting column (2) from column (1): that is, −27.32 = 3.77 − 31.09 and −19.34 = −.95 − 18.39.

and across the two investment activities – central and local projects. In some cases, the size of the reduction is considerable; for example, the weighted standard deviation value declined by over 100 percent for central projects.[13]

The smaller values of the standard deviation mean that investment behavior has become more uniform during the reform era. That is, the austerity policies during the reform era have caused the twenty-nine provinces in this study to increase their investment within a narrower band than they were able to before the reforms. This finding directly contradicts the conventional wisdom that views investment delegation and resource decentralization as leading to greater investment dispersions among provinces. That is, richer provinces are more able to increase investments than poorer provinces because they possess greater investment resources. That investment growth rates increase or decline by similar margins among Chinese provinces toward the end of the sample period further implies that during the later austerity rounds, the adjustment costs are shared more evenly in comparison with the previous austerity rounds.

There is also evidence that this behavioral uniformity is a result of the austerity policies and that the impact is most discernible in investment activities the Center attempts to discourage. For local projects during the reform era, the value of the standard deviation is smaller under austerity than it is under inflation. The amount of the reduction is relatively modest: 24.77 percent compared with 29.58 percent for the unweighted series and 10.32 percent compared with 15.42 percent for the weighted series. But other indications strengthen our conclusion. First, the direction of the reduction is uniform under both measurements and, in addition, the standard deviations for the nonproduction projects (not shown in the table) also declined.[14] Therefore the findings are internally consistent.

Second, there is a clear contrast in the way investment dispersions are related to policy shifts before and during the reforms. Before the reforms, the investment dispersions were greater during austerity than during inflation; during the reforms, the pattern reversed itself and investment dispersions declined by 5 percent when the austerity policy was in effect. Substantively, this finding implies two very different ways whereby the central government seeks to reduce local investment growth. One approach seeks a uniform reduction across all provinces; the other ties the amount of the reduction to a certain proportion of the investment growth during the inflationary period.

13. This is given by $(24.3 \div 11.4 - 1) \times 100 = 113.16$ percent.
14. There is no change in the dispersions for project commissioning.

Monitoring and investment behavior

Enforcement of investment control critically revolves around how information is distributed. Central control can be more effective if the central government knows more about local investment projects and about other relevant local conditions and is able to specify unambiguous reduction targets. But the Chinese system, and CPEs in general, produce and utilize information inefficiently.

General monitoring problems in CPEs

More than anything, effective monitoring depends on accurate information. For policy makers in China and in other CPEs, however, obtaining accurate information is a major challenge. The first reason inhibiting the flow of reliable information is the authoritarian nature of the political system, which suppresses views and opinions, which, if aired, would be valuable to decision makers and would assist them in their policy deliberations. A clear example here is the Chinese Communist Party's persecution in 1958 of Ma Yinchu, a demographer and president of Peking University, who had advocated birth control. The resultant delay in the implementation of a birth control program in China was probably the costliest economic mistake in the history of CPEs.

The institutions and procedures used in the Chinese system to monitor local officials (see chapter 4) give rise to in-house monitoring, which is subject to biases and conflicts of interest. In democratic societies, a free and independent press probably does more than anything else to help provide valuable information, especially information about official conduct. Chinese officials know that this is a source of information that they do not have. In his speech on the need to establish an auditing system in China, Han Guang (1990 [1984]: 56–57), the a secretary of the CDIC, said that many officials feared media publicity more than administrative and political censure. At this juncture in Han's speech, Wang Bingqian, China's finance minister from 1980 to 1992 and a widely respected financial expert, interceded. He related a conversation with auditing officials in an unnamed foreign country, in which the Chinese officials inquired about the power and independence of the auditing agency of that country. The conversation reveals both the kind of problems that Chinese auditing officials face and their reactions to how a democratic society deals with similar issues:

Our people asked them, "How does your auditing agency handle cases once you have detected problems?" They said that they had a lot of power and apart from wielding out punishment and levying fines, there was also media exposure, which they feared the most. Our people asked them if they had ever handled ministers and if they dared to touch the powerful, high-ranking, and senior officials. In that country, they had once censured a minister of health and it was reported in the papers. Once it was in the papers, all the papers began to say how bad this minister of health was and he was totally disgraced. We are different from them. If you censure someone, the worst thing is that he loses face but, after a few days, if he corrects his mistakes, then that's it. If the media makes the case public, then a minister in a capitalist country completely collapses and he loses all his prestige and positions.[15]

Bureaucratic coordination of the economy exacerbates the informational shortage. Because market prices do not serve allocative purposes, the suppression of the market reduces the potential amount of information available to policy makers. First, planners are often in the dark about genuine social demands. Each CPE has warehouses stockpiled with goods that are not wanted on the market, whereas there may be a severe shortage of goods actually in demand. A case in point relates to the difficulties CPEs experience in estimating consumer demand. Because prices are not set to reflect relative scarcities, planners are forced to use alternative measures to forecast demands. In the former Soviet Union, there was an attempt to use wages to forecast demand but this was less precise than prices because although wages may provide some information about aggregate demand, they reveal little about demand for specific products. An alternative is to use queuing to estimate demand, but again this is less precise, because, as Goldman (1972: 242) points out, conceivably one shopper's attempts to buy a refrigerator at seven stores may be interpreted as demand for seven refrigerators.

There are also implications with regard to bureaucratic efficiency in collecting information. In a famous essay first published in 1945, Friedrich A. Hayek (1974) argues that most economic information is inherently complex. Consumer preferences are atomistic and unique to "circumstances of place and time" and, above all, are ever changing. On the production side, the same problem arises from the heterogeneity of products and production processes.[16] In a competitive market, the virtue of prices is precisely their ability to transmit such varied data as consumer preferences, product quality, and technology relatively quickly. An additional source of efficiency in collecting and utilizing information in a market economy is that the prices also embody incentives, in addition to the valuable information they contain.

Thus two sources of inefficiency in a CPE in collecting information can be

---

15. This paragraph appears in the speech by Han Guang (1990 [1984]: 57).

16. There are important exceptions. One situation in which prices cannot serve as an efficient conveyor of information arises when the so-called intangible assets – knowledge embodied in human beings, patented technology, or any other know-how that enables cheaper production or that has appeal in the marketplace – are evaluated on the market. Typically, a market solution tends to underprice products involving intangible assets. (For a more extended discussion, see Caves 1985.)

identified. Given the unorganized and changing nature of economic knowledge, a centralized bureaucracy, however technically sophisticated, is unable to collect sufficient information or information of sufficient nuance because of its inherent rigidity. There is also a divergence of incentives. Bureaucrats strive for power or security – incentives that do not necessarily require an efficient utilization of information. Information is also inevitably lost, because it goes through many administrative layers (Lindbeck 1971: 51–52).

Monitoring problems in Chinese investment planning

From the point of view of the central government, a serious problem in investment control is that local officials have more information about the details of the investment projects they sponsor, organize, and help finance than the central government; yet the central government relies on the same local officials to enforce investment controls. This informational asymmetry in part arises from perverse incentives that encourage investors not to reveal their true investment preferences and the true social value of projects during the investment screening process; in part it is a result of the administrative complexities involved in investment management.

As noted in chapter 5, the systemic causes for excess investment demand include soft-budget constraints and negative externalities associated with investment expansions. An incidental effect of excess investment demand is distorted information in the investment application process. Because not all projects are approved – the approval rate is about 71 percent (Zheng Hongliang 1992: 25) – and approved projects carry benefits far in excess of their costs, project applications are tailored to maximize approval chances. The first source of informational distortion is the tendency to overstate social profitability or, equivalently, to understate projected economic costs in investment applications. The calculation is that once a project is under way the marginal costs of completion appear low and planners would find it difficult to turn down requests for further funding or for allowing the project to proceed, even though actual costs exceed projected costs. In Chinese planning parlance, this kind of project is known as a *tiaoyu* or "fish-bait" project. A survey of 4,117 investment projects finds that cost overruns are a significant problem. The average cost overrun for capital construction projects is about 20.5 percent; for renovation projects, it is about 31.4 percent (SPC and SSB 1992: 92).

Information is further distorted in the investment approval process because planners have no objective criteria by which to judge the relative merits of projects. Investment projects are always justified on the grounds of their contributions to the government's policy preferences at the time. In a recent survey of Chinese enterprises, 92 percent listed "fulfilling tax obligations" as their most important objective; "creating new and superior products" as the second most important objective (90 percent); "improving management" as the third (84 percent); and "increasing exports and earning foreign exchange" as the fourth (81 percent) (Zheng Hongliang 1992: 25–26). All of these objectives coincide closely with the government's industrial policies and with the mandate of those bureaucrats in charge of approving project applications.

This kind of behavior should not be surprising given the strong incentive to maximize approval chances; it does, however, have implications for the informational value of project justification. If every project is justified on similar grounds, policy makers cannot discriminate among projects on that basis. Decisions to turn down 30 percent of the project applications that find their way to the desks of investment planning officials must be guided by other criteria.

Two additional factors exacerbate the informational asymmetry. One is the inherent complexity of monitoring investment activities via administrative means, arising from the sheer number of projects under construction each year. In 1985, 32,000 new investment projects broke ground and in the first half of 1986, 11,000 new projects broke ground (Tao Zengyi 1988: 598); in 1986 as a whole a contractionary year, there were over 100,000 new and existing projects under construction (Shen Zhiqun 1988: 568). Given the large number of investment projects at any given point in time, it is simply administratively impossible for the central government to review each project carefully and to follow the project cycles at each step of the project's life. Indeed, even the provincial officials feel that they do not have sufficient information and staff resources to evaluate investment projects at the prefectural and county levels, which prompted them in 1984 to request a further delegation of review authority.

Managing investment projects is also extremely complex. Because investment is an economywide activity, numerous government agencies and enterprises are involved in the investment approval process and construction. At a minimum, other than the government agency directly sponsoring and supervising a project, the local bureaus of the MOF, SPC, Ministry of Construction, Ministry of Urban and Rural Construction and Environmental Protection, SSB, and branches of the PCBC are all involved in the planning, financing, or regulatory stages of a project. (Before 1983, there was also the State Commission on Capital Construction.) There is no single administrative chain of command to compel compliance. The central government imposes a somewhat arbitrary investment quota on each province, because it does not have detailed budgetary breakdowns to enable it to monitor projects on a case-by-case basis

(Naughton 1987: 74). The limited administrative resources of the central government further constrain its ability to assess and sufficiently discipline provincial investment behavior. A comparison with the former Soviet Union shows that the Chinese central government is understaffed. In 1987, for example, the Soviet statistical agency outnumbered its Chinese counterpart by a factor of seventy-two; Gosplan outnumbered the SPC by about two times, similar to the ratio between the size of the two central governments.[17]

Some hypotheses about local investment behavior

The first hypothesis that can be formulated about local investment behavior is that informational asymmetry makes certain planning approaches feasible while making others infeasible. The choice between alternative approaches is contingent on the amount of information they require. Because information is in short supply, the approach that tends to be chosen most often is the one that economizes on the use of information, even though it is not necessarily the best approach given the problem at hand.[18]

The second hypothesis is that a control approach that is chosen to economize on the use of information produces some perverse consequences. One such consequence is the problem known as "adverse selection." Adverse selection is a concept most often used in the insurance industry to refer to the practice of basing the selection of insurees on the ability to pay premiums. The selection is adverse because those least needing to be insured (such as the young and the healthy) are insured while those most in need (such as the elderly and the sick) are selected out.[19] In our story, adverse selection occurs when the provinces least able to reap benefits from investment expansion are compelled to bear adjustment costs proportionately more than those provinces most able to reap the benefits from investment expansion. This happens when all provinces, regardless of their previous investment performance, are required to reduce their investment growth by the same margin (in percentage terms). Implicitly, this scheme punishes the slower growers.[20]

---

17. On the SSB and the Central Statistical Agency in the former Soviet Union, see *Dangdai . . .* (1990: 78), Wang Yifu (1986: 212), and International Monetary Fund et al. (1991: 135). On the SPC, see Lee (1987: 104) and Wu Peilun (1990: 167). On Gosplan, see Aslund (1991: 119, 120).

18. This informational approach is used to explain why the Soviet reforms came later than the Chinese reforms in their comparative stages of economic development (Huang 1994).

19. For a fuller illustration of the adverse selection problem in economic life, see Akerlof (1970).

20. Suppose Province A grew by 10 percent while Province B grew by 1 percent in the previous year. In the current year, the central government requires both of them to reduce their growth by 1 percent. For Province A, this is only 10 percent of its growth; for Province B, it is 100 percent.

The third hypothesis is that "moral hazard" characterizes local investment behavior. Moral hazard refers to the conduct of an agent who performs well only in the measured dimensions, neglecting or even sacrificing other aspects of the task he is supposed to perform. This problem typically arises when the specification of a proxy measurement is problematic. In production planning, for example, when the measurement is denoted in tons, managers strive to increase the weight of the product, ignoring other dimensions. Nove (1986: 97) gives an excellent illustration of this phenomenon:

There is . . . the question of expressing the desired total output target in some ways: tons, square meters, length, thousands of units, or pairs, kilowatt-hours, etc. . . . The difficulty arises from the fact that no measure is adequate, whenever there is any sort of product mix. . . . Long ago *Krokodil* published a cartoon showing an enormous nail hanging in a large workshop: "the month's plan fulfilled," said the director, pointing to the nail. In tons, of course. It is notorious that Soviet sheet steel has been heavy and thick, for this sort of reason. Sheet glass was too heavy when it was planned in tons, and paper too thick.

Thus moral hazard is a special form of shirking behavior, and its occurrence is a function of the effectiveness with which the performance is measured. In the present case, local officials can be said to perform well (from the point of view of the central government) in those investment activities that are effectively monitored but less well in those less effectively monitored.

Monitoring and investment behavior: Empirical evidence

The analysis presented here is descriptive. That is, it focuses on the characteristics of the dependent variable – investment behavior – without explicitly linking them with independent variables, such as the distribution of information, which in this case are not directly quantifiable. Thus the second-best research strategy is to examine in detail the distributions of the data and then to determine if these distributions are consistent with the theoretical expectations.

Investment control approaches

The distribution of information affects the feasibility of the control approaches. Some approaches require more information than others, and thus a shortage of information results in the adoption of those approaches that use the least amount of information. One of the ways central planners obviate the information shortage is by bargaining with local or ministerial officials. In CPEs, bargaining is a forum for communication; information regarding supply situations and enterprises' technical capabilities is conveyed directly to planners during these negotiations (Powell 1977: 57). A Soviet planning official has the following to say about the function of bargaining in the planning process: "In the long process of coordination and confirmation, the demands and concessions made by the trading or haggling sides get rid of the obvious errors. Of course not always, but the real significance of this process of coming to agreement is very great, and it is a pity that Western students give scant attention to this point" (quoted in Gorlin 1985: 359).[21]

Economic agents, on the other hand, try to increase informational asymmetry to gain a bargaining edge. For example, the negotiations during the formulation stage of the Soviet plan tended to revolve around technical arguments. Ministries and their subordinate enterprises would bring in the most reputable engineers and technicians in their negotiations with Gosplan and Gosnab. In essence, technical complexity increases the informational gap. "If you don't defend your resource requests well," one former Soviet official has pointed out, "you can't get anything. Every request has to be technically substantiated" (Gregory 1990: 86).

Because bargaining serves a useful function in CPEs, it is a widespread phenomenon. Janos Kornai (1986b) characterizes the Hungarian economy in the 1980s as a "bargaining regime." Another Hungarian economist, T. Laky (1979: 227), comments on the scope of bargaining in the Hungarian economy:

> By now the use of the word "bargaining" has become completely general, indicating that every instruction, desire, and distribution of resources coming from the control sphere may be an object of bargaining between central organs and enterprises. There is bargaining about the extent of "expectations," the support and preferences available under various titles, the size of credits, the way of repayment, the lifting of import restrictions, that is to say, about everything in which the interests represented by the central organs may be different from that of the enterprise.

Investment bargaining in the Chinese economy is widespread. Lampton (1987a) writes about the foot-dragging and negotiations over the amount of reductions during the 1983 retrenchment period.[22] The SPC officials describe the annual investment review process as "quarrels"; local officials, on the other hand, use a more colorful phrase to describe their task when they go to Beijing to bargain over the size of their investment quota: "the essence of annual planning is a good fight" (*yinian zhi ji zaiyu zheng*) (*Dangdai Zhongguo de guding zichan touzi guanli* 1989). Not only do they bargain over investment

---

21. The American economist Paul Gregory holds a similar view: "A taut plan creates frictions as enterprises and ministries find they cannot fulfill their output targets. As they compete for more resources and for lower plans, superior organizations accumulate valuable nonprice information on relative scarcities, which enables them to make more rational decisions" (Gregory 1990: 80).

22. For a general discussion on bargaining in the Chinese system, see Oksenberg and Lieberthal (1988).

quotas, they also bargain over investment treatments. For example, enterprises bargain hard to claim tax exemptions on their capital investment loans or, equivalently, to have loan repayments counted as taxes (Walder 1992).

But bargaining can be costly. For one thing, it takes time, and if the central government urgently wants to curtail investment, it may not tolerate the delay. Also, in a bargaining situation it is necessary for the central government to have very good information to defend the policy goals it tries to impose on local officials, and when such information is unavailable, its policy goals may have to be revised. Such an outcome may not be acceptable to the central government in an emergency situation.

There are two alternative control approaches, and it takes different levels of information to administer them and different levels of embodied bargaining to make them work. The first is a uniform control approach, which mandates that each province reduce investment growth by a certain percentage regardless of its investment performance during the inflationary period and regardless of the aggregate impact on the macroeconomy. Under this approach, a slow province (say, with 10 percent growth) is required to reduce its growth by the same margin as a fast province (say, with 30 percent growth). In addition, under this scheme, the amount of the investment reduction is not tied to the relative size of the provincial economy or to the relative contribution of the different provinces to macroeconomic stability. For example, Xizang (Tibet), with 0.7 percent of the total national investment, would absorb the same amount of adjustment costs as Jiangsu, a province with a 5.2 percent share of total national investment.

A more fine-tuned control approach would take into consideration economic and investment variations among provinces. The mandated investment reduction, in percentage terms, is tied to a number of yardsticks that the central government may use to evaluate provincial investment performance. At a minimum, these crude yardsticks should include investment growth performance during the inflation-policy period and provincial investment shares (which is a proxy for the impact a province makes on the country's macroeconomy).[23] This is an indexing control approach.

There is no question that the indexing control approach is superior. In a sense, it is more fair because the adjustment costs are allocated in proportion

---

23. There could be other yardsticks as well. For example, investment efficiency and sectoral investment composition may be considered. Because I do not have adequate data regarding these two investment activities, I cannot evaluate their relevance. However, because investment speed and shares are relatively crude yardsticks, findings that crude yardsticks do not play a role can be taken as prima facie evidence that refined yardsticks are not used. If crude yardsticks are found to play a role, then we have an indeterminate conclusion.

to the benefits received from investment expansion. It is also more efficient in that it produces virtuous incentives down the road because it ties the size of investment reduction to the size of investment expansion and therefore induces some self-restraint. In contrast, the uniform control approach punishes the virtuous and promotes the perverse incentive that the best protection against investment reduction is to strive for a higher growth rate.

The chief drawback of the indexing control approach is that it requires a lot of information. This is not to suggest that the central policy authorities do not have information regarding provincial growth rates and their investment shares; however, using such information imposes auxiliary informational requirements that the Center may not be able to meet competently. For example, indexing the size of investment reduction to investment performance during the previous policy period is an open invitation to provincial leaders to make pleas for additional considerations. These pleas can be virtually infinite in range, from strictly economic ("Yes, our investment growth was fast, but it was efficient"), to strategic ("Although our growth was faster, our tax turnover was much larger") and to political ("10 percent is the minimum; otherwise we would have problems with social stability").

The argument local officials use most often against investment reduction is a fiscal one. Shandong province, for example, demanded that the SPC nearly double the planned growth target in 1986 from 8 percent to 15 percent, arguing that this was the only way to meet increased expenditures (Development Center of the State Council 1986: 6). Zhong Zhangrun (1988), an official from the Nanjing municipal government, believed that 10 percent was the minimum economic growth rate needed to maintain fiscal balance. Concerns over tax implications from economic austerity cut across poor and rich provinces alike. In the face of the central macroeconomic retrenchment in 1986, officials from Anhui and Shanghai expressed alarm over the implications for the tax situation in their regions (Anhui Economic and Cultural Research Center 1986: 53–54; Shanghai Economic Research Center 1986: 74–75).

Although such pleas can be legitimate, sorting out true from false claims and designing an investment reduction margin appropriate to these claims requires a great deal of specific and detailed information and may be quite time-consuming. This drawback of the indexing approach makes the uniform control approach all the more attractive. Systemwide, across-the-board investment reduction, or what Chinese call *yidaoqie* (literally, "slicing with one stroke"), requires no specific information about local conditions. Like the Gramm-Rudman amendment in the U.S. Congress, which aimed to cut the budget across all programs, the uniform control approach minimizes bargaining and conflicts. The uniform control approach also shows central policy resolve in that central decisions are deliberately made independent of local considerations. The result of the policy is a "hard landing."

Documentary evidence tends to support the idea that the uniform approach is applied during periods of austerity. In 1986, for example, the Center mandated a zero-growth target, and in 1989 it set forth a 20 percent reduction from the actual level achieved in 1988. It should be noted that in these two examples neither of these two objectives tied the reduction margin to the previous year's growth or to any other performance characteristics. Understandably, this approach does not sit well with local officials, especially with those from provinces with relatively low growth rates, because it requires compliant provinces to cross-subsidize noncompliant provinces. Officials from Anhui province, a relatively poor province with a small annual investment volume, were quite blunt in describing their unhappiness with the tight central monetary policy: "Loss of credit control is a problem up there [i.e., the central government] and the degree of that loss is different in different provinces. But now there is this across-the-board reduction. In effect people up there are ill, but people down here have to take the medicine; other people are ill, but we have to take the medicine!" (Anhui Economic and Cultural Research Center 1986: 53–54).

Consider now some more systematic evidence. As mentioned earlier, when information is scarce, the method that economizes on the use of information tends to be selected. Thus one should expect to see investment patterns closer to the uniform control approach than to the indexing control approach. The operationalization of this proposition revolves around two indicators. One is the relationship of investment growth rates across different policy periods and the other is the degree of investment dispersions among provinces – that is, the differences in the investment growth rates among provinces. The indexing approach requires that the reduction margin be dependent on the previous year's growth rate. Therefore a province's investment growth during an austerity period should be correlated strongly and negatively with its investment growth during an inflationary period. If fast growers in year$_{(t-1)}$ become slow growers in year$_{(t)}$ (while slow growers remain slow growers), then the indexing approach also predicts that the differences in growth rates among provinces should narrow as a result of the austerity programs. On the other hand, the uniform approach predicts a nonnegative association in growth rates between different policy periods and stability in investment dispersions between policy periods.[24] These findings are presented in tables 7.5 and 7.6.

24. This is easily illustrated with a simple example. Suppose two provinces grow at 20 and 10 percent, respectively, during an inflationary period and their dispersion is 10 percent. When the uniform control approach is in effect that requires each of them to reduce the growth rate by 5

Table 7.5. *Inter- and intrapolicy period Pearson coefficients of growth rates, unweighted and weighted measures (percentage)*

Pearson correlation	(1) Year$_{(t)}$ = austerity[a]	(2) Year$_{(t)}$ = inflation
Year$_{(t-1)}$ = inflation[b]	0.09 (0.28)	0.09 (0.04)
Year$_{(t-1)}$ = austerity	0.11 (0.10)	0.16 (0.30)

Note: Weighted measures are in parentheses. The correlation values are between previous (in rows) and current (in columns) years.
[a] Year$_{(t)}$ = current year.
[b] Year$_{(t-1)}$ = previous year.
Source: Database.

Table 7.6. *Investment growth dispersions under two macroeconomic policy regimes (percentage)*

Regime	Austerity	Inflation
Unweighted averages		
Central project	34.93	39.72
Local project	28.70	27.53
Weighted averages		
Central project	12.52	12.56
Local project	9.72	11.02

Note: Weights are the moving averages of provincial shares of NMP.
Source: Database.

Table 7.5 shows clearly that the indexing approach is not at work. All the values are positive, regardless of the direction of the policy shifts, contrary to what the indexing approach predicts. In general, those provinces with high growth rates during inflationary periods retain high growth rates during austerity periods; in addition, those provinces that resist reducing investment growth during austerity tend to do better when the macroeconomic policy becomes more permissive. There is no evidence that the rate of investment reduction in year$_{(t)}$ is negatively dependent on investment growth in year$_{(t-1)}$.

Patterns of investment dispersions further confirm this result. Dispersions

percent, one would grow at 15 percent and the other at 5 percent. The dispersion remains unchanged, at 10 percent, even though the average growth rate now is 10 percent. Under the indexing approach, suppose the first province is required to reduce its growth rate by 10 percent and the second, by zero percent; then the dispersion would be zero while the average growth rate is also 10 percent.

are measured by the standard deviations of central and local provincial investment growth rates under two alternative macroeconomic policy regimes. The two measurements are consistent in showing that macroeconomic policy shifts cause almost no change in investment dispersions in both weighted and unweighted series. The standard deviation values remain essentially the same under the two policy regimes; for example, the austerity period produces a standard deviation value of 28.7 percent for the unweighted local investment series; the inflation period, 27.53 percent. For the weighted series, the change is small, slightly more than 1 percent for local projects, while there is virtually no change in central projects.

A striking feature is the large size of the standard deviation values. In part, the absolute size of the standard deviation is accounted for by the underlying economic differences among the Chinese provinces rather than by the discretionary decisions of local bureaucrats. When investment growth is weighted by the provincial NMP shares, about two-thirds of the investment dispersions have disappeared.

Nevertheless, in both measurements investment dispersions are insensitive to policy shifts. The stability of the standard deviation values is contrasted with significant changes in the mean growth rates as a result of austerity policies. This can be illustrated by calculating the ratios of the standard deviations to the mean growth rates.[25] During an austerity period, the ratio is about 16 for local projects; during an inflationary period, it is only about 1.07. The stability of investment dispersions (relative to extreme instability in the mean growth rates) is consistent with our earlier finding that there is little dependency of investment growth rates between different policy periods. This is prima facie evidence that the uniform control approach is driving investment behavior during an austerity period. Provinces reduce their investment growth sharply during an austerity period but they do so by equal margins. Hence the *relative* distance among their growth rates remain the same, even though the average level falls precipitously.

Could it be that the margin of investment reduction is determined not so much by the investment behavior during the previous policy period but by economic or investment size? Possibly. The indexing approach links investment reduction with the aggregate impact of local investment behavior. According to this hypothesis, big provinces, because their behavior has a greater impact on the macroeconomy, should be controlled more tightly than small provinces; thus during an austerity period larger investment reduction margins are imposed on them, with the result that size should be negatively related

25. This measure is called the coefficient of variation.

to investment growth or, if it is a positive association, the magnitude of the association should decline when austerity is in effect.

The evidence disproves this hypothesis. Size can be measured in two ways. One is economic size, which is the provincial share of national net material product; the other is investment size, which is the provincial share of national investment.[26] The Pearson correlation coefficient between local investment growth rates and these two measurements of size is consistently positive under both policy regimes. Indeed, the Pearson correlation value (economic size) increases from 0.04 to 0.13 when the policy regime shifts to austerity, whereas it stays essentially at the same level when the size is measured in investment shares (0.08 under austerity and 0.10 under inflation). The positive values of the correlation between size and investment growth rates imply that the Chinese system confers an advantage on size: the bigger you are, the faster you tend to grow, an empirical finding that runs entirely counter to what the indexing approach would predict.

Adverse selection

Planning for the future always relies on the information that is available now. In a context of informational asymmetry, however, there is only a limited amount of information that planners can reliably draw upon. In investment planning, when investment reduction is not the top objective, planners allocate investment quotas among various agents in the economy by relying on the "achieved level" of the past.[27] Because of the inherent distortions in the project application process, planners often lack information about the "true" demand for investments or about the real contributions a given investment project makes to their policy objectives. In effect, the achieved level is the only piece of information that is independent of the application process. When the goal is to reduce investment growth, the past growth rate becomes irrelevant in determining an appropriate reduction margin, as the reduction margin is uniform systemwide. The uniform approach *implicitly* takes the achieved investment base as legitimate: Whatever the reduction margin, the margin is calculated on the basis of the existing investment size. Thus the achieved level still matters.[28]

26. Again, I use the moving average values of these figures to minimize year-to-year fluctuations. The intention here is to denote "size" in its stationary rather than dynamic notion. The benchmark years are 1976–79, 1980–83, 1984–87, and 1988–92.

27. An example here is credit allocation in Chinese banks. In the fourth quarter of 1984, banks issued excessive credits because the central government tied the 1985 lending quotas to the 1984 realized level (Xue Muqiao 1987).

28. For a good discussion on the generic problems with planning on the basis of achieved levels, see Hewett (1988).

That the achieved levels powerfully determine the future has an incentive effect on behavior. Local officials are strongly motivated to strive for a higher "achieved level" either to influence the size of future investment quotas in the next round of investment planning or to attain a smaller *effective* reduction margin. As noted in the last section, the best protection against the sharp edges of the austerity policies is to grow faster than other provinces during the inflationary policy period; those who shirk the adjustment costs during the austerity policy period, in general, do better than other provinces when the policies become more permissive.

This is an indication that an adverse selection problem exists in the Chinese system. The uniform approach punishes the virtuous and awards the shirkers. Shirkers are those provinces that push investment growth higher than other provinces during an inflationary period while reducing investment growth less than others during an austerity period. There are sucker provinces that do exactly the opposite. This is an adverse selection problem because benefits and costs are distributed inequitably. Inflation control is a public good and therefore shirkers cannot be excluded from enjoying all the benefits associated with lower price levels and with the restoration of economic order. But they contribute less than others, especially less than the suckers, and therefore they pass the adjustment costs onto the suckers. Shirkers also have advantages when the macroeconomic policy shifts from austerity to inflationary: because they have a higher growth rate, they are rewarded with larger investment quotas.

In numerical terms, as shown in table 7.6, the shirkers' advantages are about one-tenth of 1 percent when policy shifts from inflation to austerity and about one-and-a-half-tenth of 1 percent when the policy shift is in the opposite direction. When there is no policy shift, the advantages stay at one-tenth of 1 percent. When the effect of provincial economic size is controlled for, the shirkers' advantages become considerable, about one-third of 1 percent, and policy shifts (in either direction) produce a large jump in the size of the shirkers' advantages as compared with the absence of such shifts. Interestingly, in the weighted measurement, the policy shift terms are particularly large as compared with those in the unweighted measurement. This is an indication that the size advantages described earlier are particularly handy when a new policy regime comes into effect (during an interpolicy period); when the policy becomes the norm (during an intrapolicy period), the size advantage completely disappears.

Chinese provinces can be divided into two categories – shirkers and suckers – according to the growth rates of their local investment during an austerity period. The division is based on a number of restrictive criteria. The first is that the behavior of shirkers or suckers must be extreme in relation to the average behavior. There is no theory to suggest what constitutes "extreme" behavior; thus the shirker (sucker) can arbitrarily be defined as a province whose investment growth rate lies above (below) that of 84 percent of the observations. This demarcation value is chosen because of a statistical principle: in a normal distribution roughly 68 percent of the observations lie within one standard deviation away from the mean, which means that 16 percent of the observations lie above one standard deviation away from the mean in both directions. To put it another way, about 68 percent of the observations are considered to be normal behavior while about 32 percent of the observations are considered extreme behavior, either in the lowest or highest tiers.[29] To calculate cumulative probabilities it is necessary to convert investment growth rates into Z-scores. The appendix to this chapter details the calculation.

The second criterion is behavioral regularity, and thus I exclude those provinces that fit the definition only once during the 1977–92 period. Altogether, there were nine years in the austerity policy period (1979–81, 1983, 1986–87, and 1989–91). Third, I control for the effect of the economic sizes of the provinces and the effect of increasing levels of "inflation tolerance" during the reform period. Thus I only use the weighted measurement of local investment growth, which has the effect of removing many of the smaller provinces from the shirker and sucker categories.[30] To control for the fact that the leadership's tolerance for inflation increased during the reform era, I use two different reference categories, one for the pre-reform era and the other for the reform era. Thus the calculation automatically adjusts to the permanent upward shift in the mean growth rates since the second half of the 1980s. To take into account the switching behavior of provinces – that is, from construction to renovation investments – I use the growth of total local investment, which I define as the sum of construction and renovation investments. Thus the moral hazard conduct described earlier is modeled as a part of shirking behavior. Table 7.7 presents the results of the calculation.

The first noteworthy finding of the table is the lack of behavioral regularity of provinces in each category. Only Guangdong and Jiangsu fit with the

---

29. In essence, shirkers and suckers are outliers in a statistical distribution and the choice of demarcation value determines how "outlying" the outliers are. If we set the demarcation at two standard deviations, for example, then this means that the shirkers and suckers are only 1 percent of all the observations, respectively. There are good reasons to believe that 2 percent may be too restricting; the shirkers' sizable advantages imply that the number of observations should be more than 1 percent. Of course, setting it at 16 percent is also arbitrary, and there is no reason not to set it at 10 or 20 percent. In this case, 16 percent is chosen only because of statistical convenience.

30. This is justifiable to the extent that the aggregate impact is much greater if the shirker (sucker) is a large province.

Table 7.7. *Allocation of local investment reduction among shirker and sucker provinces during austerity periods*

Shirker provinces[a]	Sucker provinces[b]
Guangdong (5)[c]	Hebei (2)
Heilongjiang (2)	Henan (2)
Hunan (2)	Hubei (2)
Jiangsu (5)	Hunan (2)
Liaoning (3)	Jiangsu (2)
Shandong (3)	Shanghai (2)
Shanghai (3)	
Sichuan (2)	
Zhejiang (2)	

[a] Z-scores > 1 during at least two years.
[b] Z-scores < −1 during at least two years.
[c] Numbers in parentheses refer to the number of years in which the province meets the definition of each category.
Source: Database.

definition of shirker provinces for more than 50 percent of the time (i.e., five out of nine years); none of the provinces are in the suckers' category for more than two years. This result does not fundamentally change when the Z-score is lowered to allow a more liberal definition of shirkers and suckers.[31] The lack of behavioral regularity suggests that provinces adjust their behavior relatively frequently over time and that most of the provinces most of the time behave within a range that is considered normal by the definition adopted here. To some extent, the lack of behavioral regularity in the shirkers' category should be surprising, considering the fact that there are sizable shirkers' advantages in the Chinese system. One possibility is that there are mechanisms in the Chinese system that somewhat constrain flagrant shirking behavior, meaning consistent shirking; this possibility is explored in greater detail in chapter 8.

Second, there are more shirkers than suckers, which should not be surprising given the provinces' economic interests. In some years, however, there are more suckers than shirkers, whereas in other years there are more shirkers than suckers. In 1989, for example, fifteen provinces were suckers, but there were no shirkers in that year. In contrast, there were eight shirkers in 1986 but only one sucker. Thus the severity of the austerity policy definitely has an impact.

31. The benchmark Z-scores were lowered to 0.70 and 0.60 for shirkers and −0.70 and −0.60 for suckers.

Third, provinces can switch their behavior drastically. Hunan, Jiangsu, and Shanghai are classified as both shirkers and suckers and, because both categories are created to encompass "extreme" growth rates, this means that their investment growth rates varied very widely even under a similar macroeconomic policy environment. In Jiangsu province, for example, the investment growth rates were 21.8 percent in 1979, 28.57 percent in 1980, 25.41 percent in 1986, 17.64 percent in 1987, and 24.86 percent in 1991. In contrast, the growth rates were −27.42 percent in 1981 and −35.46 percent in 1989.

This highly elastic investment conduct suggests that normal economic variables do not drive short-term provincial investment behavior. Economic changes are usually gradual and incremental; the relatively stationary economic variables do not produce volatility of this magnitude. This is seen in figure 7.1, which plots the annual mean growth rates of provincial NMP, local capital construction, and renovation investments for the twenty-nine provinces against time. Investments fluctuated annually within a very wide range; the lowest rate for construction investment was −24.36 percent in 1981 while the highest was 56.69 percent in 1985. In contrast, provincial NMP growth fluctuations were far milder and almost all the points lie within a −6 to 17 percent range. The lowest was in 1989 (−5.72 percent); the highest was in 1984 (16.85 percent). Not only did the investment growth fluctuate widely on a year-to-year basis, in any given year the variability among provinces was much greater for the investment series than for the NMP growth. For every year between 1977 and 1992, the standard deviation values for local construction and renovation investment growth exceed those for NMP growth. In the late 1970s and early 1980s, the gap between them was huge and as the decade progressed, it became narrower, as shown in figure 7.2.

There are two possible explanations for the volatility of investment behavior. One is obviously the policy shift from inflation to austerity and vice versa. Not only do macroeconomic policies change from austerity to inflation or vice versa, austerity policies themselves also vary in degree of severity. In some years, the policy is firm and in other years, it is relatively soft, as explained in chapter 5. Thus high investment volatility is a function of policy changes and, by implication, the switching behavior described earlier is a function of alternations between firm and soft policy commitments.

But this explanation does not indicate why investment activity should fluctuate *more than* other economic activities; thus the second explanation points to the role of the bureaucracy in sponsoring and organizing investment projects. Compared with other economic activities, investment activity is much more of a *governmental* activity and therefore is more sensitive to government policies and to the actions of individual provincial leaders. In part, this can be borne

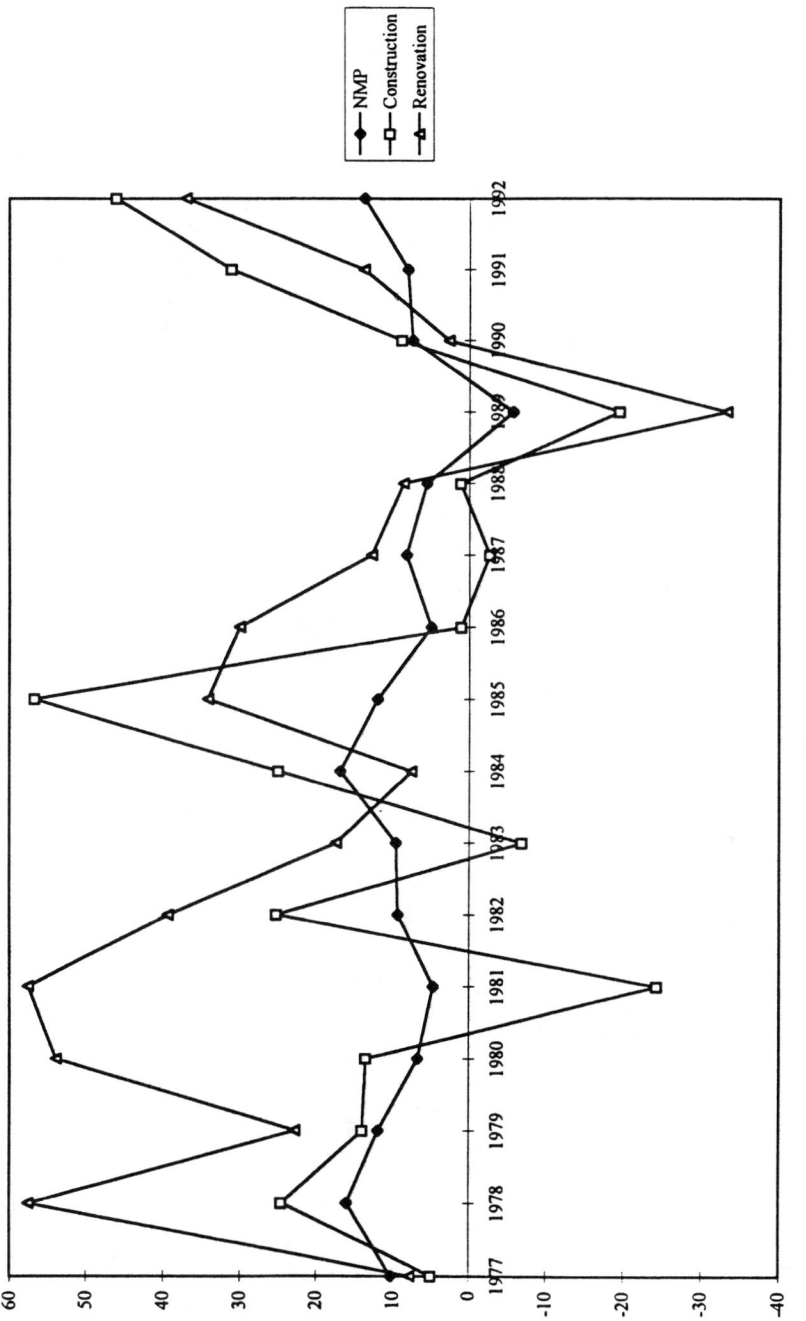

Figure 7.1 Annual provincial mean growth rates of net material product (NMP) and of local investment, 1977–92. *Source*: Database

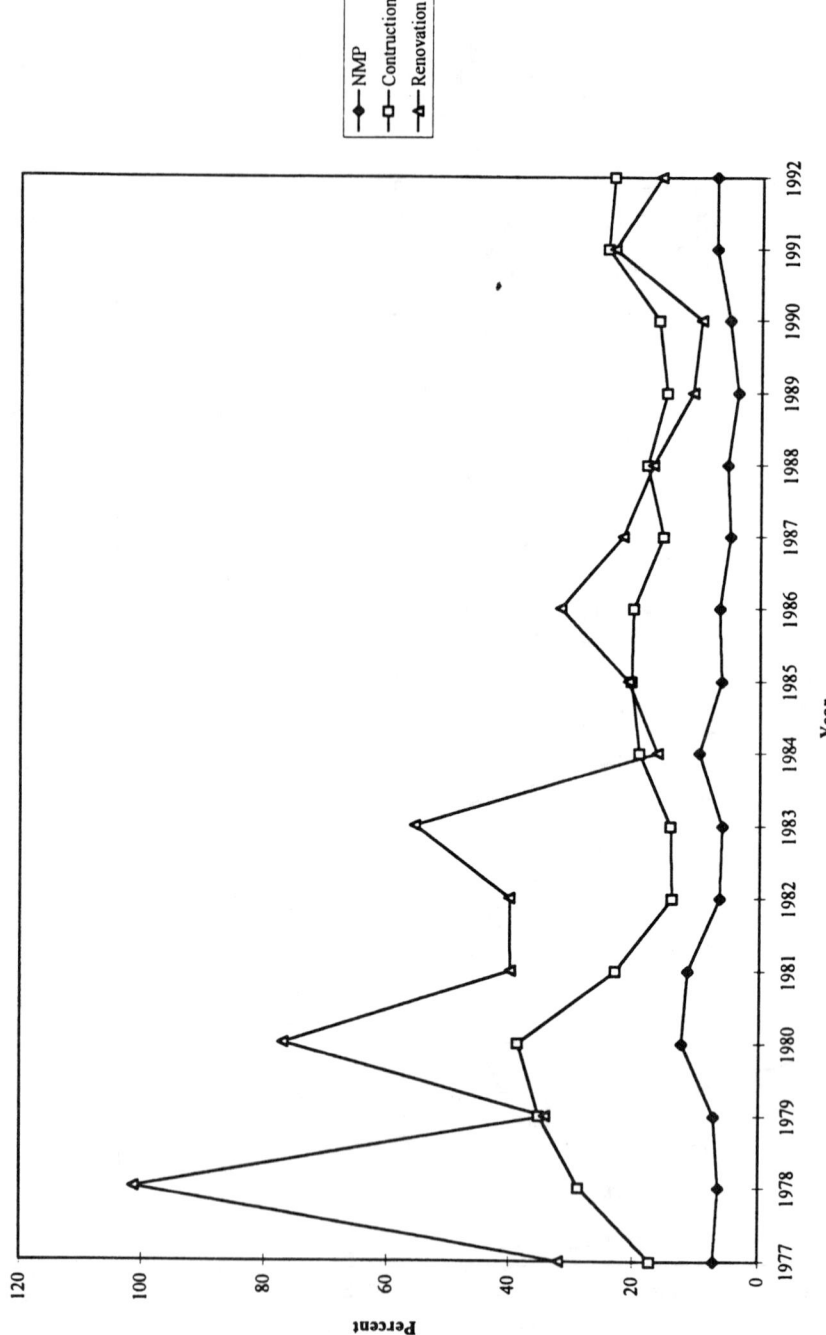

Figure 7.2 Annual growth dispersions of net material product (NMP) and of local investment, 1977–92. *Source:* Database

out by regressing local investments and a select economic series on two bureaucratic characteristics of provincial officials: appointment events and bureaucratic integration. Invariably, bureaucratic characteristics are found to be significantly related to local investments but not to other economic series.[32] The governmental nature of investment activity in part explains why the level of the dispersions for local investment far exceeds that of dispersions for provincial NMP. Different leaders implement investment policies differently. Top provincial officials have short tenures and investment behavior tends to change as provincial leaders change. This connection is examined systematically in chapter 8.

Moral hazard conduct

In Chinese investment planning, the incidence of moral hazard is a severe problem during austerity periods. Local officials reduce drastically the growth of investment activities about which the central government has better information, while maintaining a high rate of growth for those investment activities about which the central government has poor information. This can be shown by noting the contrast in local investment behavior in two investment activities: capital construction investment (*jiben jianshe touzi*) and technical renovation investment (*gengxin touzi*).

As pointed out in chapter 1, capital construction investments create new enterprises or significantly expand the capacity of existing enterprises; technical renovation investments aim to modify existing enterprises. Technical renovation investment began its steady growth in 1967, when the central government allowed enterprises to retain a portion of their depreciation funds. During the reform era, technical renovation investment grew quickly in part due to the accelerated pace of enterprise profit retentions and the diversification of funding sources. In 1978 technical renovation investment was only 33.5 percent of capital construction investment; by 1989 it had grown to 50.8 percent (SSB 1990: 21).

Two characteristics of technical renovation investments are important for this analysis. First, the traditional distinction between capital construction investments as a source of creating new capacity and renovation investments as a source of capacity modifications has been blurred considerably. In a real economic sense and in terms of their contributions to macroeconomic instability, the two investment activities are practically indistinguishable. Technical renovation investments are increasingly used for capital construction purposes.

---

32. For details of the results of the regression analysis, see the appendix to this chapter.

There are varying estimates as to the extent of this diversion. Naughton (1987: 54), for example, estimates that as much as two-thirds of the renovation investment funds are in fact used for new or expanded capacity expansions; Chinese economists, on the other hand, have come up with a lower figure. One is 54 percent (Du Hong 1987); another estimate is between 40 and 50 percent (Hei Aitang and Hu Ji 1988 [1985]: 125). More illustratively, of the 113 television assembly production lines in China, only three were incorporated into the State Planning Commission's capital investment program; the rest were built under the label of technical renovation investments (SPC and SSB 1992: 110).

Second, because technical renovation investments were initially small and were overwhelmingly controlled locally, the central government did not begin systematically collecting statistics on this investment series until the late 1970s; the investment data remained in the localities.[33] Over the reform decade, however, the central government has steadily increased its knowledge about technical renovation investments in part because of the specific efforts devoted to collecting data regarding renovation investments and in part because of an improvement in the overall ability of the SSB. In 1980 the SSB established detailed reporting procedures for technical renovation investments for state-owned enterprises; in 1981, the SSB combined data collections for capital construction and renovation investments under the category "fixed-asset investments" (*guding zichan touzi*). In 1986 the SPC began to include renovation investments under its fixed-asset investment planning, thus placing renovation investments directly under the monitoring and control scope of the central government. Starting in 1987 the SPC also made data collection on renovation investments more frequent, from a quarterly basis to a monthly basis.[34]

Armed with this knowledge, one is able to formulate three hypotheses about moral hazard in local investment behavior. First, renovation and construction investments are "substitution" activities. That is, local officials tend to sanction one activity while curtailing the other, depending on the policy regime in effect. When an austerity policy is in effect, local officials switch to an activity that is less monitored (renovation investment in this case); during an inflation period, the local officials revert to construction activity. Second, similarly monitored activities should exhibit similar behavior and, conversely, differently monitored activities should exhibit different behavior. Because capital construction investment is monitored more closely by the central government,

---

33. Naughton (1992b: 250) argues that the government "literally did not know how much investment was taking place."

34. The above discussion is based on SPC, SEC, SSB, MOF (1988 [1986]) and on *Dangdai Zhongguo de tongji shiye* (1990).

there should be more compliance in implementing reduction in capital construction projects during an austerity period as compared with renovation investments. Third, the seriousness of moral hazard conduct should be a function of time; as the discrepancy in monitoring between capital construction and renovation investments narrows over time, the moral hazard problem should dissipate gradually.[35]

To examine these hypotheses the two investment activities must be compared directly. This can be done with a "performance difference index." This index is defined as the percentage difference between the renovation values and the construction values. Thus zero means no difference between the two investment activities; the larger the score (in terms of absolute values), the more different the two activities. A negative performance difference score means a smaller renovation value and a positive score denotes a higher renovation value. As usual, both renovation and construction investment data used in the calculation are broken down by the twenty-nine provinces, and the figures are the annual averages of the twenty-nine provinces. The construction investments are local investment figures only; because renovation data are not broken down administratively before 1986, the renovation investments consist of activities by both central and local government agencies.[36]

Translating the three hypotheses into specific behavioral characteristics as measured by the performance difference index, one should see the following results:

1. Because renovation and construction activities are substitutes, they should be negatively related under both policy regimes;
2. During an austerity period, the two investment activities should behave more differently and therefore the absolute values of the performance difference index should exceed the level attained during a period of inflation;
3. During an austerity period, renovation should grow faster than construction investment and therefore the performance difference index should be positive; and
4. Because the monitoring capabilities of the central government increase over time, the behavior of the two investment activities should become more similar and there should be a reduction in the moral hazard over time as measured by the performance difference index (see table 7.8).

35. Naughton (1992b) and Halpern (1992) make a similar argument. They argue that the central government has increased its technocratic capabilities during the reform era, which enable it to attain its economic policy objectives more effectively.
36. However, the central component of the renovation investments is relatively small, and thus we can use the renovation investments as a proxy measure for local behavior.

Table 7.8. *Moral hazard in local investment conduct as measured by performance difference index, 1977–92 (percentage)*

Period	Austerity	Inflation
1977–92		
Growth difference[a]	16.10	−1.99
Dispersion difference[b]	14.07	10.98
Pearson correlation of growth	0.06	−0.01
1977–81		
Growth difference	49.71	11.48
Dispersion difference	19.41	47.66
Pearson correlation of growth	−0.02	−0.41
1982–85		
Growth difference	14.21	−7.31
Dispersion difference	3.23	6.26
Pearson correlation of growth	−0.52	−0.01
1986–92		
Growth difference	1.45	0.32
Dispersion difference	5.11	−8.52
Pearson correlation of growth	0.30	0.59

[a] Growth difference = mean growth rates$_{(renovation)}$ minus mean growth rates$_{(construction)}$.
[b] Dispersion difference = standard deviation$_{(renovation)}$ minus standard deviation$_{(construction)}$.
Source: Database.

All of the four expectations are confirmed. The investment substitution is seen in the negative values of the Pearson correlation coefficients between 1977 and 1985 under both policy regimes. Thus the two investment activities tend to be at the expense of the other. Given the fact that a substantial portion of renovation investment is in fact for capital construction purposes, the switching behavior is clear evidence that local officials are engaged in an act of evasion. During the 1986–92 period, the Pearson correlation coefficients are positive, thus indicating a complementary relationship between renovation and construction activities. The disappearance of switching behavior does not invalidate the theory because this is consistent with the fourth hypothesis.

Looking across the columns, all the growth difference scores are larger and all are positive during an austerity period. During the 1977–92 period as a whole, the mean growth rate for renovation projects exceeded that for construction projects by 16 percent. Different subperiods are associated with different growth difference scores; in the 1977–81 period it was as high as 49.71 percent during the austerity period, which is an extremely large figure considering the fact that the austerity policies were intended to reduce investment growth. The logical inference of this finding is that the implementation record is poorer – and in the late 1970s and in early 1980s, much poorer – in renovation activities than it is in construction activities.

In table 7.8 the 1977–92 period is divided into three subperiods, 1977–81, 1982–85, and 1986–92 corresponding roughly to three degrees of central monitoring stringency. The first subperiod was the least stringent and the third subperiod, the most stringent; the 1982–85 period lay somewhere in between. Over these three subperiods, a discrepancy in central monitoring and thus in the administrative control of renovation and construction activities steadily dissipated, which, according to our hypothesis, should cause the behavioral differences between the two investment activities to dissipate as well.

This is clearly borne out by the evidence presented. Especially during austerity the size of the growth difference score declined dramatically from the 1977–81 period to the 1982–85 period and continued to decline in the 1986–92 period under both austerity and inflationary policy environments. During the 1986–92 period, the two investment activities became practically indistinguishable. The monotonic magnitude of the growth difference scores follows precisely the order laid down by our hypothesis: that is, significant moral hazard is associated with the least monitoring; moderate moral hazard is associated with moderate monitoring; and the least moral hazard is associated with significant monitoring. The monotonic ordering breaks down somewhat in the dispersion scores: renovation and construction activities became more different in the 1986–92 period; however, these were differences of fairly small margins.

Figures 7.1 and 7.2 also show a gradual decline in moral hazard conduct over time. The annual provincial averages of construction and renovation investment growth and provincial growth dispersions are graphed against time. There is a clear time-dependent pattern. In terms of growth, before 1984 renovation investment activities diverged by a wide margin from construction investment. In general, renovation grew at a much faster rate than construction and in 1981, 1983, and 1987, renovation registered a positive growth while construction investment declined into the negative area. This is a salient indication of moral hazard conduct at work: on the surface, provinces complied with investment reduction policies by cutting drastically construction investment growth, while in reality they recouped all or a significant portion of their losses by investing in technical renovation projects. This kind of switching behavior became rarer in the second half of the 1980s; in 1989, for example, both construction and renovation investments declined steeply. The Pearson coefficients testify to this change in behavior. Before 1986 the Pearson coefficient between renovation and construction was -0.125; after 1986 it was 0.408.

As shown in figure 7.2, investment dispersions among provinces – another criterion of provincial compliance – steadily declined after the late 1970s. Before 1985 provinces registered widely different rates in renovation growth as compared with construction growth. In 1978, 1980, and 1983 the standard deviation value for renovation investment was more than twice that of construction investment. In 1980 and 1983 an austerity policy regime was in effect and thus the divergent standard deviation values indicate an inequitable distribution of adjustment costs among provinces as some provinces reduced their growth drastically whereas others kept a high-growth stance under the same macroeconomic policy regime. In 1983, for example, nine of the twenty-nine provinces in the sample had a negative growth record for their renovation projects (Anhui, Guangxi, Hebei, Heilongjiang, Jilin, Sichuan, Tianjin, Xinjiang, and Zhejiang); Heilongjiang reduced its renovation growth as much as 22.72 percent from its 1982 level. In sharp contrast, Fujian, Henan, Hubei, Hunan, and Xizang (Tibet) had a renovation growth in excess of 30 percent. The distribution of the adjustment costs became much more equitable after 1984, when the level of the growth variance declined substantially from the level in the first half of the 1980s.

In recent years, the Chinese government has begun to publish renovation investment data broken down administratively. This more disaggregated breakdown makes it possible to finesse the analysis, although, unfortunately, the series only begin from 1986 and thus changes in behavior cannot be examined over time. What the analysis does show is that any differences between renovation and construction investments have completely dissipated during the 1986–92 period. During the austerity period, the annual mean growth rate for local renovation projects was –2.96 percent; during the inflation period, growth resumed at 20.59 percent. Also, central renovation projects grew faster than local projects during the austerity period, whereas the opposite was the case during the inflationary period.[37]

37. I attribute these differences to the difference in central monitoring between the two investment activities and to the behavior of interest-maximizing local officials mindful of the central policy constraints they face. However, there may be a simpler explanation that stresses a "natural" growth pattern rather than the discretion of local officials. This explanation says that the faster growth in renovation investment could be due to the fact that renovation activities started from a lower base and, since growth figures capture annual increments, it is plausible that an investment activity that starts from a lower base should have a larger increment and therefore should exhibit a tendency for higher growth. Over time, as the difference between the renovation and construction bases narrows, the growth difference index should narrow as well. In economics this is known as the "convergence thesis." (Most economic studies, however, apply the convergence thesis to economic growth, not to investment growth. For some recent applications, see Barro [1991] and Barro and Sala-I-Martin [1991].) I examine this alternative hypothesis in the appendix to this chapter and show that this explanation is not consistent with empirical evidence.

Shirking and policy commitment

Recall from chapter 5 that austerity policy periods vary in terms of severity. In 1979 and 1980 the central leadership was locked in a fierce power struggle, while paying scant attention to the austerity program that was officially in effect; in 1987 and 1991 internal dissensions among central policy makers again prevented a firm policy commitment. Policy commitment affects local investment behavior in two ways. First, a weak policy commitment means that the central government is not enforcing its austerity program as rigorously as otherwise. This occurred in 1987, when credit supply hovered at a relatively high level and fund shortage was not a binding constraint on local investment imperatives. Or, as again in 1987, administrative control was not exercised tightly and central planning officials subjected investment project applications to a less strenuous approval process. Viewed this way, a weak policy commitment to the austerity program creates a more permissive macroeconomic environment; it is, in a sense, simply a modified form of an inflationary policy period.

The second way is more complex and it concerns the strategic motives of local officials. When implementing central austerity policies, local officials take into account the likely duration of the austerity round. If they believe that an austerity round is likely to be short-lived, they are reluctant to start reducing investment growth immediately. This is a rational calculation. Suppose that an austerity program is terminated prematurely and in a manner that is largely unforeseen. In such a situation, those provinces that have gone ahead with reducing investment growth would be worse off than provinces that have chosen to wait, in part because they would start another investment growth cycle from a lower base. On the other hand, if local officials believe that the austerity policy is likely to be maintained, then the incentive is to jump on the bandwagon quickly lest they stand out as recalcitrants and provoke the central government all by themselves.[38] This is the credibility hypothesis.

It is easy to argue that a higher investment growth rate should be associated with a soft policy commitment than with a firm policy commitment, but because both the easing of the money supply and the credibility problem have a similar impact on local investment behavior, distinguishing between the two forces is not easy. One way to distinguish their effects is to examine investment performance by sectors. Often, during the austerity period the central policy makers ease credit supply in order to support investment in key sectors

---

38. This pattern holds for a similar comparison between production and nonproduction projects: During the soft austerity period, nonproduction project growth exceeds production project growth by 31 percent. However, the effect on project completion and commissioning is rather weak.

and to finish existing projects; this may be especially necessary during the reform era since the Center is less able to target resources and therefore may have to resort to credit increases. In 1987, when the government eased the money supply, it intended to channel support to the energy and raw material sectors. Similarly, under a general condition of monetary stringency in 1989, the central government devised an industrial policy list stressing the so-called key sectors. In that case, one should see some specific sectoral effects such that those sectors the central government favors should be helped. In contrast, the central credibility problem merely creates a window of opportunity for local officials to pursue their own investment interests, and thus the boosting effect tends to be more apparent in sectors the central government discourages or the boosting effect should be across the board.

One could also argue that different causes lay behind different soft austerity rounds. It seems that in 1987 and 1991 the central policy makers intended the austerity programs to be less restrictive. In 1987 Zhao Ziyang believed that microeconomic reforms, by the imposition of financial discipline on firms, would help curb excess investment demand; in 1991 the central policy makers hoped to inject some dynamism to bring China out of its worst recession. The "softness" of the policy commitment was voluntary. In contrast, in 1979, 1980, and the first half of 1989 central policy makers disagreed strongly among themselves about a number of significant political and economic issues at the time (the succession, the evaluation of Mao, responses to student demonstrations, and the necessity and the purposes of the austerity programs). Thus the lack of leadership and direction from Beijing seemed to be the main factor driving local investment behavior. The softness was involuntary.

A principal difference between voluntary and involuntary softness of austerity policies is the uncertainty about central policy intentions. When the soft commitment is voluntary and is a deliberate act by the central policy makers, there is certainty about central policy intentions. In contrast, when the softness is caused by involuntary central actions, there are conflicting policy signals and therefore there is uncertainty about central policy intentions. Different levels of uncertainty are associated with different levels of investment dispersions. Certainty about central policy intentions produces uniform behavior because there is less room for varying interpretations.

When there are conflicting policy signals, there is more room for subjective interpretations and provincial investment behavior varies more. This may happen, for example, when central policy makers debate among themselves about the wisdom of the austerity policies. Some local officials may interpret these developments as a green light to go ahead with their investment plans; the more cautious may view this only as a yellow light and wait for more

Table 7.9. *Changes in policy commitment and local investment behavior, 1979–91 (unweighted measure, percentage)*

Change	Central projects	Local projects
Growth[a]	9.15	21.93
Growth[b]	−10.98	−11.65
Dispersion[c]		
Relative to austerity	9.82	3.57
Relative to inflation	3.60	13.93
Dispersion[d]		
Relative to austerity	−6.49	1.81
Relative to inflation	−6.59	−3.00

[a] Growth changes = mean growth rates$_{\text{(soft austerity)}}$ minus mean growth rates$_{\text{(firm austerity)}}$.
[b] Growth changes = mean growth rates$_{\text{(soft austerity)}}$ minus mean growth rates$_{\text{(inflationary period)}}$.
[c] Dispersion changes are measured by using the 1977–83 figures and are given by: standard deviation$_{(79,80)}$ minus standard deviation$_{(77-83)}$ during austerity or inflation.
[d] Dispersion changes are measured by using the 1984–92 figures and are given by: standard deviation$_{(87,91)}$ minus standard deviation$_{(84-92)}$ during austerity or inflation.
Source: Database.

clarification. According to this logic, the soft austerity rounds in 1987 and 1991 should be associated with less investment dispersions because they were voluntary. The involuntary nature of the commitment softness in 1979 and 1980, however, produced more investment dispersions. These hypotheses are examined in table 7.9, which presents changes in the percentage of investment growth and in dispersions between soft austerity on the one hand and firm austerity and inflationary periods on the other.

Positive figures indicate that the values during the soft austerity period are larger than those during the other two policy periods. Both the numbers in row (1) are positive, a solid piece of evidence that during the soft austerity period the growth rates are higher than they are during the firm austerity period. On the other hand, both the numbers in row (2) are negative, meaning that the growth rates during the soft austerity period are lower than they are during the inflationary period. Thus it is appropriate to describe the soft austerity period as a modified form of the inflationary period, with its severity lying somewhere between the firm austerity and the inflationary periods. There is little evidence that local investment behavior is driven by a targeted central policy during the soft austerity period. This is shown across row (1). A comparison of central and local projects clearly shows that the boosting effect is concentrated in local projects; the growth change in local projects exceeds that in central projects by some 13 percent.

Patterns of investment dispersions are shown in rows (3) and (4) in the form of changes in investment dispersions from soft austerity period to firm austerity and inflationary periods, respectively. The underlying assumption behind such comparisons is that policy uncertainty during the firm austerity and inflationary periods should be less than policy uncertainty during the soft austerity period. The reason is simple. During the firm austerity period, there is little question in the minds of local officials that the Center wants to reduce investment growth; during the inflationary period, there is little question that the Center encourages the localities to speed up economic development. The gray area, therefore, is the soft austerity period.

The hypothesis that voluntary and involuntary softness affects investment dispersions differently can be tested by looking at the soft austerity period in two separate series: the 1979–80 period and the 1987–91 period. In order to control for the effect arising from the decline in investment dispersions over time (see the last section on the impact of the reforms), the pre-reform period (1977–83) is taken as the benchmark for the 1979–80 series, and the reform period (1984–92) for the 1987–91 series. The results largely confirm the hypothesis. In 1979 and 1980, investment behavior was characterized by a high degree of uncertainty about central policy intentions and therefore by a high degree of investment dispersions, as compared with the investment dispersions during the austerity and inflation periods between 1977 and 1983. All the numbers are positive, which implies that investment dispersions were the highest in 1979 and 1980. In contrast, in 1987 and 1991 policy uncertainty was considerably less, in relation to their levels during the austerity and inflationary periods, as indicated by their negative signs. The only exception is the dispersion for local projects relative to austerity, which carries a positive sign.

This kind of behavior suggests a strategic calculus on the part of local officials. They pursue their investment interests avidly, but up to a limit. They may test central policy resolve but will never challenge it directly. Local investment behavior interacts closely with central policy intentions. When central policy intentions are reasonably unambiguous, local officials fall in line by the drove; when they are less than crisp clear, some officials switch gears quickly, whereas the more cautious ones choose to wait out the uncertainty. Whether this kind of behavior should be called incompliance depends on one's preferences; I choose to call it strategic behavior.

The presence of strategic behavior makes posturing a necessary policy instrument and imparts a high premium to unity among leaders. Naughton (1988) points out that one of the reasons investment reduction measures are adopted in the form of Central Committee of the Communist Party decisions is to show that the Center means business. In the first half of 1989, when Zhao Ziyang and Li Peng clashed openly about the austerity program, implementation was rather ineffectual. In his annual report to the NPC in March 1989, Yao Yilin, then a vice premier and chairman of the SPC, expressed his frustrations about the wavering commitment (Yao Yilin 1991a [1989]: 477): "Although there has been some progress in suspending the ongoing projects and reducing the investment scope, this year's plan is far from being fulfilled. This is mainly because quite a few localities and departments still have this wait-and-see attitude, stress their own special circumstances, and compare themselves with others."

Conclusion

This chapter has presented two broad findings. First, investment performance over time cannot be characterized as incompliance on the part of local governments. Here it helps to put this finding in two perspectives. First, local officials have a positive incentive to expand investment and lack a negative incentive to constrain investment demand. Second, they possess a host of tools to protect their investment programs. When there is a credit squeeze, they can draw on their fiscal reserves or they may resort to alternative financing sources. Guangdong province, in 1990, issued 260 million yuan in bonds to raise construction funds and solve its liquidity problems ("Guangdong's economic predicament since June 4th," 1990). Those provinces in which alternative financing is lacking may simply try to evade the recentralization of investment approvals. For example, they can break up a large project into a number of small and seemingly independent projects to ensure a local – and presumably more sympathetic – approval hearing, or they may dress up their investment applications to hide their true purposes.

Anecdotal and some statistical evidence suggests that local officials are indeed engaged in evasions. A 1990 survey revealed that 983 new projects involving an investment of less than 1 million yuan were approved by prefectural and county level governments, although according to policy regulations, all of them should have been screened by the provincial governments. Seventy-three of the projects involved office and recreational buildings, projects specifically banned by the State Council (Ma Hong and Sun Shangqing 1991). Yet, the aggregate evidence presented here suggests that these practices are not pervasive in the Chinese system. The compliance record has by and large been quite good. Moreover, there is no evidence that the far-reaching economic reforms have caused an overall decline in the ability of the central government to restore macroeconomic stability, although the evidence does show that the costs of attaining its industrial policy objectives have increased over time.

The second major finding is that informational distribution shapes behavior. Although this point is often asserted, it is seldom shown. This chapter has demonstrated the effect of informational distribution on both central and local actions, and some of the perverse consequences from these actions. In general, the empirical findings bear out our a priori conjectures about the ways in which informational considerations should affect the choice of control approaches by central policy authorities and the relative record of local implementation of central policies across investment activities.

This finding suggests that Chinese localities are not as compliant as their aggregate behavior suggests. Their compliance depends on how their behavior is monitored. All else being equal, monitoring clarity and stringency lead to compliance; a lack of these elements leads to incompliance. Furthermore, the ability of the central policy authorities to restore macroeconomic stability in part depends on a crude approach. The crudeness exhibits itself in the inequity with which the benefits and costs of adjustment are allocated among the provinces: those provinces that comply less with the central government are favored above the more compliant provinces. This is the adverse selection problem, and it is inevitable once that a method – to economize on the use of information – is chosen. Although in the short term the approach apparently achieves its intended effect, in the long run, its effectiveness is highly questionable.

APPENDIX

Provincial responses: A procedural approach

Provincial policy responses fall into several categories. The first demonstrates the political resolve to seriously tackle the problem. For example, the highest-ranking officials are put in charge of supervising investment reduction. In 1983 Henan set up an ad hoc group, headed by a vice governor, to audit all ongoing projects; the high profile given to this group was intended to settle quickly the interagency squabbles over the suspension of ongoing projects. Provincial leaders also launched campaign-style initiatives to stop construction projects. In 1987 Li Ruihuan, mayor of Tianjin, convened a rally, attended by 120,000 municipal officials, to "create momentum" (*zaocheng qiangda de shengshi*) for investment reduction. In October 1988, soon after the conclusion of the Third Plenum of the Thirteenth Party Congress, Li immediately convened another conference of municipal officials and announced the setting up of an ad hoc leadership group, headed by Nie Bichu, a vice mayor, specifically in charge of examining all the ongoing projects (Li Ruihuan 1989: 129–30) (see "Guanyu kongzhi guding zichan touzi guimo wenti" 1986: 22).

Table A7.1. *Henan's investment approval requirements, 1985 and 1986*

Year	Nature of project	Level of approval authorities
1985	Budget-financed projects by prefectures and cities	Prefectures and cities Notification to provincial authorities
	Self-financed projects, 5–10 million yuan.	Prefectures and cities Notification to provincial authorities
	Self-financed projects < 5 million yuan	Counties
1986	Budget-financed projects > 5 million yuan and self-financed projects > 10 million yuan	Provincial governments
	Budget-financed projects between 3 and 5 million yuan and self-financed provincial projects < 10 million yuan	Bureaus of provincial governments
	Below-provincial projects < 3 million yuan and self-financed below-provincial projects < 10 million yuan	Prefectures and cities

Source: Henan Local History Editorial Committee (1986: 347, 1987: 399).

Political resolve, however, must be accompanied by specific policy measures to affect actual behavior. In 1986 Li Ruihuan set a zero-growth target for capital investment (Li Ruihuan 1987 [1986]: 81); when the central government's macroeconomic policy became tighter over the course of 1986 and 1987, Li escalated the squeeze even further by announcing the goal of reducing local fixed-asset investment by 21.9 percent, mainly via the termination of projects (Li Ruihuan 1988 [1987]: 58). The results were impressive. In two months, between October and December 1988, soon after the central plenum announced a three-year retrenchment program, the municipal government terminated or suspended about 130 local projects, amounting to 869 million yuan or about 28 percent of the fixed-asset investment target originally set for 1988 ("*Quanmian qingli guding zichan zaijian xiangmu*," 1989: 400). In 1983, the Henan provincial government centralized the investment approval process in the hands of the Henan provincial planning commission and devised project-based investment quotas so as to set forth relatively unambiguous criteria against which subprovincial officials could be evaluated. In 1986 the Henan planning commission tightened investment approval requirements by raising the administrative approval threshold and devising more detailed investment categories for bureaucratic screening. During the austerity period, there was more red tape in the investment screening and approval procedures than during the reflationary period. Table A7.1 compares Henan's investment approval requirements under the two different policy regimes, in 1985 and 1986.

As can be seen in the table, the approval requirements were both more liberal and simpler in 1985, the second year in a macroeconomically expansive cycle. Provincial authorities were only notified after a decision was made on projects that were financed by the budget or were self-funded projects and required a capital commitment of more than 10 million yuan. In 1986, however, the authority to approve projects was taken away from the county governments, and the provincial governments reasserted authority over the screening and approval process. Centralizing the investment screening and approval procedures has two principal effects. One is that the economic and technical criteria used to screen and approve projects can be expected to be stricter at higher levels of administrative authorities, given the general shortage of competent administrative personnel to assess projects. Second, a higher level of approval authorities can mobilize investment resources more efficiently by reducing the number of "duplicate projects." Selecting and approving projects at the provincial level presumably can force decisions to take into account market conditions on a provincewide rather than on a prefecture or countywide basis.

Of course, not all the provinces embrace investment reduction enthusiastically; typically local officials do not complain directly about central policies but rather about the consequences of central policies. For example, Li Ping, the chairman of the provincial planning commission of Gansu, gave the following reason for the severe shortage of funds in the province: the central government "tossed" (*shuaigei*) some of its own projects to the province and cut its investment subsidies (Li Ping 1988). Behind closed doors and in muted voices, the assessment is more frank. In an internal memorandum prepared for submission to the SPC in Beijing, Shenzhen planning officials offered their opinions on the economic targets for 1990 outlined by Vice Premier Zou Jiahua (also the chairman of the SPC) in his annual report to the National People's Congress. After praising its clarity and its correct general direction, the memorandum gingerly criticized the report for too much emphasis on the old problems (such as excessive investment growth) while neglecting the new ones (such as insufficient market demand and high interest rates):

At the same time, we have this feeling, which is not necessarily correct, that the state pays close attention to those problems that have been accumulated over a long period of time, but it pays less attention to new problems and contradictions that have arisen in recent years, such as soft market demands, enterprise short-term behavior, and high interest rates. It is less clear about what effective measures should be taken, especially measures that seek to improve economic efficiency. (Shenzhen Planning Commission 1991: 90–91)

Preferences for higher growth rates translate readily into preferences for higher investment growth. Shenzhen officials, in the aforementioned memorandum, requested a larger investment quota from the central government; in 1981, the governor of Fujian province, Hu Ping, revised the investment quota in the SPC plan from 340 million yuan to 663 million yuan by invoking the policy latitude allowed for the province as a Special Economic Zone and he pledged to try to get support from the central government (Hu Ping 1981). In 1985, a work team was dispatched by the State Council to solicit opinions from various provincial officials on the appropriate pace of economic growth. One of the findings of the team was that provinces with relatively high growth rates universally demanded high investment quotas (Development Center of the State Council 1986). Planning conferences with provincial officials, even those intended to put a cap on investment growth, often end up raising the investment quotas. In May

Table A7.2. *Performance/plan ratios for central and local investment projects in ten provinces, 1981–89*

Project	1981	1982	1983	1984	1985	1986	1987	1988	1989
Local	1	26	38	59	83	74	74	129	139
Central	20	32	18	19	10	22	30	60	85

Source: Plan data are collected from various issues of: *Tianjin ribao, Shanxi ribao, Shaanxi ribao, Guizhou ribao, Hebei ribao, Henan ribao, Hunan ribao, Fujian ribao, Jilin ribao*, and *Heilongjiang ribao*.

1985, for example, at the provincial governors' conference, the investment quota was raised from 80 billion to 88.8 billion yuan (eventually it was raised to 96.3 billion yuan) for the year.

One may easily question this periodization on two grounds. One is that some of the years during the austerity period cannot be said to fall under an austerity policy regime because the austerity policy was not really binding. This is a valid objection (see the discussion in chapter 7). The other objection is that policy periods do not precisely coincide with calendar years; for example, the fourth investment reduction round was put into effect in October 1988, not in January 1989. Unfortunately, most of the data series used in this analysis are grouped annually, which makes a refined analysis impossible.

Investment performance/plan ratios

The investment/plan ratio is derived by dividing actual investment by the planned target for that year minus one. Thus, zero of this ratio denotes perfect compliance and, if central preference is to reduce investment, positive numbers imply incompliance, whereas negative numbers imply overly compliant behavior. This ratio has been used by specialists on centrally planned economies to express the degree of control planners have over economic activities (Ickes 1986) and has been applied to estimate macroeconomic behavior in Poland (Portes et al. 1987). Similarly, in this study the ratio between actual performance and plan targets measures the degree of control central leaders exercise over provincial officials; we call this ratio the performance/plan ratio. I have collected plan data for ten provinces for the 1981–89 period. A comparison with the actual investment figures for these ten provinces is presented in table A7.2.

A few interesting features emerge from this table. First, Chinese investment planning tends to be overfulfilled. All the numbers exceed one and, in some cases, such as central investment in 1989 and local investment since 1984, actual investment exceeded plan targets by wide margins. Furthermore, the Chinese performance/plan ratio is substantially greater than the ratio in other centrally planned economies. According to Portes et al. (1987), the worst deviation from the investment plan in Poland was in 1972, when actual investment exceeded the planned target by 13.41 percent. In contrast, the worst deviation in China was 85 percent (i.e., 85 percent above the planned level) for central projects and 139 percent over the planned level for local projects.

The second feature of Chinese investment behavior is that planning compliance deteriorated in the 1980s. This is especially true in the case of local investment, with the performance/plan ratio steadily increasing from around 1 in 1981 to 139 in 1989. Two exceptional years were 1986 and 1987, when investment slowed somewhat. Also, incompliant investment behavior in the local sector is much more pronounced than central investment. The degree of plan deviation at the local level is twice as large as that for central projects (69 percent compared with 33 percent).

A major shortcoming of this measure is that data, especially plan data, are not always available. Although the Chinese central government publishes annual national plans regularly, provincial plan data are much more scattered, and they are made more stringent by the requirement that the investment plan data should be broken down into central and local projects. (See "Guanyu kongzhi guding zichan touzi guimo wenti," 1986: 22). Investment plan data for the 1981–89 period are more or less consistently available for the following ten provincial-level regions: Tianjin, Shanxi, Guizhou, Hebei, Henan, Hunan, Jilin, Heilongjiang, Fujian, and Shaanxi.

There is also a more substantive shortcoming. In the Chinese system, plan targets are not taken too seriously and are often revised to accommodate actual performance (Granick 1990). As a result, local officials overshoot plan targets routinely, and it is doubtful whether plan targets are perceived to be binding central intentions. He Zhukang, governor of Henan province, set a zero-growth target for fixed-asset investment for 1984 at the beginning of the year (He Zhukang 1985: 44); yet a report by the Henan Provincial Statistical Bureau released in 1985 (Henan Provincial Statistical Bureau 1985: 64) indicates that fixed-asset investment actually grew by 30.8 percent. In 1985, another reflationary year, sixteen provinces overshot the targets for renovation investments by some 30 percent. Among the worst offenders were Sichuan (80 percent above target), Jiangsu (64 percent), Guangdong (42 percent), Shanghai (40 percent), and Beijing (37 percent).

However, the Henan report notes that central investment projects fulfilled 93.9 percent of the plan, and that local investment projects overfulfilled the plan by some 17 percent (see Henan Local History Editorial Committee 1985: 382). In any case, the emphasis on central projects proved to be ephemeral, and the trend quickly reversed itself. In 1985, the central projects experienced a sharp decline, to 61 percent. The local projects experienced a corresponding increase, to 39 percent (calculated from SSB 1990: 543).

Z-scores for investment growth rates

The Z-scores are given by

$$Z_{(it)} = \frac{(G_{it} - \overline{G})}{S_I}$$

where:

G_{it} is the investment growth in province i and in year t;

$\overline{G}$ is the mean growth rate;

S_I is the standard deviation.

Table A7.3. *Investment activity as a governmental activity*

Dependent variable, bureaucratic	$LI_{(it)}$ [a]	$IND_{(it)}$ [b]	$NMP_{(it)}$ [c]	$PCI_{(it)}$ [d]
$APP_{(it-1)}$	−0.13*	0.014	0.02	0.02
	(0.04)	(0.02)	(0.014)	(0.016)
$BINT_{(it)}$	−0.05**	0.001	0.01	0.01
	(0.023)	(0.012)	(0.008)	(0.009)
Adjusted R^2	0.12	0.001	0.03	0.07
Number of observations	413	428	433	433
D-W statistic	1.51	1.07	1.92	1.51

Note: Standard errors are in parentheses. Significance tests are one-tailed. The findings are generated by regressing these four independent variables on $BM_{(joint)}$.
[a] LI = local investments.
[b] IND = industrial output value.
[c] NMP = net material product.
[d] PCI = per capita income.
* p < 0.05.
** p < 0.1.
Source: Database.

The proposition that 68 percent of the observations lie within one standard deviation from the mean depends on the normality of the distribution of the Z-scores. A number of indicators show that the provincial Z-scores during an austerity period approximately approach a normal distribution. The mean is 6.57e − 011, very close to zero; the standard deviation is one. The skewness is 1.62 and the Kurtosis is about 6.86. The skewness and the Kurtosis measures indicate that the distribution is slightly positively skewed. The degree of the skew is not too serious, as the normal distribution score for the skewness is 0.00 and is 3 for the Kurtosis.

Investment as a governmental activity

Compared with other economic activities, investment is controlled more tightly by governmental decisions. The logical implication is that bureaucratic characteristics should be more closely related to investment activity as opposed to other economic activities. In table A7.3, I apply $BM_{(joint)}$ to four dependent variables, local investment ($LI_{(it)}$), provincial industry ($IND_{(it)}$), provincial net material product ($NMP_{(it)}$), and per capita income ($PCI_{(it)}$). All dependent variables are logged real values. The regression analysis shows that the two bureaucratic variables, $APP_{(it-1)}$ and $BINT_{(it)}$, are only significantly related to $LI_{(it)}$.

Investment convergence: An alternative hypothesis

In chapter 7 I attribute the differences in the growth characteristics of construction and renovation investments to actions of local officials under different monitoring constraints. A simpler explanation holds that renovation investment grows faster because it starts from a lower base. I examine this alternative hypothesis here.

There is strong evidence that there were differences in the base ratios between the two investment activities and that these base ratios steadily declined during the 1977–92 period. The base ratios refer to the ratios of the level of renovation investment relative to the level of construction investment in a given province. A base ratio of one indicates that the two investment activities are of the same size; values less than one indicate that renovation investments are smaller and values larger than one indicate that renovation investments are larger. Before 1981, the mean annual base ratio was 0.45 (i.e., renovation investments were only 45 percent of local construction investments); between 1981 and 1986, it was 0.99; and between 1986 and 1992, it was 1.14. Clearly, over the 1977–92 period the base ratios narrowed because renovation investments grew at a faster rate than construction investments.

Although the aggregate evidence is consistent with the convergence thesis (i.e., growth rates become similar as investment sizes become similar), it does not invalidate our hypothesis. Our expectation is a behavioral one, positing that local officials substitute renovation investments for construction investments because the former are monitored less vigilantly than the latter. To test our hypothesis, it is necessary to examine the relationship between renovation and construction activities *in a typical province*, rather than look at the aggregate performance of all the provinces. Specifically, we ask the following question: "Does a typical province tend to have a positive growth difference score because it has a lower renovation base relative to its construction base?" To answer this question, we need to study how the investment base ratios are correlated with the growth difference score. The convergence hypothesis – the alternative hypothesis – says that they should be negatively correlated: that is, a province that has a smaller base ratio tends to have a larger growth difference score.

The evidence strongly rejects the alternative hypothesis. The Pearson correlation values between the base ratios and growth difference scores is positive for every year during the 1977–92 period. For the 1977–85 period, for example, the Pearson correlation value was 0.18 during an austerity period. Substantively speaking, this means that there is a modest advantage in promoting renovation projects in a province with a larger renovation base. As an illustration, the growth difference was 49.71 between 1977 and 1981 under austerity and the associated base ratio was 0.64. If the base ratio were to increase to 1 (i.e., there is no difference between renovation and construction activities in their bases), then the growth difference would increase to 65.5.

8

Bureaucratic investment behavior

Chapter 6 outlined an investment model that seeks to link the bureaucratic status of local officials with their investment behavior. However, there is a "unique solution" problem: that is, the model itself cannot make a "unique" prediction about how bureaucratic status may affect local investment behavior. Prior assumptions about the way the Chinese political system works and about the calculus that drives individual actions lead to two equally plausible but contrary hypotheses. If it is assumed that the formal organizational layers of the Chinese political system meaningfully represent the way political power is distributed, then bureaucratic integration must restrict the investment shirking in the localities. On the other hand, if real power in the Chinese system lies with informal connections and the associated patronage ties, the opposite would be true. These hypotheses identify and stress different explanatory factors and they can both establish plausible expectations about logical links between the alleged causal force(s) and the object of inquiry in this study. Thus, prior studies alone cannot be used to rule out one of the two competing hypotheses.

The task of this chapter is to confront these two conflicting visions with the available evidence and to examine their empirical validity with the aid of multiple regression analysis, a technique widely used in social science research. The fundamental advantage of this method, as compared with a more qualitative method, is its ability to take into account the effect of many factors on an outcome of interest to researchers and to deal with a large number of cases. This helps guard against constructing ad hoc explanations. An ad hoc explanation derives some general statements about causal relationships by making observations about events without examining alternative explanations or empirical cases beyond those from which the explanation is derived. A major shortcoming of an ad hoc explanation is that it may lead to flawed general statements about causality. Since the outcome is known a posteriori, it is generally possible to pinpoint a set of factors that were both unique and

logically linked to the event under investigation.[1] But in social science research, the presence or absence of a single factor, or a single group of factors,
seldom produces a consistent outcome across repeated instances; an outcome
may result from a group of factors *in conjunction with* other factors. Because
of this causal complexity, it is necessary to examine the effect of many causal
variables as well as to employ a comparative research strategy (Ragin 1987:
chap. 2).

The second advantage of this approach is its ability to demonstrate the
hypothesized causal chains directly. So far, the argument that increased supervision and monitoring have enhanced central macroeconomic and industrial
policy enforcement (or at least have offset some of the decentralizing effects
of the economic reforms) has been supported by indirect evidence and by
inference. The central government has not "lost control" of local investment
– a fact attributed to a variable that has varied with time: the improvement in
administrative supervision and monitoring (see chapter 7). Implicitly or explicitly, time is used here as a proxy variable to deduce the effect arising from
administrative improvement. To the extent that the longitudinal variations in
local investment performance are consistent with the longitudinal changes in
administrative capabilities, it can be said that improvement in administrative
capabilities has "caused" compliance in investment conduct.[2]

However, the argument will be more convincing if a direct and explicit link
can be found between a set of bureaucratic characteristics of local officials and
their investment behavior. Such a link (or its absence) can be found by em-
ploying multiple regression analysis, which associates changes in the independent variable by one unit with changes in the dependent variable by a
certain coefficient. The coefficients generated by the regression analysis provide two pieces of information. The first concerns the direction of the association, that is, whether the associations are positive or negative. Positive
associations mean that the two variables move in the same direction; if a
variable is found to be positively related to local investments, then that variable
is said to boost local investments. Negative associations mean that the two
variables move in the opposite direction; if a variable is negatively related to
local investments, then that variable is said to constrain local investments. The
second piece of information involves the strength of the associations. Whether

---

1. For further discussion on the shortcomings of ad hoc explanations, see Olson (1982: 9–13).

2. Using time as a proxy variable is a common approach in social science research, especially
when the variable we want to examine is intrinsically unobservable but nevertheless produces a
real effect. In economics, changes in technology are often studied this way. In political science,
a recent application is Martin (1992). She tests the theory of hegemonic stability against changes
in international cooperation on sanctions over time. Because hegemonic power has declined over
time, changes over time – increases, decreases, or stationarity – in international cooperation can
be observed to assess the hegemonic stability theory.

positive or negative, the magnitudes of the associations denote how closely the movement of one variable follows the movement of the other variable; indeed, the necessary criterion used to ascertain if there is any meaningful relationship at all between two variables is that the strength of their association has to meet a certain previously set threshold.[3]

The third point to mention is that the objective here is to explain *typical* behavior, not aberrations or exceptional cases. To determine whether the phenomenon informed by one or the other hypothesis is systemwide or whether it is isolated in place or time demands the study of a large number of cases, which the statistical method makes possible. Furthermore, even if the correct causal relationship is identified, its explanatory power remains limited until it has been shown that the relationship can hold in a large number of other cases. Again, multiple regression analysis comes in handy for this purpose because of its ability to handle a large number of cases. The discussion opens with some comments about the model specifications and then proceeds to the operationalization of the variables used in the analysis and their hypothesized relationships.

Model building

Model building is about including or excluding variables for analysis and about the specific forms of such variables. The purpose of the model-building effort here is to *test* a theory or a hypothesis about causal relationships; the statistical models themselves, however, are unable to supply the causal relationships. In reality, the process works the other way around. Armed either with theory or with prior knowledge, one first specifies a theoretical model and then examines the plausibility of such a model. The question of concern here is, "Given that this is the way we hypothesize about the real world, how likely are we to observe the empirical evidence at hand?"[4] Thus the most critical step in the

3. It is quite possible, however, that our empirical analysis will not permit us irrefutably to rule out alternative hypotheses and that competing hypotheses may be found to possess different degrees of explanatory power or to be valid under different conditions. In the real world, of course, it is also quite possible that two competing hypotheses can both be valid and they need not be mutually exclusive; nevertheless, it is worthwhile to explore whether the central–provincial relationship is characterized *largely* by one or another mode of interactions. The research task here is therefore to ascertain the relative validity of competing hypotheses, to attempt to specify conditions under which one hypothesis may appear to be superior to its alternatives, and to construct an eclectic approach with the broadest possible explanatory power.

4. As Tufte (1974: 115) puts it succinctly: "The regression answers the quantitative question by estimating a parameter in a model – on the assumption that the model is correct. We choose between competing models by comparing their goodness of fit, by thinking about their theoretical underpinnings, and by adding sufficient degrees of freedom in the model to allow the data to indicate the best fit."

present model-building effort is to specify ex ante expectations – that is, those expectations that are independent of our regression results – as to how our posited independent variables and local investment behavior are linked and to assess our hypotheses in light of ex post empirical results that are generated by the regression analysis. The hypothesis will be rejected if the statistical analysis does not yield results consistent with our expectations and if it fails to meet a conventionally set criterion for acceptance. Otherwise it will be accepted.

The model described here is based on the following specifications. First, central to the theorizing effort in economics and neoclassical political economy is an assumption that individuals are "rational" in the sense that they maximize their preferences to the degree permitted by the constraints that they face. In the present case, Chinese local officials are assumed to maximize their investment preferences subject to constraints. These constraints can take economic or bureaucratic forms, such as the availability of financial resources or the stringency of central administrative control.[5]

A good model depends more on a correct specification of what the relevant constraints are than on the empirical validity of the rationality assumption itself. The rationality assumption is our "core" assumption in the Lakatosian sense. That is, if empirical evidence contradicts our hypothesis, we do not give up the rationality assumption, but we revise other auxiliary specifications connected to the hypothesis.[6] For example, if our models do not produce consistent findings about bureaucratic constraints on investment behavior, we do not question the maximal behavioral assumption of Chinese local officials and conclude that they act randomly. Instead, we respecify the models by positing other constraints or other policy preferences. This is necessary because, arguably, the rationality assumption is indispensable to social science research and it is used as a heuristic, if not as an empirical, device.[7]

The second specification involves the content of the policy preferences on the part of Chinese local officials. Although neoclassical political economy presumes consistency between preferences and deeds, it does not say what these preferences are. Policy preferences must be contextually determined and the plausibility of our models depends critically on a correct specification

---

5. Of course, there could be other constraints. Simon (1982), for example, proposes that many constraints are inherent in human intelligence itself: human beings are so limited in their capacity to gather and process information that it is difficult to examine an exhaustive range of options and compare their costs and benefits. Human beings thus engage in "satisficing" behavior. That is, they seek and adopt solutions that meet their minimum requirements for satisfaction. For analytical tractability, I ignore constraints of this kind.

6. See Lakatos (1970) for a view on this positivistic research method.

7. See Friedman (1953) for a defense of this use of the rationality assumption.

of these preferences. That is why a good deal of analytical attention has been devoted to this task in this volume. In chapters 1, 2, and 3, I presented evidence for and analyzed the reasons why the Chinese tax system, the features of the planning system, and the public goods nature of inflation control all contributed to a maximization of local investment interests and, relatedly, to efforts to evade implementation of central investment policies. An auxiliary extension of this specification is that there is a fundamental conflict between central and local governments regarding both the level and the structure of investment programs. These discussions helped lay an empirical foundation for the models in this chapter.

The third specification regards the possible relevance or direction of the independent variables. In a study on investment behavior, it is simply taken for granted that certain economic variables (to be discussed in the next section) should be included; less common is an approach that also explicitly takes bureaucratic variables into account. Chapters 4 and 6 indicated why it is important to include bureaucratic variables in a study such as this. It is somewhat more difficult to specify the direction of the effect that the bureaucratic independent variables have on local investment behavior. In part this is because there have only been a few similar studies on this topic. The bureaucratic model of local investment behavior proposes two competing hypotheses, control and bargaining; these two hypotheses posit opposite bureaucratic effects. Thus the empirical task of this chapter is to examine the relative validity of these two hypotheses by comparing their consistency with the data.

The statistical findings are meaningful when these three sets of specifications make methodological, theoretical, or empirical sense. For example, if a variable is found to be negatively related to local investment, this finding should not imply that local officials are irrational or that they act to minimize local investment interests. Instead, the negative coefficient can be said to imply that the variable in question imposes so high a cost on increasing investment that the officials perceive it to be in their self-interest to curtail their own economic demand. The relevance and the importance of correct specifications readily become apparent: to the extent that these specifications are erroneous, the interpretations of the statistical results would be flawed as well. Evaluating the soundness of these specifications in fact is the most convenient way to assess the credibility of our findings. A statement as to whether these specifications hold is equivalent to a statement about the precise conditions under which our analysis applies.

The basic approach here is to model local investment behavior as a function of both economic and bureaucratic variables. Because the analytical focus is on a set of bureaucratic variables, I include economic variables mainly as "control" or "setting" variables. In other words, they are included to control for the extraneous effect that they may have on the dependent variable and for any interaction effect between them and the political or bureaucratic variables. I will not analyze economic variables in great detail.

A note about the variables and notations is in order at this point. All of the variables are broken down by the twenty-nine provinces as well as by years. In the subscript, *it*, *i* represents a province and *t* represents a year; thus the dependent variable local investment, or $LI_{(it)}$, means local investment level in province *i* and in year *t*. The economic and bureaucratic variables in the models and the outline of the baseline models are presented next; further details about operationalization of the variables and the equation forms of the models and the notations used can be found in the appendix to this chapter.

Dependent variables

The primary dependent variable here is the level of local investments broken down by the twenty-nine provinces ($LI_{(it)}$). These are investments directly organized, financed, or supervised by the local governments. Running throughout this book is the argument that local officials have a strong incentive to maximize local investments and that the concern of the central government, especially during periods of macroeconomic stringency, is to reduce the growth of local investments. The impact on local investment behavior arising from the independent variables is an indication of the relative importance of these variables in affecting the compliance of local officials.

The dependent variable can be formulated in alternative ways. In part, this is done out of empirical interest in examining the relationship between the independent variables and other dependent variables; in part, it is motivated by methodological considerations. Testing our models on alternative dependent variables is one way to assess their "explanatory power," or their ability to explain as many phenomena as possible. Confidence in the models will increase if the findings can be generalizable to related areas.

An analogous category of $LI_{(it)}$ refers to renovation investments ($RI_{(it)}$). As argued in previous chapters, $RI_{(it)}$ is heavily controlled by local governments and is often an alternative investment outlet when the central investment policy is to restrict the growth of local capital construction investment. Because $LI_{(it)}$ and $RI_{(it)}$ have similar characteristics, our empirical examination should reveal that bureaucratic variables produce similar effects on them. As noted in previous chapters, central investment ($CI_{(it)}$) is a form of contrarian investment activity from $LI_{(it)}$ and $RI_{(it)}$. Revenue-maximizing local governments often seek to shirk undertaking central investment projects because of their low profitability and the presence of positive externalities associated with them. Thus our hypothesized behavior of local governments is that they typically seek to maximize $LI_{(it)}$ at the expense of $CI_{(it)}$. If this hypothesis is correct, then those bureaucratic variables that expand $LI_{(it)}$ should constrain $CI_{(it)}$, and vice versa.

Economic models

Consider now the independent variables. I provide three alternative models that include only economic variables; later on, when I perform the statistical tests, I add bureaucratic variables to each one of them. Because economic theories about investment behavior are somewhat underdeveloped, I have not based my specifications on economic theories; rather, they are guided by a commonsensical understanding of investment dynamics and the operations of the Chinese economic system during the reforms. (In the appendix to this chapter, the regression diagnostics show that the bureaucratic effects are completely independent of economic specifications.) In addition, a trial-and-error approach helps remove some variables or guide the specific statistical form taken by them. The overall thrust of these model specifications is to highlight the variations among provinces and to demonstrate how these cross-sectional variations in the independent variables are systematically correlated with the cross-sectional variations in the dependent variable.[8]

Lag model (LM). The first model is the simplest. It hypothesizes that the level of investments of a province in the current year is a function of its level of investments in the last year, $LI_{(it-1)}$. This simple model makes a lot of intuitive sense. Investment is a very path-dependent activity; typically, capital commitment in a given year to start a project is small, but it increases progressively during the course of the project cycle. In the literature on economic modeling of investment behavior in socialist economies, planners are hypothesized to rely on the lagged investment term in making decisions about the current year's quota (see Bauer 1978; Grosfeld 1987; and Roland 1987). Typically, planners are supposed to treat past investment levels as "planning norms," and

---

8. Several factors hamper our effort to specify a model based on economic theory. First, investment theory in economics is relatively underdeveloped and is practically nonexistent in the area of investment behavior in CPEs. Second, traditional modeling efforts about investment in CPEs are not very helpful largely because they usually are based on a set of assumptions that apply to the pre-reform CPE system. For example, one of the assumptions that is clearly inappropriate for our analysis is that central planners can set investment levels at will and thus fluctuations in the investment level are attributed to planners' reactions to macroeconomic conditions.

as such the lagged term should be smoothed to minimize short-term fluctuations. I use three-year moving average values for the lagged term.

Financial model (FM). Despite its simplicity, for both technical and substantive reasons the lag model is not satisfactory. For purely technical reasons, the lagged dependent variable typically has a large effect and because it correlates with the values of all the independent variables in year $t{-}1$, its effect on $LI_{(it)}$ represents the composite effect of all the independent variables omitted in the lag model. For this reason, when bureaucratic variables are added to Equation (LM), their effect on $LI_{(it)}$ tends to be artificially small. Substantively speaking, the relationship between $LI_{(it)}$ and $LI_{(it-1)}$ is fairly straightforward and is uninteresting to pursue both on theoretical and empirical grounds.

The financial model hypothesizes that local officials make investment decisions subject to financial constraints. There is some consensus among economists that financial considerations have become more important in driving investment and other economic behavior during the reform era; the financial model thus may be particularly suitable. Unless otherwise noted, most of the regression findings in this chapter are generated by the financial model (plus bureaucratic variables).

There are three financial variables. The first is foreign investments ($FI_{(it)}$); during the reform era, foreign investments have become increasingly important in capital formation in provinces such as Guangdong and Fujian. Another characteristic of foreign investments that warrants including it here is that foreign investments are often protected during investment reduction rounds; since we are interested in the behavior of local officials during retrenchment periods, biases may arise if foreign investments are omitted. The second financial variable is net provincial capital stock ($NKS_{(it)}$). Large capital stock tends to require large capital increments because of the large size of capital depreciation; thus it should be positively associated with annual investments. By trial and error, a quadratic term of net capital stock produces the best fit. When a quadratic term is included, this means that the effect of net capital stock on $LI_{(it)}$ is an increasing function of the size of the net capital stock.

The third financial variable is a measure of provincial revenue contributions ($RC_{(it)}$) to the Center. Because data on actual provincial revenue contributions are incomplete, I use the ratio of revenue collection to local expenditures as a proxy. Although this measure is imprecise, as it inevitably counts budgetary surpluses as revenue contributions, the bias cannot be corrected without further information. The bias should not affect the analysis greatly, as the purpose is to bring out differences between those provinces contributing revenues to the Center and those provinces receiving subsidies from the Center. By definition, provinces receiving subsidies from the Center do not have budgetary surpluses and persistent budgetary surpluses are not likely. Revenue contributions reduce the financial resources available for local investments, and thus large revenue contributions should be associated with lower investment levels. A serious defect with the financial model is that it does not include a credit variable. Loan data broken down by provinces are sparse.

Development model (DM). In lieu of financial variables, I specify what I call a development model that captures the different levels of economic development among provinces. The first variable is per capita income ($PCI_{(it)}$), calculated by dividing the provincial net material product by the provincial population. Rich provinces may invest more because they have more material or financial resources. Under the policy of tying loans to savings, for example, higher per capita income can generate more investible capital because the savings rate is high. The second variable is the size of the provincial industrial sector measured by net industrial product ($IND_{(it)}$). Because an overwhelming share of capital investments goes into industry, a large industrial sector is associated with large investments. The third variable is a measure of the resource constraints on local investments and it is given by the ratio of the provincial NMP to the utilized NMP. Utilized NMP refers to the portion of the provincial NMP consumed in the same province; thus the difference between NMP and utilized NMP denotes the net resource flows to other provinces.[9] Large net resource outflows ($NRO_{(it)}$) reduce available domestic resources and thus are associated with small local investments.

Bureaucratic models (BM)

Bureaucratic variables are the substantive variables. They are included so that their effects on $LI_{(it)}$ can be analyzed systematically and in great detail. I estimate the bureaucratic characteristics of the top and secondary officials both jointly and separately, and the regression results should be consistent with each other. In part for the sake of analytical convenience and in part because of the recognition that Party officials still play important roles in economic affairs, I combine the measures of the bureaucratic variables for Party and government officials and devise a composite index (see the appendix to chapter 6 for more details on the coding of the bureaucratic variables).

Two of the bureaucratic variables denote two broad characteristics of Chinese

---

9. In some provincial statistical yearbooks, this amount is referred to as "the NMP for the use of the whole country."

provincial officials. The first characteristics are those that shape leadership stability: the duration of tenure and a measurement of new appointments. The second pertain to the bureaucratic standing of provincial officials in the Chinese system in relation to the central Party and government authorities in Beijing. Unfortunately, because there is not enough background information on secondary officials, I cannot devise a measure for the bureaucratic standing of secondary officials.

For top officials, the tenure is the average years Party secretaries and governors have served in a province ($TENTOP_{(it)}$). The first year of appointment is 1, the second year, 2, and so on. The appointment variable is a dummy variable and takes a value of between zero and two ($APPTOP_{(it)}$). The variable is coded zero when there is no appointment; one when there is one appointment to the position of either Party secretary or governor; and two when there are new appointments for both Party secretary and governor.[10] The variable that measures bureaucratic standing in relation to the Center is bureaucratic integration ($BINT_{(it)}$), which takes a value of between one and four. One represents insider; two, outsider; three, centralist; and four, concurrent centralist. The composite index is the average value of the sum of $BINT_{(it)}$ for Party secretary and governor. This is Model $BM_{(top)}$ in the appendix to this chapter.

The model for secondary officials contains two bureaucratic variables. The first is the average tenure of secondary officials ($TENSEC_{(it)}$), measured in years. The second variable represents appointments for secondary officials, but unlike $APPTOP_{(it)}$ for top officials, the total number of secondary officials varies from province to province; therefore the appointment variable for secondary officials is calculated as the proportion of newly added officials in provincial Party and government establishments ($APPSEC_{(it)}$). For joint estimations, the tenure and appointment variables for top and secondary officials are combined to produce a composite index for tenure ($TEN_{(it)}$) and for appointments ($APP_{(it)}$).

My hypothesis, which I call control hypothesis ($H_{(con)}$), views personnel control and selection as strategic instruments for supervising and monitoring local officials. As argued in chapter 6, our fundamental premise is that when the Center is operating in an information-shortage environment, it opts for methods that demand less information. Personnel control and selection constitute such a method. There are fifty-eight top provincial officials and, since 1983 there have been about 522 secondary provincial officials in any given year. Managing these 580 or so officials is far easier than directly controlling and

---

10. See the appendix to chapter 6 for more details.

supervising 60,000 to 100,000 investment projects that routinely break ground each year. In addition, the criteria applied to evaluate provincial personnel are fewer and simpler and, most important, they vary far less on a case-to-case basis than those applied to evaluate investment or other economic activities.

My specifications of the effect of the bureaucratic terms on $LI_{(it)}$ are driven by this line of reasoning. The control hypothesis views personnel selection as equivalent to a process of performing ex ante monitoring; consistent with this reasoning, a provincial official should be least likely to engage in shirking behavior upon appointment. Appointment terms – that is, $APP_{(it)}$ – should thus be negatively related to $LI_{(it)}$. To the extent that personnel selection is equivalent to ex ante monitoring, the more distant time an official is from the time of appointment, the less stringently he is monitored in this specific sense. Thus shirking behavior should increase as tenure lengthens.[11] Long tenure is associated with less frequent ex ante monitoring and the tenure variable, $TEN_{(it)}$, should be positively related to $LI_{(it)}$. Alternatively, tenure duration and appointment events can be viewed in terms of those factors affecting leadership stability. Long tenure implies leadership stability in the provinces, whereas frequent or high ratios of new appointments imply leadership instability. An auxiliary assertion of the control hypothesis is that the signs of the tenure variables must be opposite to those of the appointment variables because they connote conceptually opposite features of Chinese bureaucratic operations.

The control hypothesis views provincial officials' bureaucratic standing in relation to the Center as a liability of the localities. Closer organizational ties to the Center facilitate administrative supervision and control; or they may reduce interest divergence between the localities and the Center: local officials whose career tracks are heavily lodged with central Party and government authorities may consider their current provincial posts to be temporary assignments en route to higher positions in the central government. They are keener to defend central investment interests than to defend local investment interests. Again, the hypothesis concerns the sign of the relevant variable; political liability is associated with a negative sign of the $BINT_{(it)}$ term, since local investment aspirations are "suppressed" on account of closer bureaucratic ties to the Center.

Of course, alternative specifications are possible, such as the bargaining hypothesis ($H_{(bar)}$) outlined in chapter 6. The main difference between the control and the bargaining hypotheses lies in the term $BINT_{(it)}$ and the

11. An alternative reasoning is that longer services in the same province tend to make an official care about local interests more than central interests because with the passage of time an official comes to identify with his region more.

Table 8.1. *Summary of hypotheses*

Independent variable	Predicted effects	Hypotheses tested
Setting		
Lag model		
Investment last year	Positive	
Financial model		
Foreign investments	Positive	
Net capital stock	Positive	
Revenue contributions	Negative	
Development model		
Per capita income	Positive	
Size of industry	Positive	
Net resource outflows	Negative	
Substantive		
Bureaucratic models		
Tenure duration	Positive	Control
Appointments	Negative	Control
	Positive	Bargaining
Bureaucratic integration	Negative	Control
	Positive	Bargaining

appointment term $APP_{(it)}$. Either because the bargaining hypothesis does not view bureaucratic integration as the real locus of power or because the bargaining hypothesis views bureaucratic integration as fostering connections and patronage, it may view bureaucratic integration as a political privilege and predict a positive relationship between bureaucratic integration and $LI_{(it)}$. Closer integration helps contribute to the fulfillment of local investment objectives. As far as the appointment terms are concerned, the bargaining hypothesis assumes an official is selected principally because he is the consensus candidate and is someone whom other local officials trust. If indeed local officials have sufficient control over the appointment process (see Manion 1985), then the process would inevitably lead to the appointment of local agents. The best time to advance local interests would immediately follow the appointment decision. Thus the bargaining hypothesis predicts a positive relationship. Table 8.1 summarizes the effects of both the economic and the bureaucratic variables on local investments.

Bureaucratic status and investment behavior

The multiple regression technique makes it possible to perform "quasi experiments" in the sense that when the effect of one variable on investment behavior is being analyzed, the effect of the other variables is held constant. This is the so-called ceteris paribus condition; thus when the regression coefficient of one variable is interpreted, it should be borne in mind that this is the effect attributable to that variable *in isolation of the effects of all other variables*. The ceteris paribus condition is critical to a political analysis of economic phenomena. Typically, it is difficult to demonstrate the effect of political variables on phenomena of a general economic nature because political data are "gappy" and are not immediately pertinent to economic events, at least in comparison with other economic factors. Thus to test the effect of political factors, it is necessary to control for the effect of economic factors.

For technical reasons, I have performed the log transformation on all of the economic variables, including all the dependent variables, and, again for technical reasons, I have created three regional dummy variables – Region$_{(east)}$, Region$_{(interior)}$, and Region$_{(west)}$, representing eastern provinces, interior provinces, and western provinces respectively – to control for the possible cross-sectional interdependence in the dependent variable.[12] All the Chinese data are collected in their current values. I have deflated them to constant values (previous year = 1) by using the provincial retail price index.[13]

The basic procedure consists of three steps. First, the two main bureaucratic variables are added to the three economic models specified in the last section. This makes it possible to analyze bureaucratic impact on investment behavior under a condition whereby structural economic differences among provinces are equalized. Second, regressions are run on top and secondary officials jointly and then on them separately. The logic of the inquiry is that individuals in similar situations should behave similarly and thus the models and the hypotheses should apply with equal force to top and secondary officials. If the findings are consistent with each other, then we have more confidence in our models and in this test procedure. Also, because of the underlying uncertainty about the investment roles of top officials in relation to secondary officials, the safer assumption is that they both affect investment behavior.

Third, I experiment with different forms of the models. One involves contemporaneous vis-à-vis lagged effects; this is especially relevant as far as the impact of an "event" (such as appointment) is concerned. Sometimes, an event may not produce an instantaneous effect for both substantive and technical reasons and therefore a lag period should be allowed. Also, different variables are tested. For example, the tenure variable is substituted for the appointment variable and developmental variables are substituted for financial variables.

---

12. I also run regressions with each province as a regional dummy. The results are not different. See the attached appendix for more technical details.

13. Ideally, I should use the investment goods price index, but it is not available.

Different dependent variables are also tested. In social science research, affirming or rejecting a hypothesis seldom depends on a one-shot test; test results are more believable if they hold in repeated trials. But performing repeated trials requires the collection of more data and thus more time in waiting; an alternative strategy is to formulate alternative dependent variables and to apply the same test procedures to them. In general, we should expect similar results when we apply our models to differently formulated but conceptually similar dependent variables; we should expect contrarian results when our models are applied to conceptually contrarian dependent variables. Analogously, conceptually similar independent variables should produce similar results; conceptually contrarian independent variables should produce contrarian results. On technical grounds, this procedure helps us detect measurement errors.

The appendix to this chapter presents a series of sensitivity analyses to examine the quality of our model specifications. I use two alternative specifications of the economic models – DM and LM – and run $BM_{(joint)}$ without any economic variables to check for possible measurement errors of the bureaucratic terms; I also apply a stepwise procedure to examine the robustness of the individual estimates and the Granger test to determine the direction of the causality. Furthermore, I explore the possible influences on BINT estimates from the inclusion of extreme BINT values for Beijing and Shanghai. The results reported next have performed extremely well against these diagnostic procedures. My baseline model is $BM_{(joint)}$ + FM: that is, bureaucratic variables jointly for top and secondary officials plus financial variables. Both the fixed and varied effects models are estimated, first on local investments and then on alternative forms of the dependent variables.

Fixed effects models

I assume that the regression coefficients remain constant across time, in other words, that the relationship between our independent variables and the dependent variable has remained unchanged over time. Later, I will relax this assumption and allow the regression coefficients to vary with a number of substantively interesting variables (e.g., the cycles of the macroeconomic policies). By trial and error, the following three best-fitting models are estimated. All the appointment variables are lagged by one year and the economic model is FM.[14]

---

14. Readers should consult the attached appendix for a systematic discussion on how I have arrived at these forms.

First it is important to determine whether the addition of bureaucratic and policy variables is warranted to help explain local investment behavior. This is done by adding the five substantive variables $APP_{(it-1)}$, $BINT_{(it)}$, $APPTOP_{(it-1)}$, $APPSEC_{(it-1)}$, and AP (austerity policy) to FM and comparing the generated R^2 values with the R^2 values generated by regressing local investments on financial variables alone. This procedure, called a partial F-statistic test, is used to gauge the additional power the models acquire in explaining investment variations when they include the substantive terms, taking into account the number of added variables and the number of total variables in the models. The partial F-statistics are presented in the last row of table 8.2. All of the F-statistics are statistically significant at the 0.05 level.

All the financial variables have the expected signs and are statistically significant.[15] Foreign investments ($FI_{(it)}$) are found to be positively related to local investments, and provinces with large net capital stock ($NKS_{(it)}$) have higher levels of local investments, as expected. This suggests that provinces able to attract more foreign investments (such as Guangdong and Fujian) and provinces with many industrial facilities (such as Shanghai) tend to have a higher level of local investments, ceteris paribus. The revenue contributions variable ($RC_{(it)}$) is negatively related to local investments; this confirms the hypothesis that revenue contributions have the effect of reducing the financial resources available for domestic capital construction, thus depressing local investments. The suppressive effect of $RC_{(it)}$ is consistent with our knowledge that localities are averse to large tax turnovers to the central coffers.[16]

All the substantive variables, including the austerity policy term (AP), are significant at least at the 0.05 level, meaning that the variations in these variables statistically "explain" the variations in local investment behavior. As far as the consistency between our hypothesis and the predicted effects of the bureaucratic terms is concerned, the two bureaucratic variables confirm the control hypothesis. The negative coefficient for $BINT_{(it)}$ means that $BINT_{(it)}$ tends to suppress local investments. Roughly, in $BM_{(joint)}$, as bureaucratic

---

15. The consistent statistical significance of the regional dummy, $Region_{(east)}$, suggests that additional factors contribute to investment growth that are not captured by our explanatory variables. Thus there is room for further improvement in the model specification.

16. The internal consistency of our economic variables and the fact that our findings are broadly consistent with other observations about the Chinese economic system suggest that the economic variables are well specified. It is quite possible, however, that the individual regression estimates are unreliable because of the multicollinearity among some of the economic variables. I ignore this possibility because I do not intend to examine the economic variables in great detail. Our findings from the bureaucratic terms would be flawed if the bureaucratic terms were found to correlate with the economic variables. As I show in the appendix to this chapter, this is not the case.

Table 8.2. *Three baseline models*

Equation	$BM_{(joint)}$	$BM_{(top)}$	$BM_{(sec)}$
Substantive variables			
$APP_{(it-1)}$	−0.13*	—	—
	(0.04)		
$APPTOP_{(it-1)}$	—	−0.02*	—
		(0.011)	
$APPSEC_{(it-1)}$)	—	—	−0.12*
			(0.037)
$BINT_{(it)}$	−0.05*	−0.065*	—
	(0.023)	(0.023)	
AP	−0.09*	−0.10*	−0.08*
	(0.016)	(0.016)	(0.016)
Setting variables			
Intercept	1.13*	1.12*	1.06*
	(0.233)	(0.23)	(0.24)
$Region_{(east)}$	0.35*	0.32**	0.34**
	(0.21)	(0.21)	(0.22)
$Region_{(interior)}$	−0.01	−0.02	−0.02
	(0.085)	(0.085)	(0.086)
$Region_{(west)}$	0.07	0.05	0.05
	(0.21)	(0.21)	(0.22)
$FI_{(it)}$	0.21*	0.22*	0.20*
	(0.03)	(0.03)	(0.03)
$NKS_{(it)}$	0.06*	0.06*	0.06*
	(0.005)	(0.005)	(0.005)
$RC_{(it)}$	−0.17**	−0.15**	−0.21*
	(0.11)	(0.11)	(0.11)
Adjusted R^2	0.63	0.63	0.62
Number of observations	399	399	399
D-W statistic	1.50	1.57	1.51
Partial F-statistic	23.42*	22.35*	27.74*

Note: Standard errors are in parentheses. Significance tests are one-tailed. $BM_{(joint)}$ = Bureaucratic model for joint officials; $BM_{(top)}$ = Bureaucratic model for top officials; and $BM_{(sec)}$ = Bureaucratic model for secondary officials.
* $p < 0.05$.
** $p < 0.1$.
Source: Database.

integration increases by one score, local investments typically decrease by 5 percent. To make this illustration more concrete, this means that, holding constant the economic variables and other bureaucratic effects, the local investment growth of a province presided over by concurrent centralists ($BINT_{(it)}$ = 4) is 5 percent lower than that of a province presided over by centralists ($BINT_{(it)}$ = 3); about 10 percent lower than that of an outsider provinces

(BINT$_{(it)}$ = 2); and about 15 percent lower than that of an insider province (BINT$_{(it)}$ = 1).[17] This is a large difference, indeed.

Our findings on the BINT$_{(it)}$ term illustrate a fundamental feature of the Chinese political system. In economic terms, Chinese provinces are in a strong position with respect to the central government. However, whether their economic strength is translated into bargaining advantages with the Center depends on the political status of the provincial officials. Bureaucratic status has a powerful effect on the incentive structures faced by provincial officials. Close bureaucratic integration reduces economic localism, whereas lesser integration promotes economic localism. This behavioral pattern by no means implies that those officials closely integrated to the central political apparatus are somehow less economically rational; it does indicate that pleasing their superiors in Beijing and advancing their careers in the central government constitute a more important objective to officials with stronger bureaucratic and political ties to the Center as compared with those officials operating on the relatively lower rungs of the Chinese bureaucratic ladder.

Are there any strategic considerations that can explain why some provinces are integrated to the Center more than others?[18] Given the negative functions of the BINT$_{(it)}$ term, one plausible hypothesis is that BINT is used to supplement the economic control (or to compensate for the lack thereof) the Center wields over the provinces. The proof of this hypothesis lies in the relationship between BINT and a set of economic variables. I examine four such variables: the level of economic development, as measured by per capita income, the provincial share of national income, the level of industrialization (measured by the share of industrial output of the provincial income), and the difference between local tax collection and local expenditures, which I use as a proxy measure for provincial tax contributions to or subsidies from the Center. I rank these four economic characteristics by the bureaucratic integration scores of the provinces. The purpose is to see if these economic characteristics systematically vary with the degree of bureaucratic integration of provincial officials. The results appear in table 8.3.

The evidence is somewhat mixed. Clearly, concurrent centralists preside over provinces that are richer and more industrialized; their per capita income is almost twice as large as that of other provinces and more than half of their

---

17. The growth differential is given by BINT coefficient × (BINT − 1).

18. Some scholars point to some rather idiosyncratic factors; Bartke (1990a: 457), for example, argues that Shanghai's representation on the Politburo in the 1970s was due to the fact that it was the political base of Jiang Qing. Explanations like this fail to take into account the fact that some provinces, such as Shanghai, Beijing, Tianjin, and Sichuan, have been represented on the Politburo more or less continuously; the predominance of Shanghai, for example, both preceded and persisted after the political era of Jiang Qing.

Table 8.3. *Economic characteristics and bureaucratic integration, annual provincial averages, 1976–92*

Governance types	Per capita income (yuan)	Industrial share (%)	Share of national income (%)	Tax contributions (billions of yuan)
Concurrent centralists	1,465	54.1	4.75	2.75
Centralists	667	42.0	3.82	2.13
Outsiders	810	42.5	2.63	−0.44
Insiders	797	44.3	4.35	0.59

Source: Database.

economies are industrial. In addition, they also contribute more tax revenues to the Center and loom large in the national economy. The economic differences among centralists, outsiders, and insiders are less significant and seem to be randomly distributed. Rankings by per capita income, level of industrialization, and share of national income do not correspond at all to the order as laid out by the bureaucratic integration values. A significant exception is tax contributions; provinces run by centralists contribute far more tax revenues to the Center than provinces presided over by outsiders and insiders. These findings suggest, tentatively, that the assignment of concurrent centralists is related to economic control considerations and the assignment of centralists is related to fiscal motives. The Center seeks to integrate more closely those provinces that are more economically developed by dispatching concurrent centralists and centralists to run them. The economic motives for assigning outsiders and insiders are less apparent; the appointment patterns may result from political considerations.

Our hypothesis views personnel selection as equivalent to ex ante monitoring and predicts that administrative localism should be inversely related to ex ante monitoring. Alternatively, we can reason that a new leader is tentative or inexperienced; the best assurance of his position lies in good performance in the judgment of those who just appointed him, namely, those at the Center. Although the negative signs of the lagged appointment terms $APP_{(it-1)}$, $APPTOP_{(it-1)}$, and $APPSEC_{(it-1)}$ are consistent with the control hypothesis, regressing $APP_{(it)}$, $APPTOP_{(it)}$, and $APPSEC_{(it)}$ actually produces *positive coefficients*, although only $APPTOP_{(it)}$ is statistically significant.[19] Thus there is some evidence that new officials, at least in the year they are appointed, tend to

19. These coefficients are 0.05 (0.042) for $APP_{(it)}$, 0.07* (0.032) for $APPTOP_{(it)}$, and 0.03 (0.033) for $APPSEC_{(it)}$. Standard errors are in parentheses.

increase local investments. This finding contradicts the control hypothesis, but it is consistent with the bargaining hypothesis.

This shift in behavior has two explanations. The first says that it is administratively very difficult to reduce investment growth when assuming office during the middle of the year. Investment plans are already decided at the beginning of the year; resources are already in the pipeline. Thus letting investments be driven by their own momentum is far easier than intervening to alter investment momentum in the middle of the year. This line of reasoning requires the effect of contemporaneous appointments to be zero.

At least for appointments of top officials, however, the effect is not zero and is positive. This suggests an alternative explanation. As noted in chapter 6, succession may trigger a "honeymoon" period during which the actions of a new leader may be less stringently scrutinized. Furthermore, if we relax the assumption that a new leader always pursues central interests ahead of local ones and posit a form of an opportunistic mentality whereby a new leader avidly placates local interests upon assuming office, then the inquiry revolves around the duration of the effect arising from leadership succession and around the possible changes in the $APP_{(it)}$ effect as time passes. The modified control hypothesis thus allows the initial boosting effect of leadership succession but it mandates a behavioral change: As the "honeymoon" period comes to an end, the boosting effect should fade as well. The modified control hypothesis and the bargaining hypothesis differ from each other in predicting the duration of the initial boosting effect arising from succession. If the boosting effect persists, then the bargaining hypothesis is confirmed; if there is a change in the direction of the effect, from positive to negative, then the modified control hypothesis is confirmed. Findings in table 8.2 strongly confirm the modified control hypothesis.

A descriptive analysis, presented in table 8.4, shows that appointment events are followed by an initial surge and then by a retrenchment of investment. In order to capture the concept of change as a result of appointment events, I devise a measure called the "local investment deviation rate," which is the difference between growth in the current year and that in the previous year. I then rank local investment deviation rates by the frequency of appointments. To test the hypothesis that the boosting effect is transitory, I also lag the effect of appointment events by one year. Because the deviation rates are highly sensitive to policy changes, I present the findings under the two macroeconomic policy regimes separately. The appointment events range from 0 to 2, with 0 representing no appointment, 1 representing the appointment of either a governor or of a Party secretary, and 2 representing the appointments of both a governor and a Party secretary.

Table 8.4. *Appointments and local investment deviation from the previous year*

Number of appointments	Inflationary policy		Austerity policy	
	Current effect[a]	Lagged effect[b]	Current effect[a]	Lagged effect[b]
2	36.4	24.9	−21.8	−21.9
1	21.4	23.8	−11.2	−13.2
0	25.2	26.0	−10.1	−9.2

Note: Local investment deviation rates = current year's growth rate − previous year's growth rate.
[a] Current effect refers to appointment events in the current year.
[b] Lagged effect refers to appointment events in the previous year.
Source: Database.

The initial boosting effect from the appointment of two top officials in the same year is enormous; during an inflation period, the investment deviation rate is 36 percent for the two appointment events (i.e., the investment growth is 36 percent higher than the previous year when there are two appointments), as opposed to 21 percent and 25 percent for one and zero, respectively. However, it seems that appointment advantages are only significant when both a Party secretary and a governor are newly appointed; when there is only one appointment, the effect is not that obvious. This again suggests that the *aggregate* shirking advantages accorded to appointment events are not that important, as there are fewer instances of joint appointments of governors and Party secretaries than there are of single appointments. Between 1977 and 1992 there were altogether thirty-seven instances of joint appointments, contrasted with 104 instances of single appointments.

Whatever the shirking advantages that accompany new appointments, they are highly transitory. The large difference between joint appointments and the other two categories under the current effect completely disappears under the lagged effect. Indeed, if a province had no appointment in the previous year, in general it can be expected to outperform the other provinces with appointment events, as shown by the negative $APP_{(it-1)}$ in the regression analysis. This is indicative of how the Chinese political system works: while newly appointed officials may want to appease local interests upon assuming office, they are quickly socialized into compliant behavior after the first year on the job. Noncompliance is rather rare, and, to the extent that it actually occurs, it occurs only when supervision is lax and a window of opportunity presents itself.

Investment behavior under an austerity policy period gives strong support to the control hypothesis. New officials, taking cues from the central government to rein in local investment growth, do so more avidly as compared with others. Whereas the difference between one and zero appointments is not great, there is an enormous difference between two appointment events and the other two categories. In general, new Party secretaries and governors reduce local investment growth by 10 percent or so more than others, and this pattern holds whether the effect is lagged or not. This behavioral shift between policy regimes is evidence of investment opportunism. During an inflationary policy period, when the central investment policy is permissible, new officials expand local investments rapidly. This is what the bargaining hypothesis predicts. But the true test comes when an austerity policy regime is in effect: new officials, as compared with old officials, reduce local investment growth by a far greater margin. In short, the investment behavior of new officials is highly sensitive to macroeconomic policy regimes; if appointments coincide with an austerity policy, new officials reduce investment growth by a far greater margin than other officials. Otherwise, they switch their behavior 180 degrees and expand investment growth far in excess as compared with other officials.

Alternative independent variables

Alternative specifications of the models can be examined by applying a number of alternative measures of our bureaucratic independent variables. I use measures of tenure duration – $TEN_{(it)}$, $TENTOP_{(it)}$, and $TENSEC_{(it)}$ – as alternative measures of leadership stability to appointment events. The tenure term denotes opposite leadership dynamics from the appointment term, for obvious reasons. The more appointment events there are, the shorter the tenure duration, and vice versa. The control hypothesis argues that appointment decisions are equivalent to ex ante monitoring by central Party and government authorities and thus appointment decisions should be negatively related to administrative localism. By this logic, tenure duration is positively related to administrative localism because tenure duration is negatively associated with the frequency of appointment decisions. This line of reasoning dictates that the effects of tenure should be opposite to those of appointment terms, and that the effect of the tenure term be positive. This is examined in table 8.5. For the sake of simplicity, I have omitted the financial variables in the table.

The three models in table 8.5 differ from the baseline models in table 8.2 in their tenure duration term ($TEN_{(it)}$ and $TENTOP_{(it)}$); clearly, tenure terms are not statistically significant, which contradicts our hypothesis. Before a

Table 8.5. *Tenure duration and local investment behavior*

Variable	$BM_{(joint)}$	$BM_{(top)}$	$BM_{(top)}(a)$
Substantive			
$TEN_{(it)}$	0.005	—	—
	(0.011)		
$TENTOP_{(it)}$	—	0.005	−0.006
		(0.007)	(0.009)
$TENTOPI_{(it)}$	—	—	0.02*
			(0.007)
$BINT_{(it)}$	−0.06*	−0.06*	−0.06*
	(0.022)	(0.022)	(0.022)
AP	−0.09*	−0.09*	−0.09*
	(0.016)	(0.016)	(0.016)
Setting			
Intercept	1.13*	1.13*	1.19*
	(0.24)	(0.255)	(0.255)
$Region_{(east)}$	0.33**	0.34**	0.34**
	(0.214)	(0.23)	(0.229)
$Region_{(int)}$	−0.02	−0.02	−0.02
	(0.086)	(0.089)	(0.088)
$Region_{(west)}$	0.03	0.04	0.03
	(0.212)	(0.228)	(0.226)
Adjusted R^2	0.62	0.60	0.60
Number of observations	418	418	418
D-W statistic	1.63	1.62	1.70

Note: Standard errors are in parentheses. Significance tests are one-tailed.
Financial variables are not presented. Models estimated are BM + FM.
$TENTOPI_{(it)} = TENTOP_{(it)} \times D_{(it)}$.
* $p < 0.05$.
** $p < 0.1$.
Source: Database.

definitive conclusion is drawn, I introduce a modification to the tenure term. It is plausible to argue that administrative localism, while increasing with tenure durations, may not do so by the same increments. For example, administrative localism may not be a problem with those officials who only serve out their average tenure (i.e., around four years), but administrative localism becomes significant with those officials who serve "abnormally" long periods of time. This happens because leaders in their posts for a long period of time may feel that they already enjoy tenure security and therefore see less need to perform well, as judged by the centrally set criteria, in order to protect their positions. Thus there should be a threshold of tenure duration; before the threshold, there is no localism, but once the threshold is crossed, administrative localism is present. In technical terms, this means that the relationship between the $TEN_{(it)}$ term and $LI_{(it)}$ is not linear; instead, the coefficient of the $TEN_{(it)}$ term is an increasing function of the $TEN_{(it)}$ term itself. To operationalize this hypothesis, I create a dummy variable representing unusually long tenures $D_{(it)}$ and an interaction term, $TENI_{(it)}$ ($TEN_{(it)}$ interaction), is created by $TEN_{(it)}$ $\times D_{(it)}$. Through residual analysis, the threshold is determined to be 5.5 years.[20] Thus $D_{(it)}$ is coded 0 when the $TEN_{(it)}$ is less than 5.5 years and 1 when it exceeds 5.5 years.

Only the long tenure term for top officials is statistically significant. The coefficient for the long tenure term is given by $TENTOP_{(it)}$ + $TENTOPI_{(it)}$ (i.e., 0 + 0.02); the term, $TENTOPI_{(it)}$, is significant at the 0.05 level. This result suggests that whereas top leaders with "normal" tenure durations are not able to act strongly on their investment preferences, those leaders with extremely long tenure durations are. An examination of the local investment deviation rate also confirms this result. On average, if a province has no appointment events for seven years in a row, its investment deviation rate – the difference between the current and the last year's growth rates – is about 5.24 percent. In contrast, during the same seven-year interval, if there have been appointment events, then the deviation rate is about −2.04 percent. Taking the findings on appointments into account, we can posit a highly complex behavioral function of local officials. Investment localism is strongest in the first year of appointment, but it quickly moderates in the next year; however, investment localism picks up again over the very long haul of an official's career. Extreme tenure stability leads to a feeling of tenure security and thus emboldens the promotion of local investment interests.

These findings also suggest that administrative localism on account of long tenure is not a pervasive phenomenon in the Chinese system. To promote local investment growth about 2 percent more than average, a provincial leader has to outlast most of his colleagues by at least more than 1.5 years. As another indication of the rarity of this kind of administrative localism, of the twenty-nine provinces in the present sample, only five provinces – Beijing, Hebei, Hunan, Neimenggu, and Xinjiang – have TENTOP values larger than 5.5

20. Residual analysis reveals that in our baseline models there is an upward bend when $TENTOP_{(it)}$ is around 5.5; this means that our baseline models tend to overpredict lower values of the $TENTOP_{(it)}$, but underpredict higher values of the $TENTOP_{(it)}$ (i.e., when $TENTOP_{(it)} > 5.5$). To some extent, the baseline models violate the zero-mean assumption of the regression analysis. Take $BM_{(top)}$ as an example. When the $TENTOP_{(it)}$ is less than 5.5, the mean value of the residual is −0.004, but when the $TENTOP_{(it)}$ exceeds 5.5, the mean value is 0.07. The corrective procedure that adds the $TENTOP_{(it)} \times D_{(it)}$ significantly reduces the mean value of the residuals, to 0.02. On technical grounds, it is a better model and as illustrated in the text, it is a better substantive model, too.

years for more than three years between 1976 and 1992.[21] Thus, although time is a friend to local officials, it is not necessarily on their side because the central government controls all the cards and has the sole authority to time appointment decisions.

Alternative dependent variables

The analysis can now be extended to two alternative forms of dependent variables. One is renovation investments ($RI_{(it)}$). As noted before, $RI_{(it)}$ is heavily controlled by the local governments, and $RI_{(it)}$ finances capacity expansion and is functionally similar to $LI_{(it)}$. Thus $RI_{(it)}$ here is treated analogously to local investments. The other is central investments ($CI_{(it)}$). As posited by our theory of investment dynamics in Chinese provinces, $CI_{(it)}$ is a contrarian investment category from $LI_{(it)}$. Thus, in the case of $RI_{(it)}$ we should expect to obtain similar results as with $LI_{(it)}$ in regard to the signs of the coefficients for the bureaucratic terms; in the case of $CI_{(it)}$, the results should be opposite. The regression estimates appear in table 8.6.

A glance at the results of column (3) reveals that none of the bureaucratic terms are statistically significant when $CI_{(it)}$ is the dependent variable. The various bureaucratic characteristics of local officials are simply irrelevant as far as explaining patterns of central investment behavior is concerned, although the signs for the bureaucratic variables are consistent with the prediction that they are opposite to those for $LI_{(it)}$ and $RI_{(it)}$. Central investments primarily reflect the decisions of the central ministries, and the bulk of financing costs are borne by them; local officials only affect these decisions or contribute to their costs marginally. Taking this into account, I formulate a variant form of $CI_{(it)}$, which is the ratio of central investments to local investments. The central/local investment ratio ($CLIR_{(it)}$) measures the trade-off relationship between central and local investments. This formulation captures the central–local investment conflicts more aptly: an increment in the rise of central investments is achieved by an increment in the decline of local investments. Local officials are depicted as having to make a choice between central and local projects in their allocative deliberations at the margin. As discussed in chapter 5, one central policy concern is the resource flows from central projects to local projects, which would produce smaller values of the $CLIR_{(it)}$. It is also a good measure of local officials' behavior inasmuch as local officials themselves apply the central/local investment ratios to evaluate the implementation of central

---

21. The number of provinces increases to twelve when the threshold is lowered to two years.

Table 8.6. *Local, renovation, and central investments and the central–local investment trade-off*

Dependent variables	$LI_{(it)}$	$RI_{(it)}$	$CI_{(it)}$	$CLIR_{(it)}$
Substantive				
$APP_{(it-1)}$	−0.13*	−0.14*	0.002	0.06**
	(0.04)	(0.036)	(0.045)	(0.042)
$BINT_{(it)}$	−0.05*	−0.02	0.03	0.05*
	(0.023)	(0.022)	(0.027)	(0.015)
AP	−0.09*	−0.05*	−0.02	0.03**
	(0.016)	(0.014)	(0.018)	(0.017)
Setting				
Intercept	1.13*	0.88*	1.01*	0.22*
	(0.233)	(0.242)	(0.327)	(0.08)
$Region_{(east)}$	0.35**	0.07	−0.04	−0.11*
	(0.21)	(0.219)	(0.295)	(0.072)
$Region_{(int)}$	−0.01	−0.10	−0.02	−0.001
	(0.085)	(0.084)	(0.107)	(0.052)
$Region_{(west)}$	0.07	−0.34**	−0.08	−0.05
	(0.21)	(0.217)	(0.292)	(0.072)
$FI_{(it)}$	0.21*	0.10*	0.07**	—
	(0.03)	(0.029)	(0.037)	
$NKS_{(it)}$	0.06*	0.08*	0.07*	—
	(0.005)	(0.005)	(0.007)	
$RC_{(it)}$	−0.17**	0.04	0.03	—
	(0.11)	(0.107)	(0.136)	
Lagged term	—	—	—	0.43*
				(0.03)
Adjusted R^2	0.63	0.67	0.35	0.42
Number of observations	399	388	399	410
D-W statistic	1.50	1.68	1.57	1.39

Note: Standard errors are in parentheses. Significance tests are one-tailed. The model estimated is $BM_{(joint)}$ + FM for $LI_{(it)}$, $RI_{(it)}$, and $CI_{(it)}$; for $CLIR_{(it)}$, the lag model is used to produce the estimates.
* $p < 0.05$.
** $p < 0.1$.
Source: Database.

investment policies. Column (4) in table 8.6 produces the regression results with $CLIR_{(it)}$ as the dependent variable.[22]

Comparisons across the rows illustrate a highly regular pattern: the coefficient signs of the two bureaucratic terms $APP_{(it-1)}$ and $BINT_{(it)}$, are internally

22. A trial-and-error approach reveals that none of the economic variables are significantly related to $CLIR_{(it)}$. Therefore I used the lag model to calculate the estimates.

consistent in similar investment categories but are different across different investment categories. Between $LI_{(it)}$ and $RI_{(it)}$, the two dependent variables that denote pursuit of local investment interests, both bureaucratic variables have a negative effect: newly appointed officials or those with stronger ties to the Center tend to constrain $LI_{(it)}$ and $RI_{(it)}$. In sharp contrast, when the dependent variable is formulated as $CI_{(it)}$ and $CLIR_{(it)}$ – roughly, a proxy for central investment interests – the coefficient signs change to positive (although the terms are not statistically significant to explain $CI_{(it)}$).[23]

The dependent variable $CLIR_{(it)}$ measures the central–local investment trade-off, and both $APP_{(it-1)}$ and $BINT_{(it)}$ are positively related to $CLIR_{(it)}$ (and at a statistically significant level). This means, all else being equal, that newly appointed officials and those with closer organizational ties to the Center are willing to favor central investment interests *at the expense* of local investment interests. Another way to confirm this result is to contrast the malleability of the bureaucratic effects with the constancy of the financial effects. When the dependent variable is changed from $LI_{(it)}$ and $RI_{(it)}$ to $CI_{(it)}$, two of the three financial variables do not change their signs; they are always positive no matter which dependent variable is used. The one that does change, $RC_{(it)}$, is statistically insignificant. Although similar economic conditions affect local and central investments similarly, similar bureaucratic conditions have a differential impact on these two types of investments because the underlying incentive structures differ.

That the central–local investment trade-off depends on the degree of central administrative control is a highly illuminating finding. As noted before, channeling resources from local to central projects constitutes one of the most important objectives of the central industrial policies, and our analysis shows that certain institutional characteristics facilitate this industrial policy of the central government. Once again, this result is consistent with our empirical evidence, which shows a positive correlation between administrative localism and investment localism. A natural inference is that administrative localism is inversely correlated with the ability of the central government to implement its investment interests *at the expense* of local investment interests.[24] The allocation of investment resources between central and local investment projects, probably at the margin, is a function of the bureaucratic incentive structures facing local officials. Investment localism – as measured both in terms of the ability to undertake local projects ($LI_{(it)}$) and the ability to do so at the expense

---

23. The austerity policy is found to boost $CLIR_{(it)}$, in contrast to its suppressive effect when the dependent variable is local investment.

24. Our earlier analysis shows that local bureaucratic characteristics do not explain central investment levels per se.

of central projects ($CLIR_{(it)}$) – is less severe in those cases in which administrative localism is curbed by frequent office turnovers and by organizational integration.

Varied-effects models

The effect of bureaucratic terms on local investments has just been examined under the assumption that the effect does not vary with regard to time or time-related factors: that is to say, the regression coefficients are constants and they stay the same across different time periods or different values of the variables. Under this assumption, our models say, for example, that the relationship between $BINT_{(it)}$ and local investments is the same during an austerity policy regime as it is during an inflationary policy regime, or it was the same in 1992 as it was in 1978. This assumption may well be questioned. As already demonstrated, the $TENTOP_{(it)}$ coefficient varies with the values of $TENTOP_{(it)}$; when $TENTOP_{(it)}$ is less than 5.5, the coefficient is zero, but it becomes 0.02 when $TENTOP_{(it)}$ exceeds 5.5. That our coefficients are not strictly linear should not be surprising, and it accords with our hypothesis that tenure security may have an implicit threshold. Before the threshold, there is no tenure security, but after the threshold, there is. Avidly pushing local investment interests is a behavioral characteristic of extreme tenure security.

In addition, the effect of our variables on local investments may also vary with other factors. For example, one might argue that the economic reforms have reduced the role of the government in the economy, thus weakening the relationship between bureaucratic terms and investment levels over time. Because the reforms have deepened with the passage of time, the size of the bureaucratic coefficients, measured in absolute values, should be a decreasing function of time. Conversely, the control hypothesis employed in this book is that although the central government has relinquished much of its direct economic control over time, it has compensated for this loss by augmenting administrative control. Thus the bureaucratic coefficients – in absolute values – should be an increasing function of time (or remain unchanged). In either case, a more realistic assumption is that the effect of the bureaucratic terms changes systematically with events that are time-dependent, such as changes in macroeconomic policies, economic reforms, or developments in bureaucratic institutions.

Our ex ante expectations are twofold. First, since the Center is likely to activate, or apply more forcefully, those instruments of control during an austerity period, the importance of those factors that normally constrain local investments can be expected to increase. This is based on the reasoning that those local officials who normally suppress local investment interests should do so more ardently when the central government makes explicit demands on them to do so. Analogously, the importance of the expansive bureaucratic variables can be expected to decline. That is to say, local officials act on their own investment interests less strongly when central macroeconomic policies disapprove of such behavior. The second expectation regards changes in the effect of the bureaucratic terms along with time-related trends. Time, as used in this book, is a proxy for many developments for which there is no direct measure. Two such time-related trends are pertinent to our analysis. One is the increased personnel supervision and monitoring that has been instituted since the 1983 personnel reforms; the other is the greater investment autonomy in the hands of enterprises as a result of the economic reforms. These two trends produce opposite effects on the size of the bureaucratic coefficients. Thus in the real world, because economic and administrative reforms work at cross purposes, the two effects may cancel out each other and the size of the bureaucratic coefficients may remain constant. To test whether changes in central macroeconomic policies, in personnel practices, and economic reforms alter the parameters of local investment autonomy, it is necessary to examine how the bureaucratic variables are related to investments by incorporating appropriate interaction terms. Our hypotheses are then tested by examining the statistical significance of these interaction terms and their directions. Our hypothesis regarding the macroeconomic policy effect is that all policy interaction terms should be negative and statistically significant; our hypothesis regarding the effect of time is that the time interaction terms should not be statistically significant.

I create two time-related dummy variables and an interaction term with each of these two dummy variables. One dummy variable is the change in the macroeconomic policy regime, alternating between the austerity and inflationary periods. It takes the value of one when the austerity policy is in effect and zero when it is not. The other is a time variable, which takes the value of one for 1976, two for 1977, and three for 1978, etc. Roughly, this time variable contains two conflicting trends – the economic decentralization that should weaken the effect of the bureaucratic variables and the administrative centralization that should strengthen it. If our hypothesis is correct, time interaction terms should not be significantly different from zero. The results appear in table 8.7.

Both of our expectations are confirmed. A macroeconomic policy change has a clear impact on the size of the bureaucratic coefficients. Of the four interaction terms, three are statistically significant and they are negative, meaning that there is a downward shift in the size of the bureaucratic coefficients

Table 8.7. *Bureaucratic coefficients as a function of austerity policy and economic reforms*

Variable	Policy interaction (with $APP_{(it-1)}$)	Policy interaction (with TENTOP)	Time interaction (with $APP_{(it-1)}$)
Substantive			
$TENTOP_{(it)}$	—	−0.005	—
		(0.009)	
$TENTOPI_{(it)}$	—	0.02*	—
		(0.009)	
Interaction term	—	−0.01	—
		(0.009)	
$APP_{(it-1)}$	−0.08**	—	−0.21*
	(0.054)		(0.11)
Interaction term	−0.10**	—	0.01
	(0.057)		(0.014)
$BINT_{(it)}$	−0.03	−0.04**	−0.09**
	(0.023)	(0.025)	(0.048)
Interaction term	−0.04*	−0.04*	0.004
	(0.009)	(0.009)	(0.005)
AP	—	—	−0.02
			(0.39)
Interaction term	—	—	−0.006**
			(0.004)
Setting			
Intercept	1.09*	1.14*	1.14*
	(0.23)	(0.253)	(0.23)
$Region_{(east)}$	0.33**	0.34**	0.34*
	(0.21)	(0.227)	(0.21)
$Region_{(int)}$	−0.01	−0.01	−0.01
	(0.08)	(0.06)	(0.063)
$Region_{(west)}$	0.07	0.04	0.05
	(0.21)	(0.25)	(0.21)
Adjusted R^2	0.63	0.60	0.64
Number of observations	399	418	399
D-W statistic	1.58	1.75	1.51

Note: Standard errors are in parentheses. Significance tests are one-tailed. The model estimated is $BM_{(joint)}$ + FM. $TENTOPI_{(it)}$ = $TENTOP_{(it)} \times D_{(it)}$. Financial variables are omitted from the table.
* $p < 0.05$.
** $p < 0.1$.
Source: Database.

during the austerity period. The interaction term for the long tenure, although also carrying a negative sign, does not reach statistical significance. During the inflationary period, the long tenure coefficient is 0.02 ($TENTOP_{(it)}$), -0.08 for $APP_{(it-1)}$, and -0.03 or -0.04 for $BINT_{(it)}$; during the austerity period, the three coefficients are 0.02, -0.18, and -0.07 or -0.08, respectively.[25] The downward shifts in the appointment and integration terms are consistent with our predictions that during the austerity period the normally constraining factors become more constraining. However, the normally expansive factor – long tenure duration in this case – seems not to be affected by the macroeconomic policy change.

The hypothesis that economic reforms and administrative centralization tend to cancel each other in terms of their effect on the bureaucratic coefficients is also confirmed. Under column (3), none of the interaction terms for the bureaucratic terms is significantly different from zero, meaning that the bureaucratic coefficients do not vary with time. Thus the relationship between $APP_{(it-1)}$ and $BINT_{(it)}$, on the one hand, and $LI_{(it)}$, on the other, has remained constant since 1976, a remarkable finding considering the enormous changes in the Chinese economic system, which is prima facie evidence of the continuous strength of bureaucratic control of the investment process despite reforms. The time-variant model can also be used to determine whether the effect of the austerity policy has varied with time by creating an interaction term between austerity policy and time. The interaction term is negative and is statistically significant at the 0.1 level. This means that the effectiveness of the austerity policy in reducing local investment has *increased* over time, a finding that directly contradicts the conventional wisdom in studies of the Chinese reforms, but this is consistent with the time-series findings presented in chapter 7. Using -0.006 to calculate the time-series changes in the effectiveness of the austerity policy yields the following result: in 1981, the austerity policy regime reduced local investment growth by about 3.6 percent; in 1986, by 6.6 percent; and in 1989, by 8 percent. Thus, in 1989 the effectiveness of the austerity policy was more than twice the level in 1981.

Conclusion

Two broad characteristics of Chinese local officials play a role in their pursuit of local investment interests. One is the political standing of top provincial officials in the political system, as measured by their organizational ties to the

---

25. These are given by $TENTOP_{(it)}$ + Interaction term, $APP_{(it-1)}$ + Interaction term, and $BINT_{(it)}$ + Interaction term. Because the interaction term for the long tenure is not statistically significant, it is zero.

Center. The other is leadership stability in the provinces, as measured by office turnovers and length of tenure of local officials.

The operational hypothesis here – that is, the control hypothesis that underlines much of the regression analysis – is that administrative control methods can be used to curb local investment demand and, by implication, to curb shirking when provinces are required to contribute to inflation control. The integration of provincial leaders into the central political machinery is said to be a mechanism by which control is imposed on provincial leaders. Offering central Party or government posts to provincial leaders forces them to take the perspective of the Center, rather than that of their provinces, if and when any policy conflicts arise between them. Dispatching centralists to run provinces, on the other hand, ensures that these top provincial leaders are first and foremost loyal to the Center, and that they will place central interests above those of the provinces of which they are put in charge. In short, the investment interest divergence between the Center and the localities is smaller in provinces run by concurrent or past centralists, but greater in provinces run by those with exclusively local backgrounds.

Our concept of leadership stability is desegregated into two components. One is leadership succession; frequent leadership successions mean frequent bureaucratic turnovers. Our hypothesis posits that bureaucratic turnovers increase central supervision and monitoring because personnel decisions are made by the Center. Conversely, long tenure services denote precisely the opposite dynamic. Long tenure durations reduce central supervision and monitoring because the Center selects personnel less frequently. In an information-constrained environment, selecting personnel is a relatively efficient control instrument in comparison with directly supervising specific investment activities.

Of course, alternative scenarios are possible. The bargaining hypothesis posits that closer provincial integration helps advance provincial investment objectives because it provides access to central decision makers and supplies channels of influence. Thus having representation at the Center or having centralists as top provincial leaders is considered a bargaining asset from the point of view of provincial investment interests. The same hypothesis also posits that bargaining plagues the personnel appointment process, and thus that newly selected officials are likely to take local interests to heart.

The empirical analysis in this chapter is broadly consistent with the control hypothesis. Formal organizational ties to the Center meaningfully constrain local investment demand. Closer bureaucratic integration, whether denoting provincial representation at the Center or a central presence in the provinces, implies more stringent administrative control by the Center or less divergence of interests, two conditions that reduce shirking behavior. This result, rather concretely and systematically, confirms the impression of a number of China scholars who view the Chinese political system as disciplined and organizationally rigorous.

Our empirical results on leadership stability support a modified form of the control hypothesis. Provincial leaders with extraordinarily long tenure durations are more likely to engage in shirking behavior and are more successful in pursuing local investment interests. Extraordinarily long tenure is defined here as service beyond 5.5 years. The analysis shows that an initial boosting effect accompanies leadership succession, which is evidence for the notion that there is a "honeymoon" period when a leader's actions are less critically appraised; typically the first year of appointment provides a window of opportunity for new officials to launch local projects, whether to placate local colleagues or to establish a name for themselves quickly. Like a honeymoon for married couples, however, it inevitably comes to an end, and in China's case it ends rather swiftly. When the local investment level is regressed on the appointment variables in the last year, the coefficients inevitably come out negative.

Recall that the average tenure for top officials is less than four years, despite the nominal provision of five-year terms in local organizational law. It is possible that provincial officials simply expect their tenure to last for about three to four years and that this expectation shapes their behavior accordingly. It is reasonable to believe that newly appointed officials would want to placate both their local colleagues and their superiors in Beijing, but when their local colleagues and their superiors in Beijing place conflictual demands on them, an optimal tactic is to time their actions strategically. It makes sense first to expand on local interests immediately after appointment, either because of less close supervision or because of the feeling that their tenure is secure; over time, it makes sense to switch behaviors and to take central interests more seriously. This increases their survival odds. Like junior faculty members, they first undertake activities that may be disapproved of, but they modify and even reverse their behavior as "tenure review" approaches. After all, they are not elected by their local colleagues: it is officials in the Department of Organization and the State Council who are calling the shots. The economic behavior of Chinese local officials reflects the fact that they operate under a tight political hierarchy in which they have little control over their destinies.

The findings that local officials' investment behavior is a function of their appointment timings is broadly consistent with the new political economy thesis that the strategic motives of politicians drive economic behavior. The "political business cycle" theory, for example, postulates that politicians manipulate economic policies in order to increase their electoral chances (Hibbs

1977; Nordhaus 1975). On the eve of an election, politicians purposely increase aggregate demand to achieve a temporary rise in income in order to get elected. Or, in a more ideological political system, left-wing politicians tend to increase public expenditures in order to reduce unemployment as a move to appease unions; right-wing politicians, on the other hand, pursue retrenchment policies to woo support from financial interests.

The preceding analysis has shown that cross-sectional variations in provincial supervision and monitoring are systematically correlated with cross-sectional variations in local investment compliance. Two inferences emerge here. First, the enhancement of central administrative control over time leads to more local compliance, all other things being equal. Second, the bureaucratic characteristics of local officials heavily shape their economic behavior. Herein lies the possible biases when an analysis focuses only on economic variables: the analyst may erroneously conclude that the central government has lost ground to local officials and is unable to assert control over the macroeconomic process. Although it is often a truism to say that politics and economics are intermingled, conventional approaches tend to stress the one explanation at the expense of the other.

APPENDIX

Model specifications

The three economic and bureaucratic models used to generate the results reported in chapter 8 are presented here in equation form. The hypothesized direction of the effect of the independent variables appear below each equation. I do not attempt to specify the direction of the intercept term (α_0 or β_0). The intercept term contains the regional effect of Anhui province, which is omitted when creating $Region_{(east)}$, $Region_{(interior)}$, and $Region_{(west)}$. Because the dependent variable is logged, the negative intercept term simply means that the investment volume is less than one hundred million yuan.

Economic models

Lag model. The lag model takes the following form:

$$LI_{(it)} = \alpha_0 + \alpha_1 MLI_{(it-1)}$$
$$\alpha_1 > 0$$

where $LI_{(it)}$ is the logged value of local investment in province i and in year t, evaluated at the previous year's prices; and $MLI_{(it-1)}$ is the logged value of three-year moving averages of local investment in province i and in year $t-1$ evaluated at the previous year's prices.

Financial model. The financial model takes the following form:

$$LI_{(it)} = \alpha_0 + \alpha_1 FI_{(it)} + \alpha_2 NKS^2_{(it)} + \alpha_3 RC_{(it)}$$
$$\alpha_1 > 0 \quad \alpha_2 > 0 \quad \alpha_3 < 0$$

where $FI_{(it)}$ is the logged value of foreign investment in province i and in year t, evaluated at the previous year's prices; $NKS_{(it)}$ is the logged value of net capital stock in province i and in year t, evaluated at the previous year's prices; and $RC_{(it)}$ is the logged value of revenue contributions by province i and in year t, evaluated at the previous year's prices.

Development model. The development model takes the following form:

$$LI_{(it)} = \alpha_0 + \alpha_1 PCI_{(it)} + \alpha_2 IND_{(it)} + \alpha_3 NRO_{(it)}$$
$$\alpha_1 > 0 \quad \alpha_2 > 0 \quad \alpha_3 < 0$$

where $PCI_{(it)}$ is the logged value of per capita income in province i and in year t, evaluated at the previous year's prices; $IND_{(it)}$ is the logged value of net industrial product in province i and in year t, evaluated at the previous year's prices; and $NRO_{(it)}$ is the logged value of net resource outflows measured in ratios of provincial NMP to the provincial utilized NMP.

Bureaucratic models

Bureaucratic models for joint officials take the following form:

$$LI_{(it)} = \beta_0 + \beta_2 APP_{(it)} + \beta_3 BINT_{(it)}$$
$$H_{(con)}: \quad \beta_2 < 0 \quad \beta_3 < 0$$
$$H_{(bar)}: \quad \beta_2 > 0 \quad \beta_3 > 0$$

Or

$$LI_{(it)} = \beta_0 + \beta_1 TEN_{(it)} + \beta_3 BINT_{(it)}$$
$$H_{(con)}: \quad \beta_1 > 0 \quad \beta_3 < 0$$
$$H_{(bar)}: \quad \beta_3 > 0$$

where $H_{(con)}$ is the control hypothesis, $H_{(bar)}$ is the bargaining hypothesis, $TEN_{(it)}$ is the average tenure of top and secondary officials measured in years, $APP_{(it)}$ is the ratio of new top and secondary officials to the total number of officials, and $BINT_{(it)}$ is the average bureaucratic integration scores for Party secretaries and governors ranging from 1 (insider) to 4 (concurrent centralist).

In addition, models for top and secondary officials are estimated separately, with the following bureaucratic variables and with the same specifications as above: $TENTOP_{(it)}$ is the average tenure of Party secretaries and governors measured in years; $APPTOP_{(it)}$ is a dummy variable of 0 when there is no appointment of top officials, 1 when there is one appointment, and 2 when there are two appointments; $TENSEC_{(it)}$ is the average tenure of secondary Party and government officials; and $APPSEC_{(it)}$ is the percentage of newly added secondary officials to the total number of secondary officials.

Regression technique

The data are structured in a manner known as the pooling of cross sections of time series. For technical reasons, the ordinary least-squares approach cannot be used. Instead, the generalized least squares (GLS) method has been used to produce all the estimates. It is likely that the threat to the homoskedasticity assumption comes from time-series trends, and therefore I use the Durbin procedure to produce p-estimates lagged by one year. To control for any possible cross-sectional influences on residual variances, I divide all provinces into three exclusive categories (minus Anhui as an implicit fourth category): $Region_{(east)}$, $Region_{(int)}$, and $Region_{(west)}$. I also run regressions with each province as a regional dummy variable (again minus Anhui); the results are not different (see the next section). For useful references on the application of the GLS, see Stimson (1985) and Hanushek and Jackson (1977).

Regression diagnostics

A number of tests can be conducted to determine the quality of the model specifications and the individual estimates. There are three areas of concern. The first has to do with measurement errors, which can change drastically our estimates when model specifications are changed. The second concern is multicollinearity among the bureaucratic variables. Multicollinearity among economic terms is less of a concern since these terms are included only to impose control for the structural factors; however, collinearity between economic and bureaucratic terms is a concern. The third concern has to do with determining the direction of the causality in the relationship between bureaucratic and investment variables.

The measurement errors are checked by specifying alternative economic models. If our bureaucratic coefficients are reasonably consistent across different model specifications, then measurement errors are not severe. Also, this procedure helps us detect any collinearity between economic and bureaucratic terms. Our baseline model is $BM_{(joint)}$ + FM; in table A8.1, I compare the findings across four specifications: $BM_{(joint)}$ + FM, $BM_{(joint)}$ + DM, $BM_{(joint)}$ + LM, and $BM_{(joint)}$ by itself.

Just as in $BM_{(joint)}$ + FM, all the economic variables are consistent with our hypothesis. Rich provinces and provinces with a large industrial size tend to have higher investment levels; the negative effect of the $NRO_{(it)}$ term is also consistent with our knowledge about local protectionism and local aversion to interprovincial trade. Trade conducted in an environment of administrative pricing reduces resources available for domestic capital construction.

As an indication of the stability and robustness of our bureaucratic coefficients, neither the signs of the coefficients nor their magnitudes depend on the underlying economic variables included in the models. The signs for the appointment and integration terms ($APP_{(it-1)}$ and $BINT_{(it)}$) remain negative across four very different economic specifications, and their magnitudes vary within a very narrow range, between -0.13 and -0.14 for $APP_{(it-1)}$ and between -0.05 and -0.06 for $BINT_{(it)}$. Similarly, the signs and the size of the coefficients for an austerity policy term remain stable across the four model specifications; the signs are negative, and the coefficients fluctuate within a narrow band (between -0.07 and -0.10).

Our calculation shows that there is complete independence between the bureaucratic

Table A8.1. *Four model specifications*

Variable	(1) $BM_{(joint)} + FM$	(2) $BM_{(joint)} + DM$	(3) $BM_{(joint)} + LM$	(4) $BM_{(joint)}$
Substantive				
$APP_{(it-1)}$	−0.13*	−0.14*	−0.13*	−0.13*
	(0.04)	(0.039)	(0.05)	(0.039)
$BINT_{(it)}$	−0.05*	−0.06*	−0.06*	−0.05*
	(0.023)	(0.02)	(0.02)	(0.023)
AP	−0.09*	−0.07*	−0.10*	−0.09*
	(0.016)	(0.016)	(0.02)	(0.016)
Setting				
Intercept	1.13*	−1.82*	0.133	4.42*
	(0.233)	(0.44)	(0.128)	(1.20)
$Region_{(east)}$	0.35*	0.21	0.05	1.56**
	(0.21)	(0.22)	(0.11)	(1.25)
$Region_{(int)}$	−0.01	0.05	−0.02	0.05
	(0.085)	(0.08)	(0.07)	(0.20)
$Region_{(west)}$	0.07	0.29**	0.02	−0.06
	(0.21)	(0.226)	(0.104)	(1.27)
$FI_{(it)}$	0.21*	—	—	—
	(0.03)			
$NKS_{(it)}$	0.06*	—	—	—
	(0.005)			
$RC_{(it)}$	−0.24**	—	—	—
	(0.11)			
$PCI_{(it)}$	—	0.35*	—	—
		(0.068)		
$IND_{(it)}$	—	0.56*	—	—
		(0.045)		
$NRO_{(it)}$	—	−0.46*	—	—
		(0.25)		
Lagged term	—	—	0.70	—
			(0.02)	
Adjusted R^2	0.63	0.57	0.80	0.12
Number of observations	399	411	410	413
D-W statistic	1.50	1.62	1.30	1.51
Partial F-statistic	23.42*	11.07*	0.72	—

Note: Standard errors are in parentheses. Significance tests are one-tailed.
* $p < 0.05$.
** $p < 0.1$.
Source: Database.

Table A8.2. *Variations of* $BM_{(joint)}$ + *FM*

Substantive variable	Baseline model	SH & BJ excluded	Provincial dummy variables
$APP_{(it-1)}$	−0.13*	−0.13*	−0.12*
	(0.04)	(0.039)	(0.04)
$BINT_{(it)}$	−0.05*	−0.06*	−0.06*
	(0.023)	(0.025)	(0.023)
AP	−0.09*	−0.09*	−0.09*
	(0.016)	(0.016)	(0.016)
Adjusted R^2	0.63	0.63	0.78
Number of observations	399	369	399
D-W statistic	1.50	1.47	1.48

Note: Standard errors are in parentheses. Significance tests are one-tailed. Only the relevant bureaucratic coefficients are presented.
* $p < 0.05$.
** $p < 0.1$.
Source: Database.

terms and economic terms. The bureaucratic coefficients generated by running $BM_{(joint)}$ alone are not different from other models that include various economic variables. This has both technical and substantive significance. Such independence gives us confidence that the coefficients of the bureaucratic terms measure what they are supposed to measure – namely, various characteristics of provincial personnel selection and control – rather than the spurious effects emanating from the economic variables. Second, because of the uncertainty in the underlying economic models for investment behavior, the statistical independence of the bureaucratic terms ensures the accuracy of the regression estimates of the bureaucratic terms, even if we specify the wrong economic variables in our investment models.

I also want to explore the possibility that our findings are influenced excessively by extreme values. As noted in chapter 6, Beijing and Shanghai belong to a class by themselves in terms of their extremely high BINT values. A legitimate question arises as to the uniqueness of Beijing and Shanghai, and it is necessary to explore whether the negative effect of BINT is confined to Beijing and Shanghai or whether it is a systemwide effect. Thus I recalculate $BM_{(joint)}$ + FM, but exclude Beijing and Shanghai. Also, as noted before, I create three regional dummy variables for groups of provinces according to their geographic locations in order to control for the cross-sectional inter-dependence in the dependent variable; a more conventional approach is to include each province (minus one) as a regional dummy. In table A8.2, I also examine the effect of changes in this coding strategy. For simplicity, I only present coefficients for our bureaucratic variables, $APP_{(it-1)}$ and $BINT_{(it)}$. Again, our regression results come out very strongly. There are no differences in the three substantive variables both in terms of their signs and of their statistical magnitudes. That our results do not depend on extreme values and on the adoption of a particular coding strategy implies that the specification of the BINT term is robust.

Table A8.3. *Stepwise procedure to check on multicollinearity*

Substantive variables	(1) Both APP & BINT	(2) APP only	(3) BINT only	(4) Both TENTOPI & BINT	(5) TENTOPI only
$APP_{(it-1)}$	−0.13* (0.04)	−0.14* (0.04)	—	—	—
$TENTOPI_{(it)}$	—	—	—	0.02* (0.009)	0.02* (0.007)
$BINT_{(it)}$	−0.05* (0.023)	—	−0.06* (0.023)	−0.06* (0.023)	—
Adjusted R^2	0.63	0.62	0.59	0.60	0.58
Number of observations	399	399	418	418	419
D-W statistic	1.50	1.50	1.67	1.70	1.65

Note: Standard errors are in parentheses. Significance tests are one-tailed. $TENTOPI_{(it)} = TENTOP_{(it)} \times D_{(it)}$. Only the relevant bureaucratic coefficients are presented.
* $p < 0.05$.
** $p < 0.1$.
Source: Database.

Another possibility to consider is whether there is multicollinearity among our bureaucratic variables. When multicollinearity is present, the individual estimates are suspect, as they can easily change when a related variable is added or dropped. I adopt a stepwise procedure to detect the presence of multicollinearity between $APP_{(it-1)}$ and $BINT_{(it)}$, and between $TEN_{(it)}$ and $BINT_{(it)}$. The results are displayed in table A8.3; for simplicity, only the relevant bureaucratic terms are displayed. Our bureaucratic coefficients are stable when the bureaucratic variables are run either together or separately. Thus there is no evidence that bureaucratic terms covary.

Throughout this book, our model suggests that the causal direction runs from bureaucratic to investment variables. However, it is plausible to argue that the causal relationship may run in the opposite direction. For example, the negative BINT term may imply that the central government promotes those officials who carry out central investment decrees more enthusiastically than others. In this section, I employ Granger test procedures, empirical consistency, and theoretical parsimony to determine the appropriate causal directions. The Granger test procedures establish the temporal sequence between two variables and thus they can establish a necessary condition for causality. The basic idea is that the current and past values of the exogenous variable should be better predictors of the endogenous variable as compared with the future values of the exogenous variable if the causation is unidirectional. In the presence of bidirectionality, the future values of the exogenous variable would also have predictive power.[26]

26. Another way of stating this condition is that future values of the exogenous variable are not different from zero in the case of unidirectionality and are different from zero in the case of bidirectionality. For a detailed explanation of this procedure and application, see Sims (1972). For a good review of different Granger tests, see Bishop (1979).

Table A8.4. F-*statistics of the future values of APP, TENURE, and BINT with one to three future lags*

Lag structure	APP	TENURE	BINT
t + 3	9.94*	2.81	0.43
t + 2	23.32*	13.61*	9.45*
t + 1	10.78*	5.09*	1.89

* $p < 0.05$.
** $p < 0.1$.
Source: Database.

Table A8.4 presents partial F-statistics. They are generated by adding the future values of the bureaucratic variable – from one to three future lags – to the current and the past values (with two lags) of the bureaucratic variables. In addition, the models include a lagged investment term (by one year) and the three regional terms. The GLS is applied to correct for the serial correlations. The results suggest the presence of bidirectionality, especially concerning the appointment terms. Of the nine F-statistics under three different lag structures, six are statistically significant at the 0.05 level. Similar results are produced when $LI_{(it)}$ and bureaucratic variables are regressed on each other alternatively as independent and dependent variables, using their current and past values.

The presence of causal bidirectionality, in and of itself, does not invalidate the conjecture that a causal relationship runs from the appointment system to local investment behavior; however it does call into question whether our conjecture is preferable to its alternatives. There are three reasons why our conjecture may be preferable. First, as Sims (1972) points out, if the exogenous variable can result in a set of expectations that may shape the movement of the endogenous variable, a unidirectional relationship is more likely to appear to be bidirectional than the other way around. Our model is expectational by attributing local investment behavior to ex ante monitoring and bureaucratic status of local officials. If our model is indeed correct, Granger-type bidirectionality should not be surprising.

The second reason applies to the $BINT_{(it)}$ term only. The $BINT_{(it)}$ term itself has already established a temporal order whereby the $BINT_{(it)}$ precedes $LI_{(it)}$ because it is constructed primarily on the basis of the administrative backgrounds of local officials. The classification of local officials into insiders, outsiders, and centralists all draws on information about their past administrative histories; only the coding of the concurrent centralists refers to their contemporaneous status. To avoid conceptual bidirectionality, I regress the $LI_{(it)}$ on $BINT_{(it)}$, excluding all the concurrent centralists. The result remains unchanged; the coefficient and standard error are −0.045* (0.026), compared with −0.05* (0.023) in column 1 of table 8.2. Given this result, the alternative conjecture that a causal relationship runs from $LI_{(it)}$ to $BINT_{(it)}$ would imply an implausible temporal sequence: namely, that contemporaneous investment behavior causes certain past bureaucratic characteristics.

The third reason is that the alternative conjectures are internally inconsistent for the APP and TENURE terms. If a causal relationship runs from $LI_{(it)}$ to bureaucratic variables, then the negative APP term may suggest that the central government takes local investment compliance into account in making appointment decisions: those officials engaging in investment shirking are more quickly removed than those compliant officials. However, the positive long-tenure term produces the conjecture that those officials who successfully develop local economies by increasing investment growth are rewarded by being kept in power longer. These two conjectures may be valid separately but not jointly. Jointly, the two conjectures would necessarily hypothesize an indeterminate reward structure on the part of the Center: local officials are rewarded for *both* promoting *and* suppressing local investments. As such, the alternative conjecture is inconsistent when both APP and TEN terms are statistically significant in a single model. When the APP term and the long-tenure term are both included (rather than separately, as in the text), the long-tenure term is positive (0.019) and is statistically significant at the 0.05 level. The APP term remains negative (−0.147) and is statistically significant at the 0.05 level.

In contrast, our conjecture that ex ante central monitoring via the appointment decisions shapes local investment behavior is consistent with both the negative APP term and with the positive long-tenure term. Although it is plausible that central appointment decisions are based on conflicting motives, on grounds of modeling consistency and parsimony, the conjecture that the causal relationship runs from bureaucratic variables to $LI_{(it)}$ is superior.

9

Conclusion: Political institutions, inflation control, and economic reforms

Among the findings of this study, perhaps one of the most significant is that Chinese political institutions are still quite authoritative. The connections between these institutions and inflation control help to explain why Chinese macroeconomic policy has differed so much from that of other reforming CPEs and why there may well be an optimal sequence for economic and political reforms. This and some of the present study's other conclusions about the large issues in the general political economy literature are the subject of this chapter.

Summary of findings

Before the relationships between bureaucratic constraints and investment behavior can be evaluated, they need to be placed in three broad contexts. First, inflation preferences systematically diverge between central and local policy authorities; in part, this systematic difference derives from the nature of inflation control as a public good and in part from some specific features of the Chinese economic system. Second, as distinct from their counterparts in the former Soviet Union, Chinese local officials have considerable operational autonomy and possess sizable economic resources to pursue their economic objectives. Third, in contrast to their economic status, Chinese local officials are dependent on central authorities for their political status and career advancement. These three broad contexts constitute the micro-foundation for the model-building efforts and empirical research described in this volume.

Inflation control as a public good

The nature of a public good is such that it is characterized by *nonexcludability*. That is to say, one person's consumption of the good cannot prevent other

305

people from consuming it. The condition of nonexcludability implies that a private provider of a public good cannot fully recoup its benefits, which further implies that the market cannot function efficiently in the provision of public goods because of the free-rider problem – that is, everybody has an incentive to understate his or her preference for the public good. This argument – known as the market failure argument – has often been used to support the government's role in providing law and order, defense, market regulations, innovations of new knowledge, and in financing their provisions with compulsory taxes.

Excessive investment produces negative externalities for local governments because they appropriate most of the investment returns – whether of a financial nature or employment related – while the costs are borne by the society at large. Narrowly, these costs can be the resource costs sunk in a failed project, or more broadly they are the economic and political costs of investment-induced inflation. In the absence of countervailing central policy actions, investment-induced inflation tends to be oversupplied.[1] Thus inflation control in China and in CPEs in general is a public good and its enforcement must be mandatory in character. Price stability, lower prices, and alleviated shortages of scarce goods – both financial and physical – are systemwide benefits that everyone, by virtue of being a member of the system, enjoys. In contrast, the costs of providing inflation control are specific to and can be highly concentrated on individual members. If, for example, Province A voluntarily contributes to inflation control by restraining its investment demand, while Province B refuses to do the same, Province A is in effect subsidizing the benefits associated with the lower level of inflation that Province B also enjoys. The more drastic the inflation control effort, the bigger the amount of such subsidies. Knowledge of the asymmetrical distribution of costs and benefits of inflation control creates a kind of prisoner's dilemma in which each member has an incentive to defect (i.e., not to control inflation), even though their joint welfare will be increased if they choose to cooperate (i.e., to control inflation).

For a number of reasons, inflation control is more of a public good and therefore the prisoner's dilemma is a more serious concern in CPEs than in market economies. In a market economy, the business community, specifically the financial sector, forms a strong political constituency for a low level of

---

1. This process is not limited to China. As Weingast, Shepsle, and Johnsen (1981) show formally, under a representative democracy there is a systematic bias toward a higher provision of projects than economic efficiency justifies. Geographically based representatives can concentrate the benefit of public projects in their regions while they spread the costs across all constituencies through generalized taxation.

inflation. Concerns about the eroding effect of inflation on the value of the business community's financial assets have priority over its concerns about the consequences of unemployment that are associated with a low level of inflation. Concerns about inflation are given a public policy voice because of the career paths of many of those in charge of making public monetary policies: many officials in the central banks have come from – and usually plan to return to – private financial institutions.[2]

By contrast, in a CPE state ownership of most or all of the productive assets implies that concerns about the long-term *real* appreciation of those assets are relatively weak. The "soft-budget" constraints, "investment hunger," and the chronic supply constraints discussed in chapters 1 and 5 can all be said to be auxiliary implications of this fundamental reality of CPEs. As the size of an enterprise or of the work force confers prestige and power on those bureaucrats in charge, concerns become stronger about the *nominal* appreciation of the assets or about the size of staff wages and benefits and about creating employment opportunities, stances that are consistent with preferences for inflation–unemployment trade-offs in favor of inflation.

To take the implication of the analogy between inflation control and public good provision one step further, it can be said that only the central government has the full incentive to control inflation. As shown in chapter 1, the central government bears disproportionate costs of the economic and political implications of inflation, whereas the other actors, including the local governments, have a strong incentive to free-ride. These conflicting incentives and central attempts to overcome them are what this book is all about.

Economic control

When there is a strong incentive in the system to free-ride and a disincentive to bear the adjustment costs, the question that immediately arises is how to enforce investment control, and by extension inflation control. Enforcement here encompasses two issues. One is how to achieve a desired aggregate level of investment volume and the other is how to allocate the adjustment costs among constituent members such that shirking is minimized. These two objectives are difficult to achieve in China because its economic reforms have placed immense economic resources and autonomy in the hands of the local authorities.

The basic facts of the Chinese economic reforms were examined in chapters 2 and 3. The important point to note here is that these reforms have enormous

---

2. For an analysis along this line, see Woolley (1985).

implications for the central–local relationship. The first and arguably the most significant of these is that local governments have acquired a separate economic identity (*jingji liyi zhuti*) from the central government. Although during the Maoist period administrative decentralization was quite far-reaching, most of the returns from investment or other activities of local governments were subject to the actual or potential appropriations by the tax and expenditure-setting powers of the central government. As the residual claimant and as the arbiter of final rule, the central government routinely adjusted in its favor the central–local balances of tax returns and of implied risks and benefits. As discussed in chapter 2, the fundamental change associated with the reforms is that the localities are now the residual claimants over investment returns. The tax contract system, which obligates provinces to turn over a fixed amount of tax and divides the residual by an ex ante formula, is probably the most pronounced manifestation of this new relationship.

This change in the governance structure between the Center and the localities has brought about incentive changes. Although local residual rights can be quite restricted and the central government often intervenes to increase its share, for example, by resorting to unserviced borrowings, the status of the residual claimants makes a huge difference in terms of how these central actions are perceived.[3] Post hoc interventions, which attenuate residual rights, constitute explicit costs on the owners' rightful claims, whereas ex ante interventions cause forgone benefits to the local governments. The incentive differences under the two alternative schemes arise because people respond to losses more strongly than to potential gains.[4] Thus local officials, as residual claimants, care about their shares of entitlements much more than they did about budgetary grants that failed to materialize. In incentive terms, the two are not yuan-to-yuan equivalents. What is relevant to our story is that requiring local officials to cut local projects and to channel resources to central projects in essence amounts to drawing down against the revenue claims of the local governments. As a result of the reforms, such actions elicit much more resistance from local officials than was previously the case.

The second implication, which is the one most studies of the Chinese economic reforms focus on, is that local officials have gained considerable economic and financial resources. These resources may be direct, as in the case of

---

3. "The rights of disposal over the residual income," Kornai (1992: 64) states, "are full if the owner can, if he or she so wishes, spend it all on personal consumption." Obviously, by this criterion, the Chinese localities only have restricted rights.

4. This is called a loss aversion function in studies of psychology. See Tversky and Kahneman (1990).

control over enterprises, tax- and revenue-setting powers, and investment approvals; or they can be indirect, as in the case of the ability to raise funds and to affect the sectoral allocation of credits and investment funds. Once local officials have greater control of resources, it is all the more difficult for central policy makers to realize their macroeconomic and industrial policy objectives. By the early 1990s China's central government was directly funding less than 50 percent of all projects under construction and approving less than 35 percent; local cooperation was thus a critical ingredient in any attempt to restore macroeconomic stability. The central government now faces severe resource constraints; this gap between its investment commitments and its resource control makes it necessary to seek local contributions (World Bank 1990b). In brief, the Center is now less economically dominant than it was before and thus has more difficulty imposing its investment preferences on the localities.

Political control

The Chinese political system, unlike its economic system, has remained fundamentally unchanged. It is still a one-party system and a highly developed form of a unitary political and bureaucratic system. In order to account fully for local investment behavior in these circumstances, it is necessary to pay attention not only to the economic resources controlled by the local officials but also to the position they occupy in the Chinese political system. How can economic and political forces that work at cross purposes be reconciled here, and how do they jointly give rise to the local investment behavior that we have observed?

The first point to note is that no matter how strong local officials have become in economic terms, they remain, as during the Maoist period, bureaucratic and political subordinates. All the top provincial officials are directly appointed by the central Party authorities and, as noted in chapter 4, the central Party authorities also closely monitor the selection of bureau-level officials. Apart from appointment power, some mechanisms of political and administrative control are also imposed on local officials. These officials typically have a short tenure, are rotated routinely among different provinces, and are carefully selected in order to produce the right mix in local Party and government establishments. Furthermore, the Center practices a strategic control approach. That is, it selectively integrates local officials into the central political apparatus. For example, the top Party officials of important provinces (such as Beijing, Shanghai, and Tianjin) are usually also Politburo members; during the reform era provincial representation on the Politburo has increased.

All of these practices are well-honed and have proven effective in the past to curb administrative localism. As also shown in chapter 4, central administrative monitoring capabilities have been enhanced by incremental and persistent efforts at building up those institutions and procedures that perform monitoring functions.

Two inferences can be made about issues involved in analyzing investment control. First, if attention is focused only on changes in the way economic resources are distributed, the potential of local officials to disobey central investment policies becomes exaggerated. Indeed, local compliance has not declined to the level that many China specialists assume from the effect of the economic reforms alone. Second, local investment behavior is a function not only of the distribution of economic resources, but also of the degree of preference divergence and of the distribution of information about the behavior of local officials. Local officials disobey central investment policies when they have a strong incentive to do so or when they think that they can get away with it. Thus the mechanisms in the Chinese system that affect incentive structures and monitoring have great bearing on the conduct of local investment.

Another point to note concerns the form of political and policy conflicts in the Chinese political system. This is an authoritarian system that discourages and severely punishes coalition building among interest groups. There are, of course, factions in Chinese politics, but very often they are based on lineage or shared ideological stances and are not marriages of convenience in the way that quid pro quo policy coalitions are.[5] Furthermore, factions cannot be explicitly organized and coordinated; a central proposal for a tax hike, for example, is not likely to enlist collective action from provincial governors opposing the scheme. Opposition is muted and is individually motivated. Also, there is a particular aversion in the Chinese political system to any attempt to form coalitions among local and military officials. In the mid-1950s, Gao Gang, chairman of the State Planning Commission, was removed as soon as it was suspected that he was forming a military and provincial political clique; one of the most serious charges leveled against Minister of Defense Peng Dehuai was that he attempted to collude with provincial officials from Hunan (See Li Rui 1989). More recently, the central government replaced Guangdong's powerful governor, Ye Xuanping, after he openly challenged Li Peng's proposal to phase out the provincial tax contract system ("Guangdong's economic predicament ...," 1990).

Because coalition-building activities are dormant, self-interest is not openly advocated. In turn, this suppression of the advocacy of self-interest – while not

---

5. On factions in Chinese politics, see Nathan (1973).

of self-interest per se – has several implications for studying local investment behavior. First, policy implementation is usually where the action is. The inability to influence anti-inflation policies during their formulation (at least in a collective and collusive manner) and the relative lack of capital mobility across regions as compared with market economies – due to the national scope of policy or to administrative restrictions – do not leave the localities many options with respect to protecting their self-interest during a period of austerity, other than not fully implementing the central policies. To paraphrase a well-known analogy (Hirschman 1970), if local officials cannot vote with their feet or with their voice, they may have to vote with their guile. Economic policy conflicts in China have little to do with street demonstrations or with debates in the corridors of the National People's Congress; these conflicts are scattered around the country, in various offices of industrial bureaucrats and firm managers.[6] In the economic arena, Chinese central officials often complain about the difficulties of bringing local officials into line with central policies: "there are policies at the top and there are counter-policies at the bottom" (*shangyou zhengce xiayou duice*) aptly captures this sentiment.

Note, too, that a shift in the arenas, from formulation to implementation, accentuates the ability of people to act on their self-interest. Influencing policy formulation suffers from the classic "collective action problems" identified by Olson (1965). The benefits of policy changes are reaped by everybody in the system; for example, a change from a restrictive to an expansionary monetary policy not only benefits those who labored to make the change possible, but also those who stood on the sidelines, waiting for the windfall. A nationally uniform policy does not discriminate among its recipients. In contrast, the political costs of openly advocating self-interest and of being perceived as a disruptive and uncooperative member of the community are both high and concentrated.[7] The benefits and costs of altering policy implementation, on the other hand, have a more symmetric distribution. The benefits of disobeying a central edict to reduce investment growth in Province A are completely absorbed by those in Province A, and they do not "spill over" into Province B. Indeed, the size of the benefits increases when Province B is compliant.

---

6. Ames (1987: 37) makes a similar point when he discusses how political structures shape the "sites" where political actions take place. He states: "Rules and structures translate interests into bargaining resources at particular sites. In industrial countries, legislatures and bureaucracies are the main sites. In Latin America, legislatures are sometimes important and bureaucracies always so, but claims are also pressed through personal and family connections, demonstrations, elections, strikes, and insurrections."

7. From this point of view, only Guangdong would have an incentive to openly oppose central tax reforms because it has a disproportionate stake in the status quo. Guangdong, in that sense, is analogous to a peak association in Olson's analysis (Olson 1965).

Reneging on an agreed-upon policy stance has its costs, of course. Sometimes these costs are merely psychological in the sense of the burden one must carry for being the recalcitrant party in the system. Or they can take the specific form of administrative punishment in more serious situations: in 1989 the State Council openly censured the municipal government of Wuxi in the Jiangsu provincial government for approving projects on the Center's ban list ("Guoban tongbao . . . ," 1989). The key issue here is that the bearing of these costs depends greatly on the probability of being detected. Provincial officials would alter the way a policy is being implemented only if they thought that they could get away with it. Variance in implementation decreases as central monitoring becomes more effective. Thus one comes full circle to the proposition derived from the political and bureaucratic dependency of Chinese local officials: monitoring is a critical condition that affects their ability to act on their self-interests and, in the present context, to act on their investment preferences.

Bureaucratic constraints and investment behavior

A number of conditions give rise to coordination problems – the oversupply of investment-induced inflation – in the Chinese economy. Inflation preference divergence between central and local governments plus informational asymmetry leads to what is known as the "agency problem": the incentive of lower-level agents to pursue actions that are suboptimal from the perspective of the principal. In our case, the agency problem arises when there is a tendency for local officials to increase investment growth and to channel investment resources in ways incompatible with central policies. This agency problem is exacerbated by the asymmetry of economic control.

Yet, China's reform experience is characterized by a conspicuous absence of large-scale coordination problems. Despite the widespread pessimism about its economic and administrative ability, the central government has been able to tame inflation *whenever* it commits itself to a firm austerity stance. In 1994, China's inflation rate was 25 percent and it declined to 16.7 percent on a year-to-year basis between July 1994 and July 1995. Although these rates are historically high for China, they pale in comparison with those for Russia (227 percent between August 1994 and August 1995) and with the best-performing East European economy, Poland (26 percent between July 1994 and July 1995).[8] Between 1988 and 1993, the high-inflation period for China, the

---

8. The latest inflation figures are from "Emerging Market Indicators," *Economist*, September 16–22, 1995.

annual inflation rate was about 13 percent, an impressive record compared with all the developing countries, except the industrializing East Asian economies.

How can one reconcile the potential for high inflation with the conspicuous absence of high inflation in the Chinese economy? How can one reconcile the abundant opportunities for agency problems with the periodic compliance of local officials? Our stylized model posits that the central government relies on political resources – namely, personnel allocation – to solve the coordination problems. Political centralization does so in several ways. For one thing, it alleviates the agency problem by converging, at least in part, inflation preferences; for another, it performs monitoring functions. Notice a sharp departure in our model from the previous research on the strength of the Chinese political system: compliance is obtained not as a result of discipline and coercion but as a result of an incentive-compatible arrangement under which it may be in the careerist interests of the local officials to comply with central policies.

The theoretical claim that local investment behavior is a function of central monitoring and interest divergence between central and local officials is both neat and elegant. The real question is, does it produce consistent empirical results that shed light on Chinese investment conduct, inflation dynamics, or the nature of Chinese political institutions?

The empirical analysis is performed in two ways and the results are in agreement. The first way is to examine variations in local investment behavior over time (time-series variations); the second way is to examine spatial variations in local investment behavior among Chinese provinces (cross-sectional variations). Although the specific techniques differ, the general approach is the same: Given a priori expectations about patterns of local investment behavior (or its relationships with other variables), are these patterns (or relationships) actually observed?

Because administrative monitoring and supervision appear to constrain investment shirking and because there has been an overall improvement in these two areas during the reform era, investment shirking can be expected to decline over time. This expectation is largely confirmed by comparing patterns of local investment behavior at different points in time during the reform era. In general, Chinese provinces have observed and carried out central investment preferences, both in terms of the level and structure of their investment programs; at the very least, this level of compliance is unexpected given the unprecedented scale of economic and fiscal devolution that has taken place during the reform decade and given the asymmetrical informational distribution. The reason for this outcome is that the informational distribution has become less asymmetrical over time and this development has led to lower bounds on investment shirking.

To be sure, it is quite possible that the overall level of investment compliance is probably not as impressive as it was in the 1950s and the 1960s; nevertheless, a fundamental feature of Chinese local investment behavior during the reform era has been compliance with the central government, *once the central government demands such compliance*. This is evident from variations in local investment behavior across different episodes of austerity policy. When the policy commitment is firm, the level of compliance increases; when the policy commitment is soft, compliance deteriorates rapidly.

This finding contradicts the prevailing view in studies of the Chinese economy, which is that the administrative division of economic decision-making powers has produced a weak state and brought about strong regional centrifugal tendencies (see, e.g., Wong 1987; Naughton 1988; Wu 1988; Wang Shaoguang 1991). In large part, these views differ because of a difference in approach. Here, it is assumed that the distribution of economic resources is not the only determinant of behavior, and that a full account must take into consideration the distribution of political resources as well. Furthermore, in this volume local investment behavior has been studied under a somewhat restricted condition – when central authorities make explicit demands for compliance. A true test of provincial economic and political independence should be the manner in which central and provincial investment conflicts are resolved: Is it the Center or the provinces that has the upper hand in these conflicts?

Such a test comes during a retrenchment period, when the central government stresses macroeconomic stability and tightens administrative and ideological discipline to attain it. In such a policy environment, the present analysis shows that provinces seldom defy the central government and, in general, comply with its wishes. However, provinces are not without economic muscle or strong incentives to evade complying. This shows up in two places. First, they engage in *opportunistic* behavior. Whenever macroeconomic policies are permissive, the provinces attempt to build up local industries in a hurry, neglecting central investment interests in the process. Provinces quickly switch their allegiance, however, when the policy environment changes from a reflationary to a contractionary one. In this instance, they comply and, in some cases, overcomply, with the central government. Second, they engage in moral hazard behavior. They comply eagerly in investment categories that the central government can monitor effectively, while shirking in other categories that the central government monitors poorly. The fundamental behavioral motto is: "Disobey whenever you can get away with it and comply whenever you cannot."

The finding that there has been overall compliance by no means implies uniformity in provincial investment behavior; some provinces shirk more than others, and the cross-sectional variations, even under similar macroeconomic policy environments, are considerable. This leads to those bureaucratic constraints that may vary across different provinces. Two such constraints are of particular interest here. One is the degree to which a provincial official is integrated into the central political and bureaucratic apparatus; the other is the leadership stability in the provinces. Since the Center has monopoly power over decisions in these two areas, their impact on local investment behavior is quite indicative of the effect of the control mechanisms built into the Chinese political system.

There is strong evidence that bureaucratic integration reduces investment shirking and that provincial leadership stability promotes it. These two findings are consistent in the sense that bureaucratic integration denotes strong central control, whereas provincial leadership stability denotes weak central control. By theoretical conjecture, these two findings are in turn reconciled with the time-series findings. To the extent that bureaucratic integration and leadership instability are positively associated with administrative supervision and monitoring, their negative relationship with investment shirking leads to the belief that an improvement in administrative supervision and monitoring over time helps reduce investment shirking.

The nature of Chinese political institutions

In analyses of economic institutions, preference divergence is usually assumed to be exogenous. This assumption serves both substantive and methodological purposes. On methodological grounds, this assumption increases analytical tractability. Instead of examining two variables, social scientists can now focus on the effect of informational distribution, ignoring preference divergence. On substantive grounds, economists are interested in studying competition and the effect of competition. In a competitive market, although society as a whole gains, there is little question that in each individual transaction and in a static situation, it is a zero-sum game. Consumers want to purchase goods at low prices; producers want to sell them at high prices. Laborers want to be paid high wages; capitalists want to pay low wages. Thus preference divergence is a given condition.

Sometimes, and under certain conditions, political divisions are less sharply drawn and preference divergence cannot be treated as given. In part, this is the outcome when one cannot reduce political games to the diametric pursuit of a single objective. In our story, although it is true that local officials generally place income objectives above macroeconomic stability objectives, some may do so more than others. Provincial investment preferences diverge sharply from those of the central government in some provinces, but in other provinces

they may converge with those of the central government. In the agency literature, because preference divergence is usually treated as a given condition,
shirking behavior is generally blamed on information imperfections. But if our
analysis allows for preference convergence, it is not enough to focus exclusively on information distribution; it is necessary to consider why investment
preferences diverge in some situations but converge in others.

Political institutions, it seems, reduce preference divergence and effective
political institutions reduce preference divergence effectively. Political institutions reduce preference divergence by manipulating the incentive structures
of agents. In the case of China, the mechanism of bureaucratic integration
orients the incentive structures of local officials in such a way that these officials perceive it to be in their own self-interest to pursue central investment
preferences. This is a particularly impressive result: the offering of political
and therefore nonremunerative incentives must overcome the sizable and
tangible economic incentives that tend to pull local officials in the other direction. This is concrete proof of the strength of Chinese political institutions.

The strength of the political institutions is also shown in other – albeit less
impressive – ways. In the Chinese system, there is a strong disincentive to be
perceived as a recalcitrant actor; thus investment compliance can switch from
extreme noncompliance to extreme compliance, depending on which macroeconomic policy regime is in effect. Because compliance does not stem from
sincere and genuine agreements, compliance can often be transitory. Also,
especially since 1984, the level of local investment compliance has become
more uniform among Chinese provinces, which indicates that there is more
interdependence in the timing of compliant behavior. This result holds despite
the fact that in my research and interviews I have not found much evidence
to suggest that the Center systematically penalizes local officials for their investment noncompliance. What then explains this bandwagoning behavior?

In his innovative work, Goldstein (1991) traces bandwagoning behavior to
three structural variables in the Chinese political system. One is the ordered
hierarchy in which actors stand in a clear relationship of super- and subordination (whether of a formally or informally stipulated kind); in such a setting,
actors have a minimum incentive to "get along" with the winning position, but
one's ability to sense and identify with the winning position ahead of others
will be amply rewarded. The second variable is the skewed distribution of
capabilities in favor of those occupying leadership positions; again, such a
distribution produces a strong incentive to comply. The last variable is the
absence of an alternative route for advancement in the Chinese system such
that those in subordinate positions must "follow a narrowly circumscribed
path," the path of supporting winners (Goldstein 1991: 45–49).

My research supports Goldstein's first two claims directly and supports his third claim indirectly. The effect of hierarchy is shown by studying the effect of bureaucratic integration, that is, by studying *variations* in the hierarchy and in the systematic relationships between the hierarchical variations and variations in investment compliance. Obviously, during the reform era, the economic distribution of capabilities has favored the provinces, not the Center, but the distribution of political and bureaucratic capabilities has been to the advantage of the Center. Herein lies a fundamental reality of the Chinese system: to translate economic resources into tangible political power requires a degree of collective action and collusion. Collective action or collusion among provinces is not possible so long as the Center maintains a tight political and bureaucratic grip on the careers of provincial officials. A province, regardless of its economic and fiscal resources, is a weaker player when facing the Center all by itself.

At the provincial level, there is no question that the Center controls all the cards for career advancement. Local officials are not elected, despite the nominal provisions for such a procedure in Chinese law. Both the appointment procedures and interprovincial transfer of personnel suggest that appointment decisions are not driven by locally specific considerations but are made at the supraprovincial level. Under this system, local officials must ultimately act on cues from the Center. Although local officials do have preferences at variance with those of the Center, there are real limits on how much local officials are able or willing to pursue their own interests at the expense of those of the Center. The Center has retained one of the key residual rights – the right to personnel allocation. That right turns out to be particularly handy when the residual rights over fiscal and economic resources have been delegated.

Political institutions, inflation control, and economic reforms

In light of the fundamental economic and political changes that are taking place in centrally planned economies and in socialist countries, can the findings here illuminate the transition process, and do they point to an optimal course for such countries? The answer to this question lies in the connections between inflation control and economic reforms, and in the connections between political institutions and inflation control.

Inflation control and economic reforms

Although policy makers and economic advisers have not yet reached a consensus on the appropriate sequences of the measures needed to convert a bureaucratically controlled economy into a market system, there is some agreement regarding the prerequisite macroeconomic policy environment under which economic reforms are to be carried out. In general, they see a need to maintain strict monetary and fiscal discipline and to bring inflation down to a "tolerable" level (Kornai 1990: 138–54; Lipton and Sachs 1990).[9] Currency conversion, trade and price liberalizations, and ownership reforms all take time to implement, and they take even longer to produce the kind of behavior that is compatible with a market mentality; inflation, to the extent that it causes people to heavily discount the future, has incentive-distorting effects that will defeat the purpose of these reforms.

The Chinese reform experience shows strongly that economic reforms can only be successfully implemented when there is economic stability. One little-noticed fact is that the Chinese government typically has taken bold reform initiatives in the wake of its austerity measures. This was the case in 1984 when the government announced far-reaching trade and enterprise reforms following the 1983 investment crackdown; in 1987 the government implemented the contract responsibility system in the urban areas on the heels of a tight monetary policy. In 1990 and 1991, in the middle of a three-year retrenchment program, the government adjusted the prices of a few key producer goods (such as steel and cement) to a more rational level, removed price controls on many consumer goods, and allowed market access for foreign brand-name products; in November 1993, soon after Zhu Rongji's austerity measures succeeded in bringing about some order to foreign exchange markets and the stock markets, the Chinese government announced an ambitious economic reform blueprint at the Third Plenum of the Fourteenth Party Congress. This close correlation in timing between economic stability and reforms is indeed remarkable because very often economic stabilization marked the political dominance of the central planners.

Such a policy sequence – that is, first austerity and then reforms – is wise economically and politically. Economically speaking, inflation tends to wipe out beneficial incentive effects; a simple example involves price adjustments. In CPEs, the prices of raw materials are misaligned with the prices of manufactured goods, and economic reforms usually require some rationalization of the relative price structure. However, the intended effect of shifting resources would be small if such a price adjustment took place in the context of an

---

9. In China, the debate has centered around "getting prices right" as opposed to getting the "micro foundation" right. The former school seeks a correction of enterprise behavior through a realignment or liberalization of prices, while the latter contends that such a measure is futile until there are changes in ownership patterns and proposes clarification and diversification of state enterprises (Hua Sheng, Zhang Xuejun, and Luo Xiaopeng 1988). In the former Soviet Union, three reform strategies – the big bang approach, the stage approach, and the conservative approach – were debated and successively tried (Nordhaus 1990: 297–301).

overall rise in prices. Politically speaking, only when the macroeconomic environment is sufficiently stable can reforms be carried out in an orderly fashion. Sometimes, the policy sequence between austerity and reforms could be the result of happenstance rather than any deliberate policy actions. Typically, austerity policies cause an overcooling of the economy or a recession (as in 1989 and 1990); economic reforms are then implemented as stimulants to increase aggregate demand.

Inflationary pressures tend to become more serious during economic transitions. Inflationary pressures are intensified in part by policy mistakes and in part by more systemic factors. In China, at the macro level, relative price adjustments have the effect of reducing profitability in state-owned industry, traditionally the largest source of the government's tax revenues (see Naughton 1991c). This leads to inflationary pressures under two scenarios. First, the reduction in revenue is not accompanied by a commensurate reduction in expenditure commitment, especially expenditure commitment in investments. The direct result is an increase in government deficit, which is financed by bank overdrafts, which in turn lead to excessive liquidity growth. Second, and probably more important, inflation is caused not by government deficit, at least not directly, but by the shift in investment financing from budgetary sources to bank credits. High investment growth during the reform era and the continuous decline in the share of budgetary investment spending in the total investment program were possible only because banks took on more financing responsibilities. Because many investment projects are directly sponsored and organized by government agencies, credit financing of investment projects makes the government deficit deceptively small and is a contributing factor to the rapid liquidity growth during the reform era, far in excess of the level that overt government deficits signify.

The microeconomic causes, however, are the basic ones driving the inflationary process. Economic reforms, at least in the short run, place more decision-making authority in the hands of local officials and enterprise managers without changing the behavior associated with state ownership. This means that the distribution of benefits and costs associated with investment expansions has become more asymmetrical: local governments and enterprises appropriate the benefits of investment expansion but push the costs of such expansion onto the society at large. Thus the immediate impact of the reforms is quite contrary to what reformers have in mind: The risks associated with capacity expansion become small, and smaller investment risks feed investment hunger.[10] This is the paradox of the reforms.

---

10. For a more detailed discussion, see Bauer (1991).

Inflation control and political institutions

Policy makers in transition economies face a difficult dilemma: Economic reforms in the short run typically intensify inflationary pressures; deepening economic reforms, however, require that inflationary pressures be brought under control. Economic demand for stabilization is compounded by the *political* difficulties of supplying it. Inflation control has significant distributional implications: the nature of the macroeconomic policies – whether accommodating to or restrictive of "excess demand" – becomes a test of political will. And herein lies the direct relevance of the political institutions.

In recent years, political economists have systematically tracked the relations between the characteristics of political or policy-making institutions, on the one hand, and macroeconomic outcomes, on the other. These institutional characteristics range from the stability of the political system, the centralization of the economic policy-making process, the nature of regimes, and political polarization to the legal or actual independence of the central bank.[11] The emerging consensus in the growing body of political economy literature is that democracies per se need not hinder and authoritarian regimes per se need not help stabilization policies or economic reforms.[12] First, weak executives, partisan politics, and fragmented economic policy infrastructure can all "delay" stabilization policies or undermine their implementation regardless of the regime types (Alesina and Drazen 1991). Partisan politics undermines confidence in the ability of governments to pursue consistent macroeconomic policies; sharp disagreements among important political coalitions make governments fragile, a situation that either leads to an inability to pursue politically difficult policies or gives rise to economic populism.

Second, relatively centralized and insular economic policy making encounters fewer difficulties in pursuing stabilization policies. The reasons are many, but they all center on the "decoupling" or independence between the political destiny of leaders, on the one hand, and the type of economic policies they pursue, on the other. Leaders in strong authoritarian regimes or institutionally strong central banks do not face electoral pressures or pressures from rent-seeking social groups using political means to protect their shares of the social product. The institutional insularity of East Asian governments – in part due to their bureaucratic meritocracy – is often viewed as one of the key reasons for prudent macroeconomic management (World Bank 1993). Third, strong

11. The political economy literature in this area is vast. For a review see Alesina (1989), Alesina and Perotti (1994), Haggard and Kaufman (1989a; 1992), and Haggard and Webb (1993). On the role of central banks, see Maxfield (1994).

12. For a summary of this consensus, see Haggard and Webb (1994). For empirical demonstrations, see Bates and Krueger (1993) and Remmer (1993).

and stable governments have a long time horizon; since there is a typical time lag between the implementation of austerity policies and the benefits associated with such policies, leaders need to believe that they will stay around to reap these benefits. Conversely, leaders in unstable societies do not have such expectations. This tends to occur in "unconsolidated democracies" where populist politicians appeal to the pent-up demand for improved living standards and pursue "economic populism" as a means of garnering electoral support. Economic adjustment is given short shrift.

The present study also focuses on the institutional variations within the same regime type rather than on the crude distinctions between authoritarian and democratic governments. It is part of this effort to understand the underlying connection between politics and macroeconomic outcomes. However, it differs from previous studies in two important respects. First, this study is about the *enforcement* of anti-inflation measures, not about whether to pursue an anti-inflation policy. In addition, there are two structural differences. Macroeconomic instability in China is not caused by external shocks or the mismanagement of fiscal or monetary policies; instead, as noted before, macroeconomic instability is rooted in such institutional characteristics as soft-budget constraints and the presence of large negative externalities. Although these are constants, economic reforms often have the effect of transforming repressed inflationary pressures into open ones. Thus, although macroeconomic instability in China may take on similar symptoms, such as trade or fiscal deficits, the underlying causal mechanisms are quite different.

Second, because of the underlying differences in the causal mechanisms, macroeconomic policies to tame inflation take different forms. In market economies, the orthodox approach is usually a combination of measures that aim at reducing expenditures, raising revenues, or stabilizing currency and whose effect is to restrict aggregate private and public spending. In China and in some of the other CPEs, these "normal" macroeconomic policy tools are too passive to be effective; in any case, the behavior of top leaders is usually not to blame for inflation. The bulk of the policy effort is exerted directly on the local governments and the enterprises to restrain investment demand or wage spending *so that* pressures on the budget or the currency are alleviated. Thus the inflation-controlling process in CPEs works the other way around from a market economy: Responsible fiscal and monetary policies are an effect of inflation-fighting measures rather than being inflation-fighting measures themselves.

The administrative nature of anti-inflation measures accentuates the importance of politics in the macroeconomic policy process. The political or administrative relationships between the anti-inflation authorities (such as the central government) and inflation-prone economic agents (such as local governments

Table 9.1. *Central governments' fiscal positions and inflation: China in comparative perspectives (percentage)*

Country	Central expenditure	Central revenue	Inflation
China	10.2^a (1990–91)	6.1^a (1990–91)	12.9 (1988–93)
			5.3 (1974–93)
Developing countries	26.4 (1985)	22.7 (1985)	51.0 (1983–87)
Low-income countries^b	20.8 (1985)	15.4 (1985)	13.0 (1983–87)

Note: Except for China, the expenditure and revenue figures are shares of GNP. Inflation is measured by the growth rate of GDP deflators. Relevant years are in parentheses. All the figures refer to annual averages.
^{a} Shares of GDP.
^{b} Excluding China and India.
Sources: For China, expenditure and revenue figures are from IMF (1994: 90, 92); inflation figures are calculated from World Bank (1995: 208–9). For developing countries, expenditure and revenue figures are from World Bank (1988: 46); inflation figures are from World Bank (1989b: 63).

in China) matter more than otherwise for the macroeconomic outcomes. As this study has shown, differences, at least in the underlying demand for inflation if not in the inflation rate itself, can be systematically traced to differences in these political or administrative arrangements. These findings are consistent with those of previous studies. This study has also shown that political polarization – modeled as interest divergence – is positively related to investment expansions, whereas centralized control is negatively related to investment expansions.

The strength of China's unitary political arrangement – defined as the effectiveness with which the Center shapes career incentives of local officials – in part explains the ability of the Chinese central government to control inflation while only commanding limited fiscal resources. Table 9.1 illustrates a basic asymmetry between the fiscal position of the central government and inflation performance in China as compared with other developing countries: China's inflation rate is lower or comparable to that of other developing countries even though the central government possesses about half of the fiscal resources of other central governments.

It is conventional wisdom in studies of public finance that the central government should be ensured sufficient fiscal resources to carry out stabilization functions.[13] The emphasis on the fiscal aspect of intergovernmen-

---

13. This is based on the reasoning that local jurisdictions either lack incentives or are ineffective in carrying out these functions owing to labor and capital mobility across jurisdictions. For a summary discussion, see Oates (1972).

tal relationships is not surprising because much of the public finance literature takes for granted political decentralization as the institutional foundation. The following paragraph from one of the most influential economic studies of federalism is indicative of this type of reasoning:

> In contrast to the conception of federalism in political science, it makes little difference to the economist whether or not decision-making at a particular level of government is based on delegated or constitutionally guaranteed authority. What matters is simply that decisions regarding levels of provision of specified public services for a particular jurisdiction (be they made by appointed or elected officials, or directly by the people themselves through some form of voting mechanism) reflect to a substantial extent the interests of the constituency of that jurisdiction. (Oates 1972: 17)

However, once political decentralization is not taken for granted, the single-minded emphasis on the fiscal aspects of intergovernmental relationships can be misleading. It would be naive to assume that fiscal allocative decisions made by elected officials do not differ from those made by officials appointed from above. Fiscal divisions between the central and local governments do not reflect the true divisions of authority if the incentive structures of local officials are such that they behave more as agents of the central government. In China, as our model suggests, the political institutions perform two important functions. One is that they reconcile policy preferences between national policy makers and local bureaucrats; the other is that they facilitate administrative monitoring. Under such a unitary arrangement, local officials act as agents of the central government, and thus the divisions between central and local fiscal shares are somewhat artificial.

These findings have explanatory implications beyond the China case. Consider the contrast between the reform courses in the former Soviet Union and China. The Soviet leadership, under Mikhail Gorbachev, launched large-scale political reforms in conjunction with economic reforms.[14] China, however, has proceeded with economic reforms while keeping the basic communist features of the political system largely intact (Goldman and Goldman 1988). Although traditionally Soviet central authorities had much greater control over the economic affairs of the republics, in the last two years of Gorbachev's rule, the political relationship shifted dramatically in favor of the republics.

The political independence of the Soviet republics, whether based on ethnic or ideological aspirations, asserted itself ahead of, or at least in conjunction with, economic independence; the Baltic republics had been clamoring for

---

14. Many of Gorbachev's earlier reforms resembled those in China, such as giving more autonomy to local officials and enterprises, allowing prices to float, and permitting enterprises to go bankrupt. The gist of these reforms was to seek a "correction" of enterprise behavior without fundamental changes in ownership. For more details, see Hewett (1988).

separation from the former Soviet Union and the then president of the Russian republic, Boris Yeltsin, was popularly elected. Political control by Moscow over its republics was tenuous at best. The connections between the macroeconomic implications and local political autonomy were then enhanced by the so-called nine-plus-one Union Treaty, which, had the August coup d'état not taken place, would have created a system of "tax farming" and would have significantly weakened Moscow's fiscal position.[15] The new Russian regime has continued to lose its political and economic grip over its republics. This is one of the reasons why the central government has become fiscally strapped and has been forced to resort to the creation of "seignorage revenues" – that is, to print money – to meet its expenditures. The inflationary consequences have been severe.

As this analysis has shown, the Chinese central government has been able to regulate the behavior of local governments effectively, despite a similar process of economic and fiscal devolutions. The main difference between Moscow and Beijing is that the latter has never lost its *political* control over its provinces; if anything, this political control has been strengthened and has proved helpful as an enforcement mechanism of central economic policies. When an economy finds that its traditional central planning apparatus is being abandoned and its economic resources are becoming more dispersed, in the short run political control can serve, in a way, as a "surrogate" for macroeconomic policy levers. The Center is able to manipulate personnel mixes and to structure the incentives and orientations of provincial officials in ways compatible with its policy objectives, one of which is macroeconomic stability.

This analysis has also shown the real limitations of the administrative approach in taming inflation. For one thing, the administrative control depicted in this book may not be a feasible option in the future as China moves away from a unitary system toward political federalism. The central government will lose the ability to rotate officials or to pick a right mix of officials to serve its economic policy objectives when personnel allocation also becomes decentralized. For example, provincial legislatures may elect provincial officials directly and make inroads into personnel management.[16] For another, using political control and bureaucratic means to attain economic ends has its costs. Bureaucratic means sometimes result in overkill as they are inherently unable to discriminate among economic activities on efficiency grounds and to engineer a "soft landing" of the economy; the recession of 1989 and 1990 is an apt

15. Tax farming allows republican governments to collect all taxes and then remit a fixed rate to the central government. In effect, this robs the central government of revenue-setting power.

16. In 1993 four provincial governors, who were not recommended by the Party Center, were elected by provincial people's congresses. See Burns (1994: 473).

example of the clumsiness of the bureaucratic approach. Because our approach is predicated on the underdevelopment of China's monetary and fiscal policies, its explanatory power will decline as economic reforms in China deepen. Indeed, the 1993 banking reforms – which separated the commercial functions from the policy functions of lending – were the harbinger of the kinds of economic reforms that may dilute the importance of our bureaucratic variables in terms of their effect on the macroeconomy.

Normative implications

Today, the basic governance issue facing China is no longer a choice between socialism and capitalism but a choice between a centralized and a decentralized system. As portrayed in this study, China already has a de facto federalist system, with the following characteristics. First, its local governments specialize in economic responsibilities and therefore they command a level of the economic and fiscal resources that correspond to their level of responsibilities. Second, the central government specializes in political responsibilities, including the management of foreign and military affairs and making personnel allocation decisions.

The current Chinese leadership has shown increasing willingness to reverse the imbalance in economic control with the localities, primarily in the fiscal area. In 1993, the Chinese government began to implement tax reforms along the lines of the principle of fiscal federalism (*fen shui zhi*): taxes are divided between central and local taxes, and separate tax collection agencies are established for the central and local governments. According to press reports, the Center hopes to increase its share from the current 30 percent of the consolidated revenue to about 60 percent, but the Center is to maintain the current 30 percent of the consolidated expenditure, thus vastly increasing its fiscal *discretion*. In the blueprint for the Ninth Five-Year Plan for the 1996–2000 period, there is also a renewed emphasis on increasing the central government's revenue shares.

Because "the Chinese style of federalism" is not codified constitutionally and is still in the process of experimentation, by tackling central–local economic and political relations in China, the present study raises a number of profound normative implications.[17] These implications ought to be considered in the context of some political and institutional fundamentals in China that are treated as exogenously given and as unlikely to change in the near future.

17. Elsewhere I have explained in detail why the current effort to recentralize China's tax system can have harmful economic and political effects. Much of the following discussion is based on Huang (1995b).

One such fundamental is China's authoritarian political system. In the presence of political authoritarianism, the Chinese de facto federalism is an optimal arrangement, in three ways. First, political centralization alleviates excessive coordination problems that might otherwise occur as a result of economic – especially fiscal – decentralization and as a result of soft-budget constraints.[18]

For CPEs in transition, the central policy authorities lack effective indirect fiscal and monetary policy instruments while state-owned firms lack the financial discipline to restrain their inflationary credit demand. In such a setting, political institutions act as constraints on the inflationary behavior and on economic opportunism of firms and their supervisory bureaucracies, and stability of political rule, in the presence of economic uncertainties, provides an anchoring point for the economy. Indeed, if one accepts the notion that moderate inflation is preferable to runaway inflation (in the sense that the former makes possible further reforms, whereas the latter inhibits further reforms), for China and for other CPEs undergoing transition, there are very good *economic* reasons to argue that political reforms should lag economic reforms. One can even speculate about the optimal length of such a lag: the lag should allow economic institutions to exert sufficient financial discipline and restraints on enterprise inflation demand so that it is less necessary to use political and bureaucratic institutions as surrogate constraints. Judged by this criterion, China today is still far from satisfying such a condition.

Second, there is considerable evidence that the independence of central banks is associated with stable macroeconomic performance and thus is a desirable institutional feature in an economic system (Alesina and Summers 1993). But in China, designing an *independent* central banking system is far less likely than designing a *centralized* central banking system. (Under a centralized central banking system, the monetary policy operations are made independent from local political authorities; under an independent central banking system, monetary policy operations are made independent from the State Council.) In this context, fiscal recentralization in effect places both fiscal and monetary controls in the hands of the State Council. Although it might be politically feasible for the central bank to resist credit demand pressures from local governments, this would be much more difficult to do with the State Council. Thus fiscal recentralization may lead to a contrarian outcome from what its advocates have hoped for – increased macroeconomic instability on account of debt monetization by the central government.

Fiscal decentralization has other economic benefits, such as harder budget

18. Here it should be stressed that this is a second-best optimality. As the following discussion suggests, once the condition of political centralization no longer holds, fiscal decentralization may be a less optimal arrangement.

constraints at the local level (Qian and Xu 1993). More fundamentally, given China's size and diversity, there are a priori reasons why many public goods are in fact local goods and their levels of provision should be determined locally. Local governments have better information about local conditions and about preferences of those living in their jurisdictions. Centralized provision of those public goods that are truly local would incur high transaction costs – the costs of information collection and the costs associated with rent-seeking activities. Centralized provision of public goods, in the presence of political centralization, can yield poor information supply because of a "bundling effect": the motive to supply information is systematically correlated with careerist incentives (Milgrom and Roberts 1990). The costs of this bundling effect can be very high.[19]

Although the present study has concentrated on the effect of politics on macroeconomic outcomes, the effect of the economic arrangement on politics can be just as profound. This is the third normative implication addressed in this volume. Fiscal decentralization is an imperfect but the only available constraining force on the political discretion of the central government; the Chinese political system itself places no formal constraints on the actions of the central government. Here it is worth recalling that during the communist period all the major events with devastating political and economic consequences (such as the Great Leap Forward and the Cultural Revolution) have been a result of the actions of the central leadership. Today, the actions of the central government can still be a source of instability. For example, it may become engulfed in power struggles that send shock waves through the economy and society; it may also commit the resources of the country to grandiose but wasteful projects such as the Three Gorges Dam; and it may pursue repressive domestic policies that provoke economically costly international reactions.

When the Center is dependent on the localities for its expenditure needs, it is less able to undertake costly and "socially bad" policies because the tax contribution effort declines in the absence of a broad consensus on the merit of the policies. Thus the central government may either refrain from undertaking these policies or strive to achieve more consensus, which makes the system more participatory and democratic. At the very least, local governments have an incentive to be involved in the deliberation of national policies, which they finance heavily. This is already happening in China. The "tax revolt"

---

19. The Great Leap Forward is an extreme example in point. The initial impact of the communization movement was magnified manyfold because lower-level officials supplied false information and enforced central policies overzealously to please their superiors. The famine that resulted – in which an estimated 30–40 million people died – would never have happened in a democracy where there is a freer flow of information (Sen 1989).

of the Chinese provinces in 1990 and 1991 in effect prevented a largely conservative central leadership from implementing a rollback of economic reforms.

The current tax reforms seek to drastically alter the relationship between the central government and local governments by replacing the tax contract system with a direct revenue collection arm for the central government. Under the tax contract system, as pointed out in chapter 2, the local governments are the residual claimants over revenue streams, but under the proposed system they are the fiscal grantees of the central government. Although, as shown in this volume, the Center often engages in ex post appropriations and some analysts have identified this as a defect with the contract system, this is a trivial criticism because it is simply unrealistic to expect a one-party, overly centralized state not to behave opportunistically. A more fundamental point has to do with the costs of the central opportunistic behavior: because the tax contract system establishes a clear target to which the Center is committed, contraventions of the tax contracts *make central appropriations illegitimate*. The clearer these contraventions are, the more illegitimate they are.

As is often the case, illegitimacy entails bilateral bargainings to create legitimacy, and the process of bargainings gives local governments a say in either fiscal or other national policies. In this respect, my analysis departs sharply from the conventional view that deplores fiscal bargainings between the Center and localities. Bargainings are a give-and-take process, and in the long run bargainings may raise demands for political participation. In the best of the scenarios, the central government may agree to give up part of its political power in exchange for an agreement from the localities to contribute more revenues, and such an exchange is easier to execute when there is an explicit contract binding the two sides.

In the long run, it is necessary to reform China's tax system so that the central government can mobilize fiscal resources to deal directly with macroeconomic problems rather than rely on inefficient administrative instruments. But designing fiscal institutions is inextricably linked with political issues and has political implications whether or not such a design is explicitly based on political grounds. Centralizing both political and fiscal controls is a highly risky strategy as it places an inordinate requirement on the honesty and rationality of the central government. China's recent history shows the hazards of concentrating too much political power in the hands of the central government, and in this regard, fiscal decentralization can be viewed as equivalent to purchasing an insurance policy against such hazards. Although like all insurance policies fiscal decentralization has its costs, these costs are well worth the benefits in the event of a catastrophic failure of the central leadership.

As an ancient poet once queried, "Who is to control the controller?" A successful political system not only gives its central government sufficient resources to carry out its functions but also has a safety feature to check and balance out its excesses. Balancing between the resource and safety requirements for successful governance is difficult but is all the more necessary in an authoritarian system and in a country emerging from a capricious past. China may not develop into a more pluralistic and democratic system by separating political power among different but equal branches of government; however, separation of economic and political powers among different levels of government may be a promising "third way."

References

Akerlof, G. A. 1970. "The Markets for 'Lemons': Qualitative Uncertainty and the Market Mechanism." *Quarterly Journal of Economics* 84 (August): 488–500.

Alchian, Armen A., and Harold Demsetz. 1972. "Production, Information Costs, and Economic Organization." *American Economic Review* 62 (December): 777–95.

Alesina, Alberto. 1989. "Politics and Business Cycles in Industrial Democracies." *Economic Policy* (April): 57–98.

Alesina, Alberto, and Allan Drazen. 1991. "Why Are Stabilizations Delayed?" *American Economic Review* 81 (5): 1170–89.

Alesina, Alberto, and Roberto Perotti. 1994. "The Political Economy of Growth: A Critical Survey of the Recent Literature." *World Bank Economic Review* 8 (3): 351–71.

Alesina, Alberto, and Lawrence H. Summers. 1993. "Central Bank Independence and Macroeconomic Performance: Some Comparative Evidence." *Journal of Money, Credit, and Banking* 25 (May): 151–62.

Allison, Graham T. 1971. *Essence of Decision: Explaining the Cuban Missile Crisis.* Boston: Little, Brown.

Alt, James, and K. Alec Chrystal. 1983. *Political Economics.* Berkeley: University of California Press.

American Economists Study Team. 1984. *Economic Reform in China: Report of the American Economists Study Team to the People's Republic of China.* New York: National Committee on U.S.–China Relations.

Ames, Barry. 1987. *Political Survival.* Berkeley: University of California Press.

Anhui Economic and Cultural Research Center. 1986. "Anhuisheng 1985 Nian Jingji Xinshi Fenxi" (An analysis of the economic situation in Anhui province in 1985). *Jingji Gongzuozhe Xuexi Ziliao* (Study Materials for Economists), no. 7: 50–54.

Aslund, Anders. 1991. *Gorbachev's Struggle for Economic Reform.* Ithaca, N.Y.: Cornell University Press.

Axelrod, Robert. 1984. *The Evolution of Cooperation.* New York: Basic Books.

Bahry, Donna. 1987. *Outside Moscow: Power, Politics, and Budgetary Policy in the Soviet Republics.* New York: Columbia University Press.

Barnett, A. Doak. 1967. *Cadres, Bureaucracy, and Political Power in Communist China.* New York: Columbia University Press.

Barro, Robert J. 1991. "Economic Growth in a Cross Section of Countries." *Quarterly Journal of Economics* (May): 407–43.

Barro, Robert J., and Xavier Sala-I-Martin. 1991. "Convergence across States and Regions." *Brookings Papers on Economic Activity* 1: 107–73.

Bartke, Wolfgang. 1981. *Who's Who in the People's Republic of China.* Armonk, N.Y.: M. E. Sharpe.

1987. *Who's Who in the People's Republic of China.* Munich: K. G. Saur.

1990a. *Biographical Dictionary and Analysis of China's Party Leadership, 1922–1988.* Munich: K. G. Saur.

1990b. *Who's Who in the People's Republic of China.* Munich: K. G. Saur.

Bates, Robert H., and Anne O. Krueger. 1993. "Generalizations Arising from the Country Studies." In *Political and Economic Interactions in Economic Policy Reform*, ed. Robert H. Bates and Anne O. Krueger, 444–72. Oxford: Blackwell.

Bauer, T. 1978. "Investment Cycles in Planned Economies." *Acta Oeconomica* 21 (3): 243–60.

1991. "The Microeconomics of Inflation under Economic Reforms: Enterprises and Their Environment." In *Managing Inflation in Socialist Economies in Transition*, ed. Simon Commander, 107–19. Washington, D.C.: World Bank.

Berliner, Joseph. 1957. *Factory and Manager in the USSR.* Cambridge, Mass.: Harvard University Press.

Billon, S. A. 1973. "Centralization of Authority and Regional Management." In *The Soviet Economy in Regional Perspective*, ed. V. N. Bandera and Z. L. Melnyk, 214–34. New York: Praeger.

Bishop, Robert V. 1979. "The Construction and Use of Causality Tests." *Agricultural Economics Research* 31 (October): 1–6.

Bo Yibo. 1983. "Guanyu Guomin Jingji You Jihua An Bili Fazhan de Jige Wenti" (A few questions concerning the planned and balanced development of the national economy). *Hongqi* (Red Flag), no. 19: 2–9.

Bowles, Paul, and Gordon White. 1993. *The Political Economy of China's Financial Reforms.* Boulder, Colo.: Westview Press.

Brzezinski, Zbigniew, and Samuel P. Huntington. 1964. *Political Power: USA/USSR.* New York: Viking Press.

Buchanan, James M., Robert D. Tollison, and Gordon Tullock. 1980. *Toward a Theory of Rent-seeking Society.* College Station: Texas A&M University.

"Buduan Gaige He Wanshan Woguo de Chuizhi Lingdao Tizhi" (Continuously improve China's vertical leadership system). 1990. In *Zhongguo Zhengfu Jigou, 1990* (Chinese government agencies, 1990), ed. State Commission on Government Establishment (SCGE), 579–81. Beijing: Zhongguo Jingji Chubanshe.

Bunce, Valerie. 1979. "Leadership Succession and Policy Innovation in the Soviet Republics." *Comparative Politics* 11 (4): 379–402.

1981. *Do New Leaders Make a Difference?* Princeton, N.J.: Princeton University Press.

Burns, John P. 1987a. "China's *Nomenklatura* System." *Problems of Communism* (September–October): 36–51.

1987b. "Civil Service Reform in Post-Mao China." *Australian Journal of Chinese Affairs*, no. 18 (July).

ed. 1989. *The Chinese Communist Party's Nomenklatura System.* Armonk, N.Y.: M. E. Sharpe.

1994. "Strengthening Central CCP Control of Leadership Selection: The 1990 *Nomenklatura*." *China Quarterly*, no. 138 (June): 458–91.

Byrd, William A. 1983. *China's Financial System: The Changing Role of Banks.* Boulder, Colo.: Westview Press.

1991. *The Market Mechanism and Economic Reform in China.* Armonk, N.Y.: M. E. Sharpe.

Byrd, William A., and Gene Tidrick. 1987. "Factor Allocation and Enterprise Incentives." In *China's Industrial Reform*, ed. Gene Tidrick and Jiyuan Chen, 6–102. New York: Oxford University Press.

1992. "The Chongqing Clock and Watch Company." In *Chinese Industrial Firms Under Reform*, ed. William A. Byrd, 58–119. New York: Oxford University Press.

Cao Erjie. 1988. "Guanyu Digongzi Gongjizhi Fenpei Fangshi He Zongxuqiu Pengzhang de Chubu Yanjiu" (Preliminary research on the relationship between the system of rationing and low wages and aggregate expansion). *Jingji Yanjiu* (Economic Research) (October): 16–26.

Cao Erjie, Li Minxin, and Wang Guoqiang. 1992. *Xin Zhongguo Touzi Shigang* (History of investment in New China). Beijing: Zhongguo Caizheng Jingji Chubanshe.

Caves, Richard E. 1985. *Multinational Enterprise and Economic Analysis*. Cambridge: Cambridge University Press.

Central Committee. 1986 [1982]. "Peibei Lingdao Banzi Yao Jianjue Zhixing Decai Jianbei de Yuanze" (The principle of emphasizing virtue and expertise must be strictly adhered to in staffing leadership positions). In *Dangde Zuzhi Gongzuo Wenxian Xuanbian* (Selection of documents on Party organizational work), ed. Department of Organization (DOO), 171–72. Beijing: Zhonggong Zhongyang Dangxiao Chubanshe.

1992 [1984]. "Zhonggong Zhongyang Guanyu Jingji Tizhi Gaige de Jueding" (The decision by the Party Center on the reform of the economic system). In *Zhonggong Zhongyang Wenjian Xuanbian* (Selections of documents of the Party Center), 281–310. Beijing: Zhonggong Zhongyang Dangxiao Chubanshe.

Central Committee, and State Council. 1986 [1983]. "Guanyu Dishizhou Dangzheng Jiguan Jigou Gaige Ruogan Wenti de Tongzhi" (Notice on a few questions about reforms of prefectural, city, and district-level agencies). In *Renshi Gongzuo Wenjian Xuanbian* (Selections of documents on personnel work), ed. Ministry of Labor and Personnel, vol. 6, 268–73. Beijing: Laodong Renshi Chubanshe.

Central Discipline Inspection Commission (CDIC). 1987 [1986]. "Guanyu Zhengdun Jilu de Tongzhi" (Circular on rectifying discipline). In *Renshi Gongzuo Wenjian Xuanbian* (Selections of documents on personnel work), ed. Ministry of Labor and Personnel, vol. 9, 124–27. Beijing: Laodong Renshi Chubanshe.

1988 [1987]. "Guanyu Dui Dangyuan Ganbu Jiaqiang Dangnei Jilu Jiandu de Ruogan Guiding (Shixing)" (Regulations on strengthening monitoring the discipline of the Party cadres [provisional]). In *Renshi Gongzuo Wenjian Xuanbian* (Selections of documents on personnel work), ed. Ministry of Personnel, vol. 10, 320–24. Shijiazhuang: Hebei Renmin Chubanshe.

Chamberlain, Heath B. 1972. "Transition and Consolidation in Urban China: A Study of Leaders and Organizations in Three Cities, 1949–53." In *Elites in the People's Republic of China*, ed. Robert A. Scalapino, 245–301. Seattle: University of Washington Press.

Chang, Parris H. 1978. *Power and Policy in China*. University Park: Pennsylvania State University Press.

1981. "Chinese Politics: Deng's Turbulent Quest." *Problems of Communism* 30 (January–February): 1–21.

1982. "The Last Stand of Deng's Revolution." *Journal of Northeast Asian Studies* 1 (June): 3–20.

Chen Muhua. 1987. *Zhongguo Muqian Jinrong Gongzuo* (Current Chinese monetary work). Beijing: Zhongguo Jinrong Chubanshe.

Chen, Nai-Ruenn, and Chi-ming Hou. 1986. "China's Inflation, 1979–1983: Measurement and Analysis." *Economic Development and Cultural Change* 34 (July): 811–35.

Chen Wenqing, and Su Kai, eds. 1991. *Dangnei Changyong Wenti Zhishi Shouce* (Handbook on common document styles in the Party). Shenyang: Baishan Chubanshe.

Chen Yizi. 1990. *Zhongguo: Shinian Gaige Yu 89 Minyun* (China: ten years of reforms and the 1989 democracy movement). Taipei: Lianjing Chuban Shiye Gongsi.

Chen Yongjian, and Sun Tao. 1986. "Shenyangshi Jiti Gongye Qiye Pochan Wenti Diaocha" (Investigation into bankruptcy of collective industrial enterprises in Shenyang). In *Gaige: Women Mianlin de Wenti Yu Silu* (Reforms: our questions and thinking), ed. Chinese Institute for the Reform of the Economic System (CIRES), 54–62. Beijing: Jingji Guanli Chubanshe.

Chen Yun. 1982. "Dui Jingji Gongzuo de Jidian Yijian" (A few opinions on economic work). In *Sanzhong Quanhui Yilai Zhongyao Wenxian Xuanbian* (Selections of important documents since the Third Plenum), ed. Document Research Office of the Central Committee, vol. 2, 1057–60. Beijing: Renmin Chubanshe.

1984a [1954]. "Jiejue Siying Gongye Shengchanzhong de Wenti" (Solve the problems arising from private industrial production). In *Chen Yun Wenxuan, 1949–1956* (Selections of Chen Yun's works, 1949–1956), ed. Central Committee, 264–71. Beijing: Renmin Chubanshe.

1984b. "Youguan Jingji Tizhi Gaige de Sandian Yijian" (Three suggestions concerning economic system reforms). In *Wenxian He Yanjiu* (Documents and research). Beijing: Renmin Chubanshe.

1986 [1982]. "Ganbu Jiaoliu Zhidu Hen Hao" (The cadre circulation system is good). In *Dangde Zuzhi Gongzuo Wenxian Xuanbian* (Selection of documents on Party organizational work), ed. Department of Organization, 369. Beijing: Zhonggong Zhongyang Dangxiao Chubanshe.

Chen Yun, and Li Xiannian. 1982. "Guanyu Caijing Gongzuo Gei Zhongyang de Yifeng Xin" (A letter to the Central Committee about financial and economic work). In *Sanzhong Quanhui Yilai Zhongyao Wenxian Xuanbian* (Selections of important documents since the Third Plenum), ed. Document Research Office of the Central Committee, vol. 1, 72–73. Beijing: Renmin Chubanshe.

China Directory. Tokyo: Radiopress, Inc. Annual.

Chinese Institute for the Reform of the Economic System. 1986a. *Gaige: Women Mianlin de Tiaozhan Yu Xuanze* (Reforms: our challenges and options). Beijing: Jingji Chubanshe.

1986b. *Gaige: Women Mianlin de Wenti Yu Silu* (Reforms: our questions and thinking). Beijing: Zhongguo Jingji Guanli Chubanshe.

Chinese Urban Economic Society. 1988. *Ershisanwei Shizhang Tan: Chengshi Gaige Yu Fazhan* (Talks by twenty-three mayors: urban reforms and development). Beijing: Zhongguo Caizheng Jingji Chubanshe.

Chow, Gregory C. 1985. "A Model of Chinese National Income Determination." *Journal of Political Economy* 93 (4): 782–92.

Clarke, Christopher, M. 1987. "Changing the Context for Policy Implementation: Organizational and Personnel Reform in Post-Mao China." In *Policy Implementation in Post-Mao China*, ed. David Lampton, 25–47. Berkeley: University of California Press.

Coase, Ronald H. 1937. "The Nature of the Firm." *Economica* 4 (November): 386–405.

Dai Qinxiang, and Cai Yulong. 1989. *Jiandu Gongzuo Shouce* (Handbook on supervision work). Beijing: Zhonggong Zhongyang Dangxiao Chubanshe.

Dangdai Zhongguo Caizheng (Contemporary Chinese finance). 1988. Beijing: Zhongguo Shehui Kexue Chubanshe.

Dangdai Zhongguo de Guding Zichan Touzi Guanli (Managing fixed-asset investment in contemporary China). 1989. Beijing: Zhongguo Shehui Kexue Chubanshe.

Dangdai Zhongguo de Tongji Shiye (Statistical work in contemporary China). 1990. Beijing: Zhongguo Shehui Kexue Chubanshe.

De Wulf, Luc, and David Goldsbrough. 1986. "The Evolving Role of Monetary Policy in China." *IMF Staff Papers*, no. 33: 209–41.

Deng Xiaoping. 1982 [1980]. "Guanche Tiaozheng Fangzhen Baozheng Anding Tuanjie" (Carry out the retrenchment principle and seek stability and unity). In *Sanzhong Quanhui Yilai Zhongyao Wenxian Xuanbian* (Selections of important documents since the Third Plenum), ed. Document Research Office of the Central Committee, vol. 1, 627–48. Beijing: Renmin Chubanshe.

———. 1986. "Sixiang Luxian Zhengzhi Luxian de Shixian Yao Kao Zuzhi Luxian Lai Baozheng" (Achievement of ideological and political lines depends on organizational lines). In *Dangde Zuzhi Gongzuo Wenxian Xuanbian* (Selection of documents on Party organizational work), ed. Department of Organization, 3–7. Beijing: Zhonggong Zhongyang Dangxiao Chubanshe.

Department of Organization. 1980 [1979]. "Guanyu Shixing Ganbu Kaohe Zhidu de Yijian de Tongzhi" (Circular on suggestions on provisionally implementing a system of cadre evaluation). In *Renshi Gongzuo Wenjian Xuanbian* (Selections of documents on personnel work), ed. Bureau of Personnel, vol. 1, 12–15. Beijing: Laodong Renshi Chubanshe.

———. 1984a [1980]. "Guanyu Chongxin Banfa 'Zhonggong Zhongyang Guanli de Ganbu Zhiwu Mingcheng Biao' de Tongzhi" (Circular on the reissuance of "The list of cadres on the *nomenklatura* of the Chinese Communist Central Committee"). In *Renshi Gongzuo Wenjian Xuanbian* (Selections of documents on personnel work), ed. Ministry of Labor and Personnel, vol. 4, 158–64. Beijing: Laodong Renshi Chubanshe.

———. 1984b [1980]. "Guanyu Zhixing 'Zhonggong Zhongyang Guanli de Ganbu Zhiwu Mingcheng Biao' Zhong Jige Juti Wenti de Tongzhi" (Circular on a few specific provisional implementation details concerning "The list of cadres on the *nomenklatura* of the Chinese Communist Central Committee"). In *Renshi Gongzuo Wenjian Xuanbian* (Selections of documents on personnel work), ed. Ministry of Personnel (MOP), vol. 4, 165–70. Beijing: Laodong Renshi Chubanshe.

———. 1984c [1980]. "Guanyu Zhongyang He Guojia Jiguan Sijuzhanqji Ganbu Renmian Shenpi Chengxu de Tongzhi" (Circular on approval procedures for appointing and removing bureau-level cadres in central Party and government agencies). In *Renshi Gongzuo Wenjian Xuanbian* (Selections of documents on personnel work), ed. Ministry of Labor and Personnel, vol. 4, 156–57. Beijing: Laodong Renshi Chubanshe.

———. 1985 [1982]. "Guanyu Zhongyang Guanli de Ganbu Renmian Gongzuo Ruogan Guiding de Xiugai He Buchong Tongzhi" (Circular on revisions of and additions to the regulations on appointment and removal of cadres on the central management list). In *Renshi Gongzuo Wenjian Xuanbian* (Selections of documents on personnel work), ed. Ministry of Labor and Personnel, vol. 5, 69–71. Beijing: Laodong Renshi Chubanshe.

———. 1986a. "Gonggu He Fazhan Shengdi Liangji Lingdao Banzi Tiaozhengde Chengguo" (Strengthen and further the successes of adjusting leadership at the provincial and prefectural levels). In *Dangde Zuzhi Gongzuo Wenxian Xuanbian* (Selection of documents on Party organizational work), ed. Department of Organization, 210–15. Beijing: Zhonggong Zhongyang Dangxiao Chubanshe.

———. 1986b. "Tiaozheng Hao Lingdao Banzi Bixu Zhuyi de Jige Wenti" (A few issues that must be paid attention to during leadership adjustments). In *Dangde Zuzhi Gongzuo Wenxian Xuanbian* (Selection of documents on Party organizational work), ed. Department of Organization, 185–92. Beijing: Zhonggong Zhongyang Dangxiao Chubanshe.

1986c. "You Lingdao You Jihua de Gaige Ganbu Zhidu" (Reform the cadre management system under the leadership and in a planned fashion). In *Dangde Zuzhi Gongzuo Wenxian Xuanbian* (Selection of documents on Party organizational work), ed. Department of Organization, 431–36. Beijing: Zhonggong Zhongyang Dangxiao Chubanshe.

1986d. "Zuzhi Gongzuo de Zhongda Zhuanbian" (A milestone in organization work). In *Dangde Zuzhi Gongzuo Wenxian Xuanbian* (Selection of documents on Party organizational work), ed. Department of Organization, 40–46. Beijing: Zhonggong Zhongyang Dangxiao Chubanshe.

1986e [1983]. "Guanyu Gaibian Xiang Zhongyang Bei'an de Ganbu Cailiao Baosong Banfa de Tongzhi" (Circular on changes in the method of reporting to the Party Center for the record on cadres). In *Renshi Gongzuo Wenjian Xuanbian* (Selections of documents on personnel work), ed. Ministry of Labor and Personnel, vol. 6, 71–80. Beijing: Laodong Renshi Chubanshe.

1987 [1986]. "Guanyu Jiaqiang Zhonggong Guojia Jiguan Sijuji Ganbu Guanli Gongzuo de Tongzhi" (Circular on strengthening bureau-level cadre management at central Party and state institutions). In *Renshi Gongzuo Wenjian Xuanbian* (Selections of documents on personnel work), ed. Ministry of Labor and Personnel, vol. 9, 322–25. Beijing: Laodong Renshi Chubanshe.

1989 [1988]. "Guanyu Shixing Difang Dangzheng Lingdao Ganbu Niandu Gongzuo Kaohe Zhidu de Tongzhi" (Circular on provisional implementation of the system of the annual performance evaluation of Party and government cadres). In *Renshi Gongzuo Wenjian Xuanbian* (Selections of documents on personnel work), ed. Ministry of Personnel, vol. 11, 119–20. n.p.: Xueyuan Chubanshe.

1992 [1991]. "Guanyu Baosong Zhongyang Guanli Ganbu Zhiwu Renmian Cailiao Jige Wenti de Tongzhi" (Circular on transmitting information on the appointment and removal of cadres managed by the Party Center). In *Renshi Gongzuo Wenjian Xuanbian* (Selections of documents on personnel work), ed. Ministry of Personnel, vol. 14, 59–62. Beijing: Zhongguo Renshi Chubanshe.

Department of Organization, and Department of Propaganda. 1985 [1982]. "Guanyu Zhongyang Xuanchuanbu Fenguan Jiaoyu Xitong Ganbu Youguan Shixing de Tongzhi" (A circular concerning provisional implementation of separate management by the central Department of Propaganda of cadres in the educational system). In *Renshi Gongzuo Wenjian Xuanbian* (Selections of documents on personnel work), ed. People's Bank of China, 366–67. Beijing: Zhongguo Jinrong Chubanshe.

Department of Organization, Department of Propaganda, and Department of the United Front. 1986 [1985]. "Guanyu Zhongyang Xuanchuanbu, Zhongyang Tongzhanbu Fenguan de Shuyu Zhongyang Guanli de Ganbu Guihua Zhongyang Zuzhibu Guanli de Tongzhi" (Circular on reverting control to the Department of Organization of cadres on the central *nomenklatura* previously managed by the Department of Propaganda and the Department of the United Front). In *Renshi Gongzuo Wenjian Xuanbian* (Selections of documents on personnel work), ed. Ministry of Labor and Personnel, vol. 8, 37. Beijing: Laodong Renshi Chubanshe.

Department of Organization, and Department of the United Front. 1985 [1981]. "Guanyu Zhongyang Tongzhanbu Fenguan Ganbu de Qingshi" (A report requesting separate management of cadres by the central Department of the United Front). In *Renshi Gongzuo Wenjian Xuanbian* (Selections of documents on personnel work), ed. People's Bank of China, 347–48. Beijing: Zhongguo Jinrong Chubanshe.

Department of Organization, and Ministry of Labor and Personnel. 1986 [1983]. "Guanyu Pifu Shengji Jigou Shezhi de Qingkuang He Yijian" (Approvals and opinions on establishment of provincial-level agencies). In *Renshi Gongzuo Wenjian Xuanbian*

(Selections of documents on personnel work), ed. Ministry of Labor and Personnel, vol. 6, 304–7. Beijing: Laodong Renshi Chubanshe.

Department of Organization, and Ministry of Personnel. 1990 [1989]. "Guanyu Shixing Zhongyang, Guojia Jiguan Sichuji Lingdao Ganbu Niandu Gongzuo Kaohe Zhidu de Tongzhi" (Circular on provisional implementation of the system of the annual performance evaluation of bureau- and division-level cadres in central Party and government institutions). In *Renshi Gongzuo Wenjian Xuanbian* (Selections of documents on personnel work), ed. Ministry of Personnel, vol. 12, 72–80. Beijing: Zhongguo Renshi Chubanshe.

1991 [1990]. "Guanyu Xiuding 'Zhonggong Zhongyang Guanli de Ganbu Zhiwu Mingcheng Biao' de Tongzhi" (Circular on revising "The list of cadres on the *nomenklatura* of the Chinese Communist Central Committee"). In *Renshi Gongzuo Wenjian Xuanbian* (Selections of documents on personnel work), ed. Ministry of Personnel, vol. 13, 35–53. Beijing: Zhongguo Renshi Chubanshe.

Dernberger, Robert F. 1986. "Economic Policy and Performance." In *China's Economy Looks toward the Year 2000*, ed. Joint Economic Committee, vol. 1, 15–44. Washington, D.C.: Government Printing Office.

Development Center of the State Council. 1985. "Zhengque Chuli Jingji Jianshe Tizhi Gaige He Tigao Renmin Shenghuo Sanzhe de Guanxi" (Correctly handle the relationships among economic construction, system reforms, and raising people's living standards). *Jingji Gongzuozhe Xuexi Ziliao* (Study Materials for Economists), no. 5: 2–38.

1986. "Jingji Xingshi He Gaige Zuotanhui Jiyao" (Summary of the minutes of the discussion on the economic situation and reforms). *Jingji Gongzuozhe Xuexi Ziliao* (Study Materials for Economists), no. 7: 3–13.

Diao Tianding, Chen Jialin, and Zhang Hou'an. 1989. *Zhongguo Guojia Difang Jigou Gaiyao* (Essentials of Chinese local state institutions). Beijing: Falu Chubanshe.

"Difang Zhengfu Zai Qiye Yingyunzhong de Jingji Xingwei" (Economic behavior of local governments in enterprise operations). 1991. *Jingji Yanjiu* (Economic Research) (August): 48–55.

Discipline Inspection Commission of Heilongjiang Party Committee. 1987. *Dangde Jilu Jiancha Gongzuo Shouce* (Handbook on Party discipline and supervision work). Beijing: Zhongguo Zhanwang Chubanshe.

Dittus, Peter. 1989a. "China: The State Investment System." Washington, D.C.: World Bank Background Paper.

1989b. "Monetary Policy in China." Washington, D.C.: World Bank Background Paper.

Domes, Jurgen. 1984. "Intra-elite Group Formation and Conflict in the PRC." In *Groups and Politics in the People's Republic of China*, ed. David S. G. Goodman. Armonk, N.Y.: M. E. Sharpe.

Donnithorne, Audrey. 1981. *China's Economic System*. London: George Allen & Unwin.

Downs, Anthony. 1967. *Inside Bureaucracy*. Boston: Little, Brown.

Du Hong. 1987. "Tan Kongzhi Guding Zichan Touzi Guimo Wenti" (On the question of controlling the fixed-asset investment scope). In *Lun Zhongguo Hongguan Jingji Guanli* (On China's macroeconomic management), ed. Gui Shiyong, Wang Jiye, and Yang Zhenjia, 600–603. Beijing: Zhongguo Jingji Chubanshe.

Dyker, David A. 1983. *The Process of Investment in the Soviet Union*. Cambridge: Cambridge University Press.

Eckstein, Alexander. 1981. *China's Economic Revolution*. Cambridge: Cambridge University Press.

Edwards, Sebastian. 1994. "The Political Economy of Inflation and Stabilization in Developing Countries." *Economic Development and Cultural Change*, 42 (2): 235–66.

Eggertsson, Thrainn. 1990. *Economic Behavior and Institutions.* Cambridge: Cambridge University Press.

Ellman, Michael. 1989. *Socialist Planning.* Cambridge: Cambridge University Press.

"Emerging Market Indicators." 1995. *Economist,* September 16–22.

Fairbank, John King. 1987. *The Great Chinese Revolution, 1800–1985.* New York: Harper & Row.

Falkenheim, Victor C. 1987. "Citizen and Group Politics in China: An Introduction." In *Citizens and Groups in Contemporary China,* ed. Victor C. Falkenheim, 1–15. Michigan Monographs in Chinese Studies. Ann Arbor: Center for Chinese Studies, University of Michigan.

Fang Weizhong. 1984. *Zhonghua Renmin Gongheguo Jingji Dashiji 1949–1980* (Important economic events of the People's Republic of China 1949–1980). Beijing: Zhongguo Shehui Kexueyuan Chubanshe.

Forster, Keith. 1986. "Repudiation of the Cultural Revolution in China: The Case of Zhejiang." *Pacific Affairs* (Spring): 5–27.

Frieden, Jeffry A. 1991. *Debt, Development, and Democracy.* Princeton, N.J.: Princeton University Press.

Friedman, Milton. 1953. *Essays in Positive Economics.* Chicago: University of Chicago Press.

Fu Caixiang, and Xu Meizheng. 1988. "Jinyibu Wanshan Zhongyang Yinhang Tiaokong Tixi" (Further improve the regulatory system of the central bank). *Renmin Ribao* (People's Daily), December 12, 5.

Fubai: Huobi Yu Quanli de Jiaohuan (Corruption: an exchange between money and power). 1989. Beijing: Zhongguo Zhanwang Chubanshe.

Gao Zhongsheng, Yang Meilian, Fei Jianjun, and Zhang Hua. 1988. "Jiaqiang Tongji Fazhi, Tigao Shuzi Zhiliang" (Strengthen the statistical law and improve the quality of data). In *Zhongguo Tongji Fazhan Zhanlue Wenti Yanjiu* (Research on China's statistical development strategy), ed. China Statistical Association, 168–77. Beijing: Zhongguo Tongji Chubanshe.

General Auditing Administration (GAA). 1986 [1985]. "Guanyu Gaijin Dui Difang Shenji Gongzuo He Sheli Paichu Jigou Wenti de Baogao" (Report on improving leadership over local auditing work and establishing direct branches). In *Renshi Gongzuo Wenjian Xuanbian* (Selections of documents on personnel work), ed. Ministry of Labor and Personnel, vol. 8, 50–52. Beijing: Laodong Renshi Chubanshe.

Gerschenkron, Alexander. 1984 [1962]. "Economic Backwardness in Historical Perspective." In *Leading Issues in Economic Development,* ed. Gerald M. Meier, 101–4. New York: Oxford University Press.

Goldman, Marshall. 1972. "Consumption Statistics." In *Soviet Economic Statistics,* ed. Vladimir G. Treml and John P. Hardt, 315–47. Durham, N.C.: Duke University Press.

Goldman, Marshall, and Merle Goldman. 1988. "Soviet and Chinese Economic Reform." *Foreign Affairs* 66 (Winter): 551–73.

Goldstein, Avery. 1991. *From Bandwagon to Balance-of-Power Politics.* Stanford, Calif.: Stanford University Press.

Goodman, David S. G. 1984. "Provincial Party First Secretaries in National Politics: A Categoric or a Political Group?" In *Groups and Politics in the People's Republic of China,* ed. David S. G. Goodman, 68–82. Armonk, N.Y.: M. E. Sharpe.

——— 1986. *Centre and Province in the PRC: Sichuan and Guizhou, 1955–1965.* Cambridge: Cambridge University Press.

——— 1993. *The Political Economy of Regionalism in China: Economic Development and the Prospects for Political Disintegration.* Working Paper 26. Western Australia: Asia Research Centre, Murdoch University.

Gordon, Robert J. 1975. "The Demand for and Supply of Inflation." *Journal of Law and Economics* 18 (December): 807–36.

Gorlin, Alice C. 1985. "The Power of Soviet Industrial Ministries in the 1980s." *Soviet Studies* 37 (July): 353–70.

Granick, David. 1990. *Chinese State Enterprises: A Regional Property Rights Analysis.* Chicago: University of Chicago Press.

Gregory, Paul R. 1990. *Restructuring the Soviet Economic Bureaucracy.* Cambridge: Cambridge University Press.

Gregory, Paul R., and Robert C. Stuart. 1981. *Soviet Economic Structure and Performance.* New York: Harper & Row.

Grosfeld, Irena. 1987. "Modeling Planners' Investment Behavior: Poland, 1956–1981." *Journal of Comparative Economics* 11 (June): 180–91.

———. 1989. "Disequilibrium Models of Investment." In *Models of Disequilibrium and Shortage in Centrally Planned Economies*, ed. Christopher Davis and Wojciech W. Charemza, 361–74. New York: Chapman and Hall.

Guangdong Statistical Bureau. 1987. *Guangdongsheng Gaige Kaifang Banian Chengjiu, 1979–1986 Nian* (Guangdong province's achievements in eight years of reforms and the open-door policies, 1979–1986). Guangzhou: Guangdong Tongjiju.

"Guangdong's Economic Predicament Since June 4th." 1990. *China News Analysis*, no. 1404 (February 15): 1–9.

"Guanyu Kongzhi Guding Zichan Touzi Guimo Wenti" (About controlling the fixed-asset investment scope). 1986. *Jingji Gongzuozhe Xuexi Ziliao* (Study Materials for Economists), no. 19: 21–23.

Gui Shiyong. 1992. "Guanyu Woguo Dangqiande Jingji Xingshi" (About the current economic situation). *Zhonggong Zhongyang Dangxiao Baogao Xuan* (Central Party School selections of speeches) 46 (10) (November): 1–9.

Guo Shuqing. 1992. *Jingji Tizhi Zhuangui Yu Hongguan Tiaokong* (Transition of the economic system and macroeconomic control). Tianjin: Tianjin Renmin Chubanshe.

Guo Wanqing. 1992. "You Qiutong Zouxiang Qiuyi" (From similarities to differentiation). *Jingji Yanjiu* (Economic Research), no. 12: 12–18.

"Guoban Tongbao Piping Wuxishi Zhengfu" (Notice by the Office of the State Council criticizing the Wuxi municipal government). 1989. *Jingji Cankao* (Economic Reference News), May 16, 1.

"Guowuyuan Guanyu Jiaqiang Gongye Qiye Guanli Ruogan Wenti de Jueding" (The decision by the State Council to strengthen the regulations of industrial enterprise management). 1990. In *Zhonghua Renmin Gongheguo Xingzheng Fagui Xuanbian* (A selection of the administrative regulations and laws of the People's Republic of China), ed. Ministry of Justice and Bureau of Law of the State Council, 1618–19. Beijing: Falu Chubanshe.

Haggard, Stephan, and Robert R. Kaufman. 1989a. "The Politics of Stabilization and Structural Adjustment." In *Developing Country Debt and Economic Performance*, ed. Jeffrey D. Sachs, 209–54. Chicago: University of Chicago Press.

Haggard, Stephan, and Robert R. Kaufman. 1989b. "Economic Adjustments in New Democracies." In *Fragile Coalitions*, ed. Joan M. Nelson, 57–78. San Francisco: Overseas Development Council.

Haggard, Stephan, and Robert R. Kaufman. 1992. "Economic Adjustment and the Prospects for Democracy." In *The Politics of Economic Adjustment*, ed. Stephan Haggard and Robert R. Kaufman, 319–50. Princeton, N.J.: Princeton University Press.

Haggard, Stephan, and Steven B. Webb. 1993. "What Do We Know about the Political Economy of Economic Policy Reform?" *World Bank Research Observer* 8 (July): 143–68.

Halpern Nina P. 1992. "Information Flows and Policy Coordination in the Chinese Bureaucracy." In *Bureaucracy, Politics and Decision Making in Post-Mao China*, ed. Kenneth G. Lieberthal and David M. Lampton, 125–48. Berkeley: University of California Press.

Han Guang. 1990 [1984]. "Zai Quanguo Shenji Gongzuo Huiyishang de Jianghua" (Speech at the National Conference of Auditing Work). In *Dangzheng Lingdao Tan Shenji* (Party and government leaders on auditing), ed. Cui Jianmin, 51–60. Beijing: Zhongguo Shenji Chubanshe.

Hanushek, Eric A., and John E. Jackson. 1977. *Statistical Methods for Social Scientists*. San Diego: Academic Press.

Harding, Harry. 1987. *China's Second Revolution*. Washington, D.C.: Brookings Institution.

Harrison, Mark. 1985. "Investment Mobilization and Capacity Completion in the Chinese and Soviet Economies." *Economics of Planning* 19 (2): 56–75.

Harrold, Peter. 1992. "China's Reform Experience to Date." World Bank Discussion Papers 180. Washington, D.C.

Hayek, Friedrich A. 1974. "The Price System as a Mechanism for Using Knowledge." In *Comparative Economic Systems*, ed. Morris Bornstein, 22–33. Homewood, Ill.: Richard D. Irwin.

He Jianzhang, and Wang Jiye. 1984. *Zhongguo Jihua Guanli Wenti* (On Chinese planning management). Beijing: Shehui Kexueyuan Chubanshe.

He Zhukang. 1982. "Shi Lun Ruhe Shixian Jingji Fazhan Sudu Yu Xiaoyi de Tongyi" (On how to combine speed and efficiency of economic development). *Zhongzhou Xuekan* (Henan Academic Journal), no. 2: 19–24.

——— 1985. "Zhengfu Gongzuo Baogao" (Report on government work). In *Henan Nianjian 1985* (Henan yearbook 1985), 42–49. Zhengzhou: Henan Nianjian Bianjibu.

Hei Aitang, and Hu Ji. 1988 [1985]. "Yasuo Guding Zichan Touzi Guimo de Jinqi He Yuanqi Duice" (Short- and long-term policies to reduce the scope of fixed-asset investment). In *Zhongguo Jingji de Dongtai Fenxi He Duice Yanjiu* (Analysis of the Chinese economic situation and policy), ed. Wu Jinglian and Hu Ji, 38–47. Beijing: Zhongguo Renmin Daxue Chubanshe.

Heilongjiang Statistical Bureau. 1987. *Heilongjiang Tongji Nianjian 1987* (Heilongjiang statistical yearbook 1987). Beijing: Zhongguo Tongji Chubanshe.

Henan Local History Editorial Committee. 1985. *Henan Nianjian 1985* (Henan yearbook 1985). Zhengzhou: Henan Nianjian Bianjibu.

——— 1986. *Henan Nianjian 1986* (Henan yearbook 1986). Zhengzhou: Henan Nianjian Bianjibu.

——— 1987. *Henan Nianjian 1987* (Henan yearbook 1987). Zhengzhou: Henan Nianjian Bianjibu.

Henan Provincial Statistical Bureau. 1985. "Henan sheng Tongjiju Guanyu 1984 Nian Guomin Jingji He Shehui Fazhan de Tongji Gongbao" (Communiqué by the Henan Provincial Statistical Bureau on 1984 Economic and Social Developments). In *Henan Nianjian 1985* (Henan yearbook 1985), ed. Henan Local History Editorial Committee, 62–66. Zhengzhou: Henan Nianjian Bianjibu.

Hewett, Ed A. 1988. *Reforming the Soviet Economy*. Washington, D.C.: Brookings Institution.

Hibbs, Douglas A., Jr. 1977. "Political Parties and Macroeconomic Policy." *American Political Science Review* 71 (December): 1467–87.

Hirschman, Albert O. 1970. *Exit, Voice and Loyalty*. Cambridge, Mass.: Harvard University Press.

——— 1985. "Reflections on the Latin American Experience." In *The Politics of Inflation and Economic Stagnation*, ed. Leon N. Lindberg and Charles S. Maier, 53–77. Washington, D.C.: Brookings Institution.

Holmstrom, Bengt. 1982. "Design of Incentive Schemes and the New Soviet Incentive Model." *European Economic Review* 17 (February): 127–48.

Holmstrom, Bengt, and Paul Milgrom. 1991. "Multitask Principal–Agent Analysis: Incentive Contracts, Asset Ownership, and Job Design." *Journal of Law, Economics, and Organization* 7 (Spring): 24–52.

Hough, Jerry F. 1980. *Soviet Leadership in Transition*. Washington, D.C.: Brookings Institution.

Hu Ping. 1981. "Guanyu 1981 Nian Guomin Jingji Jihua Anpai Yijian de Baogao" (Report on drafting the economic plan for 1981). *Fujian Ribao* (Fujian Daily), April 14, 2–3.

Hua Guofeng. 1992 [1978]. "Jiakuai Shehuizhuyi Jingji Jianshe" (Speed up socialist economic construction). In *Renmin Gongheguo Chunqiu Shilu* (Annals of the People's Republic), ed. Lin Yunhui, Liu Yong, and Shi Bonian, 1082–84. Beijing: Zhongguo Renmin Daxue Chubanshe.

Hua Sheng, Zhang Xuejun, and Luo Xiaopeng. 1988. "Zhongguo Shinian Jingji Gaige: Huigu, Fansi He Zhanwang" (Ten years of Chinese economic reforms: reflections, assessment and speculations about prospects). *Jingji Yanjiu* (Economic Research), (September, November, December): 13–37, 11–30, 10–28.

Huang Daqiang, and Liu Yichang. 1988. *Xingzhengxue yanjiu* (Administration Studies). Beijing: Renmin Daxue Chubanshe.

Huang, Yasheng. 1990. "Web of Interests and Patterns of Behavior of Chinese Local Economic Bureaucracies and Enterprises during Reforms." *China Quarterly*, no. 123 (September): 431–58.

———. 1994. "Information, Bureaucracy and Economic Reforms in China and in the Former Soviet Union." *World Politics* 47 (October): 102–34.

———. 1995a. "Administrative Monitoring in China: Institutions and Processes." *China Quarterly*, no. 143 (September): 828–43.

———. 1995b. "Fiscal and Political Decentralizations in China." Ann Arbor: Department of Political Science, University of Michigan.

———. 1995c. "Why China Will Not Collapse." *Foreign Policy*, no. 99 (Summer): 54–68.

———. 1996. "The Statistical Agency in China's Bureaucratic System – with a Comparison to the Former Soviet Union." *Communist and Post-Communist Studies* 29 (March).

Huang Yunchen, Lu Jian, and Fan Yu. 1992. "1991–1992 Nian Hongguan Jingji Taishide Panduan Yu Zhengce Jianyi" (Judgment on the 1991–1992 macroeconomic situation and policy suggestions). *Jingji Tizhi Gaige Neibu Cankao* (Internal references on economic system reforms), no. 1: 3–8.

Hubei Statistical Bureau. 1985. *Hubei Tongji Nianjian 1985* (Hubei statistical yearbook 1985). Beijing: Zhongguo Tongji Chubanshe.

Ickes, Barry W. 1986. "Cyclical Fluctuations in Centrally Planned Economies: A Critique of the Literature." *Soviet Studies* 38 (January): 36–52.

Imai, Hiroyuki. 1994. "China's Endogenous Investment Cycle." *Journal of Comparative Economics* 19: 188–216.

International Monetary Fund (IMF). 1994. *Government Finance Statistics Yearbook 1994*. Washington, D.C.

International Monetary Fund, World Bank, Organisation for Economic Co-operation and Development, and European Bank for Reconstruction and Development. 1991. *A Study of the Soviet Economy*. Paris: Organisation for Economic Co-operation and Development.

Jefferson, Gary H. 1993. "The Chinese Economy: Moving Forward." In *China Briefing, 1992*, ed. William A. Joseph, 35–54. Boulder, Colo.: Westview Press.

Jefferson, Gary H., and Wenyi Xu. 1991. "The Impact of Reform on Socialist Enterprises in Transition: Structure, Conduct, and Performance in Chinese Industry." *Journal of Comparative Economics* 15 (1): 45–64.

Jensen, Michael C. 1983. "Organization Theory and Methodology." *Accounting Review* 58 (April): 319–39.

Jensen, Michael C., and William H. Meckling. 1976. "Theory of the Firm: Managerial Behavior, Agency Costs and Ownership Structure." *Journal of Financial Economics* 3: 305–60.

Jiang Zemin. 1991 [1990]. "Zai Quanguo Sheng, Zizhiqu, Zhixiashi Dangwei Mishuzhang Zuotanhuishang de Jianghua" (Speech at the National Conference of Secretary-Generals of the Provincial Party Committees). In *Renshi Bumen Bangongshi Gongzuo Shiyong Shouce* (Handbook on office affairs of personnel departments), ed. Ministry of Personnel, 3–8. Beijing: Beijing Gongye Daxue Chubanshe.

"Jiushi Niandai Zhonggong Jingji Gaige Zouxiang Ji Wenti" (The direction and problems of the reforms of the Chinese communist economy in the 1990s). 1992. In *Zhonggong Nianbao 1992* (Chinese communist yearbook 1992). Taipei: Zhonggong Yanjiu Zazhishe.

Kaminski, Bartlomiej. 1991. *The Collapse of State Socialism: The Case of Poland.* Princeton, N.J.: Princeton University Press.

Kaufman, Herbert. 1960. *The Forest Ranger: A Study in Administrative Behavior.* Baltimore, Md.: Johns Hopkins Press.

Kemme, David M. 1989. "The Chronic Excess Demand Hypothesis." In *Models of Disequilibrium and Shortage in Centrally Planned Economies*, ed. Christopher Davis and Wojciech Charemza, 83–99. London: Chapman and Hall.

King, Gary. 1989. *Unifying Political Methodology.* Cambridge: Cambridge University Press.

Kornai, Janos. 1980. *The Economics of Shortage*, Amsterdam: North-Holland.

——— 1984. "Bureaucratic and Market Coordination." *Osteuropa Wirtschaft* 24 (December): 309–19.

——— 1986a. *Contradictions and Dilemmas.* Cambridge, Mass.: MIT Press.

——— 1986b. "The Hungarian Reform Process: Visions, Hopes and Reality." *Journal of Economic Literature* 24 (December): 1687–1737.

——— 1990. *The Road to a Free Economy.* New York: W. W. Norton.

——— 1992. *The Socialist System.* Princeton, N.J.: Princeton University Press.

Kueh, Y. Y. 1992. "Foreign Investment and Economic Change in China." *China Quarterly*, no. 131 (September): 637–81.

Kushnirsky, Fyodor I. 1982. *Soviet Economic Planning, 1965–1980.* Boulder, Colo.: Westview Press.

Lakatos, Imre. 1970. "Falsification and the Methodology of Scientific Research Programmes." In *Criticism and the Growth of Knowledge*, ed. Imre Lakatos and Alan Musgrave, 91–196. Cambridge: Cambridge University Press.

Laky, T. 1979. "Enterprises in Bargaining Position." *Acta Oeconomica* 22 (3–4): 227–46.

Lam, Willy Wo-Lap. 1989. "Li Building Own Brain Trust to Eclipse Zhao's Think Tanks." *South China Morning Post*, March 4, 1.

Lampton, David M. 1987a. "Chinese Politics: The Bargaining Treadmill." *Issues and Studies* 23 (March): 11–41.

——— 1987b. "The Implementation Problem in Post-Mao China." In *Policy Implementation in Post-Mao China*, ed. David Lampton, 3–24. Berkeley: University of California Press.

Lardy, Nicholas R. 1978. *Economic Growth and Distribution in China.* Cambridge: Cambridge University Press.

——— 1991. "Sustained Development." Unpublished Paper.

Lee, Hong Yung. 1991. *From Revolutionary Cadres to Party Technocrats in Socialist China.* Berkeley: University of California Press.

Lee, Peter N. S. 1987. *Industrial Management and Economic Reform in China, 1949–1984.* Hong Kong: Oxford University Press.

Levine, Herbert S. 1969. "Comment on Nove." In *Is the Business Cycle Obsolete?* ed. M. Bronfrenbrenner, 303–11. New York: Wiley.

Lewis, John Wilson. 1963. *Leadership in Communist China.* Ithaca, N.Y.: Cornell University Press.

Li, Cheng, and David Bachman. 1989. "Localism, Elitism, and Immobilism: Elite Formation and Social Change in Post-Mao China." *World Politics* 42 (October): 64–94.

Li, Cheng, and Lynn White. 1988. "The Thirteenth Central Committee of the Chinese Communist Party." *Asian Survey* 28 (April): 371–99.

Li, Jinyuan. 1991. *Taxation in the People's Republic of China.* New York: Praeger Publishers.

Li Kaixin. 1983. "Jizhong Wuli Baozheng Zhongdian Jianshe" (Concentrate resources and guarantee key construction). *Hongqi* (Red Flag), no. 17: 16–19.

Li Peng. 1988. "Zai Chunjie Tuanbaihuishang de Jianghua" (Speech at the spring festival celebration). *Zhonghua Renmin Gongheguo Guowuyuan Gongbao* (Bulletin of the State Council of the People's Republic of China), no. 4: 99.

——— 1989. "Jianjue Guanche Zhengdun He Shenhua Gaige de Fangzhen" (Firmly carry out rectification, and deepening of reforms). *Renmin Ribao* (People's Daily), April 6, 1–3.

——— 1990. "Zai Tingqu Quanguo Shenji Gongzuo Huiyi Huibao Shi de Jianghua" (Speech at the briefing on the National Conference of Auditing Work). In *Dangzheng Lingdao Tan Shenji* (Party and government leaders on auditing), ed. Cui Jianmin, 8–15. Beijing: Zhongguo Shenji Chubanshe.

Li Ping. 1988. "Guanyu Gansusheng 1987 Nian Jihua Zhixing Qingkuang He 1988 Nian Jihua Cao'an" (The 1987 plan implementation and the draft plan for 1988). *Gansu Ribao* (Gansu Daily), February 7, 2–3.

Li Rui. 1989. *Lushan Huiyi Shilu* (True record of the Lushan meeting). Beijing: Chunqiu Chubanshe.

Li Ruihuan. 1987 [1986]. "Zongjie Jingyan Chengsheng Qianjin Wei Quanmian Wancheng 'Qiwu' Jihua Er Nuli Fendou" (Summarizing the experience and marching victoriously striving for the full completion of the Seventh FYP). In *Tianjin Jingji Nianjian 1987* (Tianjin economic almanac 1987), 67–84. Tianjin: Tianjin Renmin Chubanshe.

——— 1988 [1987]. "Shenhua Renshi Tigao Zijue" (Deepen understanding and raise self-consciousness). In *Tianjin Jingji Nianjian 1988* (Tianjin economic yearbook 1988), 37–71. Tianjin: Tianjin Renmin Chubanshe.

——— 1989. "1988 Nian Shiyue Shiciri Zai Shiwei Wujie Erci Quanti (Kuoda) Huiyishang de Baogao" (Report at the Second Plenum of the Fifth Conference [expanded] of the municipal Party committee, October 14, 1988). In *Tianjin Jingji Nianjian 1989.* (Tianjin economic yearbook 1989), 125–37. Tianjin: Tianjin Renmin Chubanshe.

——— 1991 [1990]. "Zai Quanguo Sheng, Zizhiqu, Zhixiashi Dangwei Mishuzhang Zuotanhuishang de Jianghua" (Speech at the National Conference of Secretary-Generals of Provincial Party Committees). In *Renshi Bumen Bangongshi Gongzuo Shiyong Shouce* (Handbook on office affairs of personnel departments), ed. Ministry of Personnel, 19–20. Beijing: Beijing Gongye Daxue Chubanshe.

Lieberthal, Kenneth, and Michel Oksenberg. 1988. *Policy Making in China: Leaders, Structures and Processes.* Princeton, N.J.: Princeton University Press.

Lijphart, Arend. 1971. "Comparative Politics and the Comparative Method." *American Political Science Review* 65 (September): 682–93.

Lin, Cyril Zhiren. 1989. "Open-Ended Economic Reform in China." In *Remaking the Economic Institutions of Socialism: China and Eastern Europe*, ed. Victor Nee and David Stark, 95–136. Stanford, Calif.: Stanford University Press.

Lin Song, Liu Huirong, and Ma Chunfeng. 1989. *Jianshe Yinhang Xingdai Guanli Gailun* (A survey discussion of credit management at the Construction Bank). Beijing: Zhongguo Jinrong Chubanshe.

Lindbeck, Assar. 1971. *The Political Economy of the New Left*. New York: Harper & Row.

Lipton, David, and Jeffrey Sachs. 1990. "Creating a Market Economy in Eastern Europe: The Case of Poland." *Brookings Papers on Economic Activity* 1: 75–133.

Liu Hongru. 1987. *Zhongguo Jinrong Tizhi Gaige Wenti Yanjiu* (A study of China's banking reforms). Beijing: Zhongguo Jinrong Chubanshe.

Liu Hui, Li Qun, and Qi Mingqun. 1983. *Zhongguo Jingji Jiegou Wenti Yanjiu* (Research into China's economic structure). In *Tiaozheng Jiben Jianshe Touzi Fangxiang Cujin Guomin Jingji Jiegou Helihua* (Adjust the direction of investment and rationalize the economic structure of the country), ed. Ma Hong and Sun Shangqing. vol. 2. Beijing: Renmin Chubanshe.

Liu Jintian, and Shen Xueming, eds. 1992. *Lijie Zhonggong Zhongyang Weiyuanhui Renmin Cidian* (Biographies of the Chinese Communist Party Central Committee members). Beijing: Zhonggong Dangshi Chubanshe.

Liu Kegou. 1988. *Dangzheng Jigou Gaige Yanjiu* (Reforms of Party and government agencies). Beijing: Renmin Ribao Chubanshe.

Lou Jiwei. 1992. "On the Division of Economic Power between Central and Local Levels." *Chinese Economic Studies* 25 (Summer): 25–34.

Lowenthal, Richard. 1970. "Development vs. Utopia in Communist Policy." In *Change in Communist Systems*, ed. Chalmers Johnson, 33–116. Stanford, Calif.: Stanford University Press.

Lu Dong. 1992. *Zhongguo Gongye Jingji de Gaige Yu Fazhan* (Reform and development of the Chinese industrial economy). Beijing: Jingji Guanli Chubanshe.

Lu Feng. 1991. "Dali Tuijin Ganbu Jiaoliu Gongzuo" (Greatly promote cadre circulation work). *Dangjian Wenhui* (Selections of works on Party construction), no. 1.

Luo Gan. 1991. "Zai Quanguo Zhengfu Xitong Gongwen Chuli Gongzuo Zuotanhuishang de Jianghua" (Speech at the National Conference on Handling Documents within the Government System). In *Renshi Bumen Bangongshi Gongzuo Shiyong Shouce* (Handbook on office affairs of personnel departments), ed. Ministry of Personnel, 53–73. Beijing: Beijing Gongye Daxue Chubanshe.

Ma Hong, and Fang Weizhong. 1991. *Zhongguo Diqu Fazhan Yu Chanye Zhengce* (China's regional development and industrial policies). Beijing: Zhongguo Caizheng Jingji Chubanshe.

Ma Hong, and Sun Shangqing, eds. 1991. *Zhongguo Jingji Xingshi Yu Zhanwang, 1990–1991* (Economic situation and prospect of China, 1990–1991). Beijing: Zhongguo Fazhan Chubanshe.

——— eds. 1993. *Zhongguo Jingji Xingshi Yu Zhanwang, 1992–1993* (Economic situation and prospect of China, 1992–1993). Beijing: Zhongguo Fazhan Chubanshe.

Ma Jiantang. 1992. "Woguo Guoyou Qiye Xingwei Mubiaode Shizheng Fenxi" (An empirical analysis of objectives of China's state-owned enterprises). *Jingji Yanjiu* (Economic Research), no. 7 (July): 20–26.

Ma Qibing, and Chen Wenbing. 1989. *Zhongguo Gongchandang Zhizheng Sishinian (1949–1989)* (Forty years of rule by the Chinese Communist Party, [1949–1989]). Beijing: Zhonggong Dangshi Ziliao Chubanshe.

MacFarquhar, Roderick. 1974. *The Origins of the Cultural Revolution*, vol. 1. New York: Columbia University Press.

——— 1993. "The Succession to Mao and the End of Maoism, 1969–82." In *The Politics of China 1949–1989*, ed. Roderick MacFarquhar, 248–339. New York: Cambridge University Press.

Maier, Charles S. 1985. "Inflation and Stagnation as Politics and History." In *The*

Politics of Inflation and Economic Stagnation, ed. Leon N. Lindberg and Charles S. Maier, 3–24. Washington, D.C.: Brookings Institution.

Manion, Melanie. 1985. "The Cadre Management System, Post-Mao: The Appointment, Promotion, Transfer and Removal of Party and State Leaders." *China Quarterly*, no. 102 (June): 203–33.

1993. *Retirement of Revolutionaries in China: Public Policies, Social Norms, Private Interests*. Princeton, N.J.: Princeton University Press.

Martin, Lisa L. 1992. *Coercive Cooperation: Explaining Multilateral Economic Sanctions*. Princeton, N.J.: Princeton University Press.

Maruya, Toyojiro. 1992. "The Development of the Guangdong Economy and Its Ties with Beijing." *China Newsletter*, no. 96: 2–10.

Maxfield, Sylvia. 1994. "Financial Incentives and Central Bank Authority in Industrializing Nations." *World Politics* 46 (July): 556–88.

Milgrom, Paul, and John Roberts. 1990. "Bargaining Costs, Influence Costs, and the Organization of Economic Activity." In *Perspectives on Political Economy*, ed. James E. Alt and Kenneth A. Shepsle, 57–89. Cambridge: Cambridge University Press.

Miller, Gary J. 1993. *Managerial Dilemmas*. Cambridge: Cambridge University Press.

Ministry of Finance (MOF). 1984. *Caizheng Gongzuo Sanshiwunian* (Thirty-five years of tax work). Beijing: Zhongguo Caizheng Jingji Chubanshe.

ed. 1987. *Yusuanwai Zijin Guanli Shouce* (Handbook on managing extrabudgetary funds). Beijing: Zhongguo Caizheng Chubanshe.

1989a. *Caishui Gaige Shi Nian* (Ten years of tax reforms). Beijing: Zhongguo Caizheng Jingji Chubanshe.

1989b. *Zhongguo Caizheng Tongji (1950–1988)* (Statistics on Chinese finance [1950–1988]). Beijing: Zhongguo Caizheng Jingji Chubanshe.

Ministry of Personnel. 1989. *Zhonghua Renmin Gongheguo Sheng, Zizhiqu, Zhixiashi Dangzhengqun Jiguan Zuzhi Jigou Gaiyao* (An outline of Party, government, and mass organizations of provinces, autonomous regions, and directly administered municipalities in the People's Republic of China). Beijing: Zhongguo Renshi Chubanshe.

1991a. *Liudong Diaopei Gongzuo Zhinan* (A guidebook on cadre circulation and transfer work). Beijing: Gaige Chubanshe.

1991b. "Renshibu Gongwen Chuli Banfa Shishi Xize" (Detailed provisions of the Ministry of Personnel on official document-handling procedures). In *Renshi Bumen Bangongshi Gongzuo Shiyong Shouce* (Handbook on office affairs of personnel departments), ed. Ministry of Personnel, 245–53. Beijing: Beijing Gongye Daxue Chubanshe.

Moe, Terry M. 1984. "The New Economics of Organization." *American Journal of Political Science* 28 (4): 739–77.

Moore, Barrington. 1967. *Social Origins of Dictatorship and Democracy*. Boston: Beacon Press.

Nathan, Andrew J. 1973. "A Factionalism Model for CCP Politics." *China Quarterly*, no. 53 (January–March): 34–66.

National People's Congress. 1985a [1954]. "Zhonghua Renmin Gongheguo Difang Geji Renmin Daibiao Dahui He Difang Geji Renmin Zhengfu Zuzhifa (1954)" (The organizational law of local people's congresses and local people's governments in the People's Republic of China [1954]). In *Zhonghua Renmin Gongheguo Zuzhifa Xuanbian* (Selections of organizational laws of the People's Republic of China), ed. Ministry of Labor and Personnel, 123–32. Beijing: Jingji Kexue Chubanshe.

1985b [1979]. "Zhonghua Renmin Gongheguo Difang Geji Renmin Daibiao Dahui He Difang Geji Renmin Zhengfu Zuzhifa (1979)" (The organizational law of local people's congresses and local people's governments in the People's Republic of

China [1979]). In *Zhonghua Renmin Gongheguo Zuzhi Fa Xuanbian* (Selections of organizational laws of the People's Republic of China), ed. Ministry of Labor and Personnel, 133–44. Beijing: Jingji Kexue Chubanshe.

Naughton, Barry. 1987. "The Decline of Central Control Over Investment in Post-Mao China." In *Policy Implementation in Post-Mao China*, ed. David Lampton, 51–80. Berkeley: University of California Press.

——— 1988. "Macroeconomic Management and System Reform in China." Paper Prepared for the conference "The Chinese Developmental State: Change and Continuum," Sussex Institute for Development Studies, University of Sussex.

——— 1991a. "Industrial Policy during the Cultural Revolution: Military Preparation, Decentralization, and Leaps Forward." In *New Perspectives on the Cultural Revolution*, ed. William A. Joseph, Christine P. W. Wong, and David Zweig, 153–82. Cambridge, Mass.: Council on East Asian Studies, Harvard University.

——— 1991b. "The Pattern and Legacy of Economic Growth in the Mao Era." In *Perspectives on Modern China*, ed. Kenneth Lieberthal, Joyce Kallgren, Roderick MacFarquhar, and Frederic Wakeman Jr., 226–54. Armonk, N.Y.: M. E. Sharpe.

——— 1991c. "Why Has Economic Reform Led to Inflation?" *AEA Papers and Proceedings* 81 (May): 207–17.

——— 1992a. "The Chinese Economy: On the Road to Recovery?" In *China Briefing, 1991*, ed. William A. Joseph, 77–96. Boulder, Colo.: Westview Press.

——— 1992b. "Hierarchy and the Bargaining Economy: Government and Enterprise in the Reform Process." In *Bureaucracy, Politics and Decision Making in Post-Mao China*, ed. Kenneth G. Lieberthal and David M. Lampton, 245–79. Berkeley: University of California Press.

Nelson, Joan. 1988. "The Political Economy of Stabilization: Commitment, Capacity, and Public Response." In *Toward a Political Economy of Development*, ed. Robert H. Bates, 80–130. Berkeley: University of California Press.

Newcomb, Amelia A. 1995. "China without Deng: U.S. Debates Scenarios." *Christian Science Monitor*, February 14, 6.

Nordhaus, William D. 1975. "The Political Business Cycle." *Review of Economic Studies* 42 (April): 169–90.

——— 1990. "Soviet Economic Reform: The Longest Road." *Brookings Papers on Economic Activity* 1: 287–308.

Nove, Alec. 1986. *The Soviet Economic System*. Boston: Allen & Unwin.

Oates, Wallace E. 1972. *Fiscal Federalism*. New York: Harcourt Brace Jovanovich.

Oi, Jean C. 1989. *State and Peasant in Contemporary China*. Berkeley: University of California Press.

Oksenberg, Michel. 1969. "Local Leaders in Rural China, 1962–65: Individual Attributes, Bureaucratic Positions, and Political Recruitment." In *Chinese Communist Politics in Action*, ed. A. Doak Barnett, 155–215. Seattle: University of Washington Press.

——— 1982. "Economic Policy Making in China, Summer 1981." *China Quarterly*, no. 90 (June): 165–94.

Oksenberg, Michel, and James Tong. 1991. "The Evolution of Central–Provincial Fiscal Relations in China, 1971–1984: The Formal System." *China Quarterly*, no. 125 (March): 1–32.

Olson, Mancur. 1965. *The Logic of Collective Action*. Cambridge, Mass.: Harvard University Press.

——— 1982. *The Rise and Decline of Nations*. New Haven, Conn.: Yale University Press.

Peebles, Gavin. 1986. "Aggregate Retail Price Changes in Socialist Economies: Identification, Theory and Evidence for China and the Soviet Union." *Soviet Studies* 4 (October): 477–507.

Portes, Richard, Richard E. Quandt, David Winter, and Stephen Yeo. 1987. "Macroeconomic Planning and Disequilibrium: Estimates for Poland, 1955–1980." *Econometrica* 55 (January): 19–41.

Posen, Adam. 1994. "Why Central Bank Independence Does Not Cause Low Inflation: There Is No Institutional Fix for Politics." *Finance and the International Economy* 7: 41–59.

Powell, Raymond P. 1977. "Plan Execution and the Workability of Soviet Planning." *Journal of Comparative Economics* 1 (March): 51–76.

Pu Xingzu. 1990. *Dangdai Zhongguo Zhengzhi Zhidu* (The contemporary Chinese political system). Shanghai: Shanghai Renmin Chubanshe.

Pye, Lucian. 1968. *The Spirit of Chinese Politics*. Cambridge, Mass.: MIT Press.

Qian Yingyi. 1995. "Qiye de Zhili Jiegou Gaige He Rongzi Jiegou Gaige" (Reforms of control and financing structures of enterprises). *Jingji Yanjiu* (Economic Research) (January): 20–29.

Qian, Yingyi, and Chenggang Xu. 1993. "The M-form Hierarchy and China's Economic Reform." *European Economic Review* 37: 541–48.

Qiao Shi. 1991 [1990]. "Zai Quanguo Sheng, Zizhiqu, Zhixiashi Dangwei Mishuzhang Zuotanhuishang de Jianghua" (Speech at the National Conference of Secretary-Generals of Provincial Party Committees). In *Renshi Bumen Bangongshi Gongzuo Shiyong Shouce* (Handbook on office affairs of personnel departments), ed. Ministry of Personnel, 15–17. Beijing: Beijing Gongye Daxue Chubanshe.

"Quanmian Qingli Guding Zichan Zaijian Xiangmu" (Thoroughly Scrutinize the Ongoing Fixed-Asset Investment Projects). 1989. In *Tianjin Jingji Nianjian 1989* (Tianjin economic yearbook 1989), 400. Tianjin: Tianjin Renmin Chubanshe.

Ragin, Charles C. 1987. *The Comparative Method*. Berkeley: University of California Press.

Rajaram, Anand. 1992. *Reforming Prices: The Experience of China, Hungary, and Poland*. World Bank Discussion Papers 144. Washington, D.C.

Remmer, Karen L. 1993. "The Political Economy of Elections in Latin America, 1980–1991." *American Political Science Review* 87 (June): 393–407.

Research Group. 1986. "Zhu Baogao Gaige: Women Mianlin de Tiaozhan Yu Xuanze" (Reforms: our challenges and options – the main report). In *Gaige: Women Mianlin de Tiaozhan Yu Xuanze* (Reforms: our challenges and options), ed. Chinese Institute for the Reform of the Economic System, 15–44. Beijing: Zhongguo Jingji Chubanshe.

Riskin, Carl. 1987. *China's Political Economy*. New York: Oxford University Press.

Rohwer, Jim. 1992. "A Survey of China: When China Wakes." *Economist*, November 28, 3–18.

Roland, Gerard. 1987. "Investment Growth Fluctuations in the Soviet Union: An Econometric Analysis." *Journal of Comparative Economics* 11 (June): 192–206.

Ross, Stephen A. 1973. "The Economic Theory of Agency: The Principal's Problem." *American Economic Review* 63 (May).

Schelling, Thomas C. 1980. *The Strategy of Conflict*. Cambridge, Mass.: Harvard University Press.

Schmidt, Steffen W., ed. 1977. *Friends, Followers and Factions*. Berkeley: University of California Press.

Schram, Stuart R. 1984. "'Economics in Command?' Ideology and Policy since the Third Plenum, 1978–84." *China Quarterly*, no. 99 (September): 417–61.

Schurmann, Franz. 1968. *Ideology and Organization in Communist China*. Berkeley: University of California Press.

Sen, Amartya. 1989. "Food and Freedom." *World Development* 17 (6): 769–81.

Shambaugh, David. 1993. "Losing Control: The Erosion of State Authority in China." *Current History* 92 (September): 253–59.

Shandong Statistical Bureau. 1989. *Shandong Tongji Nianjian 1989* (Shandong statistical yearbook 1989). Beijing: Zhongguo Tongji Chubanshe.

Shanghai Economic Research Center. 1986. "Dui Shanghaishi Dangqian Jingji Xingshi de Fenxi" (An analysis of Shanghai's current economic situation). *Jingji Gongzuozhe Xuexi Ziliao* (Study Materials for Economists), no. 7: 72–75.

Shanghai Planning Commission. 1986. "Cong Shiji Chufa, Kaizhan Jingji Tiaojie Gongzuo" (Carry out economic adjustment work on a realistic basis). *Jingji Gongzuozhe Xuexi Ziliao* (Study Materials for Economists), no. 14: 17–22.

Shen Liren, and Dai Yuanchen. 1990. "Woguo 'Zhuhuo Jingji' de Xingcheng Jiqi Piduan He Gengyuan" (The shortcomings and sources of "vassal economies" in China). *Jingji Yanjiu* (Economic Research), no. 3 (March): 12–29, 67.

Shen Zhiqun. 1988. "Touzi Guimo Hongguan Kongzhi Moshi de Tantao" (On a macroeconomic investment control model). In *Lun Zhongguo Hongguan Jingji Guanli* (On China's macroeconomic management), ed. Gui Shiyong, Wang Jiye, and Yang Zhenjia, 556–64. Beijing: Zhongguo Jingji Chubanshe.

Shenzhen Planning Commission. 1991. "Dui Mingnian Quanguo Jihua Anpai de Jiben Kanfa Yu Qingqiu Jiejue de Jige Wenti" (Basic positions on next year's national plan and requests to solve a number of problems). In *Shenzhen Zhengfu Jihua Wenjian Huibian* (Selections of planning documents of the Shenzhen government), Shenzhen Planning Bureau, 90–101. Shenzhen: Shenzhen Jihuaju.

Shirk, Susan L. 1989. "The Political Economy of Chinese Industrial Reform." In *Remaking the Economic Institutions of Socialism: China and Eastern Europe*, ed. Victor Nee and David Stark, 328–62. Stanford, Calif.: Stanford University Press.

———. 1990. "Playing to the Provinces: Deng Xiaoping's Political Strategy of Economic Reform." Paper presented at the Annual Meeting of the American Political Science Association, San Francisco, Calif.

———. 1993. *The Political Logic of Economic Reform in China*. Berkeley: University of California Press.

Shorter, Edward, and Charles Tilly. 1974. *Strikes in France, 1830–1968*. Cambridge: Cambridge University Press.

Simmons, Beth A. 1990. "No Time to Cooperate: Why International Monetary Cooperation Was Unstable in the Interwar Years." Paper presented at the Annual Meeting of the American Political Science Association, San Francisco, Calif.

Simon, Herbert A. 1976. *Administrative Behavior*. New York: The Free Press.

———. 1982. *Models of Bounded Rationality*. Cambridge, Mass.: MIT Press.

Sims, Christopher A. 1972. "Money, Income, and Causality." *American Economic Review* 62 (September): 540–52.

Singh, Inderjit. 1992. *China: Industrial Policies for an Economy in Transition*. World Bank Discussion Papers 143. Washington, D.C.

Skilling, H. Gordon. 1966. "Interest Groups and Communist Politics." *World Politics* 18 (April): 435–51.

Skilling, H. Gordon, and Franklyn Griffiths, eds. 1971. *Interest Groups in Soviet Politics*. Princeton, N.J.: Princeton University Press.

Skocpol, Theda. 1979. *States and Social Revolutions: A Comparative Analysis of France, Russia and China*. Cambridge: Cambridge University Press.

Solinger, Dorothy J. 1977. *Regional Government and Political Integration in Southwest China, 1949–1954*. Berkeley: University of California Press.

Song Ping. 1984. "Dangqian Guomin Jingjizhong de Jige Wenti" (A few current problems in the national economy). *Lilun Yuekan* (Theoretical Monthly), no. 3: 1–7.

1986. "Guanyu 1986 Nian Guomin Jingji He Shehui Fazhan Jihua Cao'an de Baogao" (Draft report on the 1986 plan for the national economy and social development). *Renmin Ribao* (People's Daily), April 16, 2.

State Commission for Reform of the Economic System (SCRES). 1992. "1991 Nian Woguo Jingji Tizhi Gaige Zai Wending Fazhanzhong Jiakuai Bufa" (Accelerating reforms of China's economic system in 1991 during stable development). In *Zhongguo Jingji Tizhi Gaige Nianjian 1992* (Yearbook of reform of China's economic system 1992), ed. State Commission for Reform of the Economic System, 165–71. Beijing: Gaige Chubanshe.

State Commission on Government Establishment. 1989 [1988]. "Guanyu Zhongyang Yiji Guojia Jiguan Renyuan Bianzhi Guanli He Xingzheng Yusuan de Jige Wenti de Tongzhi" (Circular on management of *nomenklatura* and administrative expenditures of central government agencies). In *Renshi Gongzuo Wenjian Xuanbian* (Selections of documents on personnel work), ed. Ministry of Personnel, vol. 11, 638–40. n.p.: Xueyuan Chubanshe.

——— ed. 1990. *Zhongguo Zhengfu Jigou, 1990* (Chinese government agencies, 1990). Beijing: Zhongguo Jingji Chubanshe.

State Council. 1984 [1980]. "Guanyu Chongxin Heding Ge Sheng, Shi, Zizhiqu Xingzheng Zong'er de Tongzhi" (Notice on re-ratifications of the total number of administrative positions of provinces, cities, and autonomous regions). In *Renshi Gongzuo Wenjian Xuanbian* (Selections of documents on personnel work), ed. Ministry of Personnel, vol. 4, 294–95. Beijing: Laodong Renshi Chubanshe.

——— 1985 [1982]. "Guanyu Guowuyuan Ge Bumen Buyao Ganyu Difang Jigou Bianzhi de Tongzhi" (Circular requesting various departments of the State Council not to interfere with the local institutional set-up). In *Renshi Gongzuo Wenjian Xuanbian* (Selections of documents on personnel work), ed. Ministry of Labor and Personnel, vol. 5, 132. Beijing: Laodong Renshi Chubanshe.

——— 1986 [1985]. "Guanyu Gansusheng Weifan Guojia Guiding Luanfa Jiangjin de Tongbao" (Notice on Gansu province's disorderly bonus practices in violation of state regulations). In *Renshi Gongzuo Wenjian Xuanbian* (Selections of documents on personnel work), ed. Ministry of Labor and Personnel, vol. 8, 692–93. Beijing: Laodong Renshi Chubanshe.

——— 1987a [1986]. "Guanyu Jiaqiang Yusuanwai Zijin Guanli de Tongzhi" (Notice on strengthening the management of extrabudgetary funds). In *Yusuanwai Zijin Guanli Shouce* (Handbook on managing extrabudgetary funds), ed. Ministry of Finance, 126–29. Beijing: Zhongguo Caizheng Chubanshe.

——— 1987b [1983]. "Guanyu Yange Kongzhi Jiben Jianshe Guimo, Qingli Zaijian Xiangmu de Jinji Tongzhi" (Urgent circular to control strictly the scope of basic construction and review current projects). In *Zhongyao Jingji Fagui Ziliao Xuanbian, 1977–1986* (Selections of important economic regulations, 1977–1986), 576–77. Beijing: Zhongguo Tongji Chubanshe.

——— 1988 [1984]. "Guanyu Jiaqiang Tongji Gongzuo de Jueding" (The decision to strengthen statistical work). In *Tongji Zhidu Fangfa Wenjian Xuanbian (1950–1987)* (Selections of documents on the statistical system and laws [1950–1987]), ed. State Statistical Bureau, 161–65. Beijing: Zhongguo Jihua Chubanshe.

——— 1989a [1988]. "Guanyu Ganbu Guanli Youguan Wenti de Tongzhi" (Circular on issues related to cadre management). In *Renshi Gongzuo Wenjian Xuanbian* (Selections of documents on personnel work), ed. Ministry of Personnel, vol. 11, 3–5. n.p.: Xueyuan Chubanshe.

——— 1989b [1988]. "Guanyu Jiaqiang Wujia Guanli Yange Kongzhi Wujia Shangchang de Jueding" (The decision to strengthen price controls and strictly curtail price rises).

In *Zhili Jingji Huanjing, Zhengdun Jingji Cixu, Quanmian Shenhua Gaige Fagui Huibian* (Collection of laws and regulations about rectifying the economic environment, restoring economic order, and deepening the reforms), ed. Law and Regulation Editorial Office, 179–82. Beijing: Falu Chubanshe.

1989c [1988]. "Guanyu Qingli Guding Zichan Touzi Zaijian Xiangmu, Yasuo Touzi Guimo, Tiaozheng Touzi Jiegou de Tongzhi" (Notice on taking an inventory of fixed-asset projects under construction, reducing the investment scope, adjusting the investment structure). In *Zhili Jingji Huanjing, Zhengdun Jingji Cixu, Quanmian Shenhua Gaige Fagui Huibian* (Collections of laws and regulations about rectifying the economic environment, restoring economic order, and deepening the reforms), ed. Law and Regulation Editorial Office, 25–43. Beijing: Falu Chubanshe.

1991. "Guojia Xingzheng Jiguan Gongwen Chuli Fangfa" (Regulations on handling documents of government units). In *Renshi Bumen Bangongshi Gongzuo Shiyong Shouce* (Handbook on office affairs of personnel departments), ed. Ministry of Personnel, 201–14. Beijing: Beijing Gongye Daxue Chubanshe.

State Council, and State Planning Commission (SPC). 1990. *Zhongguo Gongye Xianzhuang* (The current state of Chinese industry). Beijing: Renmin Chubanshe.

State Economic Commission (SEC), ed. 1986. *Zhonghua Renmin Gongheguo Jingji Guanli Dashiji* (Significant events in the economic management of the People's Republic of China). Beijing: Zhongguo Jingji Chubanshe.

State Planning Commission (SPC). 1987. "Guanyu Zhizhi Mangmu Jianshe, Chongfu Jianshe de Jixiang Guiding" (Regulations on banning blind and repeat construction projects). In *Zhongyao Jingji Fagui Ziliao Xuanbian, 1977–1986* (Selections of important economic regulations, 1977–1986), 558–60. Beijing: Zhongguo Tongji Chubanshe.

State Planning Commission, Ministry of Finance, and People's Construction Bank. 1991 [1985]. "Guanyu Guojia Yusuannei Jiben Jianshe Touzi Quanbu You Bokuan Gaiwei Daikuan de Zhanxing Guiding" (Provisional regulations on converting all the grants into loans for state budgetary basic construction investment). In *Zhongguo Touzi Guanli Daquan* (Almanac on Chinese investment management), 852–56. Beijing: Zhongguo Caizheng Chubanshe.

State Planning Commission, State Economic Commission, State Statistical Bureau, and Ministry of Finance. 1988 [1986]. "Guanyu Jiaqiang Guding Zichan Touzi Tongji Gongzuo de Tongzhi" (Notice on strengthening statistical collection of fixed-asset investment data). In *Tongji Gongzuo Zhongyao Wenjian Xuanbian 1986–1987* (Selection of important documents on statistical work 1986–1987), ed. State Statistical Bureau, 95–97. Beijing: Zhongguo Tongji Chubanshe.

State Planning Commission, and State Statistical Bureau. 1991 [1985]. "Guanyu Tiaozheng Jiben Jianshe Touzi Jihua, Tongji Fanwei Koujing de Tongzhi" (A circular on adjustment of capital construction planning and statistical sources). In *Zhongguo Touzi Guanli Daquan* (Almanac on Chinese investment management), 842–43. Beijing: Zhongguo Caizheng Chubanshe.

1992. *1992 Nian Zhongguo Touzi Baogao* (China investment report in 1992). Beijing: Zhongguo Jihua Chubanshe.

State Statistical Bureau (SSB). 1983. "Guanyu 1982 Nian Guomin Jingji He Shehui Fazhan Jihua Zhixing Jieguo de Gongbao" (Report on the performance of the 1982 national economic and social development plan). *Renmin Ribao* (People's Daily), April 30, 2.

1986. *Zhongguo Tongji Nianjian 1986* (China statistical yearbook 1986). Beijing: Zhongguo Tongji Chubanshe.

1987a. *Guding Zichan Touzi Tongji Gongzuo Shouce* (Handbook for work in fixed-asset capital investment). Beijing: Zhongguo Tongji Chubanshe.

1987b. *Zhongguo Guding Zichan Touzi Tongji Ziliao (1950–1985)* (Statistical materials on Chinese fixed-asset investment [1950–1985]). Beijing: Zhongguo Tongji Chubanshe.

1988. *Zhongguo Tongji Nianjian 1988* (China statistical yearbook 1988). Beijing: Zhongguo Tongji Chubanshe.

1989. *Zhongguo Guding Zichan Touzi Tongji Ziliao (1986–1987)* (Statistical materials on Chinese fixed-asset investment [1986–1987]). Beijing: Zhongguo Tongji Chubanshe.

1990. *Quanguo Gesheng, Zizhiqu, Zhixiashi Lishi Tongji Ziliao Huibian* (Collection of historical data of Chinese provinces, autonomous regions, and directly administered municipalities). Beijing: Zhongguo Tongji Chubanshe.

1991a. *Qiwu Shiqi Guomin Jingji He Shehui Fazhan Gaikuang* (A survey on national economic and social development during the Seventh Five-Year Plan). Beijing: Zhongguo Tongji Chubanshe.

1991b. *Zhongguo Guding Zichan Touzi Tongji Ziliao (1988–1989)* (Statistical materials on Chinese fixed-asset investment [1988–1989]). Beijing: Zhongguo Tongji Chubanshe.

1992a. "1982 Nian Guomin Jingji Fazhan Qingkuang" (The development of the national economy in 1982). In *Bashi Niandai de Zhongguo Jingji* (The Chinese economy in the 1980s), ed. State Statistical Bureau, 13–19. Beijing: Zhongguo Tongji Chubanshe.

1992b. "1985 Nian Guomin Jingji Fazhan Qingkuang" (The development of the national economy in 1985). In *Bashi Niandai de Zhongguo Jingji* (The Chinese economy in the 1980s), ed. State Statistical Bureau, 30–37. Beijing: Zhongguo Tongji Chubanshe.

1992c. *China Foreign Economic Statistics, 1979–1991*. Beijing: China Statistical Information & Consultancy Service Centre.

1993a. *Zhongguo Guding Zichan Touzi Tongji Ziliao (1990–1991)* (Statistics on Chinese fixed-asset investment [1990–1991]). Beijing: Zhongguo Tongji Chubanshe.

1993b. *Zhongguo Tongji Nianjian 1993* (China statistical yearbook 1993). Beijing: Zhongguo Tongji Chubanshe.

1994. *Zhongguo Tongji Nianjian 1994* (China statistical yearbook 1994). Beijing: Zhongguo Tongji Chubanshe.

Stimson, James A. 1985. "Regression in Space and Time: A Statistical Essay." *American Journal of Political Science* 29 (November): 914–47.

Su, Si-jin. 1993. "Motivations of Profit-seeking Behavior and Market-oriented Growth of Chinese Firms: An Institutional Approach." Working Papers on Transition from State Socialism 92–3. Ithaca, N.Y.: Mario Einaudi Center for International Studies, Cornell University.

"Sudu Wenti Shi Yige Zhengzhi Wenti" (The issue about speed is a political issue). 1992 [1977]. In *Renmin Gongheguo Chunqiu Shilu* (Annals of the People's Republic), ed. Lin Yunhui, Liu Yong, and Shi Bonian, 1079–80. Beijing: Zhongguo Renmin Daxue Chubanshe.

Sullivan, Lawrence R. 1988. "Assault on the Reforms: Conservative Criticism of Political and Economic Liberalization in China 1985–86." *China Quarterly*, no. 114 (June): 198–222.

Szelenyi, Ivan. 1989. "Eastern Europe in an Epoch of Transition: Toward a Socialist Mixed Economy?" In *Remaking the Economic Institutions of Socialism*, ed. Victor Nee and David Stark, 208–32. Stanford, Calif.: Stanford University Press.

Tang Gongzhao. 1983. "'Tiaotiao' 'Kuaikuai' Yu Dangqian de Jihua Guanli Wenti" ("Vertical" and "regional" issues and the current situation in planning management). *Sichuan Daxue Xuebao* (Journal of Sichuan University), no. 1: 23–28.

Tang Lingyun. 1992. "Dangqian Huobi Xiandai Xingshi He Hongguan Jinrong Guanli" (On the current money supply, credit situation, and macro monetary management). In *Gaige Yu Fazhan* (Reform and development), ed. Wang Zhanxiang, 69–83. Beijing: Zhongguo Caizheng Jingji Chubanshe.

Tao Zengyi. 1988. "Kongzhi Guding Zichan Touzi Guimo de Ruogan Jianyi" (A few suggestions on fixed-asset investment control). In *Lun Zhongguo Hongguan Jingji Guanli* (On China's macroeconomic management), ed. Gui Shiyong, Wang Jiye, and Yang Zhenjia, 594–99. Beijing: Zhongguo Jingji Chubanshe.

Teiwes, Frederick C. 1971. "Provincial Politics in China: Themes and Variations." In *China: Management of a Revolutionary Society*, ed. John M. H. Lindbeck, 116–92. Seattle: University of Washington Press.

Tian Jiyun. 1986. "Guanyu Dangqian Jingji Xingshi He Jingji Tizhi Gaige de Wenti" (Issues on the current economic situation and reform of the economic system). *Renmin Ribao* (People's Daily), January 12, 1.

——— 1990 [1983]. "Zai Shenjishu Chengli Dahuishang de Jianghua" (Speech at the opening ceremony for the General Auditing Administration). In *Dangzheng Lingdao Tan Shenji* (Party and government leaders on auditing), ed. Cui Jianmin, 23–28. Beijing: Zhongguo Shenji Chubanshe.

Tian Yinong, Xiang Huaicheng, and Zhu Fulin. 1988. *Lun Zhongguo Caizheng Tizhi Gaige Yu Hongguan Tiaokong* (On Chinese fiscal system reforms and macroeconomic management). Beijing: Zhongguo Caizheng Jingji Chubanshe.

Tianjin Jingji Nianjian 1988 (Tianjin economic yearbook 1988). 1989. Tianjin: Tianjin Renmin Chubanshe.

Tianjin Jingji Nianjian 1989 (Tianjin economic yearbook 1989). 1990. Tianjin: Tianjin Renmin Chubanshe.

Tianjin Statistical Bureau. 1989. "Guanyu Tianjinshi Guding Zichan Touzi Heli Guimo de Taolun" (A discussion on the rational fixed-asset investment level in Tianjin). In *Tongji Fenxi Baogao Xuanbian 1986–1987* (Selection of statistical analysis reports 1986–1987), comp. State Statistical Bureau, 229–42. Beijing: Zhongguo Tongji Chubanshe.

Tidrick, Gene. 1987. "Planning and Supply." In *China's Industrial Reform*, ed. Gene Tidrick and Jiyuan Chen, 175–209. New York: Oxford University Press.

Tidrick, Gene, and Jiyuan Chen. 1987. "The Essence of Industrial Reforms." In *China's Industrial Reform*, ed. Gene Tidrick and Jiyuan Chen, 1–10. New York: Oxford University Press.

Tong, James. 1989. "Fiscal Reform, Elite Turnover and Central-Provincial Relations in Post-Mao China." *Australian Journal of Chinese Affairs*, no. 22 (July): 1–28.

"Toushui Loushui, Shuishi Dahu?" (Who are the biggest tax evaders?). 1988. *Jingji Ribao* (Economic Daily), December 1, 1.

Tsakok, I. 1979. "Inflation Control in the PRC 1949–54." *World Development* 7 (August–September): 865–75.

Tufte, Edward R. 1974. *Data Analysis for Politics and Policy*. Englewood Cliffs, N.J.: Prentice-Hall.

Tversky, Amos, and Daniel Kahneman. 1990. "Rational Choice and the Framing of Decisions." In *The Limits of Rationality*, ed. Karen Schweers Cook and Margaret Levi, 60–89. Chicago: University of Chicago Press.

United Nations. 1984 [1960]. "Capital Accumulation and Development." In *Leading Issues in Economic Development*, ed. Gerald M. Meier, 219–22. New York: Oxford University Press.

Vogel, Ezra F. 1980 [1969]. *Canton under Communism*. Cambridge, Mass.: Harvard University Press.

Wade, Robert. 1990. *Governing the Market: Economic Theory and the Role of Government in East Asian Industrialization.* Princeton, N.J.: Princeton University Press.

Walder, Andrew G. 1986. *Communist Neo-traditionalism: Work and Authority in Chinese Industry.* Berkeley: University of California Press.

——— 1987. "Communist Social Structure and Workers' Politics in China." In *Citizens and Groups in Contemporary China,* ed. Victor C. Falkenheim, 45–90. Michigan Monographs in Chinese Studies 56. Ann Arbor: Center for Chinese Studies, University of Michigan.

——— 1989. "The Political Sociology of the Beijing Upheaval of 1989." *Problems of Communism* (September–October): 30–40.

——— 1992. "Local Bargaining Relationships and Urban Industrial Finance." In *Bureaucracy, Politics and Decision-making in Post-Mao China,* ed. Kenneth Lieberthal and Michael Lampton, 308–33. Berkeley: University of California Press.

Wang Bingqian. 1988. "1987 Nian Guojia Yusuan Zhixing Qingkuang (Jielu)" (The implementation of the 1987 budget [excerpts]). In *Zhongguo Jinrong Nianjian 1988* (Chinese financial almanac 1988), ed. Chinese Financial Society, 20–21. Beijing: Zhongguo Jinrong Chubanshe.

——— 1990. "Guanyu 1989 Nian Guojia Yusuan Zhixing Qingkuang He 1990 Nian Guojia Yusuan Cao'an de Baogao" (Report on the implementation of the 1989 budget and the draft 1990 budget). In *1990 Zhongguo Jingji Nianjian* (Chinese economic almanac 1991), 127–36. Beijing: Zhongguo Jingji Guanli Chubanshe.

——— 1990 [1983]. "Zai Sheng, Zizhiqu, Zhixiashi Shenji Juzhang Zuotanhuishang de Jianghua" (Speech at the Conference of Chiefs of Auditing Bureaus of Provinces, Autonomous Regions, and Directly Administered Municipalities). In *Dangzheng Lingdao Tan Shenji* (Party and government leaders on auditing), ed. Cui Jianmin, 30–39. Beijing: Zhongguo Shenji Chubanshe.

——— 1991. "Guanyu 1990 Nian Guojia Yusuan Zhixing Qingkuang He 1991 Nian Guojia Yusuan Cao'an de Baogao" (Report on the implementation of the 1990 budget and the draft 1991 budget). In *1991 Zhongguo Jingji Nianjian* (Chinese economic almanac 1991), 138–47. Beijing: Zhongguo Jingji Guanli Chubanshe.

Wang Hongmo. 1989. *Gaige Kaifang de Licheng* (The historical process of reforms and opening). Zhengzhou: Henan Renmin Chubanshe.

Wang Liguo. 1989. "Xingwei Maodun de Difang Zhengfu: Lilun de Kunhuo Yu Xianshi de Xuanze" (Local governments in behavioral contradictions: theoretical confusions and real choices). *Jingji Tizhi Gaige* (Economic System Reform), no. 2: 64–68.

Wang Shaoguang. 1991. "Jianli Yige Qiangyoulide Minzhu Guojia" (Building a strong democratic state: on regime type and state capacity). Princeton, N.J.: Center for Modern China.

——— 1994. "Central-Local Fiscal Politics in China." In *Changing Central-Local Relations in China,* ed. Jia Hao and Zhimin Lin, 91–112. Boulder, Colo.: Westview Press.

Wang Shaoguang, and Hu Angang. 1993. "Jiaqiang Zhongyang Zhengfu Zai Shichang Jingji Zhuanxinzhong de Zhudao Zuoyong" (Strengthen the function of the central government during the market transition). Unpublished paper. New Haven, Conn.: Yale University.

Wang Yifu. 1986. *Xin Zhongguo Tongji Shigao* (History of New China's statistical work). Beijing: Zhongguo Tongji Chubanshe.

Wang Zhigang. 1988. *Zhengfu Zhineng Yu Jigou Gaige* (Transformation of governmental functions and reform of institutions). Beijing: Guangming Ribao Chubanshe.

Watson, Andrew, Christopher Findlay, and Yintang Du. 1989. "Who Won the 'Wool

War'?: A Case Study of Rural Product Marketing in China." *China Quarterly*, no. 118 (June): 213–41.

Weber, Max. 1958. "Politics as a Vocation." In *From Max Weber: Essays in Sociology*, ed. H. H. Gerth and C. Wright Mills. New York: Oxford University Press.

Weingast, Barry R., and Mark Moran. 1983. "Bureaucratic Discretion or Congressional Control: Regulatory Policymaking by the Federal Trade Commission." *Journal of Political Economy* 91 (October): 765–800.

Weingast, Barry R., Kenneth A. Shepsle, and Christopher Johnsen. 1981. "The Political Economy of Benefits and Costs: A Neoclassical Approach to Distributive Politics." *Journal of Political Economy* 89 (5).

Wen Jiabao. 1991 [1990]. "Zai Quanguo Sheng, Zizhiqu, Zhixiashi Dangwei Mishuzhang Zuotanhuishang de Jianghua" (Speech at the National Conference of Secretary-Generals of Provincial Party Committees). In *Renshi Bumen Bangongshi Gongzuo Shiyong Shouce* (Handbook on office affairs of personnel departments), ed. Ministry of Personnel, 21–35. Beijing: Beijing Gongye Daxue Chubanshe.

Who's Who in China: Current Leaders. 1989. Beijing: Foreign Languages Press.

Wiemer, Calla, and Xiaoxuan Liu. 1991. "Price Reform in China: The Transition to Rationality." In *China's Reform, 1978–1988*, ed. M. Dutta and Zhongli Zhang, 111–32. Greenwich, Conn.: JAI Press.

Winiecki, J. 1982. "Investment Cycles and an Excess Demand Inflation in Planned Economies: Sources and Processes." *Acta Oeconomica* 28 (1–2): 147–60.

"Woguo Guomin Jingji He Shehui Fazhan de Qige Wunian Jihua" (China's Seventh Five-Year Plan of Economic and Social Development). 1986. In *Zhongguo Jingji Nianjian 1986* (Chinese economic almanac 1986), 148–74. Beijing: Jingji Guanli Chubanshe.

Wong, Christine P. W. 1985. "Material Allocations and Decentralization: Impact of the Local Sector on Industrial Reform." In *The Political Economy of Reform in Post-Mao China*, ed. Elizabeth Perry and Christine Wong, 253–78. Cambridge, Mass.: Council on East Asian Studies, Harvard University.

———. 1986. "Ownership and Control in Chinese Industry: The Maoist Legacy and Prospects for the 1980s." In *China's Economy Looks Toward the Year 2000*, ed. Joint Economic Committee, vol. 1: *The Four Modernizations*, 571–603. Washington, D.C.: Government Printing Office.

———. 1987. "Between Plan and Market: The Role of the Local Sector in Post-Mao China." *Journal of Comparative Economics* 11 (3): 385–98.

———. 1990. "Central-Local Relations in an Era of Fiscal Decline: The Paradox of Fiscal Decentralization in Post-Mao China." Working Paper 210. Santa Cruz: University of California.

Woolley, John. 1985. "Central Banks and Inflation." In *The Politics of Inflation and Economic Stagnation*, ed. Leon N. Lindberg and Charles S. Maier, 318–48. Washington, D.C.: Brookings Institution.

World Bank. 1985. *China: Long-term Development Issues and Options*. Baltimore, Md.: Johns Hopkins University Press.

———. 1988. *World Development Report 1988*. New York: Oxford University Press.

———. 1989a. *China: Revenue Mobilization and Tax Policy*. Washington, D.C.

———. 1989b. *World Development Report 1989*. New York: Oxford University Press.

———. 1990a. *China: Macroeconomic Stability and Industrial Growth under Decentralized Socialism*. Washington, D.C.

———. 1990b. *China: Between Plan and Market*. Washington, D.C.

———. 1990c. *China: Financial Sector Policies and Institutional Development*. Washington, D.C.

———. 1993. *The East Asian Miracle*. New York: Oxford University Press.

1995. *World Tables 1995*. Washington, D.C.

Wu Deming. 1987. *Guojia Yusuan Guanli Tizhi Gailun* (An outline of the government budget management system). Beijing: Zhongguo Caizheng Jingji Chubanshe.

Wu, Jinglian. 1988. "The Strategic Options of Reform and the Evolution of Economic Theories – An Analysis of China's Example." Paper presented at the Conference on Socialist Reforms, Vienna, Austria.

Wu, Jinglian, and Renwei Zhao. 1987. "The Dual Pricing System in China's Industry." *Journal of Comparative Economics* 11 (3): 309–18.

Wu Peilun, ed. 1990. *Woguo de Zhengfu Jigou Gaige* (Reform of government institutions in China). Beijing: Jingji Ribao Chubanshe.

Xu, Chenggang. 1990. "Growth, Productivity and Bureaucratic Control of Chinese Rural Industry." Cambridge, Mass.: Economics Department, Harvard University.

Xu Gang. 1986. "Fei Shengchanxing Touzi Pengzhang" (Expansion of nonproductive investment). In *Gaige: Women Mianlin de Tiaozhan Yu Xuanze* (Reforms: our challenges and options), ed. Chinese Institute for the Reform of the Economic System, 181–93. Beijing: Zhongguo Jingji Chubanshe.

Xu Ruixin. 1991 [1990]. "Zai Bufen Buwei Bangongting Zhuren Zuotanhuishang de Jianghua" (Speech at the Conference of General Offices of a Number of Ministries and Commissions). In *Renshi Bumen Bangongshi Gongzuo Shiyong Shouce* (Handbook on office affairs of personnel departments), ed. Ministry of Personnel, 67–73. Beijing: Beijing Gongye Daxue Chubanshe.

Xu Xu. 1988. "'Zhuanhu Cunchu' Shi Yusuanwai Zijin Guanli de Youxiao Tujing" ("Specialized accounts" are an effective way of managing extrabudgetary funds). *Jingji Yanjiu Cankao Ziliao* (Economic Research Reference Materials), June 30, 46–52.

Xue Muqiao. 1983. "Muqian Woguo Jingji Xingshi de Fenxi He Zhanwang" (An analysis of the current economic situation and prospects). *Renmin Ribao* (People's Daily), June 3, 5.

1987. "Liyong Jingji Banfa Jiaqiang Hongguan Kongzhi" (Using economic methods to strengthen macro control). In *Lun Zhongguo Hongguan Jingji Guanli* (On China's macroeconomic management), ed. Gui Shiyong, Wang Jiye, and Yang Zhenjia, 5–12. Beijing: Zhongguo Jingji Chubanshe.

Yang, Dali. 1990. "Patterns of China's Regional Development Strategy." *China Quarterly*, no. 122 (June): 230–57.

Yang Guansan, Lin Bing, Wu Quhui, and Wang Hansheng. 1986. "Dangqian Woguo Qiye Ganbu Suzhi de Diaocha Yu Chubu Fenxi" (An investigation and a preliminary analysis of the characteristics of enterprise cadres). In *Gaige: Women Mianlin de Tiaozhan Yu Xuanze* (Reforms: our challenges and options), ed. Chinese Institute for the Reform of the Economic System, 270–305. Beijing: Zhongguo Jingji Chubanshe.

Yao Ruxue. 1984. "Kongzhi Jijian Guimo Baozheng Zhongdian Jianshe" (Control investment volume and guarantee priority projects). In *Henan Nianjian 1984* (Henan yearbook 1984), ed. Henan Local History Editorial Committee, 358–59. Zhengzhou: Henan Nianjian Bianjibu.

Yao Yilin. 1982. "Guanyu 1982 Nian Jingji He Shehui Fazhan Jihua Cao'an de Baogao" (Draft report on the 1982 economic and social development plan). *Renmin Ribao* (People's Daily), May 5, 2.

1983. "Guanyu 1983 Nian Guomin Jingji He Shehui Fazhan Jihua de Baogao" (Report on the 1983 national economic and social development plan). *Renmin Ribao* (People's Daily), June 25, 3.

1991a [1989]. "Guanyu 1989 Nian Guomin Jingji He Shehui Fazhan Jihua Cao'an de Baogao" (Draft report on the 1989 plan for national economic and social development). In *Shisanda Yilai Zhongyao Wenjian Xuanbian* (Selection of important documents since the thirteenth congress), ed. Document Research Office of the Central Committee, 470–90. Beijing: Renmin Chubanshe.

1991b [1990]. "Zai Quanguo Sheng, Zizhiqu, Zhixiashi Dangwei Mishuzhang Zuotanhuishang de Jianghua" (Speech at the National Conference of Secretary-Generals of Provincial Party Committees). In *Renshi Bumen Bangongshi Gongzuo Shiyong Shouce* (Handbook on office affairs of personnel departments), ed. Ministry of Personnel, 18–19. Beijing: Beijing Gongye Daxue Chubanshe.

1992a [1988]. "Tingqu Quanguo Tongji Gongzuo Huiyi Huibao Shi de Jianghua" (Speech at the briefing of the National Statistical Work Conference). In *Tongji Gongzuo Zhongyao Wenjian Xuanbian 1988–1990* (Selections of important documents on statistical work 1988–1990), ed. State Statistical Bureau, 63–64. Beijing: Zhongguo Tongji Chubanshe.

1992b [1990]. "Zai Tingqu Quanguo Tongji Gongzuo Huiyi Huibao Shi de Jianghua" (Speech at the briefing of the National Statistical Work Conference). In *Tongji Gongzuo Zhongyao Wenjian Xuanbian 1988–1990* (Selections of important documents on statistical work 1988–1990), ed. State Statistical Bureau, 636–48. Beijing: Zhongguo Tongji Chubanshe.

Yue Wei. 1988 [1986]. "Zai Quanguo Tongji Gongzuo Huiyi Kaimushi de Jianghua" (Speech at the opening of the National Statistical Work Conference). In *Tongji Gongzuo Zhongyao Wenjian Xuanbian 1986–1987* (Selections of important documents on statistical work 1986–1987), ed. State Statistical Bureau, 15–32. Beijing: Zhongguo Tongji Chubanshe.

Zang, Xiaowei. 1991. "Provincial Elite in Post-Mao China." *Asian Survey* 31 (June): 512–25.

Zhang Jun. 1991. "Xunqiu Duanque de Zhidu Yuanyin" (Institutional causes for shortage). *Jingji Yanjiu* (Economic Research), no. 12 (December): 12–21.

Zhang Keyun. 1992. "Zhongguo Quyu Jingji Yunxing Wenti Yanjiu" (Research on Chinese regional economies). *Jingji Yanjiu* (Economic Research), no. 6 (June): 52–58.

Zhang Quanjing. 1988. *Ganbu Renshi Gongzuo Gaishu* (Essentials of cadre and personnel work). Ji'nan: Shandong Renmin Chubanshe.

Zhang Sai. 1987. "Tongji Fazhan Zhanlue Wenti Yanjiu" (Research on the issue of statistical development strategy). *Tongji Yanjiu* (Statistical Research), no. 4.

1989. "Lun Tongji Jiandu Zhineng de Qianghua" (On strengthening the statistical auditing function). *Jingji Yanjiu* (Economic Research), no. 9 (September): 50–55.

ed. 1992. *Zhonghua Renmin Gongheguo Tongji Dashiji, 1949–1991* (Chronicle of events in statistical work of the People's Republic of China, 1949–1991). Beijing: Zhongguo Tongji Chubanshe.

1992 [1989]. "Qianghua Tongji Jiandu Zhineng, Chongfen Fahui Tongji Gongzuo Zai Gaige He Jianshezhong de Zhongyao Zuoyong" (Strengthen the statistical auditing function, fully develop the use of statistical work in reforms and construction). In *Tongji Gongzuo Zhongyao Wenjian Xuanbian 1988–1990* (Selections of important documents on statistical work 1988–1990), ed. State Statistical Bureau. Beijing: Zhongguo Tongji Chubanshe.

Zhang Shaojie, Cui Heming, Xu Gang, and Ji Xiaoming. 1986. "Touzi: Jizhi de Chubu Bianhua Ji Gaige Silu" (Investment: initial changes in the system and some ideas on the reforms). In *Gaige: Women Mianlin de Tiaozhan Yu Xuanze* (Reforms: our challenges and options), ed. Chinese Institute for the Reform of the Economic System, 159–80. Beijing: Zhongguo Jingji Chubanshe.

Zhang Shaojie, and Zhang Amei. 1986. "Dangqian Woguo Gongye Qiye de Jingying Huanjing Fenxi" (An analysis into the current environment for Chinese industrial enterprises). In *Gaige: Women Mianlin de Tiaozhan Yu Xuanze* (Reforms: our challenges and options), ed. Chinese Institute for the Reform of the Economic System, 58–70. Beijing: Zhongguo Jingji Chubanshe.

Zhang Xiangling. 1989. *Heilongjiang Sishi Nian* (Heilongjiang's forty years). Harbin: Heilongjiang Renmin Chubanshe.

Zhang, Xun-Hai. 1992. *Enterprise Reforms in a Centrally Planned Economy*. New York: St. Martin's Press.

Zhao Dexing. 1989a. *Zhonghua Renmin Gongheguo Jingjishi (1967–1984)* (An economic history of the People's Republic of China [1967–1984]). Zhengzhou: Henan Renmin Chubanshe.

———. 1989b. *Zhonghua Renmin Gongheguo Jingjishi (1949–1966)* (An economic history of the People's Republic of China [1949–1966]). Zhengzhou: Henan Renmin Chubanshe.

Zhao Shenghui. 1987. *Zhongguo Gongchandang Zuzhi Shi Gangyao* (An outline of the Chinese Communist Party's organizational history). Hefei: Anhui Renmin Chubanshe.

Zhao Suying. 1986. "Jingji Tizhi Gaigezhong de Qiye Xingwei" (Enterprise behavior under economic reforms). In *Gaige: Women Mianlin de Wenti Yu Silu* (Reforms: our questions and thinking), ed. Chinese Institute for the Reform of the Economic System, 1–34. Beijing: Jingji Guanli Chubanshe.

Zhao Yujiang. 1986. "Yusuanwai Zijin Fenbu He Difang Zhengfu de Guanli Xingwei" (The distribution of extrabudgetary funds and local governments' managerial behavior). In *Gaige: Women Mianlin de Wenti Yu Silu* (Reforms: our questions and thinking), ed. Chinese Institute for the Reform of the Economic System. Beijing: Jingji Guanli Chubanshe.

Zhao Ziyang. 1982a. "Guanyu Dangqian Jingji Gongzuo de Jige Wenti" (A few problems on current economic work). *Hongqi* (Red Flag), no. 7: 2–10.

———. 1982b [1980]. "Guanyu Tiaozheng Guomin Jingji de Jige Wenti" (A few questions on economic adjustment). In *Sanzhong Quanhui Yilai Zhongyao Wenxian Xuanbian* (Selection of important documents since the Third Plenum), ed. Document Research Office of the Central Committee, vol. 1, 608–26. Beijing: Renmin Chubanshe.

———. 1985. "Dangqian de Jingji Xingshi He Jingji Tizhi Gaige" (The current economic situation and economic reforms). *Renmin Ribao* (People's Daily), April 12, 1–4.

———. 1988a. "Dangzheng Jiguan Lianjie Yu Ganbu Pingjia Biaozhun" (On the honesty of Party and government agencies and cadre evaluation criteria). *Zhongguo Xingzheng Guanli* (China's Administrative Management), no. 8.

———. 1988b. "Report to the Third Plenary Session of the 13th CCP Central Committee." *Beijing Review* 31 (November 14–20): I–VIII.

———. 1988c. "Yanhai Diqu Jingji Fazhan de Zhanlue Wenti" (The strategic question concerning coastal economic development). *Dangde Wenxian* (Party Documents), no. 4: 2–7.

Zheng Hongliang. 1992. "Gaige Guochengzhongde Guoyou Qiye Xingwei" (An analysis of behavior of Chinese state-owned enterprises in the process of economic reform). *Jingji Yanjiu* (Economic Research), no. 5: 22–29.

Zheng Jiaheng. 1992 [1989]. "Jiaqiang Tongji Gongzuo, Jinyibu Fahui Tongji Jiandu Zuoyong" (Strengthen statistical work and further develop the statistical auditing function). In *Tongji Gongzuo Zhongyao Wenjian Xuanbian 1988–1990* (Selections of important documents on statistical work 1988–1990), ed. State Statistical Bureau. Beijing: Zhongguo Tongji Chubanshe.

Zhong Chengxun. 1993. *Difang Zhengfu Touzi Xingwei Yanjiu* (Research on local government investment behavior). Beijing: Zhongguo Caizheng Chubanshe.

Zhong Xingzhi. 1994. "Zouxiang Hou Deng Xiaoping Shidai Zhongnanhai Anzhong

Jiaojin" (Toward the Post–Deng Xiaoping era: Quiet power struggles in Zhong-nanhai). *Zhongshi Zhoukan* (China Times Business Weekly), no. 138 (August 21–27): 6–9.

Zhong Zhangrun. 1988. "Difang Zhengfu Lingdaoren de Xinli Zhuangtai" (The psychology of local government officials). *Shijie Jingji Daobao* (World Economic Herald), November 21, 6.

Zhonggong Nianbao (Yearbook on Chinese communism). Annual. Taipei: Institute for the Study of Chinese Communist Problems.

"Zhonghua Renmin Gongheguo Guomin Jingji He Shehui Fazhan Diliuge Wunian Jihua, 1981–1985" (The Sixth Five-Year Plan on Economic and Social Development of the People's Republic of China, 1981–1985). 1983. In *Zhongguo Jingji Nianjian, 1983* (Chinese economic almanac, 1983). Beijing: Jingji Guanli Chubanshe.

Zhou Enlai. 1984 [1954]. "Ba Woguo Jianshe Chengwei Qiangdade Shehuizhuyide Xiandaihuade Gongye Guojia" (Build up our country into a powerful, socialist, and modern industrial country). In *Zhou Enlai Xuanji* (Selections of the works of Zhou Enlai), vol. 2, 132–45. Beijing: Renmin Chubanshe.

Zhou Hanrong. 1991. *Zhongguo Touzi Guanli Daquan* (Almanac on Chinese investment management). Beijing: Zhongguo Caizheng Jingji Chubanshe.

Zhou Mubin. 1988. "Zhongyang Yinhang Shixing Chuizhi Lingdao Youliyu Hongguan Tiaokong" (Vertical leadership at the central bank is beneficial to macro regulation). *Jinrong Shibao* (Financial Times), December 5, 1.

Zhou Shulian. 1983. "Jiben Jianshe Guimo He Shehui Jingji Jizhi" (Investment scope and the social and economic system). *Jingji Lilun Yu Jingji Guanli* (Economic Theory and Economic Management) 4: 7–13.

Zhou, Xiaochuan, and Zhu Li. 1988. "China's Banking System: Current Status, Perspective on Reform." In *Chinese Economic Reform*, ed. Bruce Reynolds, 109–19. Boston: Academic Press.

Name index

Subject index

Achieved level as a source of information, 240–241
Administrative leadership relations, 29–30
Agency problems, 312–313
Agricultural Bank of China (ABC), 42
Anti-inflation policies, *see* Austerity: policies; Inflation control
Appointment system, 90, 121–122, 196, 303
Appointment variable (APP), 274–276, 279–280, 282–284, 289–290, 293–294, 298–299, 300–304
Appointment variable for secondary officials (APPSEC), 274, 279–280, 282, 298
Appointment variable for top officials (APPTOP), 274, 279–280, 282, 298; contemporaneous effects of, 277, 283, 303; lagged effects of, 277
Asymmetry: of central fiscal positions and inflation performance, 322–325; of costs and benefits of investments, 134, 143, 175; of economic control, 58, 183, 312; of information, 132 fn.7, 181–183, 213, 230–232, 234, 240, 312
Austerity: equity objective of, 216; firm policy commitment to, 165–167, 188 fn.10, 253, 255–256, 312; policies, 45, 56, 69, 127, 158, 166, 175, 213–224, 227, 239–244, 250–285, 290–299, 314, 319–321; soft policy commitment to, 158, 188, 253–257

Bankruptcy, 12, 135
Bankruptcy Law, 146
Banks, performing a monitoring role, 42
Bargaining hypothesis, 275–276, 283, 285, 295, 298
Bei'an system, 93–94
Bureaucratic integration (*also see* Organizational integration; Political integration), 189–191, 192, 194–200, 210–211, 247, 265, 274, 276, 281–282,
282, 295–296, 298, 315–317; as a political liability, 275; as a political privilege, 276
Bureaucratic integration variable (BINT), 210, 263, 274–275, 278–281, 286, 289–291, 293–294, 298–299, 300–303; high values for Shanghai and Beijing, 191
Bureaucratic model (BM), 273–276, 280; of investment behavior, 180, 186
Bureaucratic slack, 183
Bureau-level officials: management of, 92–93; selection of, 309

Cadres: evaluation of, 70 fn.6, 94–96, 119; management of, 89, 90–96, 97, 99, 119, 121, 195, 276; Party management of, 91; political rehabilitations of, 107; rotation system of, 116
Capital formation, 11, 83, 134, 138, 272
Capital mobility, 311, 322
Capitalism (*also see* Socialism), 325
Careerist incentives, and bundling effect, 327; of local officials, 322
Cellular system, 27
Central bank, 18 fn.28, 307, 320; centralization and independence of, 326
Central Discipline Inspection Commission (CDIC), 97, 99–101, 105, 121, 228
Central enterprise, definition of, 33
Central government, 3, 23, 55, 88, 270, 297; and administrative pricing, 54 fn.39; and adverse selection, 232 fn.20, 240 fn.27, 258; and austerity policies, 41, 86, 130, 159–163, 166, 171, 214–216, 221, 223, 225–227, 253, 259, 326; as balancers of the last resort, 17, 46; and bank lending, 44, 81, 240 fn.27; and cadre management, 89, 91–92, 109, 111, 120, 205, 275, 285, 288, 304, 313; and capital goods allocation, 84–85, 162, 165; and enterprises, 33, 35–37, 39, 150; in the

363